Unearthed

Rebe Taylor was born in London and grew up in Adelaide. She has worked variously as an actor, stable hand, waitress, curator, historian and television presenter since the age of seven. She completed her Masters of Arts at the University of Melbourne in 1992 and her PhD at the Australian National University in 2004. She is an Australian Research Council Fellow at the University of Melbourne and lives with her partner, Peter and their son, Hugo. Rebe no longer dreams of becoming an opera singer. *Unearthed* is her first book.

Unearthed

The Aboriginal Tasmanians
of Kangaroo Island

Rebe Taylor

Wakefield
Press

Wakefield Press
16 Rose Street
Mile End
South Australia 5067
www.wakefieldpress.com.au

First published 2002
Reprinted in this revised edition 2008
Reprinted 2019

Cover designed by Liz Nicholson, designBITE
Designed and typeset by Clinton Ellicott, Wakefield Press
Maps and genealogies by Chris Blackall
Indexed by Susan Rintoul, Professional Editing Services

National Library of Australia
Cataloguing-in-publication entry

Author:	Taylor, Rebe.
Title:	Unearthed: the Aboriginal Tasmanians of Kangaroo Island/ Rebe Taylor.
Edition:	Rev. ed.
ISBN:	978 1 86254 798 8 (pbk.).
Notes:	Includes index. Bibliography.
Subjects:	Aboriginal Tasmanians – South Australia – Kangaroo Island – History. Aboriginal Tasmanians – South Australia – Kangaroo Island – Social conditions. Kangaroo Island (S. Aust.) – History.
Dewey Number:	994.235

Publication of this book has been assisted by
Alison McDougall and Colin Telfer.

CORIOLE
McLAREN VALE

Wakefield Press thanks
Coriole Vineyards for
continued support

For Ariette, John and Chris

Contents

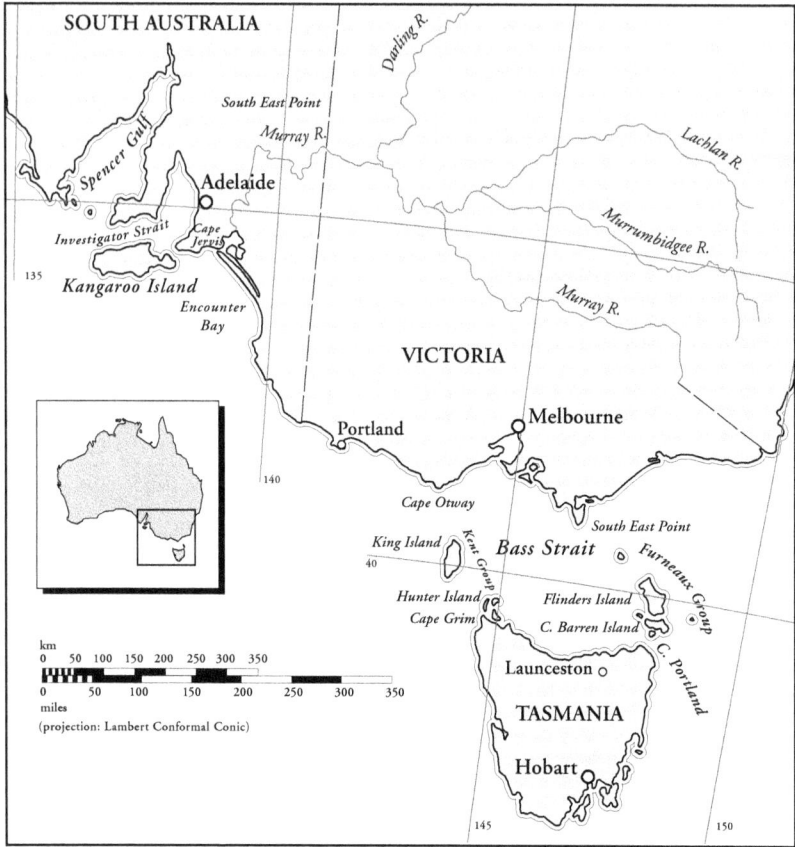

SOUTH AUSTRALIA

Darling R.

South East Point

Murray R.

Lachlan R.

Spencer Gulf

Adelaide

Murrumbidgee R.

Investigator Strait

Cape Jervis

135

Kangaroo Island

Encounter Bay

Murray R.

VICTORIA

Melbourne

Portland

140

Cape Otway

South East Point

King Island

40

Kent Group

Bass Strait

Furneaux Group

Hunter Island

Flinders Island

Cape Grim

C. Barren Island

C. Portland

km
0   50 100 150 200 250 300 350

0   50   100   150   200   250   300   350
miles

(projection: Lambert Conformal Conic)

Launceston

TASMANIA

Hobart

145

150

Southern Australia

Kangaroo Island

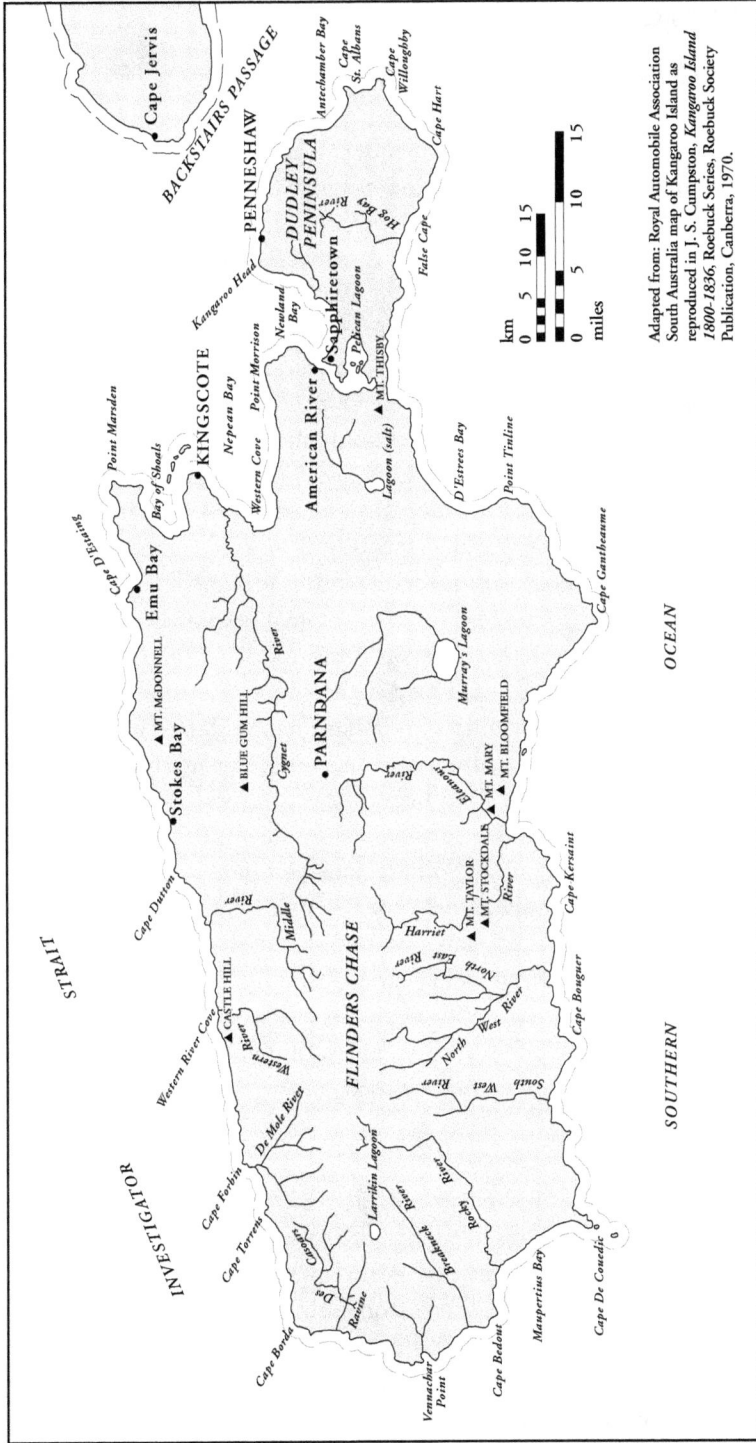

Adapted from: Royal Automobile Association South Australia map of Kangaroo Island as reproduced in J. S. Cumpston, *Kangaroo Island 1800-1836*, Roebuck Series, Roebuck Society Publication, Canberra, 1970.

km
0 5 10 15

miles
0 5 10 15

BACKSTAIRS PASSAGE

Cape Jervis

PENNESHAW

DUDLEY PENINSULA

Antechamber Bay
Cape St. Albans
Cape Willoughby
Cape Hart
False Cape

Hog Bay River

Sapphiretown

Kangaroo Head

Newland Bay

Pelican Lagoon

MT. THISBY

KINGSCOTE

Nepean Bay

Point Morrison

American River

Lagoon (salt)

D'Estrees Bay

Point Tinline

Cape Gantheaume

Point Marsden

Bay of Shoals

Western Cove

Cape D'Estaing

Emu Bay

MT. McDONNELL

BLUE GUM HILL

Stokes Bay

Cygnet River

PARNDANA

Marray's Lagoon

MT. MARY
MT. BLOOMFIELD

Elsewhere River

MT. TAYLOR
MT. STOCKDALE

Cape Kersaint

Cape Bouguer

STRAIT

Cape Dutton

Middle River

CASTLE HILL

Western River Cove

Western River

FLINDERS CHASE

Harriet River

North East River

North West River

South West River

INVESTIGATOR

Cape Forbin

Cape Torrens

De Mole River

Larrikin Lagoon

Rocky River

Breakneck River

Cassini River

De Ranine

Cape Borda

Vennachar Point

Cape Bedout

Maupertius Bay

Cape De Couedic

OCEAN

SOUTHERN

Author's Note to the Second Edition

This second edition of *Unearthed* includes a significant alteration: the real family names of all but one of the colonial descendant landowning families of the Dudley Peninsula, Kangaroo Island, have been restored: Cornelly is now Trethewey, Niven is now Buick, Richards is now Howard, Walker is now Willson and Wells is now Bates. The pseudonym 'Marshall' has remained the same. As this book traces the landownership of these six families from the nineteenth century – amounting to a history of land ownership of the Dudley Peninsula – replacing most of the real names (including in historical sources) makes this edition a more useful and accurate historical record.

I originally changed the colonial descendants' names in order to make them less easily identifiable, especially to visitors to the Island. This was because of the book's controversial nature. While *Unearthed* remains controversial, time has passed. How the colonial descendants remember the Tasmanian Aboriginal history on Kangaroo Island has changed in many positive ways, as you will read at the end of this new edition. As a result, it seems appropriate to remember them and their ancestors by their real names; their contribution to this book was invaluable.

Some further changes have been made to this second edition by request. I would like sincerely to apologise for any offence this book has caused to any of the people who have appeared in it.

There are some family names (not belonging to the Dudley 'colonial' landowners) that remain pseudonyms. They are: Chester, Sanderson, Southlyn, Whyte and Marks (formerly 'Howard' in the first edition). I have placed an asterisk next to these pseudonyms only when they first appear in the book. At the request of the Golder, Simpson and Waller families, their real names are used.

Genealogies

The family trees in this book are factual, but in some cases not all the family members have been included. Sometimes only the number of offspring and not their names are used, and in some of the most recent generations, step-children from second marriages have been excluded. The aim of these family trees is to help readers understand the relationships between the people in the story, not to provide researchers with complete genealogies.

Discovering

Three Beginnings

Mavis Golder had lived on Kangaroo Island all her life. She knew everyone in the little town of Kingscote, and almost everyone on the island. She had grown up in the same house where she now lived with her husband and two sons. Her thirty-three years had been shaped by familiarity. But in 1954 Mavis made a surprising discovery. Glancing through a copy of *Walkabout* magazine, she turned to an article headed 'Last of the Tasmanians'. Under the heading she saw a photograph of her Grandfather Joe and her Aunt Mary.[1]

Mavis was shocked. She was also confused. The photograph was clearly of Grandfather Joe and Aunt Mary, but the caption said it was of 'Tom Simpson', the 'well known ... last Tasmanian half-caste of Kangaroo Island', and his daughter. Mavis knew of no Tom Simpson, but she had known her Grandfather Joe well. She used to visit him in Penneshaw, on Kangaroo Island's Dudley Peninsula. Auntie Mary still lived in Penneshaw and often came over to Kingscote to stay. Why had their photograph been used? It made no sense. It must have been a mistake. Still, it frightened Mavis. She put the article aside and did nothing about it.

1958

In the same home in Kingscote, Mavis's 10-year-old son, Michael, was reading his 1958 edition of the *Australian Junior Encyclopaedia*. There he found an entry on 'The Old Sealing Days'. It was a brief history of the sealing industry in Bass Strait and on Kangaroo Island, and it included the following statement:

> It has been claimed that the last full-blooded Tasmanian aborigine was not Trucanini, who died in Hobart in 1876, but Mrs Seymour, who died at Hogg Bay, Kangaroo Island, at a great age in 1906.[2]

Michael was intrigued. He knew that Seymour was his grandmother's maiden name. He asked his grandmother if they were descended from the Mrs Seymour in his encyclopaedia. She told him that they were, but she told him no more.

1960

Adrian Waller was sitting at home in Adelaide reading the *Chronicle* newspaper when he came across a letter from an Edward Bates of Kangaroo Island.[3] Adrian was interested – he had lived on Kangaroo Island for ten years as a child, and he still had some family there. Bates was writing in response to an earlier piece in the *Chronicle* that had claimed Mary Seymour was the 'last Tasmanian full-blood ... to die'. Bates wrote that Mary Seymour had been a 'half-caste' Tasmanian Aborigine. He also gave a brief history of her family, beginning with her parents and concluding with a tribute to the youngest of her nephews, 'Tiger' Simpson.

The name 'Tiger' gave Adrian an unexpected jolt of recognition. Tiger had been his much-loved and well-remembered uncle.

Three beginnings; three journeys launched.

1991

The bus turned off the road and shuddered as it crossed the cattle-grid. This was nothing new; it had shuddered over corrugations and potholes all the way from Penneshaw. Mavis Golder and Adrian Waller looked out of the bus windows at an unfamiliar landscape, but one their ancestors had known intimately. It had been a long journey to get this far. Michael Golder had made endless trips to the archives to find information for his mother. Adrian had produced folders full of scribbles to unscramble a genealogy. There had been countless phone calls, meetings and letters.

The journey ended at a farmhouse, where all sixty passengers got out. The Kangaroo Island Pioneers Association had come to see Adrian and Mavis, both Association members, unveil a memorial to their ancestors. The party stood on the back lawn and watched Mavis pull back a miniature curtain to reveal a plaque that read:

Nathaniel Thomas
Arrived on Kangaroo Island in 1827 from Tasmania with an Aboriginal wife and farmed in this area. He later married Sophia Newcombe. He died in 1879 and Sophia in 1880. They were both buried nearby.

He chose a beautiful spot, Adrian thought. The farmhouse that Nathaniel had built for himself and his family stood on a headland between two white beaches, looking over the sea to Cape Jervis on the South Australian mainland.

Here, at the southern head of Antechamber Bay on Kangaroo Island's Dudley Peninsula, Mavis and Adrian at last stood on their ancestors' land. They could look at the same view Nat Thomas and his Tasmanian Aboriginal 'wife' had once enjoyed; they could hear the same sounds: the waves crashing against the rocks, the dogs barking, the breeze stirring sweet winter grass. They too could breathe in the salt air and feel the sense of timeless space.

But could they hear their history's darker secrets? Hear them whispering out of the cracks in the earth, creeping through the creek beds and whistling through the gullies? Could they smell the sadness these secrets carried on their breath?

Land, not blood, secretes memory.

The plaque Mavis unveiled was a marker of a journey begun, not ended. The journey to discover why her family did not know this land, to discover what might have been remembered in a history with less prejudice.

Memory lost, a history unearthed. In the freshly turned earth, new memories are seeded. And the roots grow deep.

Exploring

It was too late to go on shore this evening; but every glass in the ship was pointed there, to see what could be discovered.[1] The men on the deck of Captain Matthew Flinders' *Investigator* strained to see signs of life on a coast that had so far shown them none. This was unusual. For four months they had been exploring Australia's southern coast, and they had always seen *smokes or other marks of inhabitants.* But today, for the first time, they passed along an extensive stretch of coast to their south – seventy miles of high cliffs, all too exposed to anchor. When at last they rounded the easternmost point – *named Point Marsden, in compliment to the second secretary of the Admiralty –* they found a calm bay to anchor – N*EPEAN* B*AY, in compliment to the first secretary.*

Tomorrow they would explore. Tonight they could imagine. Some of the *young gentlemen* pretended to have seen *several black lumps, like rocks . . . in motion . . . which caused the force of their imaginations to be much admired.* But in the morning the imagined lumps became real. *On going toward the shore, a number of dark-brown kanguroos were seen feeding upon a grass plat by the side of the wood.* On other landings the kangaroos had bolted, but on this shore, Flinders recalled, *our landing gave them no disturbance . . . I killed ten, and the rest of the party made up the number to thirty-one . . . [T]he poor animals suffered themselves to be shot in the eyes . . . and in some cases to be knocked on the head with sticks.*

After this butchery, exploration began. Flinders *scrambled with difficulty through the brush wood . . . to reach the higher land with the surveying instruments.* But the bush was so dense that Flinders could not walk through it. He did not touch the ground, but walked on fallen timber. Although he could not see beyond the trees, the explorer concluded that *this extensive piece of land was separated from the continent.* As proof there was *the extraordinary tameness of the kanguroos.*

Which was fortunate for the ship's crew. *After four months privation from almost any fresh provisions,* the officers and men of the *Investigator* could eat *as much steaks . . . as they could consume by day and by night . . . [I]n gratitude for so seasonable a supply, I named this southern land, KANGUROO ISLAND.*[2]

Flinders had left England in July 1801 to explore, map and report on the 'unknown' south coast of Australia: from the south-western Nuyts Archipelago, named by the Dutch in 1627, to the western end of Bass Strait. He travelled via the Cape of Good Hope and first sighted Australian land at the Dutch-named Cape Leeuwin on 7 December 1801.[3]

Flinders did not always encounter Aboriginal people on his landings, but he always hoped to. He noted when he saw their fires and heard their dogs barking.[4] But on Kangaroo Island he found a bush so dense he could not walk through it, and kangaroos that looked him in the eye as he shot them. He was struck by the absence of people.

At the eastern head of Nepean Bay, where the *Investigator* was anchored, Flinders found a narrow channel of water, a mile wide but deep enough for a boat to pass. *A sandy eminence was behind it, from which alone there was any hope of obtaining a view into the interior of the island, all the other hills being thickly covered with wood.* Flinders named it Prospect Hill and climbed to the top. There he was *surprised to find the sea at not more than one and a half, or two miles to the southward.*

He was standing on a scraggy neck of land above a bladder of water that divided into two branches, east and south, each about two miles long. The eastern branch spread into a lagoon with four small islands. Flinders saw pelicans on the beaches of the lagoon, and young pelicans, still unable to fly, on three of the islands, where they were surrounded by bones and skeletons – suggesting that the islands had also *been selected for the closing scene of their existence. I named this piece of water Pelican Lagoon.*

> *Certainly none more likely to be free from disturbance of every kind could have been chosen, than these islets in a hidden lagoon of an uninhabited island, situate upon an unknown coast near the antipodes of Europe; nor can any thing be more consonant to the feelings, if pelicans have any, than quietly to resign their breath, whilst surrounded by their progeny, and in the same spot where they first drew it.*

There is poetry in Flinders' vision of this humanless sanctuary.[5] He knew it was paradise. But Flinders could see what his arrival portended: *Alas, for the pelicans! Their golden age is past.*[6]

The explorer had come and drawn his maps.

8 April 1802

> *Finally, at five o'clock, when we were both able to see each other clearly, this ship made a signal which we did not understand . . . She then ran up the English flag and shortened sail. We . . . hoisted the national flag, and I braced sharp up to draw alongside her. As they spoke to us first, they asked what the ship was. I replied that she was French. Then they asked if Captain Baudin was her commander. I was very surprised, not only at the question, but at hearing myself named as well. When I said yes, the English ship brought to . . . The English captain, Mr. Flinders . . . came aboard.*[7]

England and France were at war, but on Australia's south coast the men of Nicolas Baudin's *Géographe* and Matthew Flinders' *Investigator* met in peace, in the name of exploration. Baudin observed that Flinders *expressed great satisfaction at this agreeable meeting, but was extremely reserved on all other matters.*[8] Flinders recorded that he had *requested captain Baudin to show me his passport from the Admiralty; and when it was found and I had perused it, offered mine from the French marine minister, but he put it back without inspection.*[9]

Baudin had left Le Havre, France, in October 1800 in command of the corvettes *Géographe* and *Naturaliste*. His mission was to examine *in detail the . . . coasts of New Holland, some of which are still entirely unknown, while others are known only imperfectly.*[10] The Institut National had made its ambition clear: *we shall come to know the entire coastline of this great south land, which has seemed . . . until recently to be condemned to a sort of oblivion.* The French would also *carry out research of all kinds and perfect the natural sciences and increase the mass of human knowledge.*[11] They had departed with twenty-three artists and scientists on board.[12]

Baudin told Flinders that he had *spent some time in examining the south and east parts of Van Diemen's Land,* where he had lost a dinghy and its crew; then, in Bass Strait, a gale had left him separated from his voyage's other ship, the *Naturaliste.* But still Baudin had gone on to explore the mainland coast, beginning from Western Port, where he had found *no river, inlet, or other shelter which afforded anchorage.* This was the final stretch of the 'unknown' south coast, which Flinders was yet to explore.

After they had returned to their ships, Flinders reflected: *it somewhat surprised me, that captain Baudin made no enquiries concerning my business upon this unknown coast.* Still, Flinders had offered Baudin some charts for his journey.[13] They had agreed to remain anchored during the night and meet again at dawn.

At their second meeting both men noticed changes in one another. *He was much less reserved,* Baudin noted.[14] *He had become inquisitive,* Flinders observed.[15] It was now Flinders' turn to tell of his discoveries along the coast to the west – its *gulphs* and peninsulas, its watering places, and the large island near by.

Flinders named their meeting place Encounter Bay. Perhaps it is a marker of disappointment, the point at which each explorer's own discoveries ended. Flinders recorded that one of Baudin's officers said to him: *If we had not been kept so long picking up shells and catching butterflies at Van Diemen's Land, you would not have discovered the South Coast before us.*[16] After they parted, the explorers began to trace each other's tracks. But they did not always see things in the same way.

Baudin was at Kangaroo Island by the following evening. He did not anchor at Nepean Bay, but sailed further east. He saw no moving lumps upon the shore. The anchor would not hold, and

Baudin had to tack about throughout the night, waiting for enough light to find his bearings.[17] Next morning he travelled north-west to explore the peninsulas and gulfs of the mainland.

Three days later Baudin sailed along the island's north coast. He did not expect to find *so large an island off the mainland coast . . . as we doubled one point, another immediately appeared further on.* While *not entirely tree-clad*, the island's northern cliffs gave Baudin and his men *more pleasure than all the coast that we had seen so far.*[18]

Baudin travelled on to Nuyts Archipelago and then returned to Sydney. Nine months later, he again made for Kangaroo Island, accompanied by a smaller ship, the *Casuarina*. This time he stayed a month. He called the island *Ile Borda*, after the French mathematician and nautical astronomer. But François Péron, zoologist on the *Géographe*, gave his own name to the island: *Ile Decres*, after the French naval minister. The bourgeois Péron rarely saw eye to eye with his revolutionist captain.[19]

Baudin wanted to do what Flinders had not done – explore the island's south coast. He was disappointed. Its *sandy and treeless terrain* made it *dreary and unpleasant*. The task was completed in two days. But it was done. *If the English had the advantage . . . of having reached Kangaroo Island a few days earlier, we . . . have the advantage . . . of having circumnavigated it.* Baudin proudly added that he had determined the island's *geographical position in a way that leaves nothing to be desired for the safety of navigation.*[20]

On 6 January 1803 Baudin again anchored in Nepean Bay, this time with a reason to stay. His longboat had been smashed in Bass Strait three weeks before. His men were building another boat on deck with timber from King Island, but were making slow progress. Nepean Bay had safe anchorage and timber near by.

At sunset, with all the boats back on board, I learnt that a small port had been found at the head of the bay . . . I put further study of it off until the following day.[21] But this port was not mentioned again until a week later, when Baudin sent the petty officer in a boat to collect oysters in the Port des Pélicans. *By sunset the . . . boat returned laden with oysters, which were distributed amongst the whole crew. It likewise brought back a fairly large number of pelican's eggs and thirty or so of the birds themselves, taken from their nests.* Flinders was right. Only months after he had witnessed the young pelicans *free from disturbance of every kind*, the first act of destruction had taken place.

Perhaps because Baudin knew he was not the first man to witness this humanless sanctuary, he did not seem struck by the absence of people on Kangaroo Island. Nor did he lament that others would follow. He wanted to leave *nothing to be desired for the safety of navigation*. He also wanted to leave a marker of his presence.

Finding fresh water was difficult; there were no obvious creeks or rivers. Each day Baudin's men went east by boat to a bay they called the *Anse des Sources*, where they sank wells and filled casks.[22] As this was the only evident source of water close to the best harbour, they imagined others would follow them there. On a rock at the eastern end of the beach they etched the words: 'Expédition De Decouverte Par Le Commandant Baudin Sur Le Géographe 1803'.

Almost two centuries later, the spot is still known as Frenchman's Rock. A little white dome, like a holy grotto, houses a replica of the rock on which Baudin's men scratched their message. Next to it is a more recently crafted memorial with a drinking fountain that draws water from the same spring.[23]

Baudin also thought of what those who would follow might eat. At the same bay, he had his men release livestock into the scrub: a fowl and cockerel, a pig and sow.[24] The pigs multiplied to form a wild population.[25] The sealers who followed Baudin called the place Hog Bay, and the town that grew up on the site bore that name for more than a century before it was renamed Penneshaw.

Baudin left his animals for those who would follow, and took away the island's animals for those who would not. His aim during the voyage was not only to discover land but also to ascertain its nature. So time was given for studying the stars and the planets and for *picking up shells and catching butterflies*. But here at Kangaroo Island, Baudin wanted kangaroos. Twenty-eight of them, in fact – or at least enough for some to survive the journey back to France.

The kangaroos had grown wiser since Flinders' first landing;

they were hard to catch, and Baudin's dogs would often fatally injure them. It was also hard to keep them on deck. *One tried to escape by throwing himself in the water, but fell into our hands.*[26]

On 1 February the *Géographe* departed Kangaroo Island with eighteen kangaroos in cages on her deck, as well as two emus captured at *Anse des Sources*. Baudin took the greatest care of them, feeding them maize meal and fresh grass and leaves when he could, but only days from Kangaroo Island two kangaroos died from exposure. So Baudin ordered a pair of officers to give over their cabins to the kangaroos. His action created *two malcontents* – or at least one, for he showed his displeasure in no uncertain way. Baudin explained that it was all in the name of *the greater success of the expedition and whatever may serve our country.*[27] They sailed on to western Australia.

24 February 1803

The American captain, whom I had invited to dinner, came aboard at about two in the afternoon. Before we sat down, he asked me to give him, if possible, a map of the coast of New Holland, for he had no information that could guide him in his search for the places frequented by seals . . .[28]

Baudin had been at King George's Sound for five days when he met Isaac Pendleton, captain of the brig *Union*, which was financed by Messrs Fanning & Company of New York and had a crew of about thirty men.[29] Pendleton had been sent sealing on the strength of information passed on by Captain George Vancouver, who had sailed this coast in 1791. But Baudin recorded that *so far he had not been lucky*. In the five months since Pendleton had left America *he had obtained only three or four hundred skins. He had to have twenty thousand before thinking of heading for China*, the centre of the luxury skin trade.[30]

Vains calculs! – 'Bad move!' – Péron exclaimed when he learnt of Pendleton's itinerary. Pendleton planned to go to southern Tonga from King George's Sound and then establish himself in Bass Strait, using Port Jackson as a base to replenish his supplies, before sailing on to Canton. This *poor navigator*, Péron noted, had no idea how protective the British were of their Bass Strait and its seal colonies, which they had already begun to *devastate*.[31]

Both Péron and Baudin urged Pendleton go to Kangaroo Island. They gave him charts of Australia's southern coast and maps of Bass and Banks straits. While Péron warned that fresh water was scarce on the island, he promised Pendleton that he would find large numbers of seals there. Baudin described where they had seen *a reasonable number* and *where to find the best anchorage* on the island. But he also *recommended to him very strongly . . . to prevent his men from killing pigs and poultry that I had left there for the use of future navigators*. Pendleton promised that his men would do them no harm. The native animals were seen as a dispensable source of profit, the introduced ones as a precious source of food. After dinner, Pendleton returned to his ship to prepare for departure.[32]

∾

The rest of Pendleton's journey was recounted by the financier Edmund Fanning years later in the United States. Following the charts and advice of the French, the *Union* sailed to Kangaroo Island 'or Borders Island' and 'snugly moored' in the southern branch of the narrow channel off Nepean Bay. Pendleton called it Union Harbour, but it is known today as American River. Here Pendleton 'found both the hair and fur seals, extensive forests . . . and much game; fowls and birds of various kinds in abundance; and also excellent fish and oysters in great plenty'.[33] The human-less sanctuary was now a hunter's paradise.

The Americans feasted on birds, fish, oysters and game while they hunted the seals, which were to become hats and shoes in the fashionable centres of the world. To kill seals Pendleton's men no doubt adopted the usual technique, which was to block the seals' passage to the sea by standing on the water's edge, then go in with clubs. The hunters would slam the seals hard on the nose – their most vulnerable point, which also afforded the least damage to the pelts – then skin them with their knives.

If Pendleton was indeed sending his skins to China, he prob-ably had them dried: the blubber would have been scraped off, the flipper holes sewn up and the hide pegged in the sun. But if he wanted some to go to America or England, he would most probably have left an inch of blubber on the washed hides, then had them salted and folded into neat squares.[34] The Americans would not have had any difficulty finding salt where they were moored. In summer the lagoons behind Pelican Lagoon and Nepean Bay had up to twelve centimetres of salt, which could be easily scooped up into sacks. Salt alone would soon draw trading vessels to this bay.

About a week after their arrival, ignoring Péron's misgivings, Pendleton left one gang of sealers on Kangaroo Island and took another to Bass Strait, where they worked from early March to mid-April, seemingly without being worried by the protective British.[35]

Pendleton's gang returned to Kangaroo Island as the sealing season was ending; but it seems they had not yet secured their moiety. They decided to stay for the winter and wait for the warmer months to bring the seals back to the beaches. At American River, they built a brush hut and planted a garden of vegetables, neatly fenced to keep out the wallabies, kangaroos and possums.[36] And from the same native pine near Pelican Lagoon that the French carpenters had used, Pendleton's men built a twenty-foot schooner and called it the *Independence*. A second vessel would come to good use.[37]

In October 1803 Pendleton took the *Union* to Sydney with a cargo of skins. He found a new port connected to the world by trade. Sealing, which had begun in Bass Strait in 1798, was now booming. It was Australia's first export industry. Sealskins were as yet the only commodity that could be traded in overseas markets to procure cash and goods for the new colony of New South Wales.[38] Merchants were chartering boats to Canton, to Calcutta, to America and to England with sealskins and more – sandalwood from Fiji, flax from New Zealand and pork from Tahiti. They were coming back with tea, porcelain and silks. Here Pendleton too could trade.

He went back to Kangaroo Island, then returned again to Sydney in January 1804, this time with 6000 skins. There he met

Simeon Lord, one of Sydney's foremost sealing merchants. Luckily for Pendleton, Lord worried little about the embargo on foreign traders in this English port. Perhaps this was because, like Sydney's other two prominent sealing merchants, Lord had been a convict; he had been transported from Leeds in 1790 for stealing one hundred yards of cloth. According to historian Manning Clark, men like Lord proved that in Australia the difference between 'bond and free' was irrelevant to success.[39]

Pendleton may well have traded his 6000 skins with Lord, but another deal is recorded: Governor King paid to charter the *Union* to Norfolk Island to bring back pork. Lord stocked the American brig with his 'Tea, Sugar, &c.' – items much needed in the isolated penal colony. Pendleton possibly got a commission.

After this, Pendleton returned to where his men were sealing on Kangaroo Island's beaches; he may also have stopped again in Bass Strait. By June 1804 he had procured enough skins, and the *Union* and the *Independence* carried a collective load of 14,000 skins to Sydney. Pendleton was ready for his second deal with Lord.

This time the contract was more complicated. Lord would pay for Pendleton's 14,000 skins with the proceeds of a cargo of sandalwood that Pendleton was to procure from Fiji. Lord would finance the expedition and send his agent, John Boston, to accompany Pendleton. Under Articles of Agreement drawn up between Lord, Boston, Pendleton, a schooner master, a sealing master and the sealers, the newly built *Independence* would sail south to collect sealskins for upwards of twenty-four months. Each man on board would get a varying proportion of the profits – with the sealers getting the least.

The *Union* and the *Independence* left Sydney in August 1804, the *Union* bound for the South Pacific islands, the *Independence* to 'places southward'.[40] But for the *Union* not all went according to plan. Edmund Fanning, the distant financier, again narrates the story.

After leaving Sydney, the *Union* first landed at the 'Island of New Amsterdam, or Tongataboo' (southern Tonga) 'to engage a native, speaking the Fee Jee language, to proceed with them, to act as interpreter'. But when they arrived there, 'the captain, accompanied by Mr. J Boston ... and a boat's crew, were all most inhumanly massacred soon after landing'. Fanning gave no reason for the attack; the natives were simply 'inhuman'.

The remaining men on the *Union* returned to Sydney 'in order to replace the number of the crew recently destroyed', and the vessel 'soon again sailed for the Fee Jee Islands'. But again things went disastrously wrong. 'They experienced a heavy squall ... the brig ... got embayed among the coral reefs and every person on board either perished by drowning, or was massacred by the natives'. This time a reason is given for the massacre: 'It will be remembered these islanders are cannibals'.[41]

The little schooner, the *Independence*, returned to Sydney in April 1805 and left again to go sealing two months later, this time in company with the *Favorite*. Again the expedition did not go to plan. The *Favorite* returned to Sydney twelve months later with 60,000 sealskins, but the *Independence* was declared lost at sea.[42]

As Fanning tells it, Simeon Lord took the 60,000 sealskins to Canton and traded them for 'China goods', which he then sold in Sydney. For these skins, and for the 14,000 skins Pendleton had originally brought to him from Kangaroo Island, Messrs Fanning & Company of New York received not 'one farthing'.[43] None of the thirty Americans who left New York in 1802 ever returned home. Using information passed on from the French, they had tried to be the first to profit from sealing on an island first named and claimed by the British. They had failed. An English ex-convict got the profits instead.

24 October 1805

Joseph Murrell walked into Sydney with a spear wound in his back. It was not fresh; for some months he had been resting in Botany Bay, where he had received 'every comfort and assistance', before walking to the main settlement. Two men accompanied him, the other three crew members and all their provisions having been lost in the attack.

In May 1805, Murrell and a crew of five had set off in an open whaleboat to go sealing at Kangaroo Island. They were the first colonists to do so. News of Kangaroo Island had spread from

Pendleton's deals with Simeon Lord. But Murrell did not get far. At Jervis Bay, south of Sydney, the 'natives ... assaulted them'. The *Sydney Gazette* gave few details, but a week later it announced that Murrell was 'almost perfectly recovered' and gave a warning: 'the natives ... all along the coast, give daily proof of the actual necessity for the most guarded circumspection in approaching them, even when invited upon amicable assurances'. No reason was sought for the attack.

Murrell did eventually leave for Kangaroo Island, but no more was heard of him for another three years.[44]

2 May 1808

Two men arrived at Hunter's River, north of Sydney, having survived a 'flight of spears' that had killed three of their crewmates. William Stuart, with his boat the *Fly*, had attempted to go sealing on Kangaroo Island a month earlier. They had landed at Bateman's Bay to fill their casks with water. Natives at once surrounded them, Stuart claimed, and threw their spears as soon as the men were back in their boat. Back in Sydney, Stuart sold the *Fly*, organised a new boat and crew, and went sealing in New Zealand.[45]

September 1808

Joseph Underwood, one of Sydney's three most prominent sealing merchants, bought the *Eliza*, equipped her and sent her sealing to the south-west coast. In April 1809 the *Eliza* returned with 500 sealskins, 1000 kangaroo skins, Joseph Murrell and two of his sealers.

The *Eliza* had landed at Kangaroo Island, where it fell in with 'a gang of sealers consisting of seven persons'. They were Murrell and his men. 'The provisions were expended in three months after their landing, and having never received any supplies at all, ... for the long time of two years and nine months [they had] subsisted entirely on the flesh of wild animals'.

'This story probably explains how Hungry Beach received its name', reflects historian J. S. Cumpston.[46] Hungry Beach overlooks the entrance to American River and Pelican Lagoon. Perhaps Murrell and his gang found Baudin's pigs and fowls, though these men were hardly the 'future navigators' Baudin had intended to supply. Perhaps they found the remnants of Pendleton's vegetable garden, if the possums, wallabies and kangaroos had not already destroyed it. Or perhaps they had indeed subsisted entirely on emus, wallabies, kangaroos, oysters and even pelicans.

By the chance of meetings on a little-known coast, the same small inlet, the same beach and islets with its pelicans had now been invaded three times.

Although the *Eliza* 'fell in with ... seven persons', only three boarded her and left for Sydney. The other four stayed. Perhaps the island was now their home. Or perhaps Murrell promised to return to collect them when they had procured more skins and salt. Murrell did return after six months, and again two years later. By then there were other boats landing at Kangaroo Island. The seals, kangaroos, wallabies and salt – the stuff of profit – were by now well advertised. The British hunters had arrived and begun to devastate the island's environment. Its emus became part of the skin-hunters' diet and were extinct within twenty-five years. A kangaroo became a rare sight. This once humanless sanctuary now had a small, fluid but destructive population. There are few pelicans today at Pelican Lagoon. *Alas ... their golden age is past.*

1903

One hundred and one years after Flinders looked a 'kanguroo' in the eye and saw that no humans lived on 'this southern land', a geologist found evidence that Kangaroo Island had once had a human population. In 1903 Walter Howchin of the South Australian Museum found a small collection of stone tools on the island.[47]

Three decades later, the museum sent ethnologist Norman B. Tindale with Brian G. Maegraith and H. M. Cooper to make a further study of the island.[48] No skeletal remains or artefacts near shelters were found, nor have they ever been. But Tindale deduced from the large size of these tools that they were made by a most ancient culture. In keeping with his theories of migration,

Tindale suggested that this culture was related to the Malayans and the ancestors of the modern Aboriginal Tasmanians. He called the tools 'Kartan', after *Karta*, the name given to Kangaroo Island by the Kaurna people of the Adelaide plains. Tindale noted that there were no dingoes on Kangaroo Island, just as there were none on Tasmania.[49] These stone tools were the remains of a people who had lived on this land before the seas rose and cut it off from the mainland about ten thousand years ago. After that, Tindale claimed, the people of Kangaroo Island became extinct.[50]

'The problem', wrote archaeologist Ronald Lampert in 1981, 'had all the characteristics of a classic mystery story: a large off-shore island without people, separated … nearly 10,000 years ago, yet with abundant evidence of human population'.[51] Tindale's case was not closed. His theory of a large-stone ancient culture was thrown into question when different, smaller tools were found on Kangaroo Island. Had ancient Kangaroo Islanders become extinct or had they departed the Island voluntarily? It had taken the rising seas at least a thousand years to flood the land bridge. Were the smaller tools evidence of mainland people visiting the island by watercraft? Lampert called Kangaroo Island the 'Great Kartan Mystery'.

In 1977 archaeologist Rhys Jones suggested that Kangaroo Island had been all but abandoned after its separation from the mainland. If a more substantial population of, say, four or five hundred people had stayed for a considerable period, they would have left far more substantial archaeological remains. Perhaps one or two bands might have stayed, Jones supposed, but their small numbers would have made them vulnerable to natural disasters and would not have offered a large enough genetic pool for continuing reproduction.

There is evidence of human occupation, Jones noted, on all Australian islands, even though most had no population at the time of European invasion. The larger the island, the longer it sustained its population after the seas rose: Tasmania never lost its population. Kangaroo Island is four thousand square kilometres. Jones believed it was completely depopulated about four thousand years ago: one square kilometre for each humanless year.[52]

This is archaeological tradition. The Ngarrindjeri people of the coast opposite Kangaroo Island have another. To them Kangaroo Island is the 'land of the dead'. Muldawali, who came out of the Southern Cross, leads the spirits there across the sea.[53]

The Ngarrindjeri also have a story about the rising seas. The creation figure Ngurunderi pursued his two wives down the River Murray. They had eaten the bream fish, prohibited to women, and were escaping punishment. They travelled to the sea and ran over the land bridge to Kangaroo Island. Ngurunderi called to the waters to rise. He flooded the land bridge and drowned his wives, whose bodies became the rocky islands known as The Pages, just off the eastern tip of the island.[54]

Flinders named these islands The Pages because, like page-boys, they stand on duty to *that part of the Investigator's Strait [which] is not more, in the narrowest part, than seven miles across. It forms a private entrance, as it were . . . and I named it Back-stairs Passage.*

The waters of Backstairs Passage crash onto the cliffs of Cape Willoughby, the eastern tip of Kangaroo Island, and onto the cliffs of Cape Jervis on the mainland. They lap quietly into *the small bay where we had anchored . . . called the Ante-chamber.*[55] Flinders anchored there on his last night at Kangaroo Island. Baudin had not been able to make his anchor hold there for his first night at *Ile Borda*. Nathaniel Thomas built his house there. In 1991 Adrian Waller and Mavis Golder stood looking out to sea there, finally on their ancestor's land. He chose a beautiful spot, Adrian thought.

Arriving

Nat Thomas arrived on Kangaroo Island by accident. He had left Sydney on 17 May 1824 as a crew member on the *Belinda*, bound for the sealing grounds of the west. On 18 July the brig was wrecked on the rocks at Middle Island in Nuyts Archipelago. No lives were lost, the *Sydney Gazette* reported, but few supplies were salvaged. The crew had 'for a long time, been existing on an allowance so scanty as scarcely to admit of the prolongation of life', but, as the *Gazette* assured its readers, 'a Gracious Providence has delivered them'. In early 1825, five months after they were wrecked, the *Nereus*, 'being fortunately out sealing in that direction fell in with our hapless countrymen'. She made for Sydney with the *Belinda's* crew. On the way, she landed at Nepean Bay to collect salt, as she had done before.[1] Nat Thomas stopped at the island and never left.

Nathaniel Walles Thomas was born in London in about 1802. He would never write about himself, but on one occasion he spoke to William Anderson Cawthorne, the son of a Kangaroo Island lighthouse-keeper, who published his words in the *Adelaide Observer* in 1853. Nat told Cawthorne that his father had held a 'lucrative position in the victualling office at home', supplying the army with goods. Nat described himself as 'the scabby one' of a large middle-class family whom he left for an adventure at sea.[2] He arrived in Sydney as a seaman on the convict vessel *Shipley* on 18 November 1818. He was aged about sixteen.

Nat grew up, if he was not already a man, between the ports of Sydney and Launceston. Over the next three years he worked as a sailor, first on the *Sinbad* and then on the *Queen Charlotte*, transporting goods between these settlements.

Nat knew about the sea, and he knew about the world of cruelty that sailed upon it. He had no doubt seen men flogged, blood pouring from their wounds, perhaps had felt the pain of punishment himself. Nat would have learnt that the cruelty shown towards women, blacks and animals was no less than that shown towards men like him. Perhaps he would understand injustice differently from those who had not seen, felt and smelt this world. Perhaps Nat's pleasure was to know the sharp slap of contrast between the thick air of seaside pubs, the stench of a cargo crammed with dried sealskins, the stale smell of a cramped seamen's quarters and the whip of the Roaring Forties in Bass Strait. This was his world.

At about nineteen, Nat glimpsed a new world. In the words of W. A. Cawthorne, he went 'surveying under King'. Nat was a pilot – able to steer a ship – and could read a sextant.[3] He would have had a place on the deck of the *Bathurst* when she left Sydney in May 1821 under the command of Phillip Parker King. They surveyed the northern coast of Australia and returned in 1822 by way of the west coast.

By early that year Nat was back working the old route to Launceston, this time on the *Nereus*, the brig that would rescue him in Western Australia. He stayed working on the *Nereus* for another two years, until January 1824, when he joined the crew of the *Water Mole* bound for the sealing islands of Bass Strait. Four months later he sailed on the *Belinda* for the sealing grounds of the west and the dangers that would deliver him on to this beach at Nepean Bay.[4]

Nat Thomas would not have found Nepean Bay as it had been twelve years before – there were no *dark-brown kanguroos . . . feeding upon a grass plat*. More likely there were kangaroo, seal and wallaby skins pegged out on the beach to dry. The kangaroos, hunted in the hundreds, had long since learnt to bolt. Nor would Nat be struck by the absence of people on this beach, for evidence of their presence was all around him: perhaps some brush huts, a few spent fireplaces, the scraps of meals, a few dogs barking, the smells of cooked meat and drying pelts in the air.

The skin trade on Kangaroo Island was at its climax.[5] In almost every bay and inlet on the southern coast of the island were campsites of a few rough huts. The caves behind the beaches were stuffed with dried and salted seal, wallaby and kangaroo skins.[6] These last summer months had already seen more than half-a-dozen vessels come to take away thousands of pelts. They usually landed at the safe harbour of Nepean Bay, the central settlement, where the hunters would be ready with a moiety of skins in the camps near the beach, and where the salt could be scooped from the lagoons. Kangaroo Island salt was used by sealers all along the southern coast, and the vessels used it as ballast. Sometimes whales were killed off the island and their fat reduced on its beaches, but mostly the men went there for skins.[7] Still, men like Nat Thomas would become remembered as 'whalers'.

'Kangaroo Island, situate just through the Straits', reported the *Australian* newspaper in March 1826, '. . . has got quite a population of its own . . . It is said that there are, at present upwards of two hundred souls vegetating on this convenient spot'.[8] If there were such a number, they were scattered across the island, and possibly on the adjacent coast as well.[9] According to historian J. S. Cumpston, most of the men were employed under Articles of Agreement made with merchants such as Simeon Lord. Captain John Hart, a trader who visited the island, thought the Islanders 'had left various sealing vessels when on their homeward voyage' on the understanding that their masters would return on their next visit.[10] It was seasonal work, and few men stayed on the island longer than a few months or a year.[11] Perhaps Nat Thomas assumed he too would soon leave.

Or maybe he was in no hurry to return to the cramped rules and spaces of shipboard life. The sealers who worked under Articles of Agreement for the Sydney and Van Diemen's Land merchants only got a seventy-fifth or even a hundredth of the profits that the merchants put in their pockets. Whatever sum the sealers did get from their 'lay' was reduced by the cost of their clothing, tools and food: twelve shillings per week for seven pounds of meat (usually salted), five pounds of bread and three pounds of flour, canvas trousers, a woollen jacket, a knife and a club.

Good prices on the skin market were not always guaranteed. In 1808 the Chinese skin market had been glutted and prices had plummeted. And by the early 1820s, when Kangaroo Island's skin trade was at its peak, the boom had long passed in Bass Strait. Sealers had left most of the Australian waters after devastating the seal colonies. The traders calling at Nepean Bay for skins and salt were usually on the way to or from western Australia, New Zealand and the freezing sub-Antarctic islands.[12]

Captain Hart considered that, compared with life on board, 'this island-life had a peculiar charm for the sailors'. It was 'easy' and 'independent'.[13] Robert Newman, who had sailed with Nat on the *Belinda* and starved alongside him for the last five months in western Australia, might have told Nat about this easy life. Newman had lived on Kangaroo Island for the previous ten years.[14] He knew about living off the skin trade, about growing a garden of vegetables and crops of barley and hunting tasty game. Perhaps he had described the Aboriginal women who had been taken to the island–young women who could crew on the sealing boats, catch fish, dive for shellfish, trap wallabies, find mutton-bird eggs, and stitch jackets out of skins and shoes from the hides of seals.

But Nat had already glimpsed some of this life while working the Sydney to Launceston route. He had gone to the islands of Bass Strait on the *Sinbad* in 1819, and later on the *Water Mole*.[15] He had seen men like himself with their own islands – kings in skins. These men too lived with Aboriginal women from Van Diemen's Land who could pull mutton-birds out of holes, pluck their feathers and squeeze out their oil. By the late 1820s in Launceston these islanders were selling mutton-bird feathers to fill bedspreads, and mutton-bird oil to fill lamps. An industry and an independent community had begun to develop in the strait.[16]

Life on Kangaroo Island was not dissimilar. If Nat Thomas had walked along the beach at Nepean Bay and then gone inland about eight miles to what the sealers called Three Wells River, he would have found a significant settlement. 'Thirty men and forty black women, independent of a numerous progeny', wrote the *Australian* in March 1826, 'contrive to make themselves quite comfortable in their snug retreat'.[17] The sealers 'retired', claimed the *Hobart Town Gazette*, into a valley where they had a 'garden and huts'.[18] In this 'village', wrote Peter Cunningham in 1827, the inhabitants 'subsist upon the produce of their gardens and what game they can destroy'.[19]

The farmers at Three Wells River had been well served by Captain Baudin. They had a good number of pigs and a hundred fowls. The land was fertile, and the Islanders were able to grow an extensive kitchen garden of vegetables as well as some cereals. Captain Hart noted 'a small patch of barley for their poultry' in 1831.[20] By 1836 there were four acres of wheat. Three Wells River ran salty or fresh depending on the season, but the three wells on its banks produced a reliable supply of fresh water. The residents lived in various dwellings, including brush huts and houses of logs and bark.[21]

The supposed leader of this inland village was 'Abyssinia Jack', the *Hobart Town Gazette* claimed in 1826.[22] 'Abyssinia Jack' is often remembered as a black man, but he was probably John Anderson, an Englishman who had come to Sydney as a free settler on the *Archduke Charles* in 1815.[23] Anderson may have been confused with John 'Black Jack' Williams, a black American 'notorious for his devilry', who was also said to have led some of the first sealing gangs on Kangaroo Island. Both 'Black Jack' and 'Abyssinia Jack' eventually went to live in Bass Strait.[24]

If the Islanders ever recognised a leader, then 'Abyssinia Jack' would have been succeeded by Henry 'Governor' Wallen, one of the earliest and most established of the settlers at Three Wells River. Henry Wallen had first come to Australia in early 1815 as a crew member on the convict ship *Marquis of Wellington*. He evidently spent some time working in Australian waters; he was on the *Henrietta Packet* in the Derwent until September 1817. Two months later he was in the *Sophia* with Captain James Kelly, bound for the sealing grounds of New Zealand.

Near Otago Harbour, Wallen went into a Maori village with a party of men to buy potatoes, or so they claimed. His party was attacked and two of their number were killed. Wallen managed to make his way back to the *Sophia*, where he and the rest of the crew used their sealing knives to fight off the Maoris swarming the brig. They then took Corockar, the chief, and held him captive. When Corockar tried to escape, they shot him; he died the next day. The *Sophia* was again attacked, and Captain Kelly took retaliatory action. He and his crew entered his village armed with guns and cross-saws. They sawed up forty-two canoes and set fire to the dwellings, then left for the Chatham Islands.[25]

Wallen was not the only man on Kangaroo Island who could tell such stories. All the Islanders had experience of life in the maritime trade, in the convict transport ships or in the European naval wars.

Nat Thomas had seen much since he was fifteen. The man who would become his best mate and working partner on Kangaroo Island had seen it all since he was ten.

George 'Fireball' Bates – nicknamed for his bright red hair – had a similar history to Nat. He had been born a few years earlier, also in London. His father had been in the militia, he told a correspondent from the *South Australian Advertiser* in 1886. As a boy, George had a 'roving adventurous turn of mind', and 'his thoughts turned early towards the sea'. At ten he joined a school-ship and a year later was serving the navy in the Napoleonic Wars. He had already seen Africa and India by the time he arrived in Sydney in August 1823 as a sailor on the *Commodore Hayes*, bringing male convicts to Hobart. The 23-year-old had spent much of his childhood amid war, colonial horror and crews of hard men.[26]

Bates had arrived on Kangaroo Island a year before Nat, also on the *Nereus*. On that journey the *Nereus* stayed at Nepean Bay for three weeks while the crew loaded her hold with sixty tons of salt. Richard Wootton, the ship's boy, recalled those weeks from the relative comfort of his London upholstery shop eight years later. He told of being landed at Point Marsden, the island's eastern extremity, with two crewmen and a dozen dogs. They were ordered to hunt kangaroos for the crew while the *Nereus* sailed for Nepean Bay to moor. The party met three or four Islanders, Wootton recalled: 'I think there were some more inland; they have some black women with them'.[27]

Perhaps crew member George Bates was tempted by this island life. Many years later he told the *South Australian Advertiser* that one night during that three-week stay, when all hands on the *Nereus* got hopelessly drunk, he and his mate John Randall made their getaway. They took one of the brig's boats, some stores and three of the captain's dogs, rowed into the channel at the eastern point of the bay and hid at American River. On the first day they built a brush hut. On the second day they caught three wallabies. At sunset on the third day three men appeared over the crest of the hill, dressed all in skins. Thinking 'that they were black-fellows', Bates 'rushed for his gun, but on their nearer approach he saw they were white men'.[28] Surely at this punch-line the crusty old seaman threw back his red head and laughed, for it was not the first time he had teased his middle-class colonial audience with tales of how white seemed black on early Kangaroo Island.

It was also not Bates's only version of his arrival. As a schoolboy, Ted Bates (no relation) spent long afternoons listening to old Fireball Bates tell of his adventures. In 1960, aged seventy-eight, Ted Bates recalled Bates saying he had joined a warship that landed (inexplicably) at Hog Bay. When unloading ship, young George put the gear down for a moment to observe the new land. As punishment he was forced to stand in the sun for two hours. He 'so resented the punishment' that he made for the scrub and hid until the ship had gone.[29]

Just before his death in 1895, Bates gave a third version. He told the *Observer* that he had in fact arrived on the *Nereus* with a mate, but they had decamped hoping to find a boat to take them to Sydney and from there back to London. He never left, and never saw England again.[30]

Fireball Bates spent some time living with Nat Thomas in the place Flinders had called 'the Ante-chamber', known to the Islanders as Creek Bay.[31] The sealers' favoured landing place was at the northern end of that long white beach, but it was at the southern end that Nat eventually built himself a house and established his own farm. Nat Thomas's grandson, Stamford 'Tiger' Simpson, later claimed that in the 1830s Nat and George Bates had 'more than 500 goats, which they used for meat and milk, their skins for rugs, leather and clothing' and that they had 'erected a windmill for grinding wheat'.[32] It was more than forty-five miles overland on the roughest of tracks to Nepean Bay, where most of the ships continued to call.

Other places on the island were similarly occupied. There were huts and gardens near the salt lagoons, at Pelican Lagoon, American River and Hog Bay, where there was also a whaling station in the early 1830s.[33] The *Henry* dropped whaling supplies and a crew there in June 1832, and returned three months later to take thirteen tons of whale oil and forty-six bundles of whalebones back to Launceston. George Bates collected some whalebones over at Encounter Bay at this time; more than fifty years later, he complained that he was never paid for them.[34]

The *Henry* returned the following year, as did Captain Hart's *Elisabeth*. But the whaling was not as productive on the island as on the mainland coast. Where the *Elisabeth* procured seventy tons of whale oil over three weeks at Portland in what was later Victoria, she took only one ton away from Hog Bay.[35]

Many of the scattered settlements consisted of men in pairs. Sealers had dug freshwater wells at Point Marsden, where William Cooper lived with Peter Johnson, at the age of sixty possibly the oldest of the Islanders. Governor Wallen's long-time mate at Three Wells River was William Day. William Walker also lived near by, as did James Allen, James Everett and James Kirby.[36] And it is said that a man called Thisby lived alone by the sand-dune that bears his name. This was the dune Flinders had named Prospect Hill, and from which he had looked down on the sanctuary of Pelican Lagoon.[37]

Most of the Islanders also lived with Aboriginal women taken from Van Diemen's Land or the mainland opposite Kangaroo Island, including from Cape Jervis and Encounter Bay. These women were often abducted violently, and many of them never saw their homes again. For the men of the island, capturing the women meant the risk of having to fight Aboriginal men. But it was a risk the Islanders took, because Aboriginal women were vital to their settlements. These women could find water in a parched land and meat in a seemingly hunted-out patch; they could make their way through the interminable thick scrub and work hard at skinning and curing skins. With their help, the men could replace their worn-out canvas trousers, English boots, woollen jackets and sailor's caps with suits, hats and shoes of skin – kangaroo, wallaby or seal. In Captain Hart's words, the only money the Islanders required was 'a sovereign or two for making earrings'.[38]

In the social hierarchy on the beaches of Kangaroo Island, it was the men in skins who wielded the power. Not just over the Aboriginal women, but also over the temporary workers – the sailors who hauled salt for a few weeks, the sealers who cracked seal skulls for a summer. Perhaps the men who planted their vegetables, who risked their necks to get Aboriginal women, also had the power to determine who got the rum, tea, tobacco and sugar that the traders brought in exchange for the skins and salt. 'We used to take it out in rum and tobacco', Fireball Bates reminisced in 1895 – 'especially rum'. Men such as Fireball, Nat Thomas and Governor Wallen were empowered by their Aboriginal partners, suits of hide, fresh kangaroo and chicken meat, cabbages and potatoes. They could lord it over men who had only flour and salted meat, damp woollen coats, and the beach to sleep on. The men in skins had come up in this island world.

When Nat Thomas first arrived on the island, could he have imagined his part in this world? Could he have pictured the home he later made at Antechamber Bay? Could he have seen himself as a father, husband, landowner, grandfather – as one forgotten and remembered, reviled and honoured? At that moment of arrival, did the 22-year-old Nat stand on the beach at Nepean Bay and look into the land where he would spend his life, into the dark scrub where Flinders had stumbled? Or did he turn to face the sea and the life he had left behind?

∾

The men living in skins on Kangaroo Island – perhaps there were about thirty of them in the mid-1820s – were mostly English. Some were Irish or Scottish, and a small minority came from other places; all but a few were white. They arrived mostly in their twenties – a pack of young men full of bravado who had already seen the hard side of life.

All knew the maritime trade as a complex geographical web sustained by the ruthless hunger for profit. That hunger had landed many of them at beaches across the oceans, where some had seen – or participated in – massacres and abductions. They knew that trading was a competitive business; that if they went gently, then harder-dealing, meaner-trading men would only follow them and commit worse for a cargo of flax or Huon pine. They saw the damage their landings caused; they saw the blood on the beaches and the pain in the faces of the Tahitians, Fijians, Maoris and Aborigines, and heard stories from indigenes who worked on their boats.

The hunger for profit had brought them to the beaches of Kangaroo Island. Many would do their work of hunting and hauling and then go back to Sydney or Hobart or Britain. Not all would take part in the abduction of Aboriginal women. Not all would rape them or beat them. But seemingly few would condemn this cruelty, and all would profit from the women's passed-on knowledge.

These men would not look upon themselves as cruel or manipulative exploiters; their captains and merchants filled that role. These men had been the toilers and survivors, the poor bastards who had felt the cat on their backs and had been buggered as boys, who received a measly portion of an unguaranteed profit, who had to hustle for a swig of the bottle, a better knife, a warmer jacket. This was the life they had left for the freedom of Kangaroo Island.

Kangaroo Island, 'we suppose', the *Australian* reported cynically in March 1826, 'is in a condition to select a King and enact laws'.[39] The island, claimed for the British by Flinders, still lay beyond the practical reach of British legal codes. Many of the traders who visited the island were renowned for bending the rules in the name of profit. Its beaches were ruled by men who had been intimate with violence, often since childhood, and used it to manipulate others.

But in time Nat Thomas, Fireball Bates and the rest would become buccaneers, colourful characters, nicknamed and garbed in their skins. They would impress keen, soft visitors with boasts of their hard-learnt bush skills. They could tell their rollicking stories because they were men who had chosen freedom on this island. But what of the women whose freedom they had taken? Who would tell their stories?

1819?

Her arrival on Kangaroo Island was violent. She probably didn't know where she was going. The men may have forced her into the boat. She may have had her hands tied behind her back. She may have been raped. She may have been alone, or she may have been taken with other women from her home. She may have seen an uncle, a brother, her father, shot while defending her. Or she may have gone to work for the sealers with her family's consent, all of them thinking that she would return in a few days, bringing home mutton-bird and seal meat. She would never see her home again.

On the 400-mile journey by boat and on the beach at Nepean Bay, she would hear several languages and different accents. Perhaps she knew some English; she would soon learn more. There was a camp with huts, a few fires, some skins pegged out to dry, some barking dogs, some spent meals. A pungent smell of cooked meat and drying skins hung in the air. The scrub was dense and dark, but the trees were far smaller than in her home country. There were no deep valleys here, no roaring rivers, no mountains or rainforests. Here it was salty, flat and dry.

She was taken a few miles inland, to clearer land, and to a small river with more huts. There were fat squealing animals and small clucking birds. More dogs. Patches of yellow grass and patches of green, all surrounded with sticks in the ground. Here she would work with other Aboriginal women. Some were from near her home, but not all were her people. Some were from the land over the water that she could see from the beach. They would find a way of talking together.

Here the men wanted wallabies, kangaroos and sealskins, huge piles of them, not just for meat or for making jackets and trousers, but for trading with other men from the sea. She would make string from canvas and set wallaby traps along the low pathways in the scrub, and hunt kangaroos with fire and dogs, and pull the sinew from their tails to use as a strong thread. She would scrape the skin from hundreds of warm marsupial bodies and from the sleek seals, then salt the skins or peg them out in the sun. In summer she would also work in the lagoons, putting salt into sacks and hauling them down to the beach.

The boats would come to the bay, more over the years. They would take away the skins and the salt and leave grog and tea, sugar and tobacco. Lots of men would come and go, and different women too. Some would tell of what was happening at home; others would come from the land over the water.

Here the women could hunt better than the men, who did not know how to track animals through the scrub. She would dive for shellfish. She would go with the sealers in the boats to the smaller islands and collect mutton-bird eggs. She would sing and learn this new land, her new home. They would call her by a new name here. Betty.

∾

Betty was the great-great-grandmother of Adrian Waller and Mavis Golder. She is remembered by other names too: Bet, Old Bet, Black Bet, Betsey and Polecat.[40] The men in skins were not kind or imaginative with their nicknames. Her birth name is unknown. Her place of birth in Van Diemen's Land is unknown. Her family and her ancestors are unknown. Any woman taken from Van Diemen's Land to Kangaroo Island about 1819 could have made her imagined journey. History is imagined; it is the flesh that hangs off the bones of facts.

The plaque Mavis Golder unveiled on her ancestors' land in 1991 claimed that Nat Thomas 'arrived on Kangaroo Island in 1827 from Tasmania with an Aboriginal wife'. But the shipping records – the supposedly reliable facts on paper – piece together a story of Nat's arrival in early 1825, without any Tasmanian wives. Like old Fireball Bates's myriad tales, every story of arrival on the beaches of Kangaroo Island has more than one version. Facts on paper have little value in the currency of folklore.

It seems those who wrote the wording for the plaque had referred to a book published in 1977, B. C. Mollison's *Tasmanian*

Aborigines—a pioneering genealogical history of the Aboriginal Tasmanian descendants using a range of sources and interviews, but notorious for its unreliability.

In Penneshaw, Mollison interviewed Ted Bates, by then ninety-three, and Nat Thomas's great-great-grandson Les Simpson. They presented a story totally different from the one that emerges from the shipping records. Nat Thomas was said to have been a 'privileged prisoner' working as a pilot in the Derwent in Van Diemen's Land. He had heard about Kangaroo Island from captains and sealers and decided to 'make a run for it' in the pilot boat. He took with him several sealers and Tasmanian Aboriginal women. The party first landed in Encounter Bay, just off the mainland coast, and then crossed over and settled in Antechamber Bay in about 1827.[41] Betty, it was assumed, was among them.

It is possible that Nat Thomas has been somehow confused with another man named Thomas. According to A. L. Meston, who researched some of the Bass Strait islanders' genealogies in 1947, John Thomas was the harbourmaster at Port Dalrymple in north Van Diemen's Land. But according to local legend he was a pilot on the Tamar River. In the legendary version, this Thomas was granted a square mile of land near the Tamar, but Meston found he was in fact granted a 'location order' of forty acres in 1813. Both versions of the story share the same ending: John Thomas traded his land for rum and went to live 'among the blacks of Cape Portland'.[42]

In Wynnis Ruediger's history of Kangaroo Island, *Border's Land*, Nat Thomas simply arrived from Tasmania in an open whaling boat with fellow sealer James Everett and two Aboriginal women.[43] Variations of this idea were most often told to me on Kangaroo Island, including the claim that Nat Thomas had been a convict on a ticket of leave.[44] None of these stories gave any suggestion of his landing off the *Nereus* in early 1825, or even a version of that event.

Norman Tindale coupled his fieldwork on the ancient stone tools on Kangaroo Island with research on the Tasmanian Aboriginal women taken there, including a rough genealogy of Nat Thomas and Betty's descendants. He confidently claimed in

1937 that 'Robert Whallen took Betty from Tasmania in 1819'.[45] Henry 'Governor' Wallen has on occasion been referred to as Robert, and his surname has many variations: Whallen, Wallons, Wallon, Warley, Worley, Whalley, Wally, Walker and even Perkey.[46] But the statement that Wallen brought Betty to Kangaroo Island in 1819 seems to be merely a conglomeration of the stories Tindale gathered from interviews, novels and journals.

Tindale's notes show that he consulted Jane Watts's *Family Life in South Australia* — her published reminiscences, begun in 1837. Watts was told what was popularly believed, that the Islanders were all 'old convicts' who had escaped 'durance vile'. The first of those to arrive on Kangaroo Island was 'Whalley', who had 'made the voyage in an open boat from Van Diemen's Land' with 'Puss' and 'Polecat' some 'twenty years previous'.[47] Tindale cobbled this piece of information together with another 'fact' — that a Robert Wallen escaped custody in 1817 and arrived on the island in 1819 with 'Puss' and 'Bet' from Van Diemen's Land.[48] Tindale's confident claim has flimsy evidence.†

The shipping records tell us that Wallen was in New Zealand with the *Sophia* from December 1817. But Cumpston claims he 'was not a member of the crew of the *Sophia* when they were mustered in Sydney on 20 June 1818'.[49] Who knows what Wallen did after the *Sophia*'s sealing expedition to Chatham Islands? He may have gone to Tasmania and abducted Aboriginal women; certainly other men did. Moreover, by 1819 a Tasmanian woman had borne him a son called Henry Whalley.[50] But there is no fact, no piece of paper, no grounding shipping list or census that can tell us whether Betty was with Wallen in 1819.

There are about twenty-two named women who appear in the records as having been taken to Kangaroo Island from Tasmania. There were possibly many more who cannot be accounted for.

Missionary George Augustus Robinson, who was appointed in

---

† It seems Tindale did not learn of another local version of Wallen's arrival: Ruediger (p. 41) was told he was landed at Nepean Bay in 1816 or 1817 off the American whaling vessel *General Gates* with orders to collect skins, live pigs and fowls and a promise he would be picked up in six months. According to Cumpston (p. 59), the *General Gates* was not in Australian waters until 1819.

1829 to conciliate with the Aboriginal Tasmanians, campaigned to have all the Aboriginal women living on the islands with the sealers taken into his mission. In 1830 he went to Bass Strait with the aim of removing the women, and recorded their names and origins while he was there. Seventy-four women were accounted for in the strait, and in 1831 he was given a further fourteen names of women who were on Kangaroo Island. But Robinson did not visit Kangaroo Island himself, and Betty was not on his list.[51]

The women on Robinson's list were young, mostly in their twenties. Some would have been married when they left their homes, and some were already mothers. Robinson took down their long, beautiful names in his own system of phonetics, and also the short, ugly names the sealers had given them. He noted where they had come from, using the English names for their country's capes, ports and rivers. Robinson noted that these locations might suggest which tribes they were from, or even which bands – the more specific groups within the wider tribal boundaries where a common dialect or language was spoken.

Of the fourteen women on Robinson's Kangaroo Island list, twelve were from Tasmania's northern coasts: Cape Portland, the George River area and Launceston. Three were from the south of Tasmania, from the Nuennone band of Bruny Island. They were all sisters – in fact, they were sisters of Trukanini, the woman who would become famous for the spurious claim that she was the 'Last Tasmanian'.

If most of the known Tasmanian women on Kangaroo Island were from the north of that colony, can it be assumed that Betty was also from one of the northern tribes? Nothing can be assumed. But there is another clue. Betty spoke an Aboriginal language to her children. From the chaos of displacement, it seems poetic that only two sets of contradictory instructions have been remembered from this language. They were given to Norman Tindale by Betty's grandson Joseph Seymour in 1936:

´nina tu:´napari	you understand
lil tu:´napari	do you understand?
´bulunta	go straight ahead
ma:bir, ma:bier	go around

Joseph Seymour, Tindale noted, called his grandmother's language 'Hobart Town Speak'. But this was not what drew Tindale to conclude that Betty came from southern Tasmania. It was the word 'nina', which he thought could be the same as 'neena ... recorded for one of the southern tribes' to mean 'you'.

The appendices of Ling Roth's 1899 book, *The Aborigines of Tasmania*, include several collected Aboriginal Tasmanian vocabularies. Joseph Milligan's list of words, published in 1859, records 'neena' as the word for 'you' in the areas around Oyster Bay, Bruny Island, Recherche Bay and the south of Tasmania. But Rev. James Norman, who lived in Port Sorell on the north coast, also lists 'neener' as meaning 'you'.[52]

Nothing is conclusive, I was told by the Tasmanian Aboriginal Centre. Quote Tindale's conclusion, they said, but without his certainty, for little is certain when a European records a language that has not been spoken within its original community for over a hundred years. If it was a southern language, it may not have been the language Betty grew up with, but one shared between the Aboriginal women on Kangaroo Island.

But with most women coming from Tasmania's north-east and north Midlands, wouldn't a northern dialect or language have been dominant on Kangaroo Island? Perhaps, but many of the women whom Robinson listed as being on Kangaroo Island in 1831 were taken to Bass Strait a few years later. Only a small number of Tasmanian women stayed as long as Betty, and only two others lived about as long as she did: Make.ker.lede.de, or Sal, one of Trukanini's sisters from Bruny Island, and Suke, who was possibly from Cape Portland. Sal was also known as 'Big Sal' and as 'Bumblefoot Sal' because she had lost two toes, supposedly from sleeping too close to a fire. Because Robinson did not know of Suke, she is without an Aboriginal name. But her English name, like Betty's, has no shortage of variations: Old Suke, Sook and, confusingly, Sal.[53]

Which language was adopted for communication between the women? Did they marry English and other languages? Did all the Islanders share a general language, a creole? If so, did each woman also remember her own language? Perhaps Betty purposely spoke her mother's language to her children. But even if she did, how might it have changed in the years of finding common communication with other language speakers? The mess of colonial invasion has left the Tasmanian Aboriginal Centre yet unable to positively identify the four lone phrases. I am no linguist. Joe Seymour's phrases offer no certain conclusion as to Betty's place of birth.

∾

Betty was born into a changing world. As white settlements encroached along the Tamar River on the north coast and the Derwent River down to Hobart, Aboriginal people could no longer depend on their traditional hunting and gathering patterns or techniques. Previously without dogs, they now increasingly needed them and valued them highly. They also needed food that they did not have to hunt for, that they could store and carry.[54] Relations between tribes were also changing as resources got scarcer. They needed to adapt to survive.

By 1810, according to Lyndall Ryan in *The Aboriginal Tasmanians*, the people of the north-east 'had begun to gather each November at strategic points along the north-east coast ... in anticipation of the sealers' arrival'. By this time the remaining seal population in the strait could support only independent sealers living on the islands, not merchant traders. The sealers came at the beginning of the season in open boats, usually in groups of four to six. They were honoured with a dance, then a conference took place to decide which women would be chosen to work for them. Some of these women would go temporarily and come back with meat. Others, women who had been abducted by the host tribe from other tribes, would be traded for dogs, flour or mutton-birds.[55]

The sealers offered these opportunities for trade. As Ryan puts it, the sealers 'made no claim to Aboriginal land'. The other Europeans did, and killed for it. The sealers' goods made it more feasible to mount a guerrilla war against the other invaders. The deals with the sealers were made when choices were becoming few; deals made in an invaded country. But if the Aboriginal people could trade with the sealers, they could not control the sealers' actions. The sealers were invaders too.

Penderoin, a member of the Parperloihener tribe, told G. A. Robinson about a time (probably in about 1820) when his people were camping near Cape Grim, the most north-western corner of Tasmania. It was a favourite place to find mutton-birds, and the women and children went to gather them while the men left to hunt kangaroos. It was then that the sealers attacked. Nine of them appeared from the cave where they had been hiding in wait all night. The cliffs made escape impossible. Penderoin said that the sealers took about twelve or fourteen women, and even the mutton-birds they had collected.

But Alexander McKay, one of Robinson's convict servants, had heard from one of the sealers involved in the raid that they took only seven women that day. They included Kie.peker, Larpeeno.puric, Nie.pee.kar, Moon.dap.per, Reetar.hibar and Troe.pow.er.he.ar. McKay told of how one old man had tried to defend the women, throwing a spear from the top of a banksia tree he had climbed. The spear caught a sealer's clothing, and the white men opened fire. The old man and another elder were killed. The seven women were taken to Kangaroo Island.[56]

Tasmanian bands probably consisted of only about forty or fifty people. Take away ten of their young women, and you take away the future of the band.[57] 'The sealers', Ryan writes, 'were instrumental in the destruction of a number of Aboriginal tribes on the north coast of Tasmania'.[58] As the attacks on the Parperloihener showed, the sealers' guns also killed Aboriginal men. In 1831 G. A. Robinson noted in his journal that 'there is not a boat harbour along the whole line of coast [of northern Tasmania] but what numbers of the unfortunate native have been shot: the bones are to be seen strewed on the ground'.[59]

Trukanini's mother was murdered by sealers.[60] Her three sisters were all taken to Kangaroo Island, possibly by John Baker, 'a man of colour', in 1826. Of the three, Mur.re.ning.he or 'Kit' was reportedly later shot dead by sealer Robert Gamble in the Kent group of islands in eastern Bass Strait.[61] So too, claims one report, was Lore.we.nun.he in 1829. But another report claims she was on

Kangaroo Island in about 1831, where a third sister, Make.ker.lede.de or 'Sal', would spend the rest of her life.[62]

James Allen, an Irishman who was at Nepean Bay in the early 1830s, reportedly abducted Kal.loon.goo or 'Sarah' from Tasmania, then 'sold' her to William Dutton in the Kent group. The so-called Kangaroo Islander leader, 'Abyssinia Jack' (John Anderson), was in Bass Strait in 1831. There he told G. A. Robinson that James Allen had tied a woman called Lar.roon.er to a tree at American River, made deep incisions into her buttocks and cut off part of her ear. Anderson also said that 'Fireball' Bates had punished a 10-year-old boy for 'running away' by taking his arm and snapping it over his knee. For the same misdemeanour, Anderson claimed, Nat Thomas had cut off the ear and part of the cheek of a seven-year-old boy, the son of 'Emue', a 'Van Diemen's Land woman'. The boy died a couple of weeks later.[63] These stories of cruelty were useful to Robinson in his campaign to have the women taken from the islands. They also could be turned into colourful prose.

In 1865 W. A. Cawthorne, who had interviewed Nat Thomas in 1853, published a fictional serial in the *Illustrated Melbourne Post* depicting life on Kangaroo Island in 1823. 'Give 'em a tarnation hiding all around', one of Cawthorne's characters declares of the Aboriginal women; then he wonders, 'or slit their ears?' Cawthorne explains 'cropping the ears was considered a proper legal punishment a few years back in Christian England, so these Islanders ... had introduced the ... practice ... as one of their recognised modes of punishment amongst the women'.[64]

Such horror stories do not only feature Aboriginal women taken from Tasmania. When sealing began along the coasts of southern Australia, Aboriginal people in those places met with European invaders before official colonisation began. In the land opposite Kangaroo Island, the Ngarrindjeri and Kaurna people would get to know these unofficial invaders well.

In November 1829 Charles Sturt set out on the instructions of the New South Wales governor to travel west along the Murrumbidgee River to see if it met the 'large lagoon' near St Vincent's Gulf–Lake Alexandrina. He reached the lake three months later. There he wrote of meeting Aborigines who were hostile but feared his gun. Sturt assumed they had learnt this fear from the sealers of Kangaroo Island.[65]

When Norman Tindale borrowed the Kaurna people's name for Kangaroo Island, *Karta*, he explained that the word also meant 'lap' or 'female genitalia', according to the Kaurna vocabulary compiled in 1840 by the missionary Christian Teichelmann. The Ramong people of Encounter Bay, Tindale goes on to explain, called Kangaroo Island Kukukunga. Its literal translation is 'females (genitalia of) to'. 'This name may not be very old,' Tindale suggested; 'more than one mainland woman was forcibly carried to the island by the sealers'.[66]

The Ngarrindjeri of the Lower River Murray called the invaders *kringali kop*. A suggested translation by anthropologists Berndt and Berndt: 'white people whose noses come first'.[67] No doubt the *kringali*'s pointy, pink noses were sniffing after women.

The *Observer* quotes Fireball Bates in his 1895 obituary: 'I could blab if I liked about the old days on Kangaroo Island and afore then, but a still tongue shows a wise head'. Fireball's uncharacteristic restraint led the *Observer* to wonder. 'There were some lively rumours', the writer remarked, 'about kidnapping blacks and other dead-and-gone doings upon which the old pioneer could have thrown a light'.[68]

But nine years earlier Bates had told the *South Australian Advertiser* how he and four other men had taken a boat to Cape Jervis for a '*chasse aux femmes*'. 'Having no small difficulty in eluding the natives', they walked overland to Lake Alexandrina, behind Encounter Bay.

'Their method of capturing the women was simple', the journalist explained. When they reached a campsite they hid and waited all night. Next morning, they kept waiting until the men left to go hunting. Then 'at a signal they rushed forward and secured their prizes'. Bates said he had done this five times, and the party had taken one or two women on each occasion. 'In most cases', the *Advertiser* claimed, 'they proved useful and willing slaves'. The exception was 'Puss', named such by Bates because of her 'propensity to scratch the face of her owner when in a rage'.[69] The story reads like a ripping colonial yarn.

How might the women have told their stories, of being violently grabbed, bound and forced into sealers' boats waiting on a coast where the Aboriginal people had become so wary that men never left their women alone? How might they have told of floating over the land Ngurunderi had flooded, to the land of the dead? Here their hands were untied; this was an island, and prison enough.

From the island these mainland women could see their homes across a small stretch of water. The distance was not far–only about fourteen kilometres at the closest point. When they looked upon the islands called The Pages, which stood on guard to the entrance of the narrow Backstairs Passage, they would be reminded of the wives of Ngurunderi, who had drowned trying to escape to this land. These women would reverse the journey – there is more than one story of women who attempted to swim back to the mainland.[70]

In 1867, South Australian missionary George Taplin was told that 'it was common for native women to be . . . stolen' and taken to Kangaroo Island. One such woman was kept in a hut with other captives, with their hands tied. One day this woman burnt the cords that bound her hands, freed her companions and escaped to Cape Jervis in a boat.[71] Taplin also heard of three other women who tried to escape from Kangaroo Island in a dinghy. They found the boat was too small and one woman was left behind with her baby. She strapped the child on her back and swam. She was found dead on a mainland beach. At Point McLeay mission in 1934, a Coorong man, John Wilson, told Tindale, 'I went down to Cape Jervis.' He saw where the woman died. 'Baby died on way. Child on her back.'[72]

Albert Karloan, a Yaraldi man from the Lower Murray, told the Berndts in the late 1930s that sealers had caught a Ramindjeri woman from near the mouth of the Inman River. She had a child with her, but they left it behind on the mainland. They then took her to Nepean Bay, where she was 'passed around the camp'. After this horror, she managed to crawl away, exhausted. She hid that night and most of the next day. When she had rested enough, she swam across the strait and recovered her child.

John Bull, who was on Kangaroo Island in 1834, was told of an Aboriginal woman who, 'not satisfied with her promotion [from] slave to one of her own race to that of help to a white man ... took to the water and swam across the strait ... Despite the dangers of the powerful currents, and the multitudes of sharks ... she landed safely in her own country'. Yet she was back on Kangaroo Island when Bull was there. She was pointed out to him: 'a fine specimen of her race', he commented.[73] Perhaps this was the Encounter Bay woman who, according to Augustus Reeves in the *Observer* in 1905, tried to swim home but was caught and 'soundly thrashed for her trouble'.[74]

Bett, a woman from Rapid Bay on the mainland, also plunged into the sea at Antechamber Bay.[75] Did she make it? 'The sharks would have settled that question', Fireball Bates told the *Advertiser* in 1886. 'There is little romance in that', the journalist complained.[76]

The stories of abduction and mistreatment against the Aboriginal women were not fictional, yet they have been written in prose that would be at home in a colonial adventure novel. They are accounts intended to excite, even titillate, their audience. No effort is made to empathise with the women, or to consider the possible complexity of the relationship between them and their people and the sealers.

Fireball Bates, offering himself as a central actor, shaped his yarns for a journalist writing to entertain. He acted on a stage constructed by outsiders – journalists and schoolboy readers who wanted to be seduced by the fantastic. And so do we. We, the temporal outsiders, continue to watch the Islanders perform in the pages of a newspaper or historical record. We are wooed by the romanticism of the past.

But even before those long-dead schoolboys and the journalists who entertained them, there were the captains and merchants who met the Islanders at first hand. Despite the immediacy of their accounts, they too were voyeurs. They created the stage first. They watched the Islanders perform on the beaches from the decks of their boats, and relayed their stories to colonial journalists, who imagined the Islanders from their writing desks in Sydney or Hobart. They were separated by much more than the sea.

They were cultural outsiders, judges without knowledge. They were watching and imagining men of their race who were not of their class, and no longer of their world. These outsiders did not understand the economy and complexity of Aboriginal life, let alone that of the partly European communities on Kangaroo Island and Bass Strait. These outsiders turned Kangaroo Island into a circus, a parody of the classic nineteenth-century shipwreck story, with its mimic Robinson Crusoes and black Fridays. But in this absurd play, the Crusoes do not retain their civilised ways. They become like the Fridays; they become savages.

Judging

> They are complete savages, living in bark huts like the natives, not cultivating anything, but living entirely on kangaroos, emus and small porcupines, and getting spirits and tobacco in barter for the skins ... They dress in kangaroo-skins without linen, and wear sandals made of sealskins. They smell like foxes.[1]

So Captain George Sutherland found the Kangaroo Islanders in 1819. He bartered 4500 sealskins with the Islanders for some rum, and sold the skins in Sydney for six shillings each. Captain Sutherland could profit from these uncultivated men who apparently cultivated nothing, but he could not admire them. It appears he did not go inland from Snakes Point and find the potato patches and cabbage gardens that they grew. Sutherland mistook what he found on the beach for the Islanders' whole world. He looked on the Islanders with the same short-sighted colonial eye that had for centuries looked upon indigenous people on the beaches across the globe – the people who lived beyond the boundaries of civilisation, beyond the domain of men who wore linen.

Sutherland's sentiments were echoed seven years later by Major Lockyer, who sailed past Kangaroo Island in 1826 on an expedition from Sydney to found a settlement at King George's Sound. 'The nauseous food these people make and the miserable life they lead', Lockyer remarked, 'it is no wonder that they become actually savages'.[2]

Wild meat explained their regression; their garb of skins and foxy smell were evidence. Major Lockyer and Captain Sutherland were appalled at how *unEnglish* these Englishmen had become. Not only had they every appearance of natives, but they cohabited with native women, and had performed savage acts of abduction to do so. 'They have carried their daring acts to extremes', Sutherland explained, 'venturing on the mainland in the boats, and seizing on the natives, particularly the women, and keeping them in a state of slavery, cruelly beating them on every trifling occasion'.[3]

Savagery and criminality went hand in hand. Lockyer described the Islanders as 'a complete set of pirates', 'desperate characters', and all of them 'runaways from Sydney and Van Diemen's Land'. Armed with large knives and firearms, they roamed from 'island to island' along the southern coast and west as far as Rottnest Island, off Western Australia. Kangaroo Island, he claimed, was their 'chief resort ... a great scene of villainy' where 'a great number of graves are to be seen'.[4]

Much had already been written in the colonies about sealers and escaped convicts turning into violent and libidinous pirates. Commissioner Bigge, who was sent out from England in 1819 to review the administration of New South Wales and its dependencies, had found time to pass judgement on the Bass Strait sealers' behaviour toward Aboriginal Tasmanian women. The women, he wrote, were 'torn from their people with force of arms and with guilty violence'; in these raids, 'death is often occasioned'. After their abduction, Bigge claimed:

> The treatment of these miserable black women ... could not be believed were it not too visible ... the bruises they bear, their heads beaten and indented with the same clubs that are used to kill the seal, the scanty offals of opossums, or shell fish, which they themselves have procured and which are thrown to them after the very dogs have been satisfied, indicate this without a contradiction.[5]

Bigge's remarks, made in 1820, were quoted six years later in the *Hobart Town Gazette* to urge that 'immediate steps be taken to check the evils occasioned by boatmen and fishers in the strait'. In an emotive plea that takes Bigge's prose to an even higher pitch, the writer of the *Gazette* article appealed to supporters of the anti-slavery campaign:

> Oh, ye friends of the enslaved African – ye breakers of the chain of bondage – ye advocates of freedom, of humanity, extend your benevolent exertions to those most unhappy creatures, who, if comparatively few in number, are proportionally more wretched than the wretched negro.[6]

The sealers, 'unthinking piratical men in boats', are said to 'terrify the whole tribe . . . surround them and . . . one or two go into the throng with their clubs and the scene of slaughter ensues'. There are echoes here of Bigge's description of the women, who are also 'torn' from their tribes and have their heads 'beaten and indented with the same clubs'.

But it soon becomes apparent that, for all the journalist's excited prose, he has only marginally more sympathy for the women than for the seals. The sole redeeming feature of the communities in Bass Strait, he writes, is that the 'original natives of Van Diemen's Land may be taught and rendered serviceable', for there the women 'render their brutal masters, every service that diligence and ingenuity can perform'.[7]

If the Aboriginal women are presented as animalistic – treated like the seals, fed after the dogs – the sealers are their bestial masters, entirely unrestrained and depraved. It is as if acts of violence against native peoples and animals are seen not only as somehow comparable, but as the acts of men who have become like the natives themselves – to injure Aborigines, or 'savages', is the act of a criminal who has turned savage.

Such ideas have no place in a serious report on the issue of forced slavery. The *Gazette* article reads like a creative fantasy. But to understand why such dramatic rhetoric is employed, it is necessary to view the landscape of early Van Diemen's Land through colonial eyes.

Imagine the *Hobart Town Gazette* writer sitting in Hobart, looking north to Bass Strait, or even further – west to the uncolonised Kangaroo Island. His is a geography that maps morality and confines it to the colonised spaces, while savagery and criminality thrive in the unsettled lands. And the more savage these places are, the more civilised Hobart appears. '[W]hat will our Readers think', the *Gazette* writer worries, 'when they read from a London publication, or see it printed in Sydney without a comment, that these men may be pardoned for cohabiting with the dark daughters of the Papons . . .?'[8]

And as the writer worries about what his audience in the civilised centres might be thinking, we can see him looking over a wild and wooded landscape where white men wearing skins had roamed for years, their savage acts unrestrained by any apparent sense of Christian morality. These were the bushrangers. Such was the fear the bushrangers inspired in the Van Diemen's Land settlers that martial law was declared against them in 1816. Ten years later, when the *Hobart Town Gazette* article was published, they were still a greater threat than the Aboriginal Tasmanians would become.

The famous bushranger Alexander Pearce escaped twice from the convict settlement at Macquarie Harbour, or 'Hell's Gates'. He claimed to have eaten his entire gang. Then there was Michael Howe, who dressed in kangaroo skins, had an Aboriginal partner and even blackened his face. He was said to have carried a kangaroo-skin book where he recorded his Utopian dreams in blood. He spent his last months at large, living alone on a mountain, his beard growing long and his appearance wild. At about the time he became a myth in Hobart, his captors were carrying his head in a sack from his mountain retreat.[9]

These bushrangers, with their cannibalism, garb of skins and blackened faces, blurred the lines between what was black and white, savage and civilised, moral and immoral. They set the stage on which the sealers would later be paraded. The Bass Strait sealers became known as a 'banditti of bushrangers'.[10] James Bonwick said of them, 'on shore they would have been bushrangers'.[11]

But the sealers were on a maverick frontier of islands and wild seas far away. As they were not advancing the cause of the civilised settlers, they had to be admonished. They were Englishmen, but no heroes to colony or Empire.

So it seems that in this Hobart-devised geography, the further away men were, the worse they became. According to the *Hobart Town Gazette* in 1826, Kangaroo Island was the *'ultima thule'* of the southern seas – the furthest, unknown place. [12]

Indeed, the Kangaroo Islanders had a special place in the imagination of the *Hobart Town Gazette*. The *Gazette* claimed that they were all runaway convicts whose boats 'evade detection under the cloak of the night'. They were said to follow the coast, surviving on wildlife ('at first ... a revolting flavour') until they reached Kangaroo Island. There they gathered at the Bay of Shoals (Nepean Bay), where there was a salt lagoon and fresh water at hand. In this community, the *Gazette* continued:

> every ... labour is performed by the native women whom these unprincipled men carry off from the main ... while they themselves sit on the beach and smoke, drink, and sleep ... occasionally, perhaps, arousing to kill a young seal on the sunny beach.

Again there is a dramatic call for action to end this travesty:

> Are then these men, thus strangers to religion, strangers to principle, among whom rapine of every kind, and even murder is not unfrequent, are they to be suffered thus to debase human nature?

In this *ultima thule*, it was said, even the natives were different:

> It is to be lamented that so debased a specimen of the Christian race as these men should be the first to give an impression to the natives, who are there very numerous and of a superior class to those here. [13]

These superior natives were 'said to live in regular villages, and are all clothed with a cloak made of skins stitched together and orna-mented, and though, like all other savages, addicted to stealing, are nevertheless friendly and hospitable'. Whatever the accuracy of this description, the Ngarrindjeri or perhaps the Kaurna, have become here the natives of a faraway New World.

Distance is useful. In Hobart in 1826, the fear of bushranging was still acute, but was beginning to be superseded by fears of the Aborigines. It was politically expedient for Vandemonians to distract attention from events on their island to those on an island far away. It is therefore no coincidence that the *Hobart Town Gazette* should present Kangaroo Island as a mysterious place inhabited by 'debased' men acting out a travesty of justice to 'superior' Aborigines.

Such a representation would also become expedient after the Black War in Van Diemen's Land had ended, when the histories were being written. If the sealers were responsible for devastating several of the northern Tasmanian bands, their deeds were emphasised and exaggerated to alleviate the pressure on the official colonists. In his patriotic 1852 *History of Tasmania*, John West lists the reasons for the 'extinction' of the Tasmanian Aborigines. The sealers, ranked fifth, were described as:

> chiefly, either convicts whose sentences had expired, or such as contrived to escape. In the islands of the Straits, they indulged the boundless license of their passions, blending the profession of the petty pirate and the fisherman.

A 'chain of rocks', West claimed, led these escapees west, 'picking up the refuse of the sea and feeding on the aquatic birds'. Kangaroo Island was 'the Ultima Thule of their geography'. There, after the sealing season was over and the guns, spirits and tobacco had been traded for skins, the residents 'retired to the interior, and passed their days in alternate slumber and intoxication'.[14] Though West does not provide a direct reference, his source is clearly the *Hobart Town Gazette* article of June 1826.

About two years after West's *History of Tasmania* appeared, W. A. Cawthorne published his serial novel *The Islanders*, which was republished in 1926 as *The Kangaroo Islanders*. The later edition includes a foreword by South Australian historian Sir Archibald Grenfell Price describing pre-colonial Kangaroo Island as 'one of the most savage white communities that the British Empire ... has seen'. Cawthorne himself describes the Islanders as 'unparalleled in the most barbarous tribes of man, or the poorest sections of civilised communities'. He portrays the settlement at Nepean Bay the following terms:

The place smacked of the freebooter and the outlaw; the very scent of the locality suggested the lair of the wild beast. The resemblance was complete, and the stories of ourang-outangs capturing women and making them slaves and drudges seemed to be fully realised.[15]

Cawthorne claimed that his novel was 'fact to a very large extent'. His father, Captain William Cook Cawthorne, had been the head keeper of the Cape Willoughby lighthouse, near Antechamber Bay.[16] Nat Thomas and his son-in-law William Seymour both worked at the lighthouse under Captain Cawthorne in the 1850s.[17] Cawthorne not only met Nat when he interviewed him in 1853, but also his 'half-caste' daughter Mary and two other Tasmanian women. In a letter to the *Observer* in 1856, 'W.A.C.' – probably W. A. Cawthorne – wrote of having met and spoken with 'Betsey'.[18]

The Islanders met a mixed reception on the island when it appeared in serial form. In June 1865 the *Adelaide Observer* reported:

An *Illustrated Melbourne Post* has found its way into the hands of some of our old islanders containing Mr Cawthorne's story. They think it a queer yarn, but not very complimentary to them . . . I dare say when Mr Cawthorne revisits the island he may find hospitality at a premium.[19]

All this suggests Cawthorne's 'facts' were accompanied by hyperbole. Yet a more subtle reading shows that Cawthorne does in fact present early Kangaroo Island in quite positive terms. Literary critic Christopher Nance, who has studied *The Kangaroo Islanders*, comments that 'beneath the depreciation, emerges a sense of interested appreciation of the Islanders'. Nance quotes Cawthorne's observation that 'amidst this utter abandonment' the Islanders 'exhibited traits of heroism'.[20] Cawthorne found Kangaroo Island society no more cruel than the colonial penal system of 'civilised' England. His portrayal of the sealers' settlement as 'the lair of the wild beast' is seen through the eyes of a visitor in 1823, a middle-class man of superior rank – a Captain Sutherland or a Major Lockyer. Grenfell Price was unable to realise this subtlety seventy-two years later. Cawthorne's keen reflection of an outsider's perspective might be the most 'factual' aspect of his book.

Yet many twentieth-century writers would join Grenfell Price in accepting that the Islanders were savages. Indeed, condemning the Islanders and the Bass Strait sealers has become a historiographic tradition. In his *History of Australia*, Manning Clark claimed the sealers 'pursued a way of life as savage and elemental as the never-ending roar of that sea'.[21] He even described Henry Wallen as being 'no more capable than the aborigine of avoiding a life of degeneracy'.[22] Similarly, Geoffrey Blainey in his 1966 book *The Tyranny of Distance* described the Bass Strait of the 1830s as a 'Barbary Coast', where the 'villains ... having slaughtered most of the seals, now had more leisure to slaughter or mutilate native women and fellow sealers'.[23] John Molony's 1988 *History of Australia* echoes the judgement that the sealers were 'villains' who often treated the 'black women' they abducted 'barbarously'.[24] Robert Hughes in *The Fatal Shore*, published in 1987, describes the sealers as 'rapparees and bolters' who 'kidnapped hundreds of women from their tribes' and 'formed ... bloody, troglodytic island colonies'.[25] The savage convict sealer of Bass Strait and Kangaroo Island has become a historical 'fact'.

In early 1826 the government of Van Diemen's Land sent Captain Whyte to the islands to apprehend runaway convicts. Whyte returned in March claiming full credit for 'ridding the Bass Strait of many bad characters', but he had not gone to Kangaroo Island. The same month, the *Hobart Town Gazette* published a letter signed by W. H. Skelton, who had accompanied Whyte to the strait, expressing his hope that something would be done to 'apprehend the runaways' and 'wretched men' who 'continue their abandoned course of life' on Kangaroo Island. In late 1826 Major Lockyer called for 'immediate measures' to be taken to control the Islanders' 'lawless manner'.

But all these urgings were based on a falsehood. While the sealers may have committed crimes on Kangaroo Island, there is no evidence that any of them were escaped convicts; indeed, only a few of them had ever been convicted. George 'Fireball'

Bates told the *Adelaide Observer* in 1895 that none of the Kangaroo Islanders had been runaway convicts.[26] John Jones, a trader who visited Kangaroo Island in 1833 and met the Islanders, reported that 'no runaway convicts were among them'.[27]

Captain Hart informed Governor La Trobe that the Islanders were 'principally' sailors who had arranged with their masters to work on Kangaroo Island. He had thought 'there was another class of men' who 'probably had escaped from Van Diemen's Land', but these men lived far from Kangaroo Island, 'on islands apart from the others, some on Thistle Island, near Port Lincoln, and other islands in Spencer's Gulf'. In 1831 Hart found 'one man who had been unvisited for three years'.[28] But Hart's conclusion that these men were 'probably' escapees remains untested.

J. S. Cumpston's thorough book, *Kangaroo Island 1800–1836*, explains why Kangaroo Island was not populated by runaway convicts. 'The aim of most runaways', he writes, 'was to return to Europe or to reach America. To do this they had to get clear of the Australian coast. Perhaps the Bass Strait offered them some prospect of achieving this, Kangaroo Island did not.' Cumpston continues:

> To reach Kangaroo Island, the runaways would have had to make a 400 mile voyage from Bass Strait to Backstairs Passage across the northern fringes of the Southern Ocean. This would require a well-found whaleboat, equipped with sails and other gear, a good supply of food and water, and some knowledge of a coastline … It is a journey that could only be undertaken by a seaman and preferably not alone. Once at Kangaroo Island the escapees would be out of the track of ordinary shipping, and would have to live off the land as best they could.[29]

So the *Gazette*'s tale of escapees crawling along the coast all the way to Kangaroo Island and living only on 'revolting' wildlife was a fiction, but it proved a fiction of remarkable appeal and longevity.

Blainey, Clark, Molony and Hughes are well-known and reputable historians. What they have written about the sealers is not simply wrong – the sealers did treat many Aboriginal communities cruelly, and a few of their number, in Bass Strait at least, were convicts. Beyond that, we are in the realm of early nineteenth-century rhetoric. These historians have reused images of savagery and barbarity without questioning the political contexts that then existed, without imagining why writers in Hobart might have wanted to create such a fantastic picture for their readers.

These representations of the sealers have continued to hold currency for the same reason that they were so easily created and consumed in the early nineteenth century. They recall images that are well known and well rehearsed in the European imagination. Sutherland, Lockyer, Bigge and the journalist writing for the *Hobart Town Gazette* all described the sealers in the same way that Western explorers and colonisers had described the natives of the New World.

When Europeans first encountered indigenous people on the Canary Islands in the fourteenth century, some found the simplicity of the islanders' lives to be evidence of a Golden Age. Others found them repulsive for their diet of uncultivated food, their wild appearance and their unrestrained sexuality.[30]

But myths of Wild Men have ancient roots. The Greeks conceived of 'indiscriminate interbreedings between gods, humans and animals'. The Hebrews found such a notion abhorrent, believing it produced a 'wild and evil race of giants'. In early Christianity the biblical legend of Ham fused with pre-Christian mythology to produce the image of the 'Wild Man of the Woods'. 'Knowing neither God nor morality', writes Gustav Jahoda, 'he was a slave to his passions, and carried off women whom he ... raped'.[31] This description, like that of the Canary Islanders, is similar to the nineteenth-century descriptions of the sealers.

Cawthorne in *The Islanders* describes his central character, 'Sam' (who is possibly modelled on Henry Wallen), through the eyes of the visitor who found him in 1823: 'very hairy, so much so, that it was at times difficult to distinguish his natural hair from the hair of the skins he wore as clothes; he was a veritable Esau'.[32] The biblical character Esau, Rebekah's first-born twin son, was the 'hairy' one. He was also known as the 'son of the desert', 'devoted to the perilous and toilsome life of a huntsman'.[33]

Cawthorne's description of the Kangaroo Islanders as 'ourang-outangs' is also in a long tradition of seeing indigenes as ape-like. From the early eighteenth century, pre-Darwinian botanists, under the leadership of Carl Linnaeus, attempted to classify all living species. Mythical, biblical and cultural understandings of savagery confused the distinction between men and apes. Linnaeus's initial attempts to differentiate humans from apes included subdivisions such as the 'tailed man', *homo sylvestris*, the direct translation being from the Indonesian orang-utan. The final category in Linnaeus's 1758 *System of Nature* included six sub-categories of *Homo sapiens*, including *Homo ferus*, or 'Wild Man', based on the European myths of the people who lived in the woods.[34] Charles Darwin's *Origin of Species*, which introduced the evolutionary connection between humans and apes, was not published until five years after Cawthorne is thought to have written *The Islanders*.[35]

The European man dressed in skins has a literary history far older than the bushrangers of Van Diemen's Land. He is a central character in the stories of shipwrecks and fantastic voyages that emerged as a popular genre in the late seventeenth century, when European colonisation spread across the globe. As historian Margarette Lincoln explains, shipwrecks provided a narrative structure that could include disaster and adventure in exotic places far from middle-class drawing rooms, places where accepted European social conventions could be tested in isolation from 'civilised society'.[36]

While not the first, certainly the most famous shipwreck story is Daniel Defoe's *The Life and Strange and Surprizing Adventures of Robinson Crusoe*. First published in 1719, *Robinson Crusoe* has been widely read, translated, and reimagined many times over.[37] The white man clad in skins on an isolated island claims a central place in the Western imagination.

Cawthorne's visitor landing on Kangaroo Island in 1823 asks one of the resident sealers, 'What sort of place do you call this, Mr. Robinson Crusoe?' to which the Islander replies, 'Why, we calls this ere place a menagerie.'[38] W. H. Leigh, who visited Kangaroo Island in 1837, described the Islanders as living a 'solitary Selkirk life' – a reference to the actual story of Alexander

Selkirk, the shipwrecked mariner on whom Defoe apparently modelled his fictional Crusoe.[39] Travel writer George Angas, in his 1847 book *Savage Life and Scenes in Australia and New Zealand*, claimed the Kangaroo Islanders led 'a Crusoe-like life, without law or constraint'.[40] And when Edward Snell sailed past Kangaroo Island in 1849, he mused in his journal, 'fancy living there, must be rather a Robinson Crusoe sort of life'.[41]

But the sealing Crusoe is somewhat different from Defoe's original character. In his father's words, Crusoe was 'of the middle State, or what might be called the upper Station of *Low Life*'. 'I did not', explains Crusoe himself, 'ship myself as a sailor', but 'would always go on board in the habit of a gentleman'.

Despite his garb of skins and his long beard, Crusoe remains a 'true symbol of British conquest'. Friday, his companion, the savage cannibal, is his antithesis. After Crusoe is nauseated by the sight of a cannibal feast by Friday's people, he says, 'with a flood of tears in my eyes, [I] gave God thanks, that had cast my first lot in a part of the world where I was distinguished from such dreadful creatures as these'.[42]

But the ex-sailors and sealers were not seen as being so 'distinguished' from the 'dreadful creatures' of Van Diemen's Land or mainland South Australia. Historian John Blacket thought in 1907 that, unlike Crusoe, who confirmed his Christianity in solitude, the sealers had 'in a spiritual sense … descended almost to the level of the kangaroos'.[43] Indeed, it was suggested, their libidinous tendencies had partly caused their descent. 'Unable to secure their own civilised countrywomen', wrote historian James Bonwick, 'they were compelled to adopt the society of savages'.[44] (Crusoe, by contrast, had never a lustful thought in all the twenty-eight years that he was on his island.) The Islanders not only had sex with savages, they dressed like them and ate like them.

Far from being the ideal colonists, these Australian Crusoes went 'wild'. There is a long entry in the 1958 *Australian Encyclopaedia* under the heading 'wild white men', of whom the most famous is undoubtedly William Buckley, an English convict who escaped the penal settlement of Sorrento, in what was later to become Victoria, in 1803. Buckley lived among the Wathaurang of south-western Port Phillip Bay until 1835, when he came upon a group of John Batman's men who were investigating Port Phillip as a site for a new colony.[45] They at first assumed he was one of the natives. He could no longer speak English, was dressed in skins and was armed with traditional Aboriginal weapons. After the settlement was established, Buckley worked as an interpreter between the Aborigines and settlers, but soon became disillusioned and left to live in Van Diemen's Land.

There, journalist John Morgan held a series of interviews with Buckley, resulting in the 1852 book, *The Life and Adventures of William Buckley*.[46] Morgan wrote the book as if he were Buckley, but his protagonist is strikingly like Robinson Crusoe. 'Buckley' refers to 'my Robinson Crusoe hut', and even claims 'I was the real Crusoe'. There are also lengthy descriptions of cannibal-like practices among the Wathaurang.[47]

Morgan's *Life and Adventures* was reprinted as recently as 2002.[48] In the 1960s it was translated into German and Russian, and both editions were published under the title *The Australian Robinson*.[49] These 1960s translations also include photographs of Aboriginal desert peoples and land-rights protests. The narrative structure of *Robinson Crusoe* has become a medium through which to present a generic Australian indigenous history.

But Morgan's account also uses the narrative structure of *Robinson Crusoe* to tell how a white man, an Australian convict, became like one of the Aborigines. This is the opposite of Defoe's Crusoe, who retains his Englishness to the last, despite his garb of skins. Buckley was said to have taken Aboriginal 'wives', 'lost his native tongue', joined the Wathaurang in battles and ceremonies (except for the supposed cannibalistic rituals)[50] and adopted the name of Murrangurk.[51] Many commentators (though not John Morgan) admonish Buckley for his absorption into Aboriginal life. It seems they miss the colonial romance of Crusoe's civilising influence over Friday.

'Thirty years with a tribe!' James Bonwick opines, '. . . we may expect to witness some illustration of the elevating influence of an Englishman among the savages. But alas! we see nothing of the kind'.[52] John Pascoe Fawkner, one of the first Port Phillip colonists, expressed the opinion that Buckley was 'a lump of matter, too mindless to yield any very useful information'. A Victorian Protector of the Aborigines, William Thomas, claimed Buckley was 'more ignorant than the blacks and perfectly useless to them'.[53] 'Stupid as a bandicoot', echoes Charles Barrett in *White Blackfellows*.[54]

In 1901 George Sutherland wrote a simplified version of the story for children in his *Sixteen Stories of Australian Settlement*. In this version, Buckley remembers his loyalty to his fellow countrymen

'The Wild White Man': an impression of William Buckley from
George Sutherland, *Sixteen Stories of Australian Settlement*, 1901

when he overhears the Wathaurang planning to attack a nearby party of white men – a contingent of John Batman's expedition. He decides to warn the party of white men, and his arrival at their camp is described from their point of view:

> One morning they saw a very tall man coming towards them. He stopped at a little distance, and they had a good look at him. He was plainly not a black, although his skin was brown with exposure, his hair and beard were long and tangled, he had only a kangaroo skin to cover him, and he held in his hand some spears, a boomerang, and a waddy.

When Buckley comes in contact again with white men he is taught to speak 'his own language just as a mother teaches her child', until 'gradually from being "the wild white man", he became a civilised human being once more'.[55]

In the mid to late nineteenth century the Australian colonists genuinely feared that civilised white men who associated too closely with natives could '[fall] into savagery'.[56] It seems those who were least civilised to begin with, such as stupid convicts, were most susceptible. Of the sealers, Bonwick noted in 1870 that 'all were not runaway convicts; though, perhaps, all were of a type belonging to no high order of civilisation'.[57] For them, like Buckley, it was a shorter, more likely step from white man to 'savage'.

Here convictism merged with Aboriginality – the two fears that haunted the respectable colonists in the 'civilised centres'. The sealers, like William Buckley, might be called 'Robinson Crusoes', but they were in fact his antithesis. Lacking his bourgeois religiosity, they have been demonised by a nineteenth-century colonial moral reasoning that viewed their adaptation and adoption of Aboriginal culture as mere regression and depravity.

The nineteenth-century commentators' reasoning is recapitulated and perpetuated by Blainey, Hughes, Molony and Clark with almost no translation. By seeing these texts as recycled, we can begin to liberate men like Nat Thomas from the hyperbole of savagery, to recognise their knowledge, and begin to look out from their eyes.

Knowing

The would-be travellers could see Hog Bay from where they were stranded at Cape Jervis, but there was not a breath of wind to take them there. They waited for two long, hot days. Their skipper, local legend Nat Thomas, filled the empty hours with tales of the early days on Kangaroo Island, and filled the city listeners with anticipation for their first visit across Backstairs Passage. Among the group of tourists was W. A. Cawthorne. He was captivated:

> 'Nat' was a perfect character; he had been 32 years on Kangaroo Island; and as geologists find it difficult to account for the disposition of boulders – those erratic wanderers from respectable strata – so it may be a difficult problem to account for the singular life such a man has led ... He can give you some reminiscences of his visits or residence, of escapes and adventures, and of perils and dangers. He is a compound of sailor, sealer, farmer and wild man. He possesses all the resources of the sailor, combined with instincts of the aboriginal native. Place him on the western end of Kangaroo Island, with only a dog and a knife, and he will find his way out at the other – a feat he has done, I believe, more than once.[1]

Here is the story of a man who had changed. He had come from a middle-class English family and ended up on an island in the Antipodes; from knowing his way through the streets of London to being able to find his way through the thick scrub of Kangaroo Island. He had learnt to hunt, skin and swim, and had acquired at least one Aboriginal language.

When men like Nat Thomas first arrived on Kangaroo Island they were mostly young sailors fresh from the sea, hungry to join the gangs skinning bloody seal carcasses on the beaches. Few knew much about Aboriginal society, but they knew how to take what they wanted. And they needed Aboriginal knowledge: how to find water and food, how to hunt wallabies, kangaroos and seals. This was knowledge they would eventually acquire for themselves, and would boast of to tourists in years to come. But from the beginning their need gave complexity to their often violent and oppressive relationships with Aboriginal women. Cultural exchange requires some equality, and early Kangaroo Island was a meeting place of cultures.

The story of a trader, John Jones, illustrates this point. Jones left Launceston in charge of the *Henry* in 1833 to take gear and provisions to the whaling station at Hog Bay. He also crossed to Cape Jervis, where he found an Aboriginal community of about ten families. In a report written shortly after his journey, Jones described how he successfully negotiated with Aborigines in Cape Jervis to employ five men to work with him sealing. Of the five, two 'were with him constantly for near five months'. Jones repaid these two with pistols, powder and shot. Weapons are not given to a potential enemy. Indeed, Jones claimed that neither he nor his crew 'were ever annoyed by the natives, although some of the crew frequently slept on the shore'.

In all his time on the mainland coast, Jones 'saw their women and children only at a distance'.[2] It seems the Cape Jervis people had become wise by past experiences, and now handled negotiations on their terms. Jones arrived about twenty years after white men had first begun visiting the mainland from Kangaroo Island. Contact between the two groups had not merely resulted in submission and fear on the part of the Aborigines.

At times it was quite the opposite. George Meredith, a sealer, spent a few years on Kangaroo Island before deciding to establish himself on the eastern shores of St Vincent's Gulf, opposite

Kangaroo Island, in about 1834. He left Kangaroo Island with an Aboriginal working team, including Sal, who was later living on Kangaroo Island with Betty, and two young mainland Aboriginal men. When they reached the mainland, one of the young men killed Meredith and the three then used his boat and tools to carry out their own hunting.

With a boat in the ownership of the Aborigines on the other side of the strait, there was a sudden reversal of power – now the Islanders feared that they would be attacked. They particularly feared 'Encounter Bay Bob', a most notorious warrior, who they believed would come and kill them all. But their fears were never realised; Meredith's boat lost its moorings and was smashed at sea.[3] Ten years after the event, Sal and Suke were arrested for Meredith's murder; it was on this story that Cawthorne based his novel *The Islanders*.[4]

Meredith's is not the only story of a white man killed by Aborigines in pre-colonial South Australia. In February 1830 explorer Charles Sturt had been away from Sydney for more than three months and no news had been heard from him, so the New South Wales government dispatched the *Dart* to South Australian waters. She arrived in early March but could find no sign of Sturt. The government then instructed Captain Collett Barker in the *Isabella* to ascertain what they had hoped to learn from Sturt: whether there was a passage of water from Lake Alexandrina to St Vincent's Gulf.

In May 1831 Captain Barker found that Lake Alexandrina met the sea at the mouth of the River Murray, in Encounter Bay. He left his party and swam across the mouth of the river to explore, his compass tied to his head. He then climbed the sand-hills opposite and walked down the other side. Two hours later his party heard shouting 'as of a man in great agony'. Only one man in Barker's party could swim; he found the captain dead the following afternoon.

Barker had never heard his attackers approach. Cummarrin-geree's spear had entered his left hip and 'came out at the opposite side'. Barker, unarmed, fled into the sea and waved his hands to show his defencelessness. Pennegoora's spear entered his right

flank. Wannangetta's entered his back and came through his
stomach. The three men pulled out their spears and stabbed
Barker until he was certainly dead. They dumped his body in the
deep sea.[5]

For all their knives, guns and boats, the white Kangaroo
Islanders were in the minority, both numerically and culturally, on
this yet uncolonised coast. They were not like the invaders who
would follow them. They did not have the infrastructure or
numbers to invade Aboriginal land wholesale. They had to nego-
tiate, often on the terms set by the Aboriginal people.

In 1837 Nat Thomas explored the mainland Fleurieu Peninsula
on behalf of the new colonial settlers. He was accompanied by a
group of men including John Bull, who recorded the event. Two
horses from the exploratory team went missing, and the men set
out to find them. Nat Thomas's group travelled south, towards the
Onkaparinga River. When their water supplies ran out, Nat
assured the party: 'When we get to the top of that rise we shall see
the outlet of a river; the water is salt, but there are native wells
under the sandhills.' Bull explains that Nat 'had landed there
when sealing'.

But Nat had done more than seal near the mouth of the
Onkaparinga River. When the party followed him up the rise to
the river, they found a camp of Aborigines. The Aboriginal men,
writes Bull, 'set up a great shout' and 'brandished their spears'. Nat
was 'disconcerted'. He 'muttered, "full moon, come down to fish
and hold a corroboree; they must be Onkaparinga and Encounter
Bay blacks"'.

Nat explained to the members of his party that 'the black
woman whom he had on the island belonged to one of these
tribes, and he was aware they were not pleased at her absence'.
Nat 'understood a few of their words', wrote Bull, 'but thought it
better for him to keep as much out of sight as possible'.[6] It is not
known who this woman was, or whether she was from the
Onkaparinga River or Encounter Bay.

It is also hard to know how accurate Bull's story is. Whatever
indiscretion Nat had committed on their land and to their people,
he knew both well; he knew of their laws, their patterns of

movement, their language and their water resources. This *kringali*, this outsider, had some insight into their world.

It was George Bates who told Robert Davis, the assistant surgeon on Barker's *Isabella*, about how his captain had died. 'I have much satisfaction in stating', reported Davis, 'that G. Bates, from the knowledge he possessed of the language and manners of the natives, proved of essential service in obtaining the above information'.[7]

In 1886 George Bates told the *South Australian Advertiser* how he had taken Aboriginal women from the mainland by force – women who scratched his face in anger when their hands were unbound. But Bates also spoke of how he had invited an Aboriginal man and his son from Cape Jervis to stay with him on Kangaroo Island. They accepted, but the son died shortly after their arrival. The bereaved father asked Bates to return with him to his 'tribe', promising that 'the men would hunt for him, give him wives, and make him a chief among them'. Bates agreed, and was 'received at a grand corroboree'. He was then, he claims, 'made a member of the tribe by being thrown on his back and having all the males jump on his body in succession'.[8]

Bates also wrote to the *Register* newspaper in 1886, claiming that 'in 1827 I was living with the natives from Cape Jervis to Adelaide'.[9] The 'natives' were probably a group of Kaurna people, as St Vincent's Gulf is part of their land. He most likely travelled with a group along this eastern coast, hunting with them and learning some of the stories of their land. He told the *Advertiser* reporter in 1886 that 'the Cape Jervis people showed a mysterious dread of the Onkaparinga River, alleging ... it was inhabited by some terrible animal which would exterminate the tribe if they come within range of his sense of smell'.[10]

Bates also said that the Cape Jervis people 'never let him out of their sight, and appeared suspicious of him'. He said they looked after him well until his dogs died, when they left him to fend for himself. Soon afterwards some of his fellow Islanders, who had warned him against leaving, found him sick and starving in a cave near a beach on the mainland. Perhaps Bates without his hunting dogs was a burden to the Cape Jervis community. Or perhaps they had been right to suspect him of wrongdoing; maybe he had committed a misdemeanour. But the story shows that without the Aboriginal people's support and knowledge, Bates could not survive on their land.

'A black native will live where a white man will starve', claimed W. H. Leigh in his 1839 book *Reconnoitering, Voyages, Travels and Adventures in the Colonies of South Australia*, a detailed account of his experiences and the cultural practices of the Aboriginal people of coastal South Australia.[11] Henry 'Governor' Wallen, who became a key informant for Leigh, also spent considerable time on the mainland with the Aboriginal people.

'Governor Wallen', Leigh wrote, 'informed me of a singular ceremony which he was once permitted to witness'. It 'consisted in the lying in state of a famous old warrior chief'. While the 'chief' had died in battle, his body had been 'rescued' and 'placed in one of their huts, on a kind of bed'. But some of the captured enemies 'were hung up by the heels, over a slow fire; and as the fat melted from them, they sung and greased their waddies with it. Anticipating a cannibal banquet, he withdrew in disgust.'[12]

Again the voyeurism of the outsider creates the horror: the ceremony was told by one Englishman to another and then presented to an English audience; the 'anticipated' (not witnessed) cannibalism must inevitably disgust. But the mourning of the 'warrior chief' is presented with a sense of sacredness: Wallen had been 'permitted' to 'witness' this ceremony 'once'. That he was invited also suggests that he occupied a place in the private world of the Aboriginal people and was privileged to do so.

Wallen told Leigh of another Aboriginal sacred practice. 'They are very superstitious', he confided. 'That woman (pointing to one of his own) pretends she can turn a bubble of water into a beautiful white stone that will cure any thing.' The women, Wallen claimed, would 'throw' the bubbles on the fire, then produce round quartz stones already placed in their hands. 'Those few who possess the secret', he added, 'are treated with additional respect'.

If the bearer of a stone bubble finds the bone remains of another's meal, she will wrap them up in grass and carry them with her. Then 'the life of the unfortunate bone-picker is in [her] hands'. To 'cause his death' she only has to rub the stone and 'pronounce certain words'. A pocket of air that becomes solid stone and thus holds the power to take life as if popping a bubble seems a powerful metaphor of the impermanence and preciousness of existence.[13]

Was it a Tasmanian metaphor? Wallen lived with two, possibly three women taken from Van Diemen's Land. But he also told Leigh that a white man he knew had spent some months with Aborigines on the nearby mainland who held this belief so profoundly that they always burnt all the bones after a meal. As a result, the man's dogs were deprived of their dinner, and he had to feed them his own rations to sustain them. Eventually they died of starvation. Desperate, the man ate his emaciated dogs, and only after that did he manage to 'make his escape' from the Aborigines. Was this another version of Bates's story? If so, had Bates in fact been held captive on the mainland by the Kaurna? Perhaps this is what he implied when he said they watched 'his every move'. Did they treat him as a 'chief', as he boasted, or as an abductor who deserved to know what it was like to be an abductee?

Perhaps Bates's version of the story was simply posturing. In truth, he had been one white man in an Aboriginal community. He had to behave in their world according to their rules. If the stories of the stone bubble, the monster of the Onkaparinga River, the chief warrior laid out in his hut were accurate, they show that the Islanders had learnt something of those worlds. Such secret and sacred knowledge implies a relationship more complex than mere abduction and rape, cutting off of ears and slashing of buttocks. It suggests that the Aboriginal women spoke of their country and beliefs, and the white men listened.

By the early to mid-1830s, the heyday of the Kangaroo Island skin trade was over. Many sealers had left for Bass Strait or for the colonies and had taken Aboriginal women with them. Kangaroo Island became a quieter place. It also became a predominantly Aboriginal place.

In early 1836 Captain Hart estimated there were eight

European men, aged between thirty-three and seventy, living on Kangaroo Island. He also estimated that there were 'about sixteen native women'. He doesn't name the women or guess at their ages, but they would most likely have been in their early thirties.[14] Hart did not account for any children, but by this time at least twelve had been born on Kangaroo Island.[15] Some, like Wallen's son Henry, were in their early teens and may have already left the island. Henry junior, also known as 'Whalley', worked as a whaler in the southern seas, including the sub-Antarctic islands.[16] But most of the island-born children, including Nat and Betty's, were still toddlers under the age of five.

Hart did not account for any Aboriginal men living on the island, but there were two young Aboriginal men living at Three Wells River in 1836.[17] The racial and gender divide on Kangaroo Island, the white men's domination, was not as clear as might be assumed. The white men did not remain, if they ever simply were, cruel masters of 'willing slaves'. They became culturally changed.

'I eats everything', proclaims 'Georgy' in W. A. Cawthorne's *The Islanders*. Georgy, a character possibly based on George Bates, prepares a 'Kangaroo Island dinner' for a visitor who has come to trade some rum for salt. The dinner consists of roast 'iguano' (goanna), young dog, wallaby, raw ants' eggs, 'waikeries' (witchetty grubs) and the 'heart of a grass-tree' (yacca). The ants' eggs, Georgy proclaims, 'melts on the tongue', but can taste 'mouldy-like' if there are hatched ants in the dish.

Is this pure fiction? In 1837 W. H. Leigh was surprised to find that several of the ants' nests near Nepean Bay were hollow. Henry Wallen, his guide, explained to him that this was because they were on 'some of *his women's* favourite hunting-ground' and that they 'had pulled them to pieces to obtain the inhabitants'. Leigh later watched as some women took a 'large piece of the ant-hill' and 'jostled and shook it about till the ants were nearly all out in their hands'. They then rolled the insects into 'a ball' and threw them into their mouths 'with evident satisfaction'.[18]

But Georgy finds the grubs the most delicious. 'This here bit o' worm', he ponders out loud, 'is the soffest possible . . . and he lives on the hardest wood in the land?' To get them, he explains to the visitor, 'the blacks has a long thin stick with a hook in the end, and they puts it down and hooks 'em out'.[19]

Leigh, out walking with Wallen and others, observed how an Aboriginal man in their party kept poking a stick into a tree, then pulling it out and sucking on it. Supposing that the man was finding honey, Leigh imitated him. When the man saw Leigh 'suck the bare end of the stick', he laughed until 'he was unable to support himself'. Leigh realised that the Aboriginal man was in fact putting the stick in his mouth to tighten the grass that bound a hook. He watched the man poke the stick in a tree and pull out a fat grub 'nearly the size of my thumb'.[20]

The first Islanders, and the generations who followed them, found that wallaby tails made good eating, especially when dropped into boiling water then seared on an open fire. But wallabies were not easily shot, especially with the slow-loading muskets of the 1820s; they had to be snared. Using canvas thread or pieces of sinew about eighteen inches long, Aboriginal women made little nooses, stretched them on small Y-shaped sticks the height of a wallaby's head, and placed them along the wallaby tracks that crossed through the scrub.[21]

One day when W. H. Leigh was out walking, he was 'overtaken ... by an islander and his three black wives, (or gins, as they are called)'. The Islander, 'a resident here fifteen years', was hunting wallaby: 'having previously set snares in the path through the wood ... he hurried off to examine them'.[22] This skill, taught by the Aboriginal women, provided an essential item of trade on pre-colonial Kangaroo Island: in December 1831, John Hart anchored in Nepean Bay, where he procured salt and also bought 150 sealskins and 12,000 wallaby skins.[23] The dark, soft pelts were highly valued on the China skin market.

In Cawthorne's novel, Georgy also tells the visitor about the 'heart' of the 'grass-tree' on his menu. 'Yer chops all the leaves away', he explains, 'and gees it a smart rap, and the heart jumps out beautiful'. It is so rich in energy that 'yer can live upon it by the week'. Almost a century after Cawthorne wrote his book, the ethnologist Norman Tindale was told on Kangaroo Island that Suke had survived in the last week of her life solely upon the heart of a single 'yacca' that she had smashed out with a stone.[24] The women's survival and hunting skills were passed on to the white men. Without Aboriginal knowledge, there would have been no Islanders; no Englishmen turned 'complete savages'.

In this passage from *The Islanders*, Cawthorne clearly admires the ingenuity of the men who lived on the uncolonised Kangaroo Island. Cawthorne defends them against those who might find them 'barbarous' by claiming they had a 'high talent, in the Kangaroo Island sense'.

> To row, to fish, to swim, to fight, to endure, to devise, these were Kangaroo Island abilities, the proofs of genius, the steps of rank, the very L.L.D's and M.A.'s of their social rank. After all, of what merit are the graces of civilisation? They are only relative. It is most unphilosophical to attribute merit to the polish of polite society, for beyond its sphere it is useless.[25]

Cawthorne's 'high talent' – these 'proofs of genius' – were often traditional Aboriginal practices. So Georgy, for example, was renowned for his roast goanna and wallaby. Indeed, to Cawthorne, the truly qualified were the Aboriginal women themselves. In a scene set in Backstairs Passage, 'Black Bet' is introduced in glowing terms:

> In the bow, and pulling the bow oar, was a woman, 'Black Bet,' Sam's favourite wife. She was a Vandemonian black, and exceedingly expert as a huntress on land or water. As a fisher-woman or sailoress her abilities were unrivalled ... Black Bet ... was invaluable.[26]

The sailors were 'amazed' to see 'Black Bet' throw off her clothes and dive into the sea to catch a crayfish:

> The crayfish doubled, and Black Bet doubled hither and thither. Bet rose to the water, took an enormous gulp of air, and down she went the second time. The crayfish made for the shore, Bet after him. He then tried to hide himself in the

sand. That was a fatal mistake; Bet seized him by his large feelers, and triumphantly bore him back to the ship.[27]

Whether Cawthorne read about shellfish diving or learnt about it on the island, it is a traditional Aboriginal Tasmanian women's practice.[28] He also claimed that 'no tree was too tall or too straight for [Bet] to climb in her native fashion with a circular coil of rope made of bark'. This too is a traditional Aboriginal Tasmanian practice.

Was Black Bet based on the real-life Betty? Not only does it seem that Cawthorne had met Betty, but he also claims in the text that he did base his character upon her. Cawthorne tells of how, much later than the period in which the novel is set, 'a vessel was wrecked, and the crew and passengers got on the shore'. Black Bet was 'the means of their rescue', leading them to a native well and 'guiding them to a place of safety'.[29]

The *Osmali* was wrecked on Kangaroo Island's southern D'Estree Bay in 1853. The passengers made it safely to the beach and were saved by the arrival of Nat Thomas, accompanied by 'an Aboriginal woman' who brought them biscuits, flour and eggs. The 'Aboriginal woman' also showed the crew a freshwater spring in a gully about five miles inland. She may well have been Betty.[30] This heroic woman appears hardly to have been a chattel slave. As Cawthorne's sailors put it, she was 'invaluable'.

One of Betty's favourite camping places was at the northern end of the long white beach that the Islanders called Creek Bay. In this sheltered corner, once a favourite landing place for the sealers, the creek does not quite meet the sea. Papery eucalypts over-shadow shallow yellow water. About a hundred years after Betty camped there, her grandchildren showed Norman Tindale the place, and he dug down and found the traditional tools Betty once used to skin animals by the remnants of her fireplaces.[31]

Betty also spent time at the 'beautiful spot' where Nat Thomas had chosen to build his home. There they negotiated a relation-ship more complex than that of chattel and owner. On the plaque that honours Nat Thomas at Antechamber Bay, Betty is described as his 'wife'. Did Betty fulfil the English meaning of that word?

Did she sleep next to Nat Thomas in a bed within the walls of his small timber cottage? Did she enjoy the cool air of the rooms when he rebuilt the walls with thick stone – the walls that still stand today?

Betty often slept in traditional shelters far beyond those stone walls; for months at a time, she walked and hunted away from Antechamber Bay with the other Aboriginal Tasmanian women. Her eldest daughter was born far away on the island's south coast. All three of the children she had with Nat were brought up as Betty had been in Tasmania rather than as Nat had been in London. They grew up fishing, and hunting kangaroo and wallaby. They spoke their mother's language as well as their father's.[32]

Perhaps Nat learnt to speak Betty's language too; after all, he could speak a few words of at least one mainland Aboriginal language. Wallen's mate William Day at Three Wells River had forgotten how to speak English fluently by the mid-1830s. Perhaps for years he had spoken only an Aboriginal language, or a mix of Kaurna, Ngarrindjeri, English and Tasmanian languages.[33]

For so many years these white men had lived outside a place where the English culture or language was dominant. For so many years they had not felt cotton against their skin, eaten leavened bread or broiled mutton, or tied up the laces on a pair of boots.

Such was also the life of the men who lived with Aboriginal Tasmanian women on the Bass Strait islands. In 1837 there were six Aboriginal Tasmanian women living on the islands; their numbers had fallen by sixty-eight in less than seven years. There were also four Australian mainland women, and one woman of Maori and Tasmanian ancestry living with twelve white men.[34]

G. A. Robinson had lobbied for the Aboriginal women to be taken off the islands. But on his mission stations the Aboriginal Tasmanian people died, while on the islands of Bass Strait and on Kangaroo Island they had healthy children who survived. In 1996 Aboriginal people across Tasmania, including the Bass Strait, made up four per cent (15,322) of the State's population (474,000).[35] They are recognised and funded by the Australian Commonwealth

Government as an Aboriginal community, which many of them call the Palawa.[36]

On the Bass Strait islands the Palawa are still pulling mutton-birds out of holes, still remembering their sealing ancestors and the traditions the Aboriginal women passed on to them. But on Kangaroo Island the descendants discovered their Aboriginal and sealing ancestors by reading a magazine, a junior encyclopaedia, a newspaper. They remember their ancestors not by traditional Aboriginal practices but by plaques. Why? What happened?

Settling

At noon on 27 July 1836, the South Australian Company's *Duke of York* dropped anchor at Nepean Bay, Kangaroo Island. After taking lunch, the passengers waded to the beach, the sailors carrying the ladies and children. There they joined in a Church of England service, which Captain Morgan concluded with a prayer of thanks-giving for their safe journey. A rainbow appeared, and Morgan remarked that it was a good omen for the new settlement.[1]

This was the same bay where Flinders had looked a kangaroo in the eye and Baudin had taken eighteen away; the same bay where Captain Pendleton had sought his moiety of sealskins and so many had followed him in search of skins and salt; where sealers' campsites had been erected and abandoned, leaving a small cross-cultural community. Now these new 'settlers' stood and prayed and imagined they were the first. For this same bay was the site of a proposed settlement named 'Kingscote', in the new British province of 'South Australia'.

No one had told Nat Thomas, George 'Fireball' Bates, Henry 'Governor' Wallen, Betty, Sal or Suke. They didn't know that the South Australian Colonization Act had been passed in London in 1834, declaring their home part of a new colony. What must they have thought when they saw the *Duke of York* land with its ladies and gentlemen, followed days later by the *Lady Mary Pelham*, weeks later by the *John Pirie* and the *Rapid* and months later by the *Cygnet*, the *Africaine* and the *Tam O'Shanter*, bringing their crews and 379 settlers?[2]

The South Australian Company chose Kangaroo Island as the site of its new settlement, the Adelaide *Advertiser* claimed in 1926, because Captain Barker's murder by the natives at the Murray Mouth five years earlier 'had made people nervous' of the mainland.[3] It was also the only place that they could learn much about. Those who knew the South Australian coast at first hand were the men who had been trading in skins and salt, and most of them had spent time at Nepean Bay.

The Company's key informant was Captain George Sutherland, the trader who had thought the Islanders were 'complete savages' who smelt like 'foxes' when he came to Kangaroo Island to collect skins in 1819. Despite the Islanders' smelliness, Sutherland praised Kangaroo Island as an ideal setting for a new settlement. And so, on the strength of a report by a man who had spent seven months there seventeen years before, the South Australian Company despatched its expensive boats, stocked with whaling and fishing gear, coopers and carpenters, families and small children, to settle 'Kingscote'.

If the Islanders saw the passengers of the *Duke of York* wade onto the beach on 27 July, they did not make themselves known. The settlers' first night at Nepean Bay was spent on board. The next day they took the first step in establishing their colony. They set up tents near the beach, at what the sealers called Snakes Point, and renamed it 'South Australian Company's Point'. This cumbersome name has not lasted. It is known today as Reeves Point, after one of the new settlers.

The new settlers' most pressing need was to find fresh food and water. Captain Morgan and the Colonial Manager, Samuel Stephens, ventured east from Nepean Bay and found an estuary, but it was disappointingly salty. They followed the inlet upstream for about five miles, hoping it would at some point become fresh. It was Three Wells River, but they did not go far enough inland to find Henry Wallen's farm. Assuming the river was their own discovery, Stephens christened it with a little brandy and called it 'the Morgan'. This name has not lasted either. It is known today as Cygnet River. Morgan and Stephens returned to their beach-camp late that night.

The next morning, a chilly winter's day, the new settlers woke with alarm to the sound of 'natives' laughing at them in the scrub and making ready to attack. A couple of kookaburras were greeting dawn.[4] This place of thick scrub and salt water was confusing and uncertain.

That day, Stephens ordered that wells be dug on the beach to procure fresh water. He then led a party back up Three Wells River to hunt for fowl, as he had seen plenty of ducks and swans the day before. The Islanders had been watching the settlers. Two men and several Aboriginal women approached the settlement at Snakes Point with wallaby, vegetables and watermelon. The men introduced their Aboriginal partners to the party and explained that they had all lived on the island for about twenty years. Morgan did not record their names; he assumed that they were ex-convicts, although they seemed 'good fellows'. It was lucky that the Islanders had thought to bring food to the new settlers. Stephens and his party returned late that day, exhausted, with only a crow.[5]

The Islanders who went to Snakes Point may have come with goods from Henry Wallen's farm, but it seems that Wallen did not go himself. Morgan first encountered Wallen three days later. Morgan and Stephens were again searching for fresh water when Morgan looked up to see Wallen on the other side of Three Wells River. He wrote in his journal: 'I saw a man like when a boy I have seen Robinson Crusoe with long hair and beard, a stick in his hand and very little apparel.' What came alive on the other side of the river was a fictional character from his boyhood, not a man changed by new cultural encounters, a man who had found fresh water in this land long before Morgan.

W. H. Leigh, the surgeon on the *South Australian*, who spent time talking with Wallen in 1837, described him in his journal as 'the august Robinson Crusoe (an excellent personification)'. Leigh extended the analogy to the two Aboriginal men living with Wallen at the farm, describing them as his 'Man Fridays'.[6] On this occasion, Wallen had given Leigh and his party a bed for the night at Three Wells ('fleas, fleas, nothing but fleas!', Leigh remembered).[7] In the morning Wallen served them a breakfast of tea and wallaby tails, then took them out to shoot ducks. While Leigh noted the adaptations, his only point of reference was a fictional text he had once read.

Leigh drew a picture of himself and a companion sitting around a fire with the three Aboriginal women who lived with Wallen. They are depicted as thick-set and moustached, dressed in men's shirts and woollen hats, and smoking pipes in the shelter of a wind-break. Thanks to Leigh's curiosity, we have an image of cultures adapted and shared in South Australia's first colonial year.

W. H. Leigh, 'A night scene in the bush, Kangaroo Island', from his 1839 book *Reconnoitering, Voyages, Travels and Adventures in the New Colonies of South Australia*

While Wallen met the new settlers only days after their arrival, it took Nat Thomas, living at Antechamber Bay, a little longer to learn that they had arrived. According to Fireball Bates, who told the story to the *South Australian Advertiser* in 1886, Nat saw the *John Pirie* arrive in September 1836. Bates's memory was only a little rusty – it landed on 16 August. Bates claimed that Nat rushed to Hog Bay, where Bates was then camping, to tell him that he had seen 'a large ship crowded with people'. Early next morning, the new immigrants emerged from their tents on the beach to see

Nat, Bates, three Aboriginal women and a pack of dogs coming towards them. Shouts of alarm were raised and there was a 'general stampede of men, women and children' up the cliff from the beach – they thought the 'natives' were attacking.[8]

Their fear and confusion are reminiscent of Bates's story of his own arrival on Kangaroo Island in 1824, also told in the same newspaper article. He said he had reached for his rifle when he first encountered Wallen, Everett, Kirby and an Aboriginal woman dressed in skins, thinking they were all 'blackfellows'. But in this story, Bates is now one of the 'blackfellows'. Again we can picture the red head thrown back in laughter at the moment of confusion between what is black and white. Bates is clearly amused that he and Nat, 'clothed in opossum skin shirts, and with coats, trousers, and boots made of the skin of the red kangaroo, were mistaken for savage inhabitants of the new country'. He liked the idea that they had lost so much of their Englishness that they were no longer distinguished from the Aboriginal women with them. That they had become so *unEnglish* that they triggered the settlers' fear of the unknown.

Mary Thomas, a South Australian Company settler who arrived at Nepean Bay in the *Africaine* in November 1836, felt this fear. She saw Nat Thomas rowing out to greet the ship in his skins and with matted hair. He fell overboard and when he scrambled on the deck of her ship, she noted in her diary, he 'shook himself as a dog does when just out of water'. She thought that 'he was more like a savage ... than an Englishman'.[9]

When Captain Morgan was introduced to Wallen's friend Day, an ex-sailor, he found he was 'quite nativefied. His voice appears to have lost his native tongue'.[10] Morgan could only hear a language lost. He could only hear the silence of the culture he knew, not the sounds of a new culture encountered.

Morgan's personal reflection and W. H. Leigh's appeal to a British reader both used the century-old image of Robinson Crusoe to describe Henry Wallen. In so doing they echoed earlier descriptions of the Islanders as dislocated and abstracted from all that whiteness should be. But unlike those previous writers, Morgan, Leigh and Mary Thomas did not lambast the Islanders for their way of living. As the new, official settlers, they interpreted the Islanders' lack of culture as a lack of legitimacy.

Although the settlers had known from Sutherland's report that there were sealers and Aboriginal women living on Kangaroo Island, they still believed they were the first settlers in a new country. They did not realise that this island had placenames and a known geography. They did not seem to remember it had once been an important part of a prosperous industry, that it had older relationships with Bass Strait and the other colonies, and with the indigenous communities of the mainland. They did not regard this as a place that other people called home.

∾

When the British House of Commons passed the South Australian Colonization Act in 1834, it established the framework for the founding of a free colony to be administered jointly by the Colonial Office and a Colonization Commission. The Commission would effectively be appointed by the gentlemen enthusiasts who had proposed the venture. It was to be an exercise in social engineering, influenced by Edward Gibbon Wakefield's notions of 'system-atic' colonisation. To ensure a secure supply of labour, land in the new colony would be sold at a price sufficient to put it out of the reach of most of the colonists in the short term, and the proceeds would be used to finance free immigration. The South Australian Company raised the finance and helped to screen the would-be emigrants who applied to take part in this social experiment.

But matters did not proceed in quite the orderly manner that the Company had planned. In 1835 Sir George Grey and Lord Glenelg became jointly responsible for the Colonial Office in London. Both men had close links with the anti-slavery movement and missionary bodies, and it was with these interests in mind that they questioned the South Australian Colonization Act. They were concerned that the Act did not recognise Aboriginal rights to the land, and they insisted that it must do so before the colonists could depart.

The Commissioners were worried; the Company's ships were already preparing for their journeys, and there was no obvious way out of the problem. Their entire scheme rested on the assumption that the colonial authorities would have unimpeded control over the allocation of land. But Robert Torrens, the chairman of the Commission, surpassed even the Colonial Office's expectations. He stated that the cession of land was to be 'perfectly voluntary' and that Aborigines who ceded land would be supplied with subsistence and religious and moral instruction.[11] A Protector would be appointed who would determine whether any land for sale was 'in the occupation or enjoyment of the natives'. If it was, and the Aborigines did not want to surrender it, then the Protector would be responsible for ensuring that their rights to occupation were fully protected.[12] Historian Henry Reynolds, who deals with this issue at length in *The Law of the Land*, observes that the Torrens amendment to the 1834 Act was the first constitutional recognition of Aboriginal land rights in Australia.

But Reynolds adds that in practice the amendment 'meant nothing'. Torrens had informed Lord Glenelg that the Aborigines' right to property would be protected '*should such right be anywhere found to exist*' [my italics]. The Commissioners did not believe such a right would be found.[13] The Commissioners' First Report to Parliament, sent after the ships' departure in April 1836, found that the Aborigines were 'not attached to the soil as cultivators' and did 'not appear to manifest the instinctive apprehension of some of the inferior animals'.[14] This sleight-of-hand permitted the South Australian Company's ships to set their courses for Kangaroo Island.

The introduction to the Commissioners' First Report, which gave the final outline of their land rights policy, also ushered in South Australia's unofficial settlers:

> The colonisation of South Australia by industrious and virtuous settlers, so far from being an invasion of the rights of the Aborigines, is a necessary preliminary to the displacement of the lawless squatters, the abandoned sailors, the runaway convicts, the pirates, the worse than savages, that now infest the coast of New Holland, and perpetrate against the defenceless natives crimes at which humanity revolts.[15]

This is hyperbole whipped to its most ludicrous. There were no hordes of pirates along the coast in 1836, only about eight middle-aged European men on Kangaroo Island. If the Commissioners did not know the precise number and ages of the Islanders at the time of writing, they at least knew that the sealers had never formed a pandemic of pillagers. The Company's chief source of information, Captain Sutherland's report, was included in the 1831 *Plan of Company*. The following year, the Commissioners interviewed Sutherland. The transcript, published in *Evidence Respecting the Soil, Climate, and Productions of the Coast of South Australia*, included the following exchange:

> Q. [Commissioners] Were you ever molested by these Sealers?
> A. [Sutherland] No, I never was interfered with at all by them, they used sometimes to come on board my vessel.
> Q. How many were there?
> A. About twelve, chiefly Englishmen, convicts and runaway sealers.[16]

This was eighteen years after Sutherland had met the Islanders. In his report, written for the Company in London the year before, he concluded his comments on the Islanders by stating 'there are few even still on the island', as if they were already an anomaly.[17]

The hyperbolic introduction to the Commissioners' First Report was even more obviously at odds with its Supplement, which included a letter from Commissioner John Morphett from Kangaroo Island. Morphett described the Islanders as 'intelligent, quiet men, having spots of land under cultivation; growing a little wheat, with potatoes, turnips, and other vegetables ... they have all expressed pleasure at the opportunity of entering into the relations of civilised life'.[18]

The Islanders had become puppets in a game of textual borrowing. The Commissioners' First Report undoubtedly has a flavour reminiscent of the *Hobart Town Gazette*. It is interesting how texts borrowed for new reasons can contradict their original uses. Where the Van Diemen's Land press viewed Kangaroo Island as the '*ultima thule*', the furthest known and least desirable place, the *Plan of a Company* described Kangaroo Island as 'a point of great importance' and 'a very desirable place'. The colonisation of this 'desirable' place was justified in the same language that had made Kangaroo Island undesirable. These textual contradictions were born out of geographically different perspectives. From Sydney or Hobart, Kangaroo Island seemed habitable only to a savage, but from faraway London it seemed a fresh place for a civilised new settlement.

In his book *Early Experiences in South Australia*, John Bull recounts the story of New South Welshman C. W. Stuart, who successfully applied for a preliminary section of land 'in a new colony to be called South Australia'. Although Stuart's friends strongly advised him against such a speculative venture, the persistent Mr Stuart went to Sydney in 1836 to organise his passage. There he found the name 'South Australia' was barely known, and communication with Kangaroo Island non-existent. Nevertheless, he approached the owner of the schooner *Truelove*, which was due to sail for western Australia, to see if he might have her call in at Nepean Bay on her way.

The owner was astonished; Mr Stuart recorded that he 'seemed to think that I had been duped, and advised me not on any account to go to Kangaroo Island till I knew positively that some vessels had arrived there from England'. The captain of the vessel gave Stuart much the same advice, but, seeing him so determined, promised to take him to Nepean Bay and see if there were indeed ships harboured at Kangaroo Island. Should there be none, he would take Stuart to Swan River and return him to Sydney at no extra charge.

When they reached Nepean Bay, the captain was surprised to find four ships in harbour: the *Rapid*, the *John Pirie*, the *Cygnet* and the *Africaine*. But the settlement was so short of provisions that the Colonial Manager bought the *Truelove*'s entire stock and sent her back to Sydney for more.[19]

In the first few days after their arrival, it was apparent that the South Australian Company's first settlers had come ill-prepared. In this salty, dry and scrubby land they could find little fresh water or food. When John Morphett said of the Islanders, 'I have no doubt we will find these men of great use', he was right.[20] The Islanders had welcomed the newcomers with fresh vegetables, watermelon and wallaby. Morphett later recorded that he had 'purchased turnips' from the Islanders 'at sixpence a dozen', and claimed 'their wheat is excellent'.[21] When the *Rapid* arrived in August, Nat Thomas, Henry Wallen and George Bates offered the passengers fresh wallaby for sale. Despite finding these 'enormous rat[s]' disgusting to look at, one settler was 'extremely grateful' to have fresh meat after months of ship's fare.[22]

George Bates told the *South Australian Advertiser* in 1886 how he and not Thomas were invited to lunch in the Colonial Manager's tent on the same day they met the new settlers. They spoke about the climate and soil of Kangaroo Island, and told him that the island was 'not flowing with milk and honey, and rich in gold and other minerals' as Sutherland had led him to believe.[23]

When the colony's Surveyor General, Colonel Light, arrived on Kangaroo Island in August 1836, he was shocked that the Company had made such a poor choice of site and had sent settlers before the land had been properly surveyed. From Charles Sturt's exploratory reports of six years earlier, Light had already imagined that the eastern shores of St Vincent's Gulf, where Adelaide now stands, would have been a wiser choice.[24] The Islanders told him the same thing.

Light employed four Islanders on his trips to the mainland. With his Aboriginal partners, William Cooper acted as interpreter, and one of his partners hunted kangaroos for Light's surveying party.[25] George Bates was employed by the Company to help build huts (in his personal opinion, the employees were hopeless).[26] Nat Thomas could not only offer advice on the reefs off Kangaroo Island, but, like other Islanders, was also able to predict the weather and advise when storms were due.[27] He went looking for the new colony's only two horses after they wandered off on the Fleurieu Peninsula in 1837, assisting in the 'exploration' of a land he already knew.[28]

The Islanders held valuable knowledge. They were sailors who knew the seas and had seen the coasts. They could interpret Aboriginal language and cultural meanings. They knew the land and how to survive in it. They made the new settlers look paltry.

While the settlers at the Company's camp had little fresh food and water, and were cold and some sick in their tents, only a few miles away was Wallen's fertile farm. 'A settler' who arrived on the *Duke of York* described it as 'a most beautiful park' with trees 'twenty feet round and ninety feet high'. He or she saw the house Wallen shared with William Day – 'the savages, as Captain Sutherland terms them in his book' – and described it as a picture of civility. It was made of trees 'driven into the ground ... pointed with clay and thatched'. Wallen hospitably spread a 'wallaby skin table cloth' and produced a 'leg of pork' for their dinner. Afterwards, he and Day escorted them 'round their estate', with its 'four acres of very fine wheat, and a large kitchen garden filled with every description of vegetable, as in England'. There was also a 'large lagoon' of fresh water 'sufficient to supply them and their stock throughout the year' and a farmyard with pigs, poultry and 'everything pertaining to a farm'. In a separate house 'lived three black women, two natives of the main and one of Van Diemen's Land'.[29]

After the tour, they partook of tea made from a 'native tree', which the settler remarked was 'as good as any tea I ever drank'. Wallen informed the settler that it was 'their only beverage', for he and Day believed liquor was 'the only cause of wretchedness of man'. Wallen then impressed the settler by baking damper in the ashes of the fire.[30]

While Wallen enjoyed home-baked bread and ate on a table-cloth, the Company settlers still suffered the discomforts of huts, tents and poor-quality food. So Stephens, Colonial Manager and pompous Wesleyan, decided that Wallen would hand over his farm to the South Australian Company. He sent a man up to give Wallen twenty shillings and order him off his estate. According to W. H. Leigh, Wallen took his coins to the wine-shop and temporarily forgot his promise to abstain.[31] In the 1950s, when Francis Bauer was studying the geography of Kangaroo Island, he was told that Stephens 'acquired the property for a song after plying the partners – Wallen and Day – with rum'.[32]

But was it so simple? Could twenty shillings really repay the years of work Wallen had invested in his beautiful farm? Was his abstinence so easily swayed? Or did Stephens's men threaten him, even with violence? While these questions cannot be answered, they beg to be asked.

Perhaps the very settlers who had admired Wallen's farm also profited from his loss. His eviction suggests the extent of their desperation. It also marks their true arrival. It was official power that gave them the right: Wallen was a squatter in a new province. And, as if the loss of his land were not enough, when Wallen decided to farm another spot, closer to Nat Thomas, he found the prices of his own stock so inflated that he could not afford to buy them back.

Stephens, the Colonial Manager, was mean not only because he was desperate, but because he was offended. An old insult had festered in him since his first encounter with Wallen. W. H. Leigh recounted the story as it had been told to him. After Stephens had 'landed with his cargo', Wallen apparently 'went down to the beach' to find out who he was. Stephens asked him, 'Who are you?' to which Wallen replied, 'I am the governor.' This prompted an immediate argument: 'You are no such thing,' said the 'enraged' Stephens who, assuming a grander title than that of Colonial Manager, claimed '*I* am governor.' Wallen remained stubborn: 'I tell you I am,' he replied. 'Who made you governor? You a governor! Why you are not even one of King John's men; you don't stand four feet in your stockings.'

'This', explains Leigh, 'was the first interview between the contending governors; and if any see this who know the parties, they will recollect that truly ludicrous scene'.[33] Indeed it is: the tall man in his kangaroo skins towering over the little pale man in his stockings, mocking him, showing him up, laughing at his pretentiousness.

Wallen had more reason to mock the scrawny Stephens as his settlement quickly turned into a debacle. It had not taken long for them to realise that Sutherland's rapturous report was bunkum. Stephens himself found 'almost every word of it a complete lie'.[34]

Sutherland had claimed that he and his men had dug a well at Nepean Bay and struck water 'as clear as chrystal ... I never tasted better'.[35] But when Stephens had wells dug there, they only found salt water. The settlers had to ferry water to the campsite every day from Point Marsden, more than four miles west, where they found freshwater wells dug by the Islanders.[36]

Sutherland had asserted that he had circumnavigated the island twice by sea and walked across it once, accompanied by two sealers. He claimed to have found on that journey hundreds of acres of open country with a few large trees, interspersed with fresh waterholes. The emus and kangaroos had grazed the grass short, and the soil seemed to Sutherland 'as good as any I have seen in Van Diemen's Land'.[37]

Sutherland's report, which included a map of his alleged journey across the island, was printed for the benefit of all the new settlers and the shareholders of the South Australian Company. On 1 November 1836, when the *Africaine* came in sight of the western coast of the island, six young men, keen for adventure, requested that they be put ashore at what is now Hanson Bay, on the south coast, and take Sutherland's route across the island to Nepean Bay. They landed in the evening and travelled a mile inland through thick scrub before setting up camp for the night. Starting at six o'clock next morning, they continued through the scrub for some hours, then rested, hot and thirsty, to examine Sutherland's report once more. 'When this belt of wood is passed', one of the men read out loud, 'you come on to an open country, covered with grass, where there are often hundreds of acres without a tree'.[38] So on they went, using a small hatchet to cut a path. They had not brought drinking water, just salt beef, biscuit and guns.

On 10 November four of the six men arrived at Nepean Bay, thoroughly exhausted from their nine-day ordeal. They had drunk the blood of seagulls and sucked the water off gum leaves. The other two were never found alive. Aboriginal women tried to track them; one was out for sixteen days. All they found was a set of tracks that seemed to go in circles, suggesting that whoever had made them had gone out of his mind. In 1858 a horseman found the skeletons of the two men, Slater and Osborne, near the north coast of the island, fifteen miles from fresh water.[39] 'I have now no hesitation in declaring', one of the survivors wrote in 1837, 'that nearly the whole of Captain Sutherland's report is one mass of

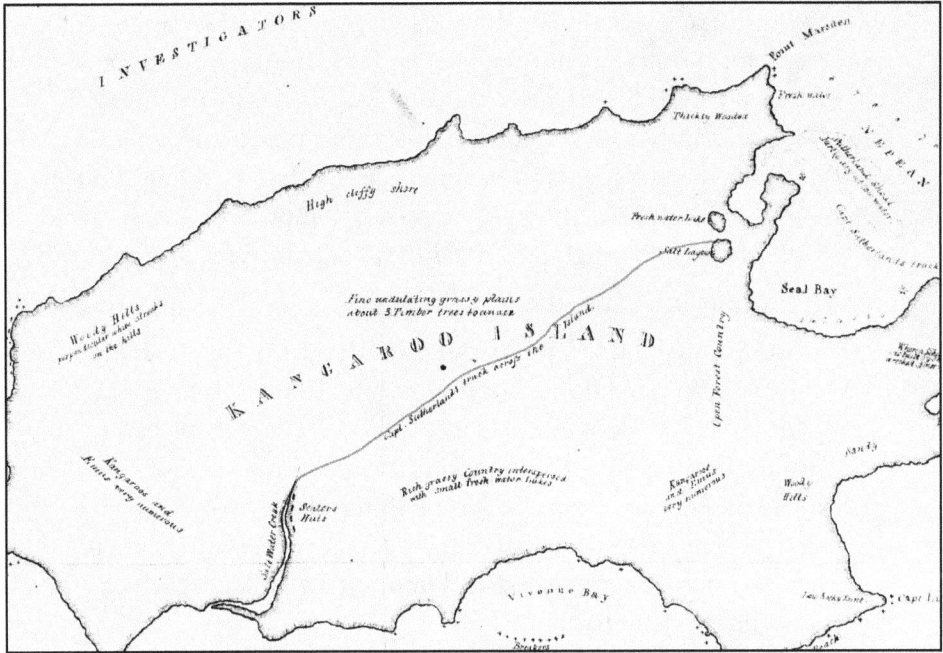

Captain Sutherland's map of Kangaroo Island, 1819, showing his
alleged journey across the island. National Library of Australia

falsehood'.[40] It was an Islander who later explained that Sutherland
'never was across the island at all'.[41]

The fisheries and attempts at hunting whales and seals were
found to be unproductive, and the Company's sealing and fishing
equipment soon lay discarded and rotting on the beach. The
scrub remained thick around the Company settlement, and
building was slow. Stephens insisted on paying the workers only in
promissory notes that had been printed in London. When they
downed tools, he produced a gun to force them back to work.

The temper of the settlement soon grew volatile. In September
1836 Stephens issued free rum to all the men to celebrate his
wedding. It caused a near-riot. Wesleyan though he was, Stephens
was prone to bouts of heavy drinking, when he would shout
abuse at the workers. It seemed all the men took to the bottle –
not surprising, when water was so scarce. In January 1837 a
Commission of Inquiry was held into 'the Lawless State of Society
on Kangaroo Island'. It was found that 'a system of disregard of

everything like even the outward observance of religion [had] prevailed for months . . . nothing can be more hopeless . . . there is no water, no land, nothing but drunkenness and demoralization'.[42]

The situation did not improve. Five months later the original Islanders decided to take the law into their hands. At midnight on 5 June 1837, some of them apparently attempted to evict the new settlers. W. H. Leigh described the incident in his journal:

> Great disturbances took place last night. Some of the wretches who have resided on the island, gaining for years a precarious existence, hurried down upon our tents at midnight, with fire brands, with a view of burning us all out. The villains had set fire to the country, in many places in a circumference of three miles; and conflagration, at such an hour, the uproar caused by the capture of some of the ring-leaders, the shouts of men, and screams of women and children, formed a scene, which I wish never again to witness.[43]

It seemed the 'intelligent, quiet men' of Kangaroo Island had been pushed beyond the point of hospitality. And perhaps in their angry actions they were influenced by the Aboriginal women. Aborigines had often used eviction by fire against explorers and settlers. Captain James Cook had encountered the same kind of protest on 19 July 1770 at Endeavour River in Queensland. After a dispute on board the *Endeavour*, a group of Aboriginal men went to a spot where some of Cook's crew were drying the nets and 'linnen', and set fire to the grass. Cook felt 'obliged to fire a musquet' to disperse them.[44]

Some seventy years later at Flinders River in Queensland, explorer Lort Stokes recorded that Aboriginal people had used a 'simple and ingenious' method of burning scrub to 'lure' his party away from where their dead lay.[45] In January 1838, Francis Henty of Portland Bay in Victoria noted in his journal that a group of Aborigines had 'fired the hills when they left' after being refused hospitality on his family's farm.[46]

On Kangaroo Island it seems the same Aboriginal practice was being used, but by white men – unofficial settlers – in an effort to evict the drunken and disorderly official colonists. Who were the 'worse than savages' now?

The meeting between the 'contending governors' exposes this irony. In this 'ludicrous scene' on the beach, two characters meet from two different histories. The sealers' history, the history of seas and beaches and cultural adaptation, meets the historical beginning of South Australia, with its dreams of order, profit, open grasslands, crystal-clear water and large shady trees. At this moment of ludicrous reality, all these absurd fantasies shatter. Far from being 'worse than savage', Wallen is found to be more 'industrious' and 'virtuous' than the man who was meant to supersede him. Kangaroo Island is found not to be the 'desirable place' the South Australian Company had promised, but neither is it the *'ultima thule'* lambasted in the *Hobart Town Gazette*.

As the two histories met, Kangaroo Island fell out of both of them. It is only a footnote to the narrative of the Aboriginal Tasmanian community of Bass Strait, as told by Lyndall Ryan and other historians. It was cordoned off, roped into the colonial narrative of South Australia. But it is only a footnote in that story as well. When the South Australian narratives of arrival and birth-places came to be written by the men now memorialised in the street names of Adelaide, Stephens's debacle at Nepean Bay was conveniently forgotten.[47] Despite Captain Morgan's sense of occasion on 27 July 1836, when he led the prayers at Nepean Bay and saw a rainbow (a good omen, he thought), it was Glenelg beach on the mainland that became remembered as the birthplace of South Australia. On 27 July 1926, ninety years after the *Duke of York* landed at Nepean Bay, the Adelaide *Advertiser* reflected: 'as every schoolboy knows, the official date of the founding of the province ... was December 28, 1836'. It was merely a quirky fact that there was a settlement called Kingscote before that date.[48] In 1991 the South Australian Parliament recognised that Kangaroo Island was the first official settlement in the Province of South Australia. Still it remains little more than a quirky fact for most of the South Australians who even know it.[49]

If pre-1836 Kangaroo Island has been left out of the historical narratives of Tasmania and South Australia, what place in history can Henry Wallen, Nat Thomas, George Bates, Betty, Suke, Sal and the other Islanders now claim? Have they been relegated to the obscurity of shipping records, to the reports of visiting captains, first settlers and the newspaper articles to be rediscovered by a handful of historians more than a century later? Or is there a place for them in the living memory of Kangaroo Island?

Remembering

Lubra Creek

The car shudders as it leaves the road and crosses the cattle-grid.
This is nothing new; it has shuddered over corrugations and pot-
holes all the way from Penneshaw. A child on the hot back seat,
I look out of the car window.

It is still a long drive to the farmhouse. The anticipation
makes it seem even longer. After another year in the city, I wait for
the familiar moment – after the dusty road's final turn, just before
the last cattle-grid – when I can see the amazing view, the shock of
blue. A vast sky and sea, sparkles on the tips of the waves, the
island's coastline snaking east and west, and then, directly north, a
distant line of strangely still, white foam hugging the cliffs of
Cape Jervis – an Uluru in the ocean. We always gasp and cheer at
seeing that view. It is the true moment of arrival.

Just before the farmhouse we pass the shearing shed. I can
smell its thick, secret smells: the sweet wool mixing with the sour
dung dumped under the boards; green paint peeling off huge
sheets of corrugated iron. It's always a bit scary inside – suddenly
dark after the sharp sun, and when the shearing is on, we're afraid
of getting in the way of the blokes who always seem to be shouting
about something. It's best when it's empty and we can use the
thick chunks of marking chalk to draw on the greasy boards. But
the yards are best. We love to 'help' with the drenching, sitting on
the fences watching the dust clouds fly around dogs and sheep.

The drive to the farmhouse runs under the branches of
a thick, dark line of pine trees. Then there are flowers around a

patch of grass with a Hills Hoist. The back door acts as the front door. We unceremoniously pass a line of boots and thongs. A green National Trust plaque screwed into rough old stone reminds us this place has history.

This is the place where Nat Thomas made his home at Antechamber Bay, and where I spent every summer holiday as a child. My parents made friends with a couple in Adelaide who invited us to rent one of the cottages on their farm. I first went when I was about seven, and we kept returning every year. Antechamber Bay became a place I loved; at nineteen, I fell in love there. Then the land and my love became one. I wanted to be swallowed, consumed, owned and defined by this land. The love affair soon ended, but a durable link with Antechamber Bay lasts to this day, a relationship with its history.

I am the youngest of three children born in London to a north-England father and a Dutch mother. We came to Adelaide when I was five and moved to Melbourne when I was eighteen. My family has never lived in a place where we implicitly *belong* – where we are grounded by our history.

We were without the weight of history that anchors most Anglo-Australians. We were not burdened by generations sprung from pioneering legends. Floating over ground untrodden by our ancestors, we observed Australian landscapes like paintings, unsure of our place within them.

Though we eventually seemed to fit into the grooves made by the once British-colonial families, the grooves were not our own. We still carried within us a sense of disconnectedness. We felt too light; we yearned for the weightiness of history to ground us to this place. We yearned for our own ancestral tracks in this soil. So we tried to make them ourselves at this 'beautiful spot', this place Matthew Flinders had called the Ante-chamber, but the Islanders had called Creek Bay.

We went on walks that took an entire afternoon. Mum would stick a hat on my head and we would ask if we could take some of the eager dogs with us. They would run off after sheep while we frantically tried to bring them to heel. We were totally inept tourists in a place we knew as paradise. We bent the tops of wire fences and gate hinges to cross the paddocks and follow tracks that we had invented. Another 'walk worked out' – another link, another loop, another spectacular view over cliffs, another moment of overwhelming joy standing on an open yellow hillside with the smell of summer grass in the breeze.

It was a different world, a disconnected piece of land to which we felt deeply connected. We were no longer observers; we had found a place in this landscape. Going on our walks and drawing the day's events in the journal became respected rituals. We made ourselves heavy with invented tradition. Special moments inspired placenames exclusive to our family – places to which we could navigate instantly when we went home. The landscape was full of our memories. In this place we had a history.

But ours was not the only history in the land at Antechamber Bay. Far thicker strata lay beneath our fresh crust of memories.

Sitting on the sheep-yard fences, I heard stories about a man who was buried under the dark pines behind the farmhouse, where the sheepdogs yelped and pulled on their chains. I was too small to venture under there. I was told he was the man who built the farmhouse a long time ago. It was 'the oldest inhabited house in South Australia'.

Nat Thomas's house at Antechamber Bay, the 'oldest inhabited house in South Australia'. Rebe Taylor, 1994

I can still see Nat Thomas in the way that I first imagined him: a tall, mythical figure dressed in skins. I knew he lived with Aboriginal women and that he killed seals. I was told how the women had been taken – 'stolen' – from the mainland, and that they cured the skins with their teeth (I still don't know if this is true). I was told Nat Thomas built his house on the headland between Antechamber Bay beach and Red House beach so that he could see all the boats crossing Backstairs Passage and then trade his teeth-tanned skins with the sea captains for rum. I imagined Nat climbing over the rocks where I fed the crabs with shellfish, or bartering his skins for big barrels of rum on those empty beaches where we built our sandcastles.

Nothing about him was very clear. The stories were filtered and flavoured by years of telling. Our friends, who had owned the farm since the 1950s, had heard the stories from neighbours whose ancestors had taken up land more than a century earlier. The stories remembered by this family were not only about Nat but also about the Aboriginal women, about his daughters and their husbands. But we had no genealogy, no historical context with which to understand these abstracted characters. We just knew the land where they had lived. The stories were attached to places in the farm, places with strange names.

In Wab's Gully a thin corridor of cleared land, a pass for bringing through sheep, divides two scrubby hills. Wab, we were told, had been an Aboriginal woman who had lived alone in the gully in the time of Nat Thomas. Deep in the dense scrub is a low dry-stone wall, the remains of her home. It seemed to us a desperately lonely place. This was where Wab had 'lived out the last of her days'.

Wab's Gully opens into cleared paddocks that sweep east until they meet the steep, tree-topped sand-dunes of Antechamber Bay. In the middle distance stands Nat's Shed – a three-walled stone and iron shed still used to house the tractors. Beyond it, at the foot of the dunes, stands a Southern Cross windmill, beneath which, I was told, lies Nat Thomas's son-in-law, William Seymour. He had suddenly dropped dead in the dunes and his wife, Nat Thomas's daughter Mary, had rolled him down the dunes and buried him at the bottom.

'Wab's Gully', Antechamber Bay: all that is left of the home of
'Wab', an Aboriginal Tasmanian woman said to have died here alone.
Rebe Taylor, 1994

'Nat's Shed', built by Nathaniel Simpson, c. 1900, Antechamber Bay.
Rebe Taylor, 1994

From the house Nat Thomas built, an old path led to a tiny beach, snug between the rocks of the headland. The path took us under a vast fig tree so old that its branches swept the ground and formed a cavern. Etched in the trunk were the words 'planted Hannah Simpson 1857'. Hannah, we were told, had been the other of Nat Thomas's two daughters. We knew little about Hannah, but her married name seemed to give meaning to Simpson's Paddock, just above the fig tree, and Simpson's Cottage, just beyond the paddock.

Red House Beach, view from 'Simpson's Paddock' towards 'Simpson's Cottage'. Rebe Taylor, 1994

My favourite place at the farm was the crossing at Lubra Creek. Here a canopy of melaleucas sheltered a soft white sand floor interspersed by a few green limestone pools. However blustery the weather, the air at Lubra Creek was always still and quiet. The light filtered by the trees' narrow leaves was soft but remarkably clear.

I used to wonder if places could feel intrinsically sacred without the learnt stories and respect that we bring to them. I think now they can, but we certainly went to Lubra Creek with both. We were told it had been a stone tool factory for the Aboriginal occupants of Kangaroo Island from thousands of years ago. We often found Aboriginal flint stones turned up by the sheep in the sand. A friend of the farmer who had spent his honeymoon on the farm was an amateur collector and had taken some of the stone tools to the South Australian Museum. I recently enquired after them. Among a collection of over a million stone tools is a small box on which is written 'Lubra Creek, section 391, Hundred of Dudley'. The name Lubra Creek is not officially mapped; it exists only in the memories of a few and on a box among hundreds of others.

We also thought Lubra Creek had been the gathering place for the Aboriginal women who lived near Antechamber Bay. Although we can only half-remember being told this, it certainly seemed an appropriately private place.

But there was another story about Lubra Creek. It was said that an Aboriginal woman had tried to escape by swimming across Backstairs Passage from the mouth of the creek. On realising she couldn't make it, she turned back. There she was caught by Nat Thomas and beaten 'for her troubles'. These words have echoed through the generations of telling. Their shocking brutality could turn the serenity at Lubra Creek into an eerie silence.

Lubra Creek, near Antechamber Bay.
Rebe Taylor, 1994

We didn't know that the story of Lubra Creek was just one among many stories of attempted escape by Aboriginal women to the mainland. We didn't even know that 'lubra' was a common, derogatory word for an Aboriginal woman. If we had been born and bred in Australia, we would have known this word. If we had been born and bred on Kangaroo Island, we would have known the stories of escape. We thought the name and the story of Lubra Creek were unique, and that we were somehow more special and attached to this land by knowing them.

The story of Lubra Creek, like all the stories at Antechamber Bay, gave us an opportunity to engage with the history of the land. These stories seemed to have been produced out of the earth itself, encrusted with mystery. This was the past we had yearned for, our excavated rusty anchor to ground us to this country. An older history surfaced from its deeper place to become part of our fresher layer of memories, to take its place among the points by which we plotted our own history in the land. We drank in the legends as if swallowing the land itself, thirsty for its soul within us.

I began imagining this history when I was a little girl, peering into the dark pine trees where a mythical character lay under yelping dogs. I began with the stories made smooth by generations of handling before I gathered any hard and sharp facts. I found what was left of the history in the earth before I started unearthing it in the archives.

These remnants of history in a land I loved became the 'topic' for my Masters thesis at the University of Melbourne. In the La Trobe Library in Melbourne, I began reading about early Kangaroo Island, the sealing industry and the South Australian Company. I read about Nat Thomas – where he was born, the versions of his arrival and the claims that he had been a convict. I discovered what was written about the Aboriginal women, and about Nat Thomas's house and farm at Antechamber Bay. I learnt that he had three children with 'Betty' and that his two daughters, Mary and Hannah, married and had children.

But it was hard to work out how many children they had, let alone what had happened to them. In fact, it seemed dismally impossible until I read Jean Nunn's 1989 history of Kangaroo

Island, *This Southern Land*, and discovered that a descendant of Nat Thomas was still living in Kingscote.[1]

Mavis Golder was happy to see me when I arrived a few months later. Her house was a tangle of cats and a lifetime's collection of bits and pieces that might one day come in handy. Next to her armchair was a pile of newspaper clippings, photocopied archival records and books, the titles I had ordered at the La Trobe library weeks before.

I began to ask Mavis my questions. Did she know the same stories that I heard as a child? Did she know the farm at Antechamber Bay well? Had she inherited any Aboriginal Tasmanian language or traditional culture? I was insensitive with curiosity.

Mavis knew none of these things. She told me about discovering her Aboriginal Tasmanian ancestry by reading *Walkabout* magazine in 1954. She had her eldest son Michael to thank for the pile of information by her armchair. He told me his story later, when we met in Adelaide. He was six when his mother had made her discovery. He told me about his own discovery four years later in the *Australian Junior Encyclopaedia*.

This had been the only scrap of information Michael had, and he hung on to it. When he went to Adelaide to go to university, he took his scrap with him to the archives and libraries. Shipping records, certificates of birth and death and marriage gave him a story at last.

Through Mavis I gained an introduction to Adrian Waller, her cousin and a descendant of Hannah Simpson. Adrian and Mavis had known each other years before when he lived on Kangaroo Island; they had met again through their efforts to find family members. Adrian told me about his serendipitous discovery of his Aboriginal Tasmanian ancestry reading the *Chronicle* in 1960. Some years later his son, Neil, had gone to the archives to piece together a narrative for the family. When I met them, they too had a pile of notes, books and a handwritten genealogy.

After so many lost years, learning about their history had brought the Golders and Wallers to Antechamber Bay a few years earlier. In the mid-1980s Adrian, Neil and Mavis joined the

Kangaroo Island Pioneers Association and became active members; Mavis was invited to be their patron and Neil became their president. They unveiled the plaque to honour Nat Thomas at Antechamber Bay in 1991.

But the history extending from the pre-colonial settlers of Antechamber Bay to Nat Thomas's descendants does not unfold from conventional historical sources. It is not revealed in the displays in the Penneshaw museum or the plaques and memorials that have been erected across the district. Rather, it has entered into the annals of an island history known only by those who are born or marry into Kangaroo Islander families. Talk to those people and a paddock, a gully, a message etched in a tree or the ruined remains of a house are revealed as the surviving threads of a history. Pull on these threads and the layers peel back to reveal how the colonial descendants have shaped the way their local Aboriginal history is remembered.

When Mavis and Adrian stood on that land in 1991, they did so not knowing many of the stories that were remembered within it. The farmer showed them the fig tree, but they did not find out about Simpson's Paddock and Simpson's Cottage. They had never heard of Wab's Gully or Nat's Shed. They did not know what it was like to feel the eerie silence in Lubra Creek and imagine the story of Nat Thomas beating a woman 'for her troubles'.

But there are Kangaroo Islanders who do know these things – the families whose ancestors settled on the eastern end of the island in the colonial period and who passed on the stories I heard as a child. Along with the title deeds to their land, they have inherited the stories it contains. The Golders and Wallers inherited neither. The reason for that is another story they did not know. Only the colonial descendants could tell it to me. Only they could tell me how to hear a connection between the eerie silence of Lubra Creek and the continuing absence of Nat Thomas's descendants.

The Hundred of Dudley

The eastern end of Kangaroo Island, where Nat Thomas lived, is almost an island in its own right. When Matthew Flinders climbed Prospect Hill and looked down upon Pelican Lagoon, he was surprised to see that the neck of land he was standing on was only about a mile wide.

In 1874 this almost-island was officially proclaimed the Hundred of Dudley. That year the whole of Kangaroo Island had been gazetted as the County of Carnarvon. Counties are the largest land divisions in South Australia. They are divided into hundreds, an old English term meaning an area large enough to raise one hundred fighting men. Hundreds are divided into sections, which in urban areas are divided into lots.

Today the Hundred of Dudley still only has one urban area: the town of Penneshaw, as Hog Bay was renamed in 1884. The 21,975 agricultural sections, ranging in size from about 350 to 634 acres, have changed little since they were surveyed between 1874 and 1876.[1] Nor, it seems, have their owners changed. Today, most of the land in Dudley is owned by the members of six families, all of whom have been there since the colonial period. Their names are Marshall [pseudonym], Willson, Buick, Bates, Trethewey and Howard. This list is in the chronological order that they began leasing land on Kangaroo Island. Thomas Marshall★ took up his first lease of ten square miles at Antechamber Bay in 1858. In the same year, Nat Thomas was granted a lease of the same size next door. But the Marshall family is still there: it was

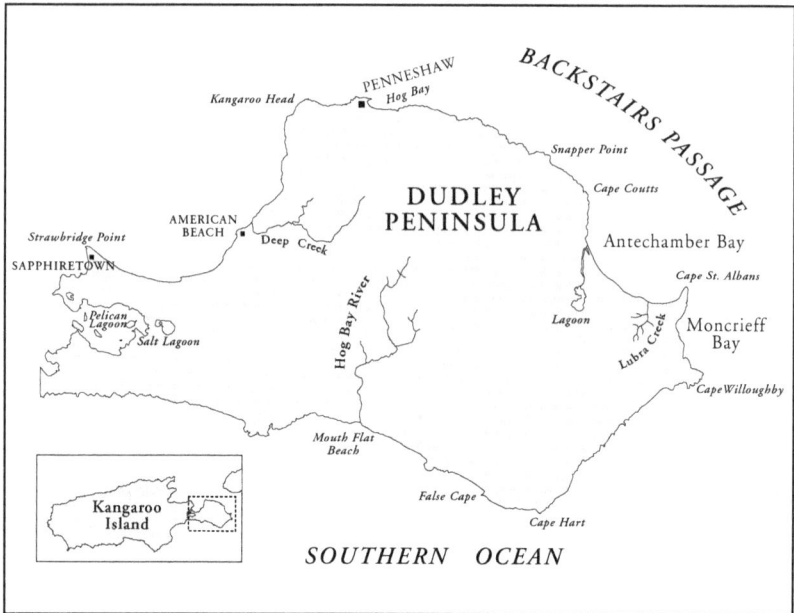

Dudley Peninsula, Kangaroo Island

the descendants of Thomas Marshall who passed on the stories I heard as a child.

I have been talking to members of these six families about the history of Nat Thomas, Betty and their descendants since 1993. My conversations with them, along with the Thomas descendants, shape my telling of this story. And, because much of it happens in Dudley, in many ways it is also the story of that district.

'Was He a Darkie?': Dave Buick

It wasn't our first meeting. I had met Dave Buick and his wife Monica a year earlier at their home in Penneshaw. Both were descended from Dudley colonial settlers. Monica told me that she had moved three times in her life, and never more than half a mile at a time. She had grown up on the land settled by her great-grandfather and spent her married life on the land first taken up by her husband's great-uncle.

Dave and Monica wanted to tell me what they thought I had come to hear. John spoke of his life working his land, of the long days working alone in distant paddocks, and of how he had seen his family through Depression and hardship. Monica told me of the difficulties of child-rearing in a rural district; she had lost two of her ten children. These are important stories, but I wanted to know about a family that was not in Dudley any more – the Aboriginal family, the descendants of Betty and Nat Thomas.

Dave and Monica told me stories passed on to them by their parents, and spoke of their own memories of Nat and Betty's grandchildren and great-grandchildren – where they had lived, whom they had worked for, what sort of characters they had been. This was history dense with personalities, relations and places, and I was grateful for their intricate knowledge. I took the information home and tried to piece it together. I tried to match genealogies with maps; I read in libraries and searched in archives. After a year I was hungrier with questions.

When I returned to Penneshaw I learnt that Dave was in Kingscote Hospital. He sat with me in the sunroom and, competing with the noise of a vacuum cleaner, spoke to me with remarkable clarity. He could remember eighty years ago as if it were last week. But when we began to talk about Nat Thomas, John forgot something. He stopped me and asked, 'Was he a darkie?'

The question surprised me. I told Dave that Nat Thomas had been an Englishman and let the moment pass. I wish I hadn't. At home, with the interview transcript in front of me, I saw the significance of his question. I wished I could recapture that moment and try to understand it better. I began to see it as a slip of his memory into that blurry place between what Dave thought a 'darkie' was like and how he remembered Nat Thomas. For Nat, who had dressed in animal skins, partnered an Aboriginal woman and had Aboriginal children, defiled all the notions of civility Dave attached to the word 'English'.

Our moment of confusion and surprise recalled the confusion and surprise of the colonists who encountered Nat Thomas in 1836; it recalled the words of Mary Thomas, arriving at Nepean Bay in the *Africaine*, when she saw Nat Thomas and thought 'he was more like a savage ... than an Englishman'. Mary's perception has been echoing in the minds of the colonial descendants ever since.

Mavis Golder

I went to see Mavis Golder at her home in Kingscote seven days after I saw Dave Buick. Though I did not know it, this would be our last meeting. Perhaps with some unwitting premonition, I asked if there was anything about her history that she particularly wanted to be remembered. She said to me, 'I would like Nat Thomas remembered as an intelligent man.' She picked up one of the history books she kept by her armchair, and found the reference to Mary Thomas's diary. She explained:

> She was talking about Nat Thomas ... and how he was a savage and all that. That used to make me mad, and it came out like that was the only thing said about him, and I think he had more things going for him than that.

Mavis told me she wanted to see Nat remembered as a pioneer, a farmer, and as the true beginning of Kangaroo Island history.

Prehistory

In the moment when 'governors' Wallen and Stephens challenged each other on the beach at Nepean Bay two characters met from two histories – Tasmanian and South Australian – and Kangaroo Island became a footnote to both their narratives. Since then, the Island's colonial descendants have been able to take this footnote and script their own narrative of colonisation. The absence of indigenous Aboriginal people on Kangaroo Island meant they could imagine their island to have been a true *terra nullius*, and be free of the burden of guilt that other colonial Australians might carry. But it also meant they could create their own frontier by remembering the Islanders as their own indigenes. The colonial descendants could take the rhetoric that was once used by Tasmanian journalists and the South Australian Company and use it in their own historical script. In their script, the Islanders are stuck in what is always the first chapter in standard histories about Australian colonisation – the chapter on the Aborigines who then disappear from the text after settlement. The history of beaches and cultural encounters is reduced to a parochial prehistory of Kangaroo Island.

On 27 July 1986 the Kangaroo Island Pioneers Association staged a re-enactment to celebrate the hundred-and-fiftieth anniversary of the South Australian Company's first landing at Nepean Bay. It was a highly choreographed affair. Each participant had a role to play and a costume to wear. Colonial Manager Stephens was there, and Captain Morgan. Even Henry Wallen made an appearance on the beach.

But the Pioneers did not act out the ludicrous scene between the contesting governors, or the Islanders greeting the new settlers with gifts of wallaby and fresh vegetables. Henry Wallen appeared flanked by two women dressed in hessian sacks, with blackened faces and wallaby skins over their shoulders. One carried a stick with pelts on it. Wallen himself wore ripped jeans, a kangaroo skin and a Davy Crockett-style possum-skin hat. He was posed on one knee with a gun aimed, ready to shoot.

The photograph on the following page is one of a series of images of the 1986 re-enactment that appear in Neville Cordes's book, *Kangaroo Island: 184 Great Years in Photographs*. The caption reads: 'Margaret Patterson, Ian Howard … and Suzanne Heywood emerge from the scrub to put fear into the hearts of the new settlers as Wallen and his entourage did in 1836.' But Wallen did no such thing. He towered over Stephens and mocked him. He offered the hungry settlers food he had grown on his farm, while Stephens could find only a crow. So why did he appear so hostile in a so-called historical re-enactment?

Because this event was not a re-enactment but an original performance. It remembered the line drawn in the first settlers' minds between civilised whites and savages, but it made that line into a colonial frontier – a frontier where the moment of contest is not ludicrous, but a heroic event from which a grand narrative unfolds. It placed a gun in the Islander's hand, substituting force for reason, hostility for generosity.

This performance honoured the South Australian Company's rhetoric about industrious and pious settlers displacing the worse than savages. But here the Islanders are not perpetrators of crimes *against* the natives: they *are* the natives. With his rifle at the ready, Wallen is defending his indigenous soil against the colonisers. It is

Henry Wallen and 'his' two Aboriginal women as they were
represented by the Kangaroo Island Pioneers Association in their
1986 re-enactment of the South Australian Company's landing
at Nepean Bay. Neville Cordes, *Kangaroo Island: 184 Great Years
in Photographs*

a strange image, not just because of the Davy Crockett look-alike and the bad make-up, but because this man, who is accompanied by 'Aboriginal' women and clearly defending his soil, is *white*; yet his figure fits neatly with our imaginings of a *black* native on the other side of a colonial frontier. One hundred and fifty years have made Wallen a savage. He is ready, with costume already fitted, to play the part of the reprobate blackfella.

'Was he a darkie?' Dave Buick's question reverberates.

∾

At the Penneshaw Folk Museum, history is preserved and presented under the direction of the tradition of storytelling in Dudley. The panels on the east wall are devoted to the histories of the major colonial families. Each family has its own space, with its own photographs of early homesteads and/or ancestors. Some early farming tools are scattered about.

I helped to finish this display in 1996. A friend and I were paid by the History Trust of South Australia to complete some of the displays on the colonial families, and to organise the collections' catalogues. To the text and photos I added drawings of the families' plots of land. I used a computer to create huge colour maps showing colonial land ownership in Dudley. I knew how the families wanted their history to be reflected: as continuous, traditional and successful.

It had been a different matter two years earlier, when I had suggested some changes to the display about the island's Aboriginal history. I criticised the displays about Nat Thomas, Betty and their daughters. They were hanging on another wall, excluded from the continuing success story, and they stopped after the first generation.

My comments brought a sharp response. I was reminded that the term 'folk' meant a history of the people (the people, it seems, who established the museum) and that 'the non-white settlers (a very small minority compared to European settlers . . .) are already well documented and relevant history displayed'.[2] Nat Thomas, it seems, is categorised among 'the non-white settlers', not among the 'European settlers'.

Attached to his panel is his rifle, a seal skull and shoulder blade, a compass and Matthew Flinders' chart of Kangaroo Island, a sketch of sealers hunting on some rocks, and a small reproduction of a watercolour of Nat Thomas's home by W. A. Cawthorne. The text reads:

'Sailor, sealer,
   farmer . . .
     . . . wildman'

The first settlers on Kangaroo Island were not farmers but sealers.

To men like Nat Thomas this isolated, uninhabited outpost offered an escape from authority.

Nat was the 'scabby one' of a respectable family in England. He ran away to sea and after several years whaling and sealing around Tasmania came to Kangaroo Island about 1824. He was accompanied by a full-blood Tasmanian woman, Betty.

At Antechamber Bay he set up camp, trading seal and kangaroo skins to passing ships. When these animals became scarce, he turned to fishing, farming and trapping wallabies for skins.

A visitor in 1853 described Nat as 'a compound of sailor, sealer, farmer . . . and wildman.' His weatherboard home was 'nice and clean' with 'about sixty pigs, chattering parrots, twenty or thirty dogs, a dozen mountain ducks, goats, geese, wallabies, etc. etc.' The visitor was given a good look around and 'a first rate cup of tea'.

We are told that Nat had escaped 'authority', but who this authority was and why he supposedly had to escape it is not clear. We are told he was 'accompanied' by a 'full-blood' Tasmanian, Betty, and can only assume the so-called racial composition of her 'blood' is mentioned because it is rare. We are told that Nat set up a 'camp' from which he could hunt and trade. A house is later mentioned along with sixty pigs. This could suggest a serious enterprise, but it is the odd collection of other animals that one senses are meant to capture our imagination – to give the impression that this is still a 'camp', and an odd setting in which to be served a 'first rate cup of tea'. After all, this cannot be a farm: the 'first settlers on Kangaroo Island were sealers, not farmers'. At the time of viewing the display, I didn't realise how this claim is contradicted on the panel itself by the inclusion of Cawthorne's watercolour, 'View of Kangaroo Island'. As it was greatly reduced and in black and white in the museum, it was not until I looked at the original in the Mitchell Library that I saw that it is clearly a picture of a farm: it includes Nat Thomas's home, complete with cattle, buildings and cultivated land.

The quotations used on the panel are from Cawthorne's article published in the Adelaide *Observer* in 1853. This was the only time that Nat's words were directly recorded. But here in the museum

Nat's voice is taken from him. His description of himself in 'his own emphatic language' as 'the scabby one' is made to sound like someone else's words. And so vanishes the tension in the original article between the reporter as audience and Nat as performer.

The quote taken as the title of the panel, 'sailor, sealer, farmer ... wildman', and again quoted in the final paragraph, also has a subtly different meaning when it is replaced in its original context:

> He can give you some reminiscences ... of escapes and adventures, and of perils and dangers. He is a compound of sailor, sealer, farmer and wild man ... Place him on the western end of Kangaroo Island, with only a dog and a knife, and he will find his way out at the other.

Throughout this passage I can hear the bravado of Nat's voice – a man in his early fifties, telling stories of adventures in which he is always the hero. The journalist Cawthorne too is performing to an audience. He is trying to capture the mood, the character of Nat. He uses the well-known images of wild man and farmer to try to explain this extraordinary individual. But that is almost completely lost in the museum, where these quotes merely give a veneer of authenticity to the version of Nat remembered by the 'folk' of Dudley – as an Englishman turned darkie.

Bruce Bates

On a cold winter's day in 1993 Bruce Bates and I sat before an open fire in the front room of his house, which had been built by his grandfather on a steep hill overlooking Penneshaw. It was June, the day before my first meeting with Dave and Monica Buick.

Bruce is also a descendant of colonial settlers, and like Monica has lived his life on the land his great-grandfather settled. But Bruce did not tell me rehearsed stories of hardships and pioneering. He asked forthrightly what I wanted. I told him I wanted to know about the descendants of Nat Thomas. Bruce became one of my richest sources of information, telling me a wealth of names, personalities and incidents that covered the Dudley district dating since his childhood. And, delving back further, he took out an exercise book in which he had written down the stories his grandfather told him.

Through the window was the view of a dark, rain-swept Backstairs Passage, but the fire was warm. I let the tape recorder take the stress of note-taking while Bruce read me a story he had recorded in his neat cursive hand:

'My Grandfather's Story Concerning Nat Thomas's Snares'

Grandfather set out for Cape Willoughby taking with him a number of wallaby snares, and as he walked along he set a few of these in likely places where the wallabies were seen to be running as they do on the unmarked trails, intending to pick up anything he may of caught on the way back. Having spent some time at Willoughby – I don't know how long, possibly overnight – he returned and was just beginning to take up his snares when he found himself confronted by Nat Thomas and George Bates, two of the old inhabitants of KI, who were rather piratical fellows, not too pleased to find the island invaded by legitimate official settlers.

It seemed that the confrontation actually took place at Nat's house, which was on the south end of Antechamber Bay, where he and George Bates had a couple of Tasmanian native women. Nat was very angry when he saw Grandfather and shouted in a very menacing, shivery kind of voice, which Grandfather demonstrated for me: 'You're the man who set your snares across mine' – that is to say, he set his snares so as to catch the wallabies before they reached Nat's snares ... Nat then called in a loud voice to his native woman: 'Suke, bring me my scissors, I'll have his windpipe out.' This thoroughly frightened Grandfather, and no doubt it was intended to do so, but George Bates broke in, saying loudly, 'For God's sake Nat, don't! For God's sake, don't.' Grandfather decided it was time to go before Nat got his scissors, and took off as quickly as he could, picked up his snares and was very careful after that not to set snares anywhere near where Nat Thomas might be.

Bruce demonstrated Nat's menacing, shivery voice for me, as his grandfather had for him. It captured a moment that had more to do with lore and with the act of storytelling than with anything else.

This story is part of Bruce's inheritance; it came with the land, the house and the family name. Knowing this story is a part of his experience of being one of a community of colonial descendant families. But confirming his sense of belonging also means placing Nat and George on the other side of an imagined frontier. He is reaffirming that his ancestors were 'legitimate and official settlers', while Nat and George were not. Although the story comes from a time when the island was already 'invaded', as Bates puts it, Nat was still angry. His anger was heard in Bruce's shivery voice, and it has been echoing in the Bates house for three generations.

At first, as when I missed the moment with Dave Buick, I didn't pay enough attention to this echo. I could see only the similarities between the representation of Nat in this story and the representation of Wallen in the 1986 performance. Certainly the similarities are there: the frontier has been imagined, Wallen's gun has become Nat's scissors, and Nat too is given 'his native woman'. (Interestingly, we don't hear the name 'Betty' called, but 'Suke', suggesting that the women moved around.) In this story, Suke is Nat's chattel, a Girl Friday fetching for a 'piratical' fellow. The cultural blindness of the first official settlers is remembered, as it was by the actors in the re-enactment.

But is the comparison so clear? Bruce's grandfather was setting wallaby snares, a skill passed on by the Aboriginal women, and Bruce knew this. When I asked him who first taught his grandfather to snare, he said he 'would have learnt it from those people who were here already and they might have learnt it from the Aboriginal women ... I used to go with him ... it was [a] traditional thing'.

This 'traditional thing' pre-dates the colonial era. Bruce's storytelling is a mastery of the voice of the 'invaded'. Here the frontier runs close between the settler and the Islander: they are both employing an Aboriginal practice on the same land. But one is legitimate and one is not. The legitimate settler may take this Aboriginal practice, this land and this encounter, and make it his own, part of his memory, part of how he proves his legitimacy. The other may not.

Only three days earlier I had asked Mavis Golder: 'Wallaby snaring – is that something your family did?'

'No,' she had answered, 'not in our family.'

'Not even further back?' I asked.

'No, not as far as I know. My Auntie Mary, in the Depression times, she used to make kangaroo-tail soup.'

Henry Wallen had served wallaby-tail soup to his colonial settler guests in 1837.[3] Perhaps he learnt from the Aboriginal women he lived with; perhaps Auntie Mary's soup *was* Mavis's tradition, even if she wasn't told so.

Back home, when I listened again to Bruce's voice on my tape recorder, I realised something obvious but significant. This was not Mavis Golder's voice. This moment did not occur in her living room. It could not, because this 'traditional thing' is part of Bruce's history, not hers. Bruce's performance was not original; it has been practised for three generations. It is far more powerful than any staged re-enactment.

The Pioneers Association was established in 1982. It has members mostly in Adelaide and Kingscote, descendants of the passengers on the South Australian Company ships. They hold a dinner in Adelaide on 27 July each year. But Nepean Bay is not in Dudley. In Dudley the colonial settlers, including Bruce Bates's and Dave Buick's ancestors, were pastoralists who arrived over a number of years. In Dudley they don't have particular arrival dates, obvious moments from which grand narratives unfold. In Dudley they don't re-enact their history; they remember it.

Creek Bay

The display on Nat Thomas in the Penneshaw Museum describes him as both a 'farmer' and a 'wildman', but it gives the impression that he was more wild than he was productive and that his home was more a camp than a serious agricultural interest. How true is this? Had Nat adopted Aboriginal practices to the extent that he no longer had any interest in European uses of the land? Did Nat do little more on his land than snare wallabies? Or is it possible to see him as Mavis Golder asked he be remembered – as one of the first pioneers of rural Kangaroo Island?

Fortunately, there is some recorded information that may help answer this question. First, W. A. Cawthorne did not just write about Nat's place in the early 1850s; he also painted it. This is the watercolour reproduced on Nat Thomas's panel in the Penneshaw Museum. Cawthorne shows us Antechamber Bay, and below it, what he calls 'Old Nat's'. Rolling hills of thick scrub break into a patch of cleared ground where two houses are standing. The bigger house is Nat's, and has a crop sown in front of it in a neat square. The smaller house was probably occupied by Mary, Nat's elder daughter, and her husband, William. (Mary had married William Seymour – who was also known as Joe – in 1849.) In the foreground is another strip of cleared land that Cawthorne calls the 'road from light house'. On it is a man carrying a staff, walking with two cattle or oxen pulling a cart, and what appears to be another man with some stock behind him. Nat did own a bullock team – is this perhaps him with a family member?[4] 'Old Nat's' looks like an ideal rural setting.

'View of Kangaroo Island'
by W. A. Cawthorne, c. 1853.
Mitchell Library, State Library
of New South Wales

(detail)

Nine years before Cawthorne wrote his article, Police Inspector Alexander Tolmer visited Creek Bay. He was there to set up headquarters to search for some smugglers who were at large in the district (not an uncommon problem on Kangaroo Island); he even made one arrest near by.[5] Tolmer wrote that Creek Bay had 'a considerable extent of good country ... high and undulating ... in the interior'. He described how 'a river of excellent water' ran 'the whole year' past Nat's house.[6]

There is no river running there today. It is unlikely Tolmer was describing Lubra Creek, which is a good walk from Nat's house. I can't work out where this river might have been, though it is possible that the landscape and its waterways have changed considerably since 1844. But fresh water can still be found beneath the limestone behind the dunes right next to Nat's house. There is a windmill there now – the same one under which William Seymour is said to be buried. Nat's grandson, Tiger Simpson, claimed that Nat had a windmill for grinding wheat in the 1830s, and by at least 1863 Nat and his family had a windmill to pump water. It may have been in the same place as the one that stands today.[7]

Police Inspector Tolmer met Betty and their three children, then five, eleven and fifteen. To him, Betty was the 'woman who catches wallaby' for Nat, and their children were 'very interesting' for having 'combined the intelligence of the white with the activity of the native'. He describes a scene of happy domesticity.

Tolmer thought Nat had built a 'good house'. Nine years later, Cawthorne found Nat's weatherboard 'nice and clean'. And by 1877 Nat had apparently improved his home further. The survey book of that year describes Nat's house as being not of weatherboard but of stone, with limestone walls twenty inches thick, a thatched roof and a flagged floor. The kitchen measured fourteen feet by eleven-and-a-half, and a weatherboard lean-to with a galvanised roof had been added. The value of the house was estimated at £25.

According to Tolmer Nat had an 'excellent farm' with a 'great number' of fowls, a flock of three hundred goats and a dairy. Cawthorne wrote of finding pigs and goats among other animals, and added some cattle or oxen and other stock in his painting. Nat might have owned horses as well, for it seems he knew how to work them. Historian Wynnis Ruediger writes of being told that Nat could hold down an unbroken colt with his bare hands when he was an old man.[8] It is a story at least accurate in its sense of Nat's boastfulness.

The farm at Antechamber Bay may not have been large, but neither were any of the other island farms in the 1850s. It seemingly had enough animals to provide more than a subsistence, and by the time Mary and William were married and could help Nat, Creek Bay was no less serious a venture than the other local farms.

In 1998 I met Ellen Marks★, another descendant of Nat and Betty, who gave me a short memoir written by her mother, Mildred Chester★. Mildred had been the granddaughter of Mary and William Seymour, and she wrote that her grandparents 'ran a sheep and cattle station ... at Antechamber Bay'.[9] It seems that as Nat grew older, Mary and William increasingly took over the farm, adding sheep to its interests. In 1877, Thomas Willson described Nat's place in the *South Australian Register* as 'a small run' where, 'with the aid of a widowed half-caste daughter and a numerous family of quadroon grandchildren', Nat had 'succeeded in raising a small flock of sheep, which is their support'.[10]

In 1992 the farmer who now owns Nat's place was digging a drain by his house when he found a lead stencil with the letters 'N T' cut out of it. He showed the stencil to me and we imagined that it might have been used to identify bales or sacks. This made us wonder if Nat and his family had sold wool or grain. We put the stencil in the Penneshaw Museum. The earth seems to grow history in Dudley.

Nat and his family's entrepreneurial interests extended beyond farming. Close by their houses, according to Tolmer, a bituminous pitch 'oozed from between the rocks'. Ruediger was told it was called 'Bun gum' by some of the first boat-builders, who used it to caulk their boats.[11] When Tolmer returned to Creek Bay some years later, he revisited the oily pitch with Nat Thomas and Mary Seymour, and three mineral leases were made in his and their names. But nothing profitable eventuated.[12]

Mildred Chester remembered in her memoirs how her

mother, Nat's grand-daughter, sometimes had the job of lighting the lamp at Cape Willoughby, and when short of the proper fuel 'she used to get oil from around the rocks by the lighthouse' where it naturally seeped out. It seems Mildred's mother was continuing a contact between her family and the Cape Willoughby lighthouse that had been established years before. While Nat Thomas and his family evidently worked at it with some seriousness, farming was not their only source of livelihood.

The Lighthouse

On 1 April 1852 W. A. Cawthorne wrote in his diary: 'Mother has just gone ... to Kangaroo Island to live with Mr. C ... shall perhaps not see them for months perhaps a year or so'. 'Mr. C' was Cawthorne's formal way of referring to his father, Captain William Cook Cawthorne, head keeper of the Cape Willoughby lighthouse, which had been lit only months earlier.

Over the following years the Cawthorne and Thomas families came to know each other well. Late in her life, Nat's daughter Mary Seymour remembered how Mrs Cawthorne taught her and her younger sister Hannah to read and write English.[13] It seems the lessons at the lighthouse went two ways – from his visits to his parents, W. A. Cawthorne learnt much about the cross-cultural community of early Kangaroo Island.

Nat and his son-in-law William Seymour were among the locals who worked on the contruction of the lighthouse. When the first log books were started in 1853, Nat Thomas was listed as the second keeper with the title of 'vice' and his son-in-law, William, as the third keeper. They worked under head keeper Cawthorne. Nat's responsibilities included taking charge of the light when on his watch and, like William, lighting, oiling and trimming the lantern and lights and checking expenditure records.[14] In 1857 Cawthorne took leave, and Nat took over the running of the light in his absence. The job involved a high level of responsibility, and required reasonable literacy skills.[15]

W. A. Cawthorne wrote in the *Observer* in 1853 that the conditions of the 'poor keepers' were very rough. They had 'no regular communication with town' – the Hog Bay mail run was not established for another six years – and were 'frequently very hard up for the want of provisions'. Salt meat was the 'staple', except when Nat could provide some goat or pork from his home. 'Wallaby hunting and fishing require a great deal of time', Cawthorne added, 'more than they can spare'. He found the keepers drinking coffee made of roast peas and smoking hops for tobacco.[16]

Then, in October 1857, W. A. Cawthorne wrote in his journal: 'Nat Thomas has got dismissed from the light house – things rather unsettled there'.[17] According to the lighthouse log book, Nat had 'resigned'. But it seems Cawthorne's account was more accurate. Relations between the families were strained. About sixty years later the *Kangaroo Island Courier* claimed Nat suffered from the smoke and oil of the lamp, but there were also complaints at the time that Nat had let the light become dirty and sooty. He may have been negligent with its cleaning during Cawthorne's leave of absence.[18]

Nat certainly lost favour with the managers of the lighthouse, the Trinity Board in Adelaide. When the Board's secretary wrote to W. C. Cawthorne of Nat's resignation, he ordered that:

> Should you find N. Thomas interferes with either of the underkeepers, or in any way takes advantage of his contiguity to the light house you will send me a special report of his conduct for the information of the Board.[19]

After Nat resigned, the Trinity Board also instructed Cawthorne to 'pay particular attention to Seymour's attendance to his duties and to observe whether he allowed himself to be in any way influenced by Thomas, and if so to report same to the President'.[20] Perhaps William did allow himself to be influenced by his father-in-law. In February 1858, only months after being promoted into Nat's position of second keeper, William resigned – or was perhaps also dismissed. Cawthorne's difficulties were not yet over. Donald McArthur, who had come with his family to replace Nat a few weeks after his dismissal, could not read or write and often reported sick.[21]

Thomas Simpson, an English settler in Hog Bay, had also worked on the building of the lighthouse.[22] In 1859, he was appointed the postmaster for Hog Bay, and in that role he took the mail to Cape Willoughby once a week. It seems he was accepted as one of the Thomas family by the end of that year; he married Hannah Thomas in February 1860. In late December 1859 Simpson told Donald McArthur's stepson, Collin MacLachlan, that there was a government dispatch and letters directed to the lighthouse waiting for the Head Keeper in Hog Bay. On learning this, W. C. Cawthorne sent Collin to Hog Bay on horseback. After travelling twenty miles on a hot day, the boy arrived in the evening to find, in Cawthorne's words, that 'no vessel had been there for some time'; if any letters had arrived, they would 'have been sent on as they usually have done' – once a week in Simpson's delivery service.

Collin returned the next day exhausted from riding in the extreme heat and was unwell for several days afterwards. 'Simpson', deduced Cawthorne, 'made the Report Maliciously as he had been forbidden to remain during the Sabbath day in MacArthur's [sic] cottage much to the annoyance of himself and his family' – the family he was soon to marry into. Cawthorne requested the support of his superiors to deal with the matter: '[As] this person threatens to give the Station as much annoyance as possible I trust the board will take measures to abate the nuisance. False Reports made to Govt. Station are punishable by Law'.[23]

The nuisance was possibly abated, but it seems Nat Thomas then took up the cause. In January 1860 he was 'cautioned', Cawthorne reported, 'from interfering with Lightkeepers or any thing what ever belonging to the Station'. Donald McArthur was also 'warned . . . not to encourage N. Thomas or any of his Family at his cottage'.[24] It seems Nat Thomas and his sons–in–law joined together to give W. C. Cawthorne 'as much annoyance as possible'. It was a vendetta of filial allegiance. Nat Thomas, the lone sailor of 1825, was now surrounded by family.

Ownership

From 1 January 1859 Nat Thomas was also the legal holder of the land he had occupied for the previous thirty years. He became one of the first lessees in the Dudley district when he was granted ten square miles at Antechamber Bay.[25] The Real Property Act, passed in 1858, stipulated that all land leased or sold in South Australia had to have its boundaries clearly set out in registered dealings, with deeds lodged both in the Lands Titles Office and with the lessee or owner.[26] But the Dudley leases were drawn up on unsurveyed land, and their boundaries were at best approximate. They were also huge. Other than the two small cleared patches near the seafront, most of Nat's ten square miles consisted of the scrubby rolling hills of Cawthorne's painting.

Since the South Australian Company had aborted its dismal settlement in Kingscote in 1839, there had been little interest from prospective settlers in Kangaroo Island. The Company had left behind a store, a manager and a few families; American River or Hog Bay had even less. There were about a dozen people living in Hog Bay during the 1840s, and the island's entire population was about eighty.[27]

There were a few formal expressions of interest in taking up pastoral land on Kangaroo Island in the 1840s, and the government issued a small number of licences.[28] The first pastoral leases were issued in 1856. By 1861 the population on the island had more than doubled to 175.[29]

So it was that, in the year Nat was granted his land, he also got neighbours. The Marshall brothers, Thomas and George, had arrived in Adelaide in the *Victoria* fourteen years earlier. They were soon the sole occupants of Thistle Island, off Port Lincoln, where they attempted to farm a small flock of sheep. Their venture was short-lived, and within months Thomas Marshall was working as a butcher in Mitcham near Adelaide. But Thomas finally realised his original intention in 1858, when he was granted a ten-square-mile lease on the north-east of Dudley. By 1860 he had another three leases in Dudley, including land at Antechamber Bay and on the south coast. Thomas died that year and his holdings, a total of forty square miles, were transferred to his widow.[30]

The Willsons followed the Marshalls. Thomas Willson and his family had emigrated from Lincolnshire about 1850 and spent their first years in Adelaide. They then moved to Yankalilla, near the coast opposite Kangaroo Island. Here Thomas Willson became

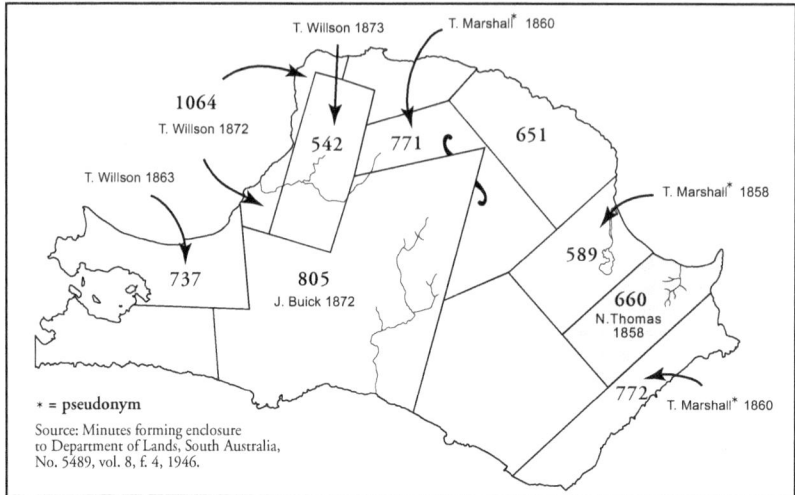

Land ownership of the Hundred of Dudley 1858–1876

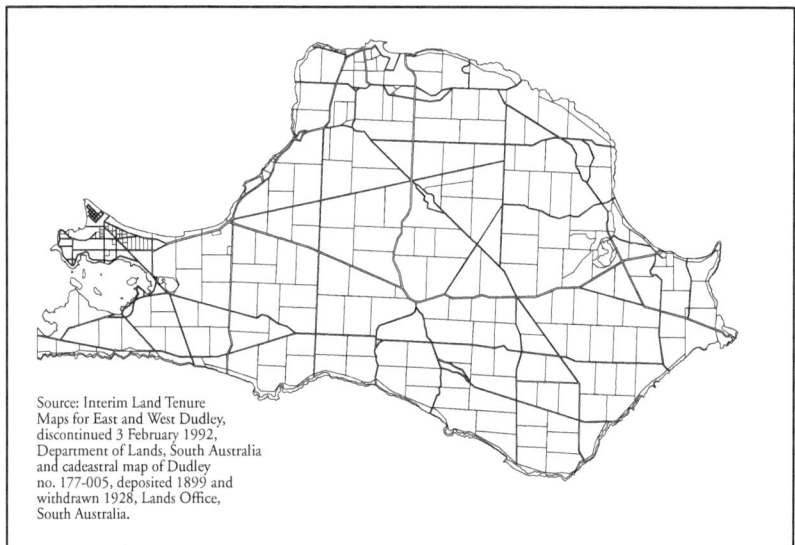

Cadastral Map of Dudley 1876–1904

the local storekeeper, corn merchant and publican, building the Yankalilla pub in 1857. He also began farming there. In 1863 he moved his family to Kangaroo Island to continue farming, leasing ten square miles in Dudley near American River. He leased an adjacent mile along the coast in 1872 and a year later took another ten-square-mile lease in the inland.[31]

By contrast, John Buick had been living on Kangaroo Island for about thirty years before he took up his two vast leases in Dudley in 1875. He had come out from Scotland in 1844, and soon after was living at American River. He helped build two cutters, the *Kangaroo* and the *Petrel*, which were mainly used to ship salt from the island to the mainland. From about 1854 he was clearing land near American River. His two leases, granted twenty years later, covered thirty-six square miles.[32] By that time, almost every acre of Dudley Peninsula was leased in the name of Marshall, Willson, Buick or Thomas.

In 1874 Kangaroo Island was officially gazetted as the County of Carnarvon, and the Hundred of Dudley was proclaimed. From the late 1870s Dudley farmers had to apply for leases or freehold grants of the newly surveyed, smaller sections. The nominal area of their holdings shrank, but they had been farming only small portions of their huge leases. Just like Nat Thomas and John Buick, who were there when the first pastoral leases were divided, these early settlers stayed where they had built their homes and had begun clearing land when the Hundred of Dudley was surveyed into farming blocks.[33]

But whether Nat Thomas was going to stay at his home seemed questionable. Like the other three landholders, he too resumed his original lease of ten square miles in 1875, but the landholdings in Dudley were being redivided in response to an increased demand for land. Settlers looking for land found little near Kingscote, for the small amount of good soil there had been mostly taken up by the South Australian Company. From the 1860s the eastern end of the island, especially the land near Hog Bay, became a natural choice, with its superior soil and slightly better annual rainfall.[34]

Rising demand for land across South Australia had resulted in the 1872 Waste Lands Alienation Act, which altered the original definition of the lands at the disposal of the Crown to include leases where less than one-fifth was utilised for the production of crops.[35] Nat Thomas, almost eighty years old, failed this requirement. His homestead was to be placed on the market.

But Thomas Willson opposed Nat's removal. In February

1877 he wrote to the *South Australian Register* to protest at what he described as the 'ungenerous and harsh' treatment of 'an old tar'. He told the story of how Nat had been 'wrecked' over '54 years ago' on the Western Australian coast before landing on Kangaroo Island and establishing his 'small run' near Cape Willoughby where he was helped by his 'widowed half-caste daughter and a numerous family of quadroon grandchildren'. Later in 1877, Mary moved with her children to Penneshaw. But even if old Nat had been alone at the time, Willson may have still asserted that he 'ought not be disturbed'.

Willson's worthy sentiments were somewhat tarnished when he added that if Nat 'was monopolizing good land, it would alter the case'. Still, Willson assured his readers, 'his is proverbially the worst land hereabout, but being near his cherished element, the sea, it suits him, and it is . . . unfeeling to turn him out of it'.[36]

It was kind of Willson to take action against the 'unfeeling' civil servants, even if he evidently did not consider Nat – the 'old tar' – to be a legitimate farmer who deserved good land. But as Tolmer had pointed out in 1844, and as the family who now farm it have told me, the land surrounding Nat's house is good. It was lucky that Willson did not know this. It may have been partly due to his efforts that by the end of 1877 Nat Thomas had been granted fifty-one acres of freehold land surrounding his homestead.[37]

Governor Wallen and Fireball Bates

Henry Wallen had not been so lucky. After the South Australian Company forced him off his lovely farm at Three Wells River, the 'Governor' had spent his remaining years near Kingscote living off what he could trap and hunt. In about 1854 he helped James Goodiar, a surveyor, to establish a sawmill on the site of his old farm. But in early 1855 Wallen took ill. On Goodiar's advice, Wallen went for treatment to Adelaide, where he died in May 1856 aged sixty-two.

At the inquest into his death, Goodiar testified that Wallen had been 'a quiet, inoffensive and most well-behaved man'. He had always kept a Bible at his side, Goodiar claimed, even when hunting, and had studied it closely. 'He was a very successful hunter', and earned good money, but 'when he visited Adelaide his kind and jovial disposition would generally lead him to spend it among friends'. Wallen's body was returned to Kangaroo Island at Goodiar's expense and buried in the Kingscote Pioneer Cemetery. A tombstone remembers 'Henry Wallen, affectionately known as Governor. The first farmer in South Australia.'[38]

After 1836 George Bates settled in Hog Bay and built what people claim is the first stone house in South Australia. This was the house where Ted Bates used to sit after school and listen to old Fireball's yarns.

In the 1840s Bates worked on the Port Adelaide wharves loading ships. In the 1850s he went to Bendigo in Victoria to try his luck at gold mining, 'without much success'. W. A. Cawthorne wrote in the *Observer* in 1853 that Nat Thomas had claimed 'an old Islander' at Hog Bay had four Aboriginal women. Perhaps he meant Bates.[39] But by 1870 Bates had married a white woman.

As they grew old together, George and his wife Elizabeth, apparently without children, were unable to support themselves. In 1889 Elizabeth was admitted to the Destitute Asylum in Adelaide, where she died three years later.[40] Bates, who had boasted to Tolmer in 1844 that he 'never had a day's sickness' on Kangaroo Island, found he was getting feeble.[41] He and Elizabeth had both been dependent on Destitute Board rations for some years before she left for Adelaide, and it was not long before Bates followed her to the asylum. He died there in September 1895 at ninety-five years of age. The *Observer* dedicated a long obituary to him, including a large photograph. The writer described him as a 'man of the sea and a hunter' and possibly the 'oldest of South Australian settlers'. In the Destitute Asylum, Bates had been 'the recipient of constant kindly services from visitors', who read him books and listened to his stories.

Bates's body was returned to Kangaroo Island, where he was buried in the Penneshaw Cemetery. The costs of passage, coffin and tombstone were mostly funded by the charity of those who knew him. But the *Observer* still concluded his obituary with a plea for funds: 'We shall be glad to take charge of any donations old colonists may see fit to send to perpetuate the memory of a genuine and historical pioneer'.[42] Just as Henry Wallen had been remembered as the first 'farmer' in the 1850s, so George Bates was remembered as a 'pioneer' in the 1890s. The idea of who could claim those titles changed radically over the next hundred years.

Nat's Death

Nat Thomas died without tombstone, obituary or donations to 'perpetuate' his memory. He had not entertained schoolboys with yarns of the old days, shared his earnings with his friends on the mainland, or even lived in a town. Unlike Wallen and Bates, he died surrounded by family. He had property to pass on to them, and no doubt stories and memories as well.

But the memories of Nat Thomas remained local. Only those who remained in Dudley continued to tell the stories. His own descendants had to return there to hear them. Only Nat Thomas's commemoration, more than one hundred years after his death, befitted the celebration of their return.

Nat Thomas died in 1879 at the age of seventy-seven. Betty died months earlier in 1878, according to what her grandson, Joe Seymour, told Norman Tindale.[43] In the short intervening period, Nat married a white woman, Sophia Newcombe. I don't know how long Sophia and Nat had known each other; I know very little about her, other than that for years she confused historians who thought she was Nat's Aboriginal 'wife'.[44] Soon after their marriage, Nat made out his will, leaving his estate, including land, house and livestock, jointly to Sophia and his grandson Nathaniel Simpson, Hannah and Thomas's eldest child.[45] But young Nathaniel soon received the whole estate: Sophia died a few months after Nat. She may have been ill when she married, for her death certificate states she died of 'congestion of the lungs' – tuberculosis.[46]

Nat did not write his will himself, but he did sign it. This was at a time when many people could only leave a cross for their name. For Mavis and her son Michael, this is significant. Mavis said to me, 'Being such a good writer, having a wonderful handwriting, Michael has said, "I think he must have come from a well-to-do, intelligent family and they've probably kicked him out because he drank rum." But I'd like anybody who was writing anything about Nat Thomas to mention his wonderful handwriting and that he was an intelligent man.'

In a letter to me, Michael wrote:

> NT ... could still sign his name, which in itself is suggestive of at least some education (and perhaps more than one might expect from an antipodean sealer born c. 1800).

In case I found Nat's signature a little scrawly, Michael had already explained to me that it was probably because Nat was 'approaching death and rather ill and "shaky" of hand'. Michael is also wary of how Nat is remembered:

> If we must make judgements about the 'character' of NT then we need to do so only on the evidence. I guess my mother would at least like to see his memory being given the 'benefit of the doubt'![47]

Nat could do more than sign his name. He had crossed the world as a teenager; he was a ship's pilot, could read a sextant, predict the weather, speak at least one Aboriginal language, manage a lighthouse and a farm and secure his property ownership. As Kingscote resident Sandy Alexander wrote in her 1997 book *Kangaroo Island – A Brief Chronological History*, 'unlike most of the white men', Nat Thomas 'took great care of his Aboriginal family, having had a respectable upbringing'.[48] This comment is indicative of some change of thinking in more recent years. But even this is frail defence against the colourful and well-rehearsed stories told in Dudley.

While these stories do not have any empirical support, let alone give Nat the 'benefit of the doubt', perhaps we ought not to cast them aside as unhistorical. For they are in every way historical: they are how Nat's history is remembered today in Dudley. Despite the veneer of celebration, Nat Thomas does not have the same standing as the colonial settlers. Just as Thomas Willson regarded Nat as the 'oldest colonist' yet not one of his own class, so too do some of Willson's descendants. Nat cannot straddle the cultural divide. Even with the harder evidence – his nice farm, his intelligent children and his 'educated' if 'shaky' hand – Nat remains on the other side of the frontier. Just as Henry Wallen was ready with his gun in the 1986 re-enactment, so Nat is ready to cut out a windpipe with his scissors – a wild man lurking in the scrub, a 'darkie'.

The Shadows

The Aboriginal women who were taken to Kangaroo Island by the pre-colonial settlers are remembered as it is imagined they were once treated: the appendages have become appendices. Sometimes named, they are always a presence: blank, black spaces, the shadows of the white Islander men. But without 'abducted chattels' the men cannot be imagined as brutal. Without Aborigines by their side, they cannot be imagined as savage, and the frontier between uncivilised and civilised cannot so clearly be drawn. White cannot be made to seem black. The shadow makes the man.

In 1836 Captain Hart estimated that sixteen Aboriginal women were living on Kangaroo Island. Eight years later Inspector Tolmer thought there were twelve. He guessed they were aged between forty and fifty.[1] By the 1860s, the number of Aboriginal women, excluding Mary Seymour and Hannah Simpson, was only about nine.[2] What happened to all these women? Who were they and how did they live?

All the women remembered or recorded as being on Kangaroo Island after 1836 lived on the Dudley Peninsula, although this can't have entirely been the case, since a ration depot for Aborigines was operating in Kingscote in 1866.[3] Of the Kaurna and Ngarrindjeri women taken to the island from the South Australian mainland, only three are remembered as living on Kangaroo Island after colonisation: Puss, Sally Walker and Sarah, or Kalinga. All three women were apparently living near Hog Bay. It is not clear where the other women taken from the mainland went, but it is possible some of them returned to their homes.[4]

Anthropologist Philip Clarke thinks one or more Aboriginal Tasmanian women left Kangaroo Island to live with mainland Aboriginal people after 1836. He explains that at least one Ngarrindjeri family in the Lower Murray region has an Aboriginal Tasmanian ancestor. He also thinks some Tasmanian women may have gone home. In a letter to the *Observer* in 1871, Thomas Willson claimed that 'several' of the Aboriginal Tasmanian women on Kangaroo Island had been 'taken back to Tasmania by Captain Duff and others'.[5] Duff had captained the South Australian Company's *Africaine* from London in 1836, and in 1840 became the owner of the *Guiana*, which operated the route from South Australia to London.[6] But there appears to be no record that he or anyone else took these women back to Tasmania.

It seems that many, if not most, of the Tasmanian women who were on Kangaroo Island in 1836 stayed. The best remembered are Betty, Suke and Sal, although they were not the only ones. In 1853, when W. A. Cawthorne stopped at the 'hut' of Nat's son-in-law, he met 'Nat's big daughter and a baby' – presumably Mary Seymour with her first child – sitting with 'Long 'un' and 'Old Wab' – 'native Van Diemen's Land women'.[7] 'Long 'un', or Wore.ter.lee.pood.yen.nin.ner, was originally among those listed by G. A. Robinson as living with James Allen on Kangaroo Island in 1831.[8] Apart from this report, there appears to be no other mention of her on Kangaroo Island. But 'Old Wab' is remembered by her gully near Nat's home, which has the remains of her shelter. Inspector Tolmer employed 'Old Wauber' in 1844 to track smugglers in return for tucker and tobacco.[9] G. A. Robinson never knew of Wab, and Philip Clarke concludes her origins are uncertain.[10] But I think Wab was Tasmanian. Not only did Cawthorne claim she was, but sitting with 'Long 'un' and Mary, and living close by in her gully, she would have been the odd one out at Antechamber Bay if she had not been from Tasmania.

For it seems there was a distance kept between the mainland women and the Tasmanian women. It was said that Sally Walker of Hog Bay had 'no associations with the Tasmanian women'.[11] In his obituary of Mary Seymour, Herbert Basedow quoted her as saying that the Tasmanian women 'regarded themselves as much superior in every respect' to the women from the mainland. For that reason 'the Tasmanian women kept to themselves and hunted in separate parties'.[12] Betty may have been quite emphatic on this point. Since W. A. Cawthorne met her and Nat's daughters, it is perhaps no coincidence that the character 'Sam' in *The Islanders* remarks of 'Black Bet': 'I wouldn't take six lubras of the main for one of these Vandiemans'.[13]

By the time the South Australian Company arrived at Kangaroo Island in 1836, most of the Aboriginal people in Van Diemen's Land had died. None were living as they once had on their traditional lands: apart from the women in the Bass Strait islands and the children living with pastoralists or in the Hobart Orphan School, all the Aboriginal Tasmanians were living on Robinson's mission on Flinders Island, where they were dying through disease and poor living conditions.[14]

Perhaps, even given the choice, the Tasmanian women did not want to return 'home'. Kangaroo Island might have been considered a refuge. After twenty years, it may even have become a home.

But to me as a child, everything about the Aboriginal women remembered in the land at Antechamber Bay seemed tragic. My family felt the sadness in Lubra Creek as we imagined a hell so complete a woman would risk her life to escape from it; a hell remembered over five generations.

In Wab's Gully I imagined the sadness of a woman, old and forlorn, dying far from wherever her home may once have been, with no one to tend to her, no one to bring her food or build up her fire. Only a little wall to provide a shelter from the wind. Behind this wall, I imagined Wab lay curled up, cold and lonely.

This same sadness was remembered in the conversations I had with the colonial descendants. Fiona and Robin Marshall live in the original, restored Marshall homestead behind the dunes of Antechamber Bay, down the hill from Nat Thomas's house. I remember when it was just a ruin off a densely overgrown path. There was a swing in the wild garden that I played on. It seemed secret and magic.

Fiona, once the curator in Penneshaw Museum, has a strong interest in the local history. When I talked with her and Robin over a typically hospitable island dinner of home-grown roast and a bottle of red, we speculated about how these Aboriginal women had lived on Kangaroo Island after settlement. Fiona pointed out that her reading suggested the women had been independent of the European Islander men. 'They kept to themselves,' she explained to me. 'They used to hunt and to fish in little groups, and they'd take the children with them and they'd speak their own native tongue most of the time ... In that sense they were probably trying to keep their culture alive.'[15]

But Fiona's research had also led her to ask her husband's family some questions, and they told her stories about the Aboriginal women, passed down through the generations. Because the Marshalls had married into several other early colonial farming families, these stories span the whole district. Robin's aunt, Mildred Willson (née Howard), told Fiona that when Robin's great-grandmother was a little girl, she and her brothers and sisters would shut the doors and the windows of their Antechamber Bay home against an 'old Aboriginal woman' who 'frightened' them when she came looking for food.

She also told Fiona how in the 1870s Robin's maternal great-great-grandmother, Mrs Willson, was living at the eastern head of Nepean Bay when an Aboriginal woman called at her house for food. Mrs Willson refused to give her any, so she walked to the home of Robin's paternal great-great-grandmother, Mrs Buick, at American River and told Mrs Buick that she had not received anything from that 'debil debil' Mrs Willson. Perhaps this was the same 'old woman' who always put the bread and honey Mrs Buick gave her under her hat. It may also have been the same 'old woman' who once complained to Mrs Buick that she did not feel well – for 'she could only eat "turteen" eggs that morning!'[16]

These stories, handed down over five generations, show the Aboriginal women as begging old fools. It is how Aboriginal people appear in stories set in nineteenth-century pastoral areas across Australia – tragically comic. It was an impression reinforced for Fiona when she researched the records of the Sturt Lighthouse on Cape Willoughby, east of Antechamber Bay.

In his monthly report to the Trinity Board (the lighthouse managers) in Adelaide in June 1859, W. C. Cawthorne wrote of 'the few wandering destitute women that still linger on the Island'. He claimed they often 'lighted fires' in the scrub, a hazardous practice. One woman was 'totally blind', Cawthorne wrote, and 'her companion nearly so'. He claimed he had 'interrogated Old Bet' as to the welfare of these two 'poor creatures' and could only gather from her that one was possibly dead. They were probably Sal and Suke.

'I mention their circumstances', Cawthorne explained to the board, 'to show the inhumanity of those men who formerly had the services of those women when young'. He complained that 'now that [the women] are Old and blind' those men had simply 'abandon[ed] them to the fate of starving in the scrub'. They should either 'be made to provide for' the women or 'at all events keep them from wandering and starting fires where ever they care to'.[17]

Cawthorne's report had an effect. The Secretary of the Trinity Board asked the Treasurer's Office that the conditions of the Aboriginal women be brought to the attention of the Protector of Aborigines.[18] In August 1859 the Treasurer's Office replied that the Commissioner of Crown Lands and Immigration, 'empathizing with the conditions in which these aborigines are described to exist', had directed half a ton of flour, two bags of rice, a bag of sugar and two dozen pairs of blankets to be 'sent to the Head Keeper ... for distribution at proper times'.[19] The lighthouse at Cape Willoughby then became a Government Store for Natives from 1859 to 1863, which was after William Seymour and Nat Thomas had stopped working there. The journal entries record issuing flour, rice and blankets to women including Betty and 'Sally'.

I discussed this over dinner with Fiona and Robin, asking if they thought increased settlement, clearing and fencing might have made it difficult for the Aboriginal women to continue their hunting lifestyles, but Fiona and Robin felt this should not have been the case. Settlement had not been dense. There were few homesteads, fewer fences and little cleared land – there was no shortage of meat to be found in the bush.

Perhaps, Fiona conjectured, the women collected rations out of 'laziness, a handout mentality. It's just so much easier to walk to the lighthouse and get a handout ... than to go out and get it yourself.'

'Certainly in the latter part of their lives', Robin asserted, the women 'had hung around this area because of the supplies'.

Fiona also wondered if Betty 'might have been a drawcard' to other women in the district because 'she was in ... a relationship with a white man' – suggesting, I supposed, that Nat was another source of 'handouts'. The other women, Fiona claimed, were 'vagrants to a certain extent ... not attached to a particular man', and if Betty 'stayed in this area' because of Nat, then perhaps 'they tended to come to her and stick together'.

Robin may have got this impression from his mother as much as from Fiona's research. Agnes Marshall had told me that Nat Thomas's 'place' (as many Islanders called it) had 'quite a settlement of black people' living on it. I was reminded of these comments when reading in Sandy Alexander's 1997 book that 'unlike most of the white men', Nat had taken 'great care of his Aboriginal family'.[20]

Ultimately it is dependence on white people that explains the presence of the women in the district. The popular image of the 'lazy' Aborigine seeking a 'handout' wins out. But she is not only 'lazy', she is also a victim – 'abandoned', as W. C. Cawthorne had put it, by 'unhuman' white men.

When I learnt that Nat Thomas married Sophia Newcombe, I too worried that he had 'abandoned' Betty, because I couldn't understand why he had married months before his death and indeed months before her own. George Bates had married Elizabeth about twenty years before they died. But why had Nat married? I gained the impression that they were men grasping for respectability in a changed, colonised world; that they, like all white men, would always prefer a woman of their own race – that they had partnered black women because they were the only women available at the time. When they 'abandoned' these women, their callousness was complete: not only were the women old and useless, but also, in this new colonial settlement, they were no longer socially acceptable.

This concludes a longer narrative in which the women were always passive: first abducted, then reduced to chattels and finally abandoned. A progression from Lubra Creek to Wab's Gully. Jean Nunn writes: 'clearly, at least some Aboriginal women were abandoned to live out their lives as shadows on the fringe of Kangaroo Island settlements'.[21] The pre-colonial men's cruelty is sustained to the last – the black shadow continues to make the savage white man.

But the savage white man would never have been made were it not for Aboriginal knowledge. While the Aboriginal women on Kangaroo Island were treated violently at first, they were also the original providers of food, and had always spent much of their time hunting in the bush. It seems that after 1836 they wanted to continue living in this traditional way. Perhaps it was less that they were 'abandoned' by the white men, and more the other way around. Perhaps they spent so little time in their partners' houses that Nat and Bates sought the company of other women.

The arrival of pastoral settlers had not ended the skin trade on Kangaroo Island. In 1844 Inspector Tolmer claimed that seals were still being killed and the skins sold in Adelaide for ten shillings apiece.[22] But the most hunted animal was the wallaby. Henry Wallen sometimes earned 'as much as £100 or £150' from the sale of wallaby skins in Adelaide. One of his largest hauls was 1500 pelts in three months, which were sold for shoe leather.[23] In 1844 Tolmer wrote that wallaby pelts were worth sixpence each in Adelaide, and wallaby rugs of forty skins, stitched with sinew, forty shillings.[24] Wallaby skins were even used on the island to make moccasins; John Buick of American River is said to have worn them in the 1850s.[25]

In 1865 wallaby skins were the second-largest source of income on Kangaroo Island after farming.[26] Wallabies became a staple meat supply because the settlers couldn't afford to slaughter the few sheep they had shipped over. For the same reason, wallaby hunting was hugely popular during the Depression.[27] But even when times were not tough, it remained a popular pastime – Robin Marshall told me he trapped wallabies as a child in the 1950s.[28] When researching on Kangaroo Island in the 1950s, Francis Bauer was told by a local that the only thing the Vivonne Bay Jetty was good for was 'to peg out [wallaby] skins'.[29]

Wallabies are protected today but, as their numbers grow, Kangaroo Island is again considering killing wallabies and selling the meat commercially. I wonder if the islanders will trap them, and again remember a tradition passed on by the Aboriginal women.

From the late 1830s to the 1870s, not only did white settlers use Aboriginal knowledge, but Aboriginal women such as Sal, Suke and Betty continued to do a lot of the work. Wallen did not earn his profits on his own. Tolmer wrote that Bates and 'Warland' (Wallen) were the 'masters' of two Aboriginal women whom they 'employed' to 'considerable advantage in taking wallaby for them, which they make a profit by selling the skins'.[30] He described Betty as the 'woman who catches wallaby' for Nat Thomas. In 1932 an Islander remembered in the Adelaide *News* that Sal 'hunted wallabies and dressed and exchanged them with the settlers for little comforts'.[31] Two years later another Islander told reporter Ernestine Hill that Sal had 'rambled the bush, bringing in a few furs for food'.[32] By working in this way, the women were able to do their own trading on Kangaroo Island.

Snaring was not the women's only skill or source of income. Tolmer also wrote of how they collected large numbers of 'sea-bird eggs' – another traditional Aboriginal practice – presumably for the Adelaide market.[33] And Tolmer had not only given Wab tucker and tobacco for tracking, but had also employed two unnamed 'native women', for whose assistance he had paid Bates and Wallen one pound. They were 'of signal service to the Police', Tolmer claimed; without them 'the object of the expedition must have failed'.[34]

Looking for information about how the Aboriginal women lived after settlement, I found quite an extraordinary story about Betty, in which she emerged as an entrepreneurial woman with a wicked sense of humour. In 1906 the *Observer* newspaper reprinted a letter sent forty years earlier from Australian explorer and entrepreneur, Captain Cadell, who stated that he had visited W. C. Cawthorne at the Cape Willoughby lighthouse. The *Observer* explained the context of the letter: exactly forty years and one month before, 'a black lubra, known on Kangaroo Island by the decent Christian name of Betsey ... sent in a preliminary claim to the Government reward promised to the discoverer of a goldfield!' Cadell had written that 'Cawthorne personally conversed with Betsey' about the find, which was about thirty miles from the Cape. The *Observer* noted that the report might sound 'ludicrous' – not for the idea of gold being found on Kangaroo Island, but that an Aborigine had made the claim – but the journalist asked, 'Did not a blackfellow find ... a wonderful mass of quartz which set half England a-longing to visit New South Wales?'

'Betsey', the *Observer* continued, knew perfectly well what gold looked like from seeing nuggets brought back by Islanders who had gone to the goldfields of Victoria and New South Wales. 'Me see him plenty like it that yellowfellow stone', she had apparently said. She was also said to claim that when her son 'was a piccaninny she, with another lubra, procured numbers of [such stones] and beat them out, or "made them long" as she expressed herself'.[35]

But if Betty was capable of lodging a claim with the Gold Research Committee, she was also capable of pulling a swift one. Two days later the *Observer* reprinted the letter that had followed Cadell's. 'W.A.C.' – presumably W. A. Cawthorne – claimed that it was he who had in fact spoken with 'Betsey', but 'cautioned' the public about accepting her story 'on account of her imaginative conceits on other occasions'. Cawthorne deduced that the discovery of her gold must have occurred '18 or 20 years ago' and not in the district that Cadell claimed.

Inspector Tolmer also had written in response to Cadell's report. He claimed that when he had been on Kangaroo Island in 1844, he had 'headed into the interior' and found a 'country different from the unusual character of the island – a stringybark range well wooded, and quartz rocks in abundance'. One of these quartz stones he picked up had gold in it, and he took it with him. But since the gold rushes had not yet begun in the other colonies he thought little of the find, and even lost the stone before he left the island. He asserted that if the land where he found the gold originally 'is identical with the district indicated by Betsey, I claim priority, as I registered my claim for the discovery some months since'.[36]

Although it seems Betty's gold claim was never a serious attempt to strike it lucky, she and the other Aboriginal women did seek other sources of subsistence – tracking for tucker or seeking 'handouts' at farmhouse doors and government ration stations. But this was not a distinct change from the pre-settlement years. On the beaches they had dealt with traders who exchanged skins for flour, salted meat, tea, sugar, rum and tobacco. It is not surprising that they had acquired a taste for these commodities; they had supplemented their traditional diet ever since they arrived on the island.

But many miles separated the farmhouse doors and ration stations, and as the women travelled by foot they must have depended primarily on traditional foods. The *South Australian Register* reported in 1869 that the women 'live by their wits and their waddies'. Although they were 'rationed by a paternal Government ... they rarely come in to claim their dole, preferring to it the wallaby and other small game which they take for themselves'.[37] In 1932 a settler on the south coast remembered how one of the women used to come to his farm with a 'peculiarly shaped club' and carried edible grubs in her 'grizzled hair'.[38]

So it is not surprising that the store for natives at the lighthouse did not solve the 'problems' that had inspired W. C. Cawthorne to establish it. In 1862 he reported that Sal and Suke were still living in the scrub. They were rarely seen by settlers, but several residents had raised concerns that their fourteen dogs would run wild when the women died. A few months later, the *Observer* reported complaints that Sal and Suke had again set fire to the scrub, endangering several properties.

It is possible that Sal and Suke were using fire to hunt kangaroos. 'Firestick farming' – clearing land to create areas where kangaroos will graze – had been an Aboriginal practice in Tasmania. Dogs had been used to catch kangaroos since before

Kangaroo Island was colonised; the fact that the women had fourteen dogs suggests that they were continuing this practice, and trading kangaroo as well as wallaby skins.

Settlers called for the women to be removed from the island and given aid.[39] There was no general understanding of the traditional life the Aboriginal women were living alongside the new settlers, and misunderstanding turned to fear as terrible stories were spread. In 1880 a reporter for the Adelaide *Advertiser* was told that Sal and Suke had 'killed Mrs Thomas [Betty] ... on account of some grudge they had against her, or perhaps at sheer envy at her happy condition' (being in a relationship with a white man – Nat Thomas). In 1932 Tindale was given information passed on from an elderly Islander that 'little Sal hit Betty over the head with a stick' and that Betty died later as a result.[40]

It was even reported in the *South Australian Advertiser* that Sal and Suke 'stole the little child from the lighthouse keeper at Cape Willoughby and ate it'.[41] In 1871 Thomas Willson wrote to the *Observer* that 'anxious mothers' were 'suspicious' of Sal, 'from the fact of two children having disappeared after her visits'. Sal was 'supposed to be *non compos mentis*', he continued, 'but this very day she has put in an appearance at my station and I don't perceive anything seriously amiss with her'.[42]

Thomas Willson's station was west of Cape Hart, on the southern coast. Sal was seen at other stations as well.[43] Sal and Suke also spent a lot of time on the island's north coast, about sixty miles from Cape Willoughby, where they received 'government' rations at Henry Snelling's property on Middle River, according to Snelling's son. At John Stokes's property at nearby Stokes Bay, they received supplies in return for work.[44] The Secretary of the Trinity Board had given explicit instructions to W. C. Cawthorne that stores must only be distributed to Aboriginal women who 'cannot procure any work'; it was 'not the ... wish of the Government to maintain any in a state of idleness'.[45]

The women were far from idle. Although Robin and Fiona Marshall thought the Aboriginal women had 'hung around' near Cape Willoughby because the ration station was there, in fact they had been there before the ration station was established: it was their presence that had inspired W. C. Cawthorne to write to the Trinity Board. The lighthouse was also a practical place for stores to be delivered, as boats had to land there with supplies for the keepers and the light anyway.[46] In fact, most of the supplies for the residents of the peninsula's east end were delivered by sea to Cape Willoughby or the nearby Red House Beach.[47]

The Aboriginal women must have depended on their traditional skills, brought from their own lands, and adapted to suit this place – home for most of their lives. They travelled long distances by foot, and continued to hunt and live by the skin trade. Despite the claims to the contrary, the Aboriginal women were, in Philip Clarke's words, 'fiercely independent'.[48]

If Betty was an 'abandoned shadow on the fringes' of society, she knew how to manipulate the system for her own amusement. The 'victims' appear not to have been so passive. I now think of Wab's Gully in a new way. Perhaps it was less a tragic place than a peaceful place. It was not like the mission station of Flinders Island. It was not a place of contempt where Wab was subjected to a poor diet and exposed to epidemics of disease. In her gully, Wab was free.

Outlasting

When Trukanini of the Nuennone died in 1876, her race was declared extinct. She was said to have been the 'Last Tasmanian'.

Trukanini is an Australian icon. She is better known than most of the official colonists after whom our rivers, mountains, cities and streets are named. She has been the subject of books, poems and songs. Her face has appeared on posters, on a postage stamp and in countless books. Trukanini's skeleton, disinterred from her grave, remained on display in the Royal Society of Tasmania Museum until 1947, when it was placed in storage. On the centenary of her death, Trukanini was cremated and her ashes scattered in D'Entrecasteaux Channel, finally respecting her last wish.[1] The film of the ceremony formed the opening scene of Tom Haydon's hugely popular 1978 film *The Last Tasmanian*.

Tasmania is considered one of Australia's most bloody historical chapters—a one-sided colonial war that had no indigenous survivors. For this reason Trukanini is also made to represent all Australian colonial wars and all indigenous people. Her story offers an appealing kind of shame, simple, neat and comprehensible. It lets the colonisers feel guilt without complication, and their descendants guilt without the tug of compensation.

Trukanini marked the end of only one story in Tasmania. Between 1831 and 1835, the missionary G. A. Robinson worked zealously to remove all the Aborigines from Tasmania to his new mission at Flinders Island. He was never completely successful in removing all the women from the sealer's settlements in the Bass Strait.

About two hundred Aborigines went to Flinders Island. Only forty-seven came back when the mission station was moved to Oyster Cove near Hobart twelve years later. By the time Trukanini died, the mission was empty.[2] But to claim she was the last Aboriginal Tasmanian is to forget the parallel and continuing story of the women living on the islands of Bass Strait and on Kangaroo Island. It is also to forget the story of Fanny Cochrane Smith. Fanny was born in the Wybalenna mission on Flinders Island in 1831 or 1832 to Tanganutura and Nicermenic. She grew up to be a successful businesswoman in the D'Entrecasteaux Channel, south of Hobart, and had eleven children with her husband, William Smith. She died in 1905, thirty years after Trukanini.[3] Before her death, scientist Count Strzelecki claimed Fanny was a half-caste; that her father had been a sealer. Though Fanny defended her 'full-blood' status, scientists and historians have continued to remember her as a 'half-caste'. Her many descendants still live mostly in the D'Entrecasteaux Channel.[4]

Many Australians do not know the stories of Fanny Cochrane Smith and the women of the Bass Strait and Kangaroo Island, and many more do not accept them. It seems many Australians don't want to recognise the Aboriginal Tasmanian survivors. They don't want their neat narrative messed up. For them, Trukanini remains the last *real*, the last really black, really tribal Aboriginal Tasmanian. Even Tasmania's official tourist literature applies to her a biological definition no longer officially recognised in Australian law: we are told she was the last *full-blood* to die.[5] This idea, while fiercely challenged, lives on. Twenty or thirty years ago, any dissenting voices were silent or silenced. Then it was a 'fact' that the Aboriginal Tasmanians became extinct in 1876. Yet even within the racist definition of 'full-blood', it was not true: there was the story of Fanny Cochrane Smith. But even if Fanny is 'scientifically' categorised as a half-caste, Trukanini still cannot take the claim of the last 'full-blood'.

In *Walkabout* magazine of January 1954, H. A. Lindsay told a story passed on from his grandfather, Arthur Lindsay, chairman of the Destitute Board of South Australia. In 1890 Arthur met a visiting scientist at a meeting of the Royal Geographical Society in Adelaide and told him that his Board was 'issuing rations to an aged Tasmanian native living on Kangaroo Island':

> 'You should go across to see her', he suggested. 'I'm sure she could give you a lot of information. It will be lost forever when she dies'.
>
> Unfortunately, the visitor was obstinate and arrogant. 'Rubbish!' he growled. 'She can't be Tasmanian. The last of them died years ago.'
>
> My grandfather was very irascible by nature. Upon being contradicted in this fashion he left the meeting in a furious temper, and so a priceless opportunity was lost.[6]

Six months later journalist Ernestine Hill wrote in *Walkabout* claiming she could 'corroborate' Lindsay's story. This was the article Mavis Golder read. Hill wrote of visiting Kangaroo Island nineteen years earlier and speaking to George Bell of Stokes Bay, on the north coast. Bell had told Hill how in the 1890s Sal and 'Sook' used to come and work for John Stokes, the property's first owner, in return for food.

Bell also told Hill the story of how the two women died. He said Sal died suddenly twelve miles from his family's farm in 1893. Sook, by then blind, tried to show the Bells where Sal was – '*tracking with her feet*', Hill adds in italics. Sook lived a year alone, 'a pitiful sight, often astray', Bell remembered. He quoted her as saying: 'I want I stop. Too long I stay.' One morning they found Sook dead on the farm. 'Though everyone knew of Truganini', Hill reflected, 'for little Sook no claim was made to fame'.

Poor little 'Sook' – no one eulogised her death, stole her skeleton, displayed it in a museum or used her to symbolise the guilt of white Australia. Perhaps Trukanini would have preferred simply to be found one morning and left to rest in peace.

But did Suke really die in 1894, eighteen years after Trukanini? Was she receiving rations from the Destitute Board in 1890? In the records of the Destitute Board, there is a memo from the Protector of Aborigines in 1894 saying that three Tasmanian

Aborigines (presumably Betty, Sal and Suke) had claimed rations on Kangaroo Island 'for many years', but the last of them had died 'about six years ago'.[7] The memo is dated 1894, which would make 1888 the date of death of the 'last' Aboriginal Tasmanian to die on Kangaroo Island. The woman is not named. But many have treated as fact the claim that she was Suke, and that she died in 1888.

In his 1937 article 'Tasmanian Aborigines on Kangaroo Island, South Australia', Norman Tindale confidently claimed that the 1894 memo is an 'official document' that 'indicates the probability that the last Tasmanian survived on Kangaroo Island until 1888'.[8] In another article, this time in *Quadrant* magazine in 1961, H. A. Lindsay quoted the Destitute Board docket stating that 'Sukey' survived 'Truganina' for twelve years. 'If somebody had written down her reminiscences!' Lindsay exclaimed, still full of regret, 'but nobody bothered to do it'.[9]

In her 1981 book *The Aboriginal Tasmanians*, Lyndall Ryan takes us over fourteen chapters from pre-contact Tasmania to the death of Trukanini, then suddenly tells us that 'Truganini was not in fact the last "fullblood" to die.' It was Suke, Ryan explains, who died on Kangaroo Island in 1888. 'Nevertheless,' Ryan immediately continues, 'for Aborigines Truganini has become a symbol of struggle and survival; for Europeans she has become a useful scapegoat for the extermination of the Tasmanians'.[10] Ryan's source is Tindale's 1937 article.

Jean Nunn reflects that the Tasmanian women living on Kangaroo Island 'must have suffered a great deal as a result of being abducted from their tribal homes and people', but she adds, as if it were compensation, that they 'survived Truganini by many years'. Nunn's notes for her book show that she went to the archives herself to read the Destitute Board memo of 1894. From this she somehow concluded that Suke was taken to the Adelaide Destitute Asylum and died there in 1888.[11] The *Encyclopaedia Britannica* claims that Trukanini 'was the last full-blooded Aborigine in Tasmania' but adds that 'another Tasmanian woman is said to have survived on Kangaroo Island in South Australia until 1888'.[12]

But in 1880 the *South Australian Advertiser* wrote that, although 'the last aboriginal native' had died in Tasmania several years before, she 'left survivors in Kangaroo Island, and the last of them only lately passed away':

> There were three old hags of that race, who having outlived the ex-whaling or convict lords and masters, used to roam about together ... At last one of the trio died, and the remaining two were inseparable ... One of these women lost her eyesight, and one day she came into one of the settlements and reported that her companion was dead. The poor wretch that remained though blind, could find her way about in an astonishing manner, but suddenly disappeared, and no trace of her has ever been seen, and so vanished the last Tasmanian aboriginal.[13]

Here is Bell's story of 'Sook' and Sal, thirteen years before he claimed it happened.

It seems that Sal died in 1874, two years before Trukanini, somewhere near Middle River. Tindale was told it took a week for Suke to report Sal's death, during which time she 'apparently lived only on the heart of a single "yacca" (grasstree)' – a claim that echoes that of the character Georgy in W. A. Cawthorne's *The Islanders*. Betty's grandsons, Joe Seymour and Tiger Simpson, thought Suke was buried at Cape Hart, but others believed she stumbled over a cliff, and Roland Snelling of Stokes Bay claimed she was burnt in her wurley.[14]

To tell Suke's story is to unravel a knot of historical sources. It is to tell the story of how the Aboriginal Protector's no-doubt-hurried note became an authoritative 'fact' that was endlessly recycled; of how a grandfather's anecdote inspired a badly researched narrative. But does not the 'fact' still remain that the last 'full-blood' Tasmanian died after Trukanini – if not eighteen or twelve years later, at least about four? Is this not still significant? Does it disturb the narrative that the Tasmanians were, as Lindsay put it, 'killed off or died out' in 1876? Hardly. For Trukanini is defined both by the purity of her rare blood and by colonial borders. She died on her indigenous soil, the island of the Black War. Her death closed a book that was quickly rewritten. Trukanini remains the iconic figure, Suke the ironic figure. Suke supplies a twist to the narrative of Tasmanian extinction, but she does not threaten it. As Ernestine Hill said, 'For little Sook no claim was made to fame'.

Lyndall Ryan too presents Suke as an aside; it is Trukanini who 'has become a symbol of struggle and survival'. Ryan is not telling us the story of Tasmanian extinction but that of Tasmanian survival. To dwell on which 'full-blood' Tasmanian died last is to validate the racial definition that makes the narrative of extinction possible in the first place. Suke is necessarily pushed aside.

Suke is pushed aside for the same reason that she has been the centre of Lindsay's and Hill's narratives: because she is an addendum to a chronology popularly thought to end in 1876. Fanny Cochrane Smith doesn't have to become an addendum; she was classed a half-caste. But Suke, with neither a supposed sealer father nor the trappings of civilised society, is recognised as a full-blood. So she has been reduced to a date, be it 1894, or 1888 or 1880 – to the year when she died.

But Suke also lived. She was more than a date, more than the composition of her blood, more than a story of historical sources, more than an ironic, quirky fact to be celebrated, or avoided, for its historical irregularity.

∾

William Lanne is not as famous as Trukanini, but he too is remembered for his death. Lanne, Trukanini's husband, was believed to be the last Aboriginal Tasmanian man. He died in the Dog and Partridge public house in Hobart in 1869. He had been very ill for some days, and was getting dressed to go to the Hobart General Hospital to seek treatment when he died. They took him to the hospital all the same.

The motives for placing him in the hospital's death-house were not good. William Crowther, the hospital surgeon, cut Lanne's skull from his head and replaced it with that of another cadaver. A few hours later Crowther's rival, fellow surgeon Dr George Stokell, removed Lanne's hands and feet. The bones of a man defined by the purity of his blood were prestigious items in scientific and museum circles.[15]

Lanne was given a state funeral. No ceremony in the Victorian era could supply a text richer in symbolic meaning. What remained of Lanne was placed in a coffin. The pall was a possum-skin rug; the decoration two native spears and waddies, around which were 'twined', a contemporary journalist noted, 'the ample folds of a Union Jack'. Lanne had been a crewman on the *Runnymede* whaling boat, so four of his Caucasian Van Diemen's Land-born crewmates carried his coffin. Three black men were his pallbearers. They included Alexander Davidson, an Afro-American, John Bull, a Sandwich Islander, and Henry Whallen, a 'native of Kangaroo Island'.[16]

Whallen, born in 1819, was the son of the 'Governor' and an Aboriginal Tasmanian woman. He was given the role of pall-bearer at Lanne's funeral because he was a 'native'. Whallen was made native to a place that was supposedly without indigenes. How many there that day knew that Whallen could identify as being native to the same land as the man they were burying?

∾

Betty died in 1878 – two years after Trukanini. She was not buried with Nat Thomas near his house on the headland, but at the other end of Antechamber Bay beach, where she had once lived, where Chapmans River doesn't quite reach the sea and papery gums overshadow shallow yellow water. Her grave is not marked, and exactly where she lies is not known. There is a reason for this gap in our knowledge.

In *Walkabout* in July 1954 Ernestine Hill wrote that she had met Tom Simpson, the 'last Tasmanian half-caste', in Penneshaw. She had in fact met Tom's cousin, Joe Seymour, the grandfather of Mavis Golder. It was Joe's photo that so shocked Mavis when she picked up the magazine.

Hill wrote that 'Tom's' mother was buried at Antechamber Bay. But if this had referred to Betty, 'Tom' would have been well over a hundred years old. Hill also wrote that in 1935 'a visiting anthropologist from the University of Adelaide had ... offered [Tom] £5 if he would take him to her grave'. Tom had at first agreed, 'but a shovel on the truck disclosed the irreverent intention to dig up a valuable skull. "I wouldn't like diggin' my mother's skull," he said, "so I just backed away".'

Norman Tindale came to Kangaroo Island in 1930 to research the remnants of its ancient population. He returned in 1931–32 and 1936 to investigate the Aboriginal Tasmanian women who had once lived there, including Betty's descendants. His research interested the Adelaide press, who also talked to local Islanders.

Arthur Daw, who had 'lived on Kangaroo Island for more than 74 years', told a *News* reporter in March 1932 that 'Little Sal', not Suke, had in fact been the 'last of the Tasmanian aborigines'. But two days later the Adelaide *Mail* asked, 'Was Little Sal a Tasmanian Abo?' The paper had interviewed another local, Roland Snelling, who claimed that 'Little Sal' had in fact been an 'Australian' (mainland) Aborigine. Tindale assured the *News* that if Little Sal's bones could be found they 'will be sent to specialists who, by exhaustive mathematical tests, will be able to prove definitely whether she was a Tasmanian'.[17]

A week later Tindale told the *News* that 'Little Sal' was not Tasmanian, that Suke was last to die and that Betty had descendants living on Kangaroo Island. The article was headed 'Hot on the Trail of Our Vanished Race'.[18] The day before, Tindale had been quoted in the *News* saying he hoped Betty's descendants 'will be able to give details of the Tasmanians'.[19] Four years later Tindale went to Kangaroo Island and met Mary Seymour's son, Joe, and his cousin Tiger Simpson.

Joe and Tiger took Tindale to 'the sealer's hut at Cape Hart' on the island's south coast. There, Tindale wrote in his journal, he 'tried to learn from Joseph Seymour the site of the burial of the last Tasmanian on Kangaroo Island but he would not describe its location in detail sufficient for anyone to find it'.[20] Perhaps Joe and Tiger knew that Tindale was 'hot on the trail', and that Suke's remains, should they be found, would be exhumed to be sent to 'specialists'. Trukanini had pleaded to be buried at sea to avoid the same fate.[21]

Joe and Tiger also showed Tindale 'the approximate site' of their grandmother's grave. Tindale recorded that it was 'in a small field opposite the point where the main road turns abruptly northwest away from the banks of Chapman River'. It is a long way from where Joe's mother had claimed Betty was buried. In 1905 Mary Seymour told E. H. Hallack, who wrote a pamphlet about Kangaroo Island, that Betty had died ten years after Nat Thomas and was buried at Cape Borda, the island's most north-western corner.[22] Perhaps she too was hoping to lead prospective grave-robbers astray. But Joe and Tiger did take Tindale to the mouth of Chapmans River at Antechamber Bay, and told him their grandmother had first lived there. Tindale described it as a 'landing place favoured by sealers who visited Antechamber Bay'.[23]

Two hundred metres behind the beach, just north of the mouth of Chapmans River, Tindale dug into a 'thin layer of undisturbed debris on the site of what was once a hut'. He unearthed some flint implements, the remains of shellfish and kangaroo bones, a hand-carved kangaroo-bone tool, some broken glass and half a homemade domino piece – Aboriginal tools and European games mixed in together.[24]

If Tindale asked Joe and Tiger for a more specific location of Betty's gravesite, they didn't show him. Tindale probably had a shovel in the back of his truck, but Joe Seymour gave him no chance to use it for graverobbing. While Tindale's visit was made the year after the one in which Ernestine Hill claimed she met 'Tom', it is possible she got the date of her trip wrong – she got so many other 'facts' wrong. But it is almost impossible to find out; Hill's notes were all taken in a kind of shorthand that is illegible to almost anyone today.[25] Perhaps half-made-up quotations and factual assertions shaped a text Hill hoped no one would know enough about to question, unaware that 'Tom's' granddaughter would read it and become frightened and confused. Adding to the mystery is what Robin Marshall told me – that 'back in the thirties or forties' someone had been 'walking around in the scrub' near Chapmans River and 'actually picked up a skull'.[26] Was it Betty's?

In her 1951 history of Kangaroo Island, Margaret Ayliffe wrote that before there was a cemetery reserved in Penneshaw a number of people were buried at Chapmans River in Antechamber Bay.[27] The YMCA used to have a campsite there, and every year I went to camp for two weeks with other girls near where Betty was buried. I loved it. I learnt to kayak on the yellow waters of

Chapmans River and skinny-dipped in a secret beach where a whale's skeleton lay. We didn't know about Betty, but there were two graves of a local family with white crosses under a willow tree near the tents – possibly remains of the cemetery that Margaret Ayliffe remembered – and every night at nine o'clock when we walked back from supper in the mess, we heard a woman's piercing scream. We were sure the place was haunted.

Shortly after the plaque to honour Nat Thomas was erected in 1991, Neil Waller approached the Department of State Aboriginal Affairs to fund a memorial to Betty near her unmarked grave. The Dudley council agreed to the project and in 1993, the International Year of the World's Indigenous People, a plaque was erected beside the Cape Willoughby Road at the bottom of Antechamber Hill, near the 'approximate site' that Joe Seymour had shown Tindale. The inscription reads in part:

> Early settlers in this area included Nat Thomas [and] his Tasmanian Aboriginal wife Betty ... [their] elder daughter was the first documented child of a European born in South Australia.
>
> While not always well treated, the Aboriginal companions of the pre-1836 settlers made a significant contribution to the early development of the island.
>
> Betty died in 1876 [sic], and while the actual site of her grave is unknown it is believed to be in this vicinity.

When I had dinner with Robin and Fiona Marshall I asked them what they thought of the memorial.

'It's in the wrong place', Robin answered. 'It's about two miles out.'

Was Betty buried closer to the mouth of Chapmans River, I asked?

'Yes,' Robin replied.

When I had visited the Marshalls the year before, Robin had shown me a photograph of the site where Betty was 'supposedly' buried, which had been shown to him by his father. I recognised it from my YMCA camps. It is a long way from the paddock on the Marshalls' property where Joe Seymour claimed Betty was

Betty's memorial on the Cape Willoughby Road near Chapmans
River, erected in 1993 by Neil and Adrian Waller, with the support of
the Dudley Council and the Department of State Aboriginal Affairs.

Rebe Taylor, 1994

buried. Perhaps Joe made the 'approximate' site very approximate in order to keep away grave robbers. But how would Joe have felt knowing that his descendant had to learn about Betty's grave in an ethnological article while the Marshalls could claim it as inherited knowledge?

'It really doesn't matter where it is,' Neil Waller told me. 'It's the symbolic thing that's more important.'

No one can know where in Tasmania Betty was born, who her parents or ancestors were, or what name they knew her by. But we can return to the land where she spent about fifty years of her life. Her own descendants can make that symbolic act of erecting a plaque in her memory, and they can do more. They can walk where she walked, know the land she knew, stand where she died, and speak the words she once spoke – the four phrases that Joe Seymour told Tindale in 1936:

´nina tu:´napari	you understand
lil tu:´napari	do you understand?
´bulunta	go straight ahead
ma:bir, ma:bier	go around

It could be a poem, an ode to understanding this history. It could be a message. *Lil tu:´napari – do you understand?*

149

The
Descendants

Mary

Mary Thomas, the elder daughter of Nat and Betty, was born on 11 September 1833 at Hog Bay River on the south coast of the Dudley Peninsula, where sealers had once camped and where the Tasmanian women continued to hunt and fish.[1] Mary was three when the South Australian Company arrived at Kingscote to colonise her home, but she saw little of the settlers. She spent most of her childhood with her sister, brother and mother on the island's south coast. Mary's was a world dominated by Aboriginal women. Together they trapped wallaby, collected shellfish and caught kangaroo, possum and fish. She and her brother and sister spoke to their mother only in her Tasmanian language.[2]

But then Mary's life became harder. When she was about twelve, her brother left. Mary called him Sam, the name of their grandfather in England. Others remember him as Nat, their father's name, and others again call him Lorne.[3] In old age Mary told her physician, Herbert Basedow, that Sam joined a whaling vessel at Antechamber Bay when he was sixteen.[4] In 1856, about ten years after he left, the *Observer* claimed that 'Betsey' had a son called 'Nat' who was 'a sailor now in England'.[5] Mary received one letter from her brother after he left. He wrote from Liverpool saying he was bound for China. She never heard from him again.[6]

Sam crossed the world at about the same age his father had. It was his father's one-way journey in reverse – from the scrub of Kangaroo Island to the streets of English towns. Or was it? One colonial descendant told me quite a different story; that 'sealers,

Nat Thomas and Betty

Sam
(also known as Nat)

Mary
m. William Seymour

Hannah
m. Thomas Simpson
(see separate
family tree p. 195)

Emma
m. Frank Barrett
(see separate
family tree p. 176)

Joseph
m. R. Josephine Butterley
(née Ebert)

Jane
unmarried

Annie
m. Arthur Harry

Mary
m. Frank Abell
no children

Mavis 📖
m. Les Golder

Michael 📖
m. Wendy

Larry 📖

Brentley 📖
m. Glenda

James   **Fleur**

Joey

**Nathaniel
Thomas**

**Samara
Annie**

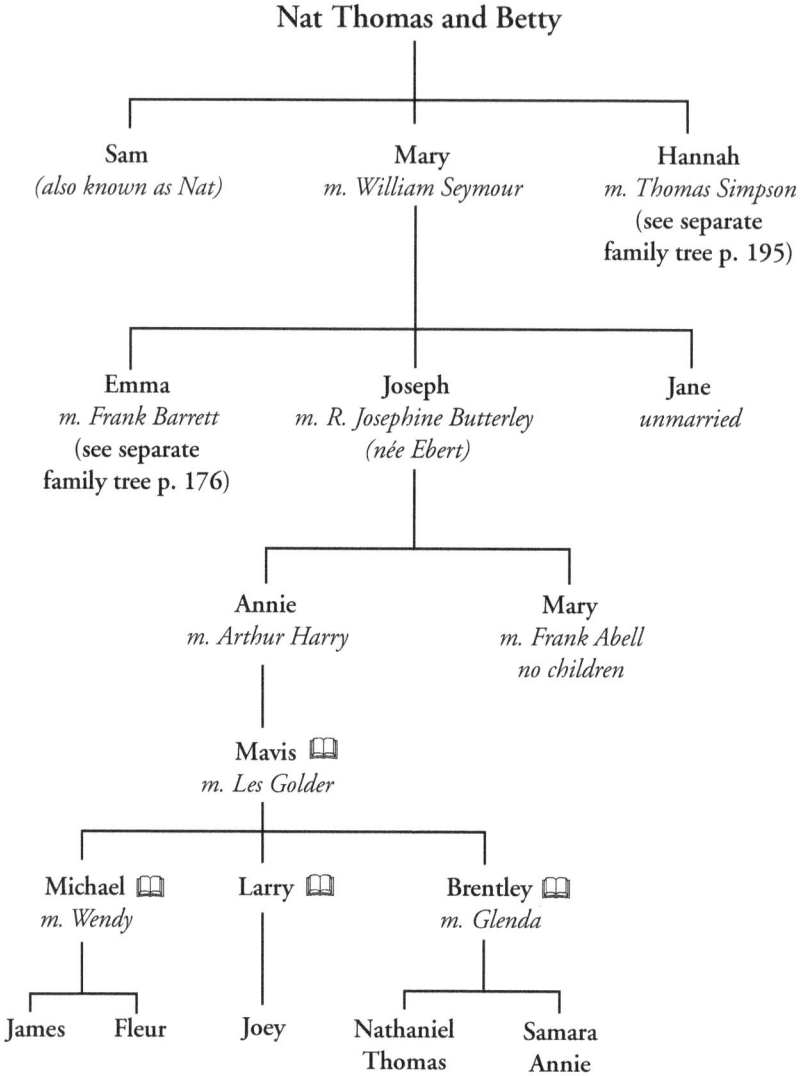

📖 = informants   * = pseudonym

the whalers', or 'somebody came here' and found that Nat Thomas's son 'was a wonderful swimmer'. They 'kept making him dive for things', I was told, 'until he became exhausted and got drowned'.[7]

At sixteen, Mary also travelled from one world of knowing to another. She married William Seymour, an Englishman many years her senior.[8] They were married in her father's house by the Venerable Archdeacon Morse. Fiona Marshall told me that Mary was remembered as a good, hard-working woman, but her husband was not. Mary's feelings towards William are remembered only in the story of his death. 'Trust the old bugger to die there' was all she apparently said when, after nineteen years of marriage, he was found dead in the sand-dunes at Antechamber Bay. But there was no resentment remembered when Mavis Golder told me how her great-grandfather 'went to Adelaide on a ... fishing boat, and came back a few days later and my grandfather, who was twelve years old ... went down to meet him at Antechamber Bay, and he found him dead on the track leading up to the house'.

Mary was about thirty-five. She would spend most of her life a widow.

In their years together, Mary and William lived a few yards from her father's house, in a small stone cottage overlooking Antechamber Bay, as W. A. Cawthorne had shown in his painting. A stubble of stone poking through tufts of grass is all that remains today. Mary was twenty-one when she had her first child, Emma. Joseph (Joe) followed, then Jane, who it was said fell off the kitchen table as a baby. A mentally disabled and dependent child was added to Mary's hardships.

Three years after their marriage William began to work at the Cape Willoughby lighthouse, a position he held for six years. It was during this time that Mrs Cawthorne, the head keeper's wife, taught Mary and Hannah to read and write English. William and Mary also worked with Nat Thomas on his farm, and did much of the work themselves in the later years. Mavis Golder thought that after William died Mary continued to do the work herself. Mavis told me: 'My great-grandmother had a farm out there, a little farm'.

Mary's children were adolescents when William dropped dead in the sand-dunes. She continued living with her father and running her 'little farm' at Antechamber Bay for about another ten years. Then, three years before her father died, Mary left the farm. Her sister Hannah had left for Hog Bay with her husband seventeen years before. Betty may have been absent much of the time as well.

But perhaps Nat was not alone. He may have been already living with his soon-to-be-wife, Sophia Newcombe. His grandson Nathaniel, Hannah's eldest son, spent an increasing amount of time at Antechamber Bay.[9] Only Sophia and Nathaniel would be remembered in his will.

If she already knew this, then perhaps Mary left Antechamber Bay disheartened. Mary's great-granddaughter Ellen Marks remembered that her mother, Mildred Chester, had spoken of 'a bit of dissension' in her family. Ellen thought Mary's elder daughter, Emma, was 'a bit put out by Nat Thomas the elder giving . . . the grandson [Nathaniel Simpson] all the property'. It was 'just a feeling', she told me; an injustice Ellen felt might best be explained by the fact that 'in those days . . . there wasn't any women's rights'.

But this woman Mary was brave. At the age of forty-four she took her experience of farming and what money she had, and made a credit agreement to buy a 268-acre block near Hog Bay. Surveyed the year before, section 112 cost one pound an acre, plus 26 pounds, 10 shillings in interest.[10] With the help of Emma and Joe, Mary told Herbert Basedow, she built a stone house on her section, cleared twelve acres and 'started a farm'. 'Mary . . . could handle a plough as well as any man', Basedow wrote, 'but although she worked with a will, she ultimately found it necessary to sell out'. After six years of effort Mary surrendered her credit agreement back to the Crown without completing her payments. Three years later Thomas Willson took out a credit agreement on her land, and by 1905 he had completed the payments.[11]

By 1885 Mary had bought a one-acre suburban section in Hog Bay. The town had been renamed Penneshaw the year before, but it would be at least another generation before the

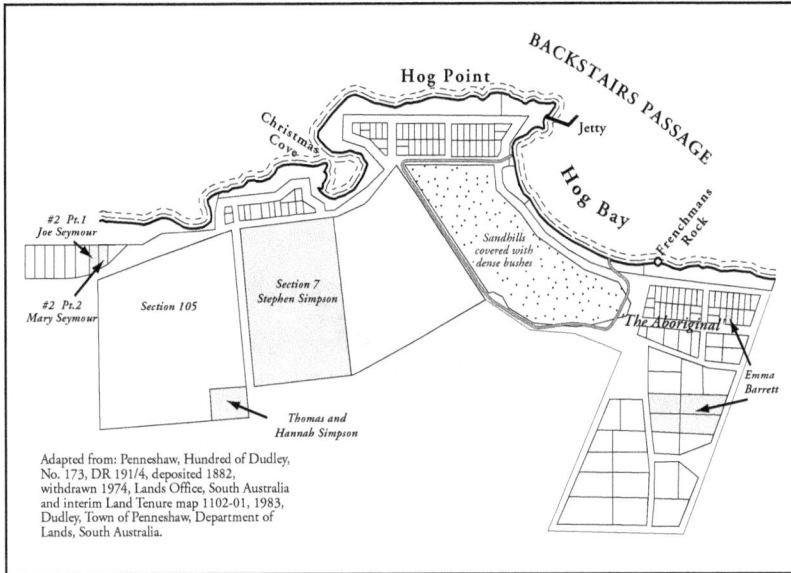

Penneshaw township showing the property holdings of the
Barretts, Simpsons, Seymours and Wallers

new name found local currency.[12] Perhaps Joe, by then a 26-year-old stonemason, helped her build the stone cottage that still stands today.[13] Mary's cottage was on the edge of the sea, over-looking Backstairs Passage. The road that passed near by could have taken her west up the hill to the cemetery where she would be buried, or east, past Christmas Cove, a natural marina and the centre of the small town.

While Mary was now living in town, it seems she did not entirely forget the traditional Aboriginal lifestyle she grew up with. In the Penneshaw Museum, among other photos of her family, I found an old picture that, although unidentified, looks very much like Mary taken in the 1880s or 1890s. She is sitting in a campsite, neatly dressed and surrounded by her dogs. A rusty pin mark stains the photo – I wonder who remembered Mary by hanging this picture in their home?

A year after Mary was granted her acre in Penneshaw, she sub-divided it and transferred two-thirds to her son-in-law Frank Barrett, Emma's husband, keeping the one rood and nine perches on which the house stood.[14] By 1894 Joe Seymour was living next

Christmas Cove, Penneshaw. Rebe Taylor, 1994

This photo is unidentified, but the curator of the Penneshaw Folk
Museum said that since it was in their collection, and it showed a
close likeness, it is most likely of Mary Seymour, camping, in the
1880s or 1890s

View over Penneshaw, including Backstairs Passage and the
mainland Cape Jervis. Rebe Taylor, 1994

Christmas Cove, c. 1906. Courtesy of Keith Southlyn
[pseudonym], who told me that one of the vehicles is
Thomas Simpson's mail cart

door on Frank's section, in his own house.[15] Emma lived on the other side of Hog Bay beach; Hannah and her family were a short walk up the hill behind Mary's house; and Jane, Mary's disabled daughter, was still living with her mother.

In 1891 Mary began to find it hard to provide for Jane, and asked the Dudley council to recommend that Jane receive rations from the Adelaide Destitute Board. The Board, which housed many poor in its Destitute Asylum, often issued rations to people in country areas on application by a local authority.[16] The Dudley council described Jane Seymour as an 'imbecile' and argued she was a 'most deserving case'. Within a month the Destitute Board approved the application.[17]

Still Mary continued to try and earn a living. A month later, at the age of fifty-eight, she became the only woman to tender for a road-construction contract with Dudley council.[18] She was unsuccessful.

By the age of sixty-one Mary was struggling to support herself. It is unlikely that Emma or Joe could have easily cared for her. By then Emma had five children with a sixth soon to come. Her husband owned a small amount of land and worked casually as a labourer for the council; he found it hard to provide for his family.

Joe was married to Rachel Josephine Ebert, who had seven children from a previous marriage, but seemingly brought only one daughter, Rachel, to live with Joe. By this time she and Joe had had two girls of their own – a two-year-old and a baby.[19] Joe could not have earned very much working as a stonemason in a town as small as Penneshaw.

Perhaps Hannah's family might have provided some assistance to Mary, but it is possible that she wanted to retain her home and independence.

In 1894 Frank Barrett wrote to the Dudley council on behalf of his mother-in-law to request that they organise Destitute rations for Mary. Thomas Willson, the Dudley council chairman, who was still paying off the land Mary had once farmed, interviewed Mary and then put her case to the Destitute Board.[20] 'Mary Seymour ... is a half-caste Tasmanian born on the Island, and is

Mary Seymour outside her home in Penneshaw, c. 1910.

The Penneshaw Folk Museum

now over 60 years of age and has no income,' Willson wrote, 'but owns a very decent cottage and an attachment of land'. Its value, according to the council, was £50. 'This property she states she will hand over to the Government in exchange for rations during her life,' Willson explained. He added with approval: 'This proposal the Council thinks is an equitable one.'[21]

It was also a standard one. Most applicants to the Destitute Board, as Mary and Willson had no doubt learnt, offered the deeds of their properties in exchange for being admitted to the asylum for the rest of their lives or, like Mary, receiving rations.[22] It was a system that ensured some return to the government. The Destitute Persons Act stipulated that the Board had the right to sell or to take charge of the property of a destitute person, or of a responsible relative. For the Act also stipulated that it was the duty of 'the father, grandfather, mother, and grandmother and the children and grandchildren of every … destitute person' to support their relatives, or pay the Board for the cost of their rations and board.[23]

This put the family of Mary's sister Hannah beyond legal responsibility, but no one called on her children Emma, Joe or their children either.[24] Thomas Willson explained to the Board: 'These people are very improvident as a rule and there is no children to aid them'. He also explained that Jane Seymour was already receiving rations. No doubt Willson knew that the Board did not always pursue relatives in 'improvident' families who could not meet their legal responsibilities, especially when a member was already receiving rations.[25] Willson concluded his letter by 'hoping' the board would 'act promptly in this case as it is urgent'.[26]

Willson's politic support might have produced the desired result had he not described Mary as 'a half-caste Tasmanian born on the Island'. The Destitute Board considered Aborigines to be outside their concern.[27] Although at that stage there was no Act in South Australia defining an Aborigine (the first was passed in 1911), the Destitute Board sent a memo to the Protector of Aborigines asking if Mary might come within the ambit of his office. As she was 'a 1/2 caste aboriginal born in South Australia', the Protector thought she would.

The Protector then sent a memo to the Minister of Agriculture requesting authorisation to issue rations to Mary. But the Minister then returned a memo to the Protector with the question: 'Is this applicant of South Australian aboriginal blood? If she is not is there any precedent for considering her as within the scope of this department?' Denied rations by one department for not being white enough, Mary seemed doomed to starvation for not being the right kind of black. But the Protector replied:

> The applicant is not an aboriginal of South Australian blood, but it has been the practice to assist aborigines from the other Australian Colonies when located in South Australia. There were three Tasmanian women, native blood, living on Kangaroo Island for many years, the last of these aborigines died about six years ago, and she was receiving rations from the Department. The present applicant is believed to be the very last of this race, and on the ground of Intercolonial reciprocity would, I submit, have some claim on South Australia for assistance.[28]

This was the docket that Norman Tindale read, and from which he concluded that Suke, the 'last' of the three, had died in 1888. It presents a senseless argument. How could Mary have claim 'on the ground of Intercolonial reciprocity' when the Tasmanian colonial government did not recognise that it had any Aborigines, and had not since the death of Trukanini in 1876? It had declared the Tasmanian native people extinct eighteen years before. But still, seemingly for the sake of compassion, in a system where Aboriginal 'blood' was defined by colonial and political boundaries, Mary became 'the very last of this race'.

The Minister was not troubled by such contradictions. He approved the application on 10 September 1894. Ten days earlier, at a council meeting in Penneshaw, Willson had already been informed that the Destitute Board had deferred Mary's case to the Protector of Aborigines. He had told Mary of this and reported her response: the minutes record that she strongly objected.[29] Perhaps Mary objected to being dealt with on the basis of her race when the issue was her poverty. Or maybe she knew that the Aborigines Office would not support her as well as the Destitute Board.

Willson resolved to meet the Destitute Board chairman in Adelaide to try to resolve the matter. If he set out to convince the chairman to take on Mary's case, he was unsuccessful. Mary's freedom to determine her identity was subordinate to her need for food and clothing. On 13 October Willson announced to the council that the Protector of Aborigines would supply Mary with rations for the rest of her life on condition that she signed the transfer of her property to the Crown. Willson then obtained a letter from the Protector ensuring that Mary could stay in her house for the rest of her life. Two days later, she signed a declaration transferring all her property 'to Her Most Gracious Majesty Queen Victoria'.[30]

The transfer was not entered in the Land Titles Office until almost two years later. On 16 May 1896 the Dudley council unanimously agreed that, 'being a destitute person', Mary Seymour should be struck off the assessment record.[31] She no longer had to pay rates, and all her needs – food, water, clothing, fuel and house maintenance – became issues of government administration. The council was responsible for allocating her food and seeing to any repairs to her house. Her son-in-law, Frank Barrett, carted thirty-six gallons of water to her home for three shillings a week. Her son, Joe, once repaired her house for thirty shillings. Her firewood was delivered, and she received winter clothes, boots, blankets and a new water tank.[32]

As I looked through the entries in the Dudley Council minutes, all of Mary's needs appeared to have been well attended. I found only two occasions when Mary took issue with her care: twice she complained to the council about the meat in her rations. Her first complaint was in 1899 about the 'condition' of the meat supplied by the storekeeper at Salt Lagoon, a small settlement near Pelican Lagoon. All the council minutes record is that the clerk would see that 'better arrangements' were made 'for sup-plying meat in the future'.[33] Four years later, Mary again com-plained about the 'quality' of her meat. This time the minutes record that the chairman, William Howard, promised to discuss the matter with the storekeeper.[34]

These two scant entries perhaps seem insignificant, but they point to a bigger underlying problem. When I spoke to Mavis

Golder about Mary's destitute status, she told me, 'There was one person who . . . benefited' from it.

'Do you mean that he ripped her off?' I asked.

'Yes,' Mavis replied. 'I don't know fully the story . . . but when she was applying for all this help he did something . . . he got some of the goods . . . I don't know how.' Mavis remembered her mother and aunt 'talking about it and . . . saying he did all right out of it.'

'Was he a councillor or a storekeeper?' I asked.

'He was everything in Penneshaw,' Mavis answered. 'Quite a well-known figure.'

'Who was he?' I asked.

'No, I couldn't,' Mavis said. 'He was a friend of the family.' She then added, 'I'll tell you if you turn that off.'

I turned off the dictaphone and Mavis told me that 'he' was the storekeeper who supplied Mary's rations, and 'he' was indeed 'everything' in Penneshaw.

I won't use his name here, but will call him Ralph Whyte. When Ralph was still a boy, he worked briefly for John Trethewey, who ran stores in both Salt Lagoon and Penneshaw. Ralph may have learnt a few lessons in meanness from his boss. John Trethewey's nephew, Roe, told me that his uncle had once suspected a young local boy of stealing from his Salt Lagoon store, which was only open on Saturdays, so he set a loaded rifle to be triggered if the door was opened during the week. The boy's testicles were shot off.

This infamous incident may have prompted Trethewey to leave for Sydney in 1900. By the second time Mary complained about the meat, Ralph Whyte was running his own shop in Penneshaw.[35] He was also the harbour-master for twenty years, the Penneshaw Cemetery curator in 1910, the district pound-keeper in 1915–16, the district council clerk from 1911 to 1916 and again for ten years from 1938, a councillor from 1917 to 1921 and 1930 to 1933, the chairman of the council in 1920, a Justice of the Peace and a freemason.[36]

He could get away with corruption. Mavis told me that her mother, Annie, worked as an assistant in his shop before she was married. Annie knew he was not giving her grandmother her due, and that he was profiting from the difference. Two days after talking to Mavis, I spoke to Mildred Willson, a colonial descendant of Mavis's generation, who told me many in the community had considered Ralph Whyte dishonest. Her father had said to her that if he was a freemason, then the freemasons were all bad. But Mildred did not want his name repeated either. If little will be said about him now, it seems even less was said then. The man who was 'everything in Penneshaw' controlled a conspiracy of silence.

Ralph not only abused his influential position but also, it seems, his relationship with the Seymour family. Roe Trethewey told me that Ralph had been 'associated with the Aboriginal mob', and that Ralph's father had 'lived with them for years'. More specifically, he told me that Ralph's father had lived with Mary Seymour's daughter Emma, although he added cautiously that he was not absolutely certain of this. If it was only hearsay, it is possible to see how the rumours were fostered. Frank Barrett, Emma's husband, died in 1901. Emma lived near Ralph's father, and in 1906 she sold him the home she and her husband had occupied.[37]

Ralph was related to the Seymour family by marriage. His grandmother, Hannah Charlesworth (her maiden name), married three times. The eldest daughter from her second marriage married Joe Seymour. Ralph's daughter even described Mavis Golder as 'a descendant of my great-grandmother Hannah Charlesworth'.[38] Ralph also remained, as Mavis put it, 'a family friend'. Emma Barrett's daughter, Ellen Marks, told me that in his later years Ralph moved to Adelaide and used to visit her mother, who lived near by. This 'friend' held Mary to ransom for his profit margin. It seems her family feared that protesting would only exacerbate the situation.

Perhaps none of this would have happened if Mary had received rations from the Destitute Board as she had requested. Unlike the Aborigines Office, the Destitute Board had clear rules and regulations stipulating that:

> Destitute persons in country districts, who are in receipt of rations are required to sign their names in full to the printed

forms of receipt at the foot of each account – the signature being witnessed but not by the person who supplied the rations – and the accounts certified by the Chairman of the District.[39]

Even this system could have been rorted if the chairman was also the council clerk and the storekeeper, as Ralph Whyte was, but perhaps not quite as easily. It seems Mary had been right to protest about receiving Aboriginal welfare.

While South Australia had a far more charitable welfare system than most Australian colonies, it was still unfair, and unfair for all. The requirement that recipients hand over their property made them even more vulnerable and left the next generation with little to inherit or bargain with, a situation Mary's children were yet to face. But at least Mary's story offers one consolation. Mary lived another nineteen years after handing over her property deeds. The cost of her rations, carting water, repairing her house and buying her boots, clothes and a new 600-gallon iron water tank amounted to at least three times the revenue the government got from the eventual sale of her property.[40]

In February 1913 Jane Seymour went to live in the Parkside Asylum in Adelaide, where she died of senile decay and cardiac disease almost a year and a half later, aged sixty-one. She only just outlived her mother.[41] The Protector of Aborigines received a telegram from Penneshaw on 9 September 1913 stating: 'Mary Seymour died today do you pay funeral expenses?'[42] It was two days before her eightieth birthday. It seems the death of a woman who had seen so much change in her life was simply an administrative matter. The Destitute Board paid for funerals, the telegram implied; did the Protector of Aborigines do the same? Did his office, like the Destitute Board, observe the 'strictest economy' in 'pauper funerals'?[43] Mary was buried in an unmarked grave.

'Old Dudley'

Seventeen members of the Australasian Association for the Advancement of Science boarded the steamer *Governor Musgrave* in January 1907 and took a three-day tour of Spencer Gulf, including Kangaroo Island. Some on board had a particular interest in local ornithology, some in botany and geography, and others in the Aborigines and their customs.[44]

When the *Governor Musgrave* anchored at Hog Bay, anatomist Professor Richard Berry walked west from the jetty, past Christmas Cove and up the hill to the house where Mary and Jane Seymour lived. 'In all probability', the opening of his subsequent article declared, 'it has not been the lot of any living British anatomist to gaze on a living representation of the extinct native Tasmanian race'.[45]

It seems to have escaped Berry that the words 'living' and 'extinct' were in direct contradiction. How could Mary 'represent' a race that had supposedly died out? Berry might answer, because only 'full-blood' Tasmanian Aborigines were *members* of the race. Mary, although 'a genuine half-caste Tasmanian' and 'one of the oldest, if not the actually the oldest' Tasmanian half-caste, was merely 'a representation'. She was 'an interesting anthropological problem'.[46]

Berry had not known that he would have an opportunity to meet Mary. He regretted not having brought the 'necessary instruments' to make any 'craniometrical measurements'. To compensate, he listed in his article the physical descriptions of Aboriginal Tasmanians given in James Bonwick's 1884 book *The Lost Tasmanian Race*. This list, he claims, was 'very accurate', because the Tasmanians' extinction (which he claims was in 1868 – not 1876 as it usually is) 'just about coincides with the birth of anthropology as an exact science'. This is despite the fact Bonwick was a historian, not an anthropologist.[47]

As if it were a revelation, Berry found that 'the subject' showed 'many striking resemblances' to Bonwick's 'pen picture'. He particularly noted 'the colour of the skin, the width of the mouth and nostrils, the weak chin, and the dark eyes'. Mary's hair, 'though distinctly woolly', had 'departed from the racial type consequent on the admixture of the white blood'.

Berry finds Mary's 'good looks' debatable, but 'there can be no two opinions as to her intelligence'. His evidence: the 'absolute purity of her English speech'. When he heard her speak, Berry 'could not have believed that such intelligence could have been derived in one generation from a race ... believed to have been one of the most degraded and brutal in the world'. Berry also quotes E. H. Hallack's pamphlet about Kangaroo Island, written two years earlier: 'Mrs. William Seymour is ... of a bright and happy disposition, a most entertaining conversationalist, and, withal, extremely apt at repartee'.[48]

Mary was friendly to the stranger. She sat for Berry's photographs and spoke to him of her life. But in the title of his article she was reduced to 'A Living Descendant of an Extinct (Tasmanian) Race'. Berry was fascinated by Mary because she was alive. But her *life*, her knowledge and her feelings were irrelevant.

They weren't irrelevant to Herbert Basedow. In Mary's obituary notice in 1914, Basedow remembered Mary's life: from hunting with her mother on the south coast, to marriage at sixteen, to farming alone. 'She was an interesting character to converse with', he remembered, 'and graphic were her accounts of

Mary Seymour with her daughter Jane outside her home in Penneshaw, c. 1907. A copy of this photograph was supplied by Jean Nunn, but it seems the photographer was anatomist Richard J. A. Berry

experiences in the pioneering days of South Australia'. She also had 'a keen intellect combined with a determined will; both of these characteristics being well known to persons who had had the privilege of her acquaintance'. Basedow had treated Mary for chronic rheumatism and a fractured kneecap, the results of a life-time of hard work. Despite her pain, 'she always displayed a cheerful disposition'. He was impressed with her strength.

But the opportunity to write about Mary as a rare racial spec-imen was not lost even on Basedow. After all, he was the 'local correspondent for ... the Royal Anthropological Institute of Great Britain and Ireland'. Her obituary was published in the anthropological journal *Man* under the heading 'Relic of the Lost Tasmanian Race'.[49]

'Mrs. Seymour was a woman of short but robust nature', writes Basedow. The 'deep notch below the glabella and the root of the nasal bones' betrayed a 'Tasmanoid inheritance'. Her hair was 'silken, white, and wavy', her eyebrows 'bushy', but her lips and chin 'remarkably free from hairs'. Her skin was 'bronze-brown' and 'wrinkled'. The lower jaw was 'well developed' and had a 'big loose flap of skin attached to it that produced a very noticeable double-chin'. Her 'keen, small eyes lay deep within their sockets'.

She was 'a true half-caste Tasmanian', concluded Basedow. But at least he gave Mary a voice to describe herself: 'Mary claimed to be "the first woman born on Kangaroo Island"'.

Is this true? Nancy Allan, described in Launceston in 1836 as 'a native of Kangaroo Island', was thought to have been born in about 1822.[50] Other girls may also have been born before 1833. But perhaps that is not the point. Mary embodied other people's con-tradictions. In Michael Golder's 1958 *Australian Junior Encyclopaedia*, Mary was 'the last full-blooded Tasmanian aborigine'.[51] To Berry she was the last living representative of an extinct race. The Aboriginal Protector argued in 1894 that she should have received rations 'on the ground of Intercolonial reciprocity' even though he thought she was 'the very last' of the Tasmanian race. The con-tradictions were born from a lie: Tasmanian Aboriginal extinction was declared in 1876, but it did not happen.

Mary Seymour shortly before she died, c. 1913.
Basedow Collection, South Australian Museum

Mary claimed she was a beginning, not an end.

In 1993 I visited the Penneshaw Cemetery and took a photo-graph of Mary Seymour's once unmarked grave. In the late 1980s two small, round granite stones were placed to form her head-stone, on which was mounted a plaque:

> Mary Seymour, nee Thomas, Born at Hog Bay River Sept 11, 1833, died Sept. 9, 1913, the first white girl born on K Is. Daughter of Nat Thomas and Betsy, a Tasmanian full blood Aboriginal.

And so Mary, the 'last Tasmanian half-caste to die', became the first 'white girl' to be born on Kangaroo Island.

When I later went to see Mavis Golder, I told her how I was surprised to see Mary described as 'white'.

'That's not right, is it?' Mavis responded, surprised. She had forgotten what the plaque exactly said. It was erected about ten years earlier when a resident near Kingscote saw an article in the *Islander* about Mavis's family history. He showed Mavis the two stones that he wanted to use as a headstone. He said he wanted

Mary Seymour's headstone, Penneshaw Cemetery.
Rebe Taylor, 1994

something 'different', Mavis remembers, to 'stand out in the cemetery' and honour the fact 'she was the first born on Kangaroo Island'.

Mavis was touched at such 'a lovely thought'. Fiona Marshall, who was working in the Penneshaw museum, picked up the stones from Mavis's house. Robin Marshall attached them and put them in the cemetery.

'Things were different,' Mavis reflected. 'There wasn't the Pioneers Association and it wasn't brought out to the fore.'

So Mary was remembered as white. 'Well, she was a half-caste', Mavis reasoned, 'but that doesn't make you white, does it?'

It does if the word 'white' does not refer to skin colour but is used to mean 'settler', 'one of us', 'part of our history'. The plaque concedes that Mary had Aboriginal 'blood', but it does not allow for the suggestion that Mary may have *been* Aboriginal. If that were acknowledged, then the word 'first' would no longer be apt. The word 'first' was not used as Mary had used it, but within a context of retrospective colonial white history. An Aboriginal cannot be the first in a white beginning. Aboriginal people are not part of white history, of linear time. They belong on the other side of the frontier, the counterpoint to civilisation.

And so remembering Mary not as a 'living representative of an extinct race' but as the 'first white child born' seemed a positive attempt to welcome Mavis into the progressive, celebrated island history. The plaque did not attempt to question the border between pre-colonial and post-colonial, or black and white. It merely accepted them and put Mary on the side of the orthodox.

It was a frontier created to forget injustice. But Mavis Golder had not forgotten. Although she was emphatic that she did not wish to cause offence, Mavis did remember her mother's anger at the treatment of Mary. And it was not simply pointed at the storekeeper who ripped Mary off, but at the community in Penneshaw. 'I think she was sort of pushed aside a bit,' Mavis said of Mary. 'She wasn't helped as much as she should have been.' She even said to me that Mary 'wasn't helped at all'.

'I think', Mavis also told me, 'there might have been a little bit of trouble with the Penneshaw council about land ownership.'

'What sort of trouble?' I asked.

'Well, I sort of had the feeling that they weren't given the opportunities of ... perhaps if you was a Buick or a Willson ... they'd get help and the pick of any land or anything, whereas Mary didn't. I just have that idea but of course ... it was a different feeling towards dark skins in those days ... you really can't compare it with today.'

Perhaps if Mary had been a white man, a Mr Buick or a Mr Willson, she would have been successful as a farmer. She might have been a councillor, a council chairman, or even a storekeeper. But others defined Mary and decided her destiny.

'I don't think that was fair at all,' Mavis complained. 'After all, she was a Kangaroo Islander through and through, really, wasn't she? Wherever your parents came from, and she had these three little children, no husband ...'

She told me: 'People didn't worry about whether she was the first or anything in those days.'

No, they didn't. In those days the locals called Mary 'Old Dudley', the name the peninsula had been given when it was declared a Hundred in 1874. Mary was the *old* Dudley; she preceded the name. She was of the time before the land was surveyed and subdivided, before there was a council, before there was an Aboriginal Protector. She marked the end of the time when Kangaroo Island was Aboriginal, when there were sealers and a link with Tasmania. She bridged two cultures.

She 'never spoke to her mother in other than the native Tasmanian tongue', Basedow wrote. 'Even in later life Mary preferred the language her mother had taught her.' But she had also learnt to read and write English with 'absolute purity'.

Mary was born when there was no South Australia; in her old age, she became vulnerable to the colony's administration. But with her 'determined will' she succeeded in adapting to these changes. She learnt to read and write the language of the colonisers. She ploughed her land, built her houses, cared for her disabled child. She was a widow, a farmer, a destitute person. She was a half-caste; she was a white girl. She was an ending; she was a beginning.

'My ancestor ... Mary was the first child born on Kangaroo Island', Mavis told me, 'that's the start of everything, isn't it?'

∾

Just before this book went to press, Mavis Golder's son Larry phoned me from his Adelaide home to say he had recently been to Kangaroo Island and visited the Penneshaw Cemetery. He took a chisel and a hammer and removed the plaque from Mary Seymour's grave. He has since replaced the plaque with a more accurate inscription. 'I was not *desecrating* her grave,' Larry said. 'I was *consecrating* it.'

Larry did not think a white girl could be born of a black woman. He made this point in a confessional letter to the editor of the local *Islander* newspaper. 'What are they going to do,' Larry asked me, 'send me to Tasmania?'

Emma, 'The Aboriginal'

'I was born ... in a small cottage near a beach ... near Frenchman's Rock ... we had a nice beach to play on and we used to fish from the rocks.' So remembered Emma Barrett's daughter, Mildred, late in life.[1] Mildred, born in 1893, was fifth in a family of six. She was preceded by Gilbert, Thomas, Oliver and Clara, and followed by Lewis. The year before Mildred was born, her father bought a small lot on which they built their home, and the following year Emma added another two adjoining sections, giving them almost one acre of land directly behind Frenchman's Rock.[2]

Also in 1893, Frank Barrett was issued a lease with the right to purchase thirty-two acres at Pigs Head Flat, a few miles inland from Penneshaw. Like Hog Bay and also Porky Flat, its name was another legacy of Nicolas Baudin. 'Barrett's Corner', now forgotten, became a placename near Pigs Head Flat. Frank cleared five acres of the land for a small farm. Mildred remembered:

> It had two dams and apple and pear and almond trees. We liked going out there so my mother built a shack so that we could stay overnight. The cows and horses had to stay out too. There were plenty of cranberry bushes out in the scrub and we used to pick them and mother made jam, which was good.[3]

This was not all the land the Barretts owned. In 1895 Frank was issued with a lease of seven agricultural sections south of Antechamber Bay, near Cape Hart, and one section just east of the

Nat Thomas and Betty

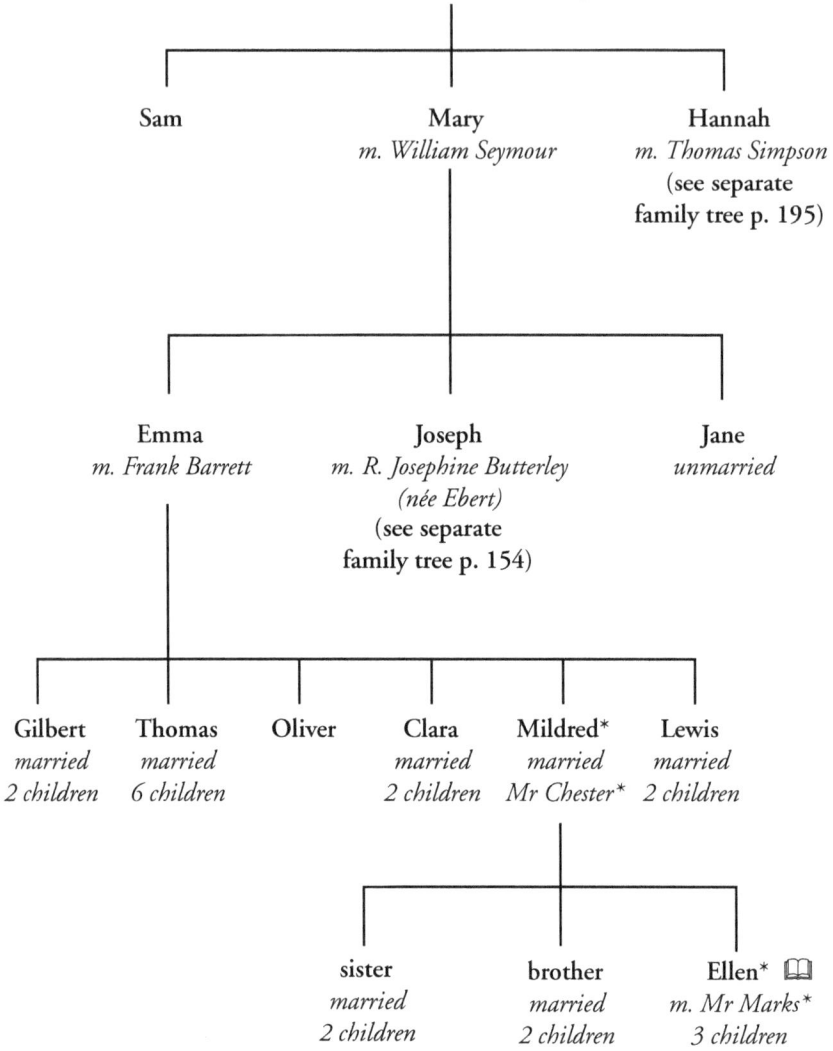

Sam

Mary
m. William Seymour

Hannah
m. Thomas Simpson
(see separate
family tree p. 195)

Emma
m. Frank Barrett

Joseph
m. R. Josephine Butterley
(née Ebert)
(see separate
family tree p. 154)

Jane
unmarried

Gilbert
married
2 children

Thomas
married
6 children

Oliver

Clara
married
2 children

Mildred*
married
*Mr Chester**

Lewis
married
2 children

sister
married
2 children

brother
married
2 children

Ellen* 📖
*m. Mr Marks**
3 children

📖 = informants   * = pseudonym

Dudley Isthmus, near Pelican Lagoon – a total of nearly 3000 acres. The sections adjoined the leases of Hannah Simpson's sons.[4] While it was an impressive amount of land, little of it was cleared and much of it was on poor limestone or sandy soil (see map on page 203). If he cleared any of it, he may have used it for some limited sheep grazing.

In 1898 Frank and Emma sold two of the three adjacent lots behind Frenchman's Rock held in her name and bought another suburban block further west, opposite the site where the Penneshaw Hotel was later built.[5] They sold this in 1900 and bought another small lot behind Frenchman's Rock, further inland from the beach. This later became Emma's home.[6] In 1901 Emma bought another five sections behind Frenchman's Rock, giving her a total of eight-and-a-half acres, which they may have used to grow vegetables.[7]

Frank also worked for the council as a labourer, as curator of the cemetery from 1890 to 1896 and as the District Ranger (which included checking stock that were licensed to graze on Council lands) from 1891 until he resigned in 1900. Emma then took over the position and held it for another four years.[8] Emma had assisted in lighting the lantern at Cape Willoughby, sometimes using the oily bitumen that oozed from the rocks near by, the bitumen from which her mother, grandfather and Inspector Tolmer had tried to profit.

But the Barretts' work and land apparently were not sufficient to support their large family. Their son Oliver suffered from 'fits' for several years, and by 1892 his condition was getting worse, so Frank requested that the council ask the Destitute Board to admit his son to the Adelaide hospital as a patient without fees. The Board agreed, but Oliver later died. The Barretts were still receiving support from the Destitute Board two years later.[9]

In 1901, when only Gilbert was of working age, their father, Frank Barrett, died. The following year the Destitute Board refused to issue Emma with any rations, in spite of repeated pleas from the council that her case was most 'deserving'.[10] Frank's land near Cape Hart and Pelican Lagoon was transferred to James Waller, the nephew of Emma's cousin.[11] The small lot where they had originally lived was transferred to Emma, although she sold it to the storekeeper's father five years later.[12]

The Pigs Head Flat farm was also transferred to Emma. 'Having a small farm helped,' Mildred remembered. 'We looked after the cows and fowls and in those days things were very cheap. My mother worked hard.' Emma rented out Pigs Head Flat for a fee; by 1912 she had paid off the lease, and the following year the land was transferred to her son Gilbert.[13]

Emma still had the five sections near her house behind Frenchman's Rock, but in 1911 she transferred the one with her house on it to her son Thomas, and went to live with her mother in order to look after her.[14] When Mary died two years later, Emma wanted to stay on in her house, but the property had been passed on to the Crown nineteen years earlier in return for rations. Emma could not inherit it. Indeed, the day Mary died, the Protector had forwarded a memo to the Commissioner of Public Works: 'Aboriginal Mary Seymour having died this date the land and house may as well be sold and the proceeds paid into Revenue'.[15]

Nonetheless, Emma asked William Gunson, a solicitor who represented many of the Islanders over labour and property issues, to make inquiries about the possibility of remaining in her mother's home.[16] Two weeks after Mary had died, Gunson went to see the Protector of Aborigines. Perhaps on the Protector's advice, Gunson wrote him a letter later that same day requesting that 'Mrs. Emma Barrett ... be allowed to remain in occupation of her late mother's house'. He explained:

> She is ... in poor circumstances and has no house and it would be a great thing to her to have the old place as a home during her departure. For many years she was in constant attendance of her old mother and during the latter's last days attended to her both day and night and is now completely broken down.[17]

The Protector responded sympathetically. He forwarded a memo to the Commissioner of Public Works amending the docket he had sent the day Mary died. 'Mrs Barrett being an old woman and a descendant of Aborigines', he explained, 'I would respectfully suggest that she may be allowed the use of the property during her life'.[18] He also said that the house and land were worth 'about £20 only'; this was £30 less than the council's original estimate in 1894. But a low value was in Emma's interest. As the Protector suggested, the sum involved was too petty to warrant worrying an 'old woman' out of house and home.

Just over three weeks later the Protector went to Penneshaw to make 'inquiries', and completely shifted his position. On his return to Adelaide, he reported to the Commissioner that 'residents, including Mrs Barrett ... find that the house is of no use to her'. He had also spoken to Mr Gunson, who claimed the Protector had been 'misled by a resident of Hog Bay'. The Protector's closing recommendation was to sell the house 'in the usual manner'. Beneath the typed script was the handwritten addition: 'I have an offer of £50 for it and another of £35'.[19]

But when offers were publicly invited two days later, Emma Barrett, again represented by William Gunson, made a bid of £30. There is a sense of heartbreak and sadness in his accompanying letter. 'You are aware of the circumstances', wrote Gunson, '[and] we feel sure that you will do what you can to assist our client to get the property back which she and her mother largely assisted to get together originally.'[20]

What had happened? Who had spoken to the Protector in Penneshaw? Was it more than coincidence that one of those offering to buy Mary's cottage was family 'friend' and relative Ralph Whyte?

The Protector did not entirely lose sympathy with Emma's cause. When he sent the list of offers to the Commissioner of Public Works, he wrote in parentheses after Emma's name '(daughter of the late owner Aboriginal Seymour)' and added a note to 'draw the attention' of the Commissioner to Gunson's accompanying letter arguing for compassion in her case. But someone in the Commissioner's office circled R. E. Bates's offer of £60 and wrote the word 'highest' beside it.[21]

Five months passed without the offers being taken up; then another offer came in, this time for £62. The Commissioner forwarded it to the Protector, asking him 'to please make a definite recommendation'. The Protector replied that he did not think Crown land could legally be sold privately without the approval of the Surveyor General. He concluded: 'the property is of no further use to the Department'.[22] There was no mention of Emma Barrett.

It seemed to be time to collect the money and end the matter. The Surveyor General approved a cash sale of the property with a reserve price of £60.[23] But since nothing had been announced publicly for several months, Emma Barrett again wrote to the Protector requesting that she have the property as her own until her death.[24] Gunson offered another bid on her behalf, this time for £40.[25] Then, in August 1914, Emma's brother Joe wrote to the Surveyor General:

> I was under the impression [my mother] owned the property at the time of her death but I have received information that prices have been called for the property. What I want to know is the date of the transfer of the property from her to you. If there is any cost such as a search fee … let me know.[26]

It must have been hard for Joe, who had possibly helped build his mother's house thirty years before, to learn that it had been the possession of the Crown for twenty of those years, and even harder to witness the property going under the hammer on 8 October 1914. It was sold to Ann Bates for £60 5s, and remained in the Bates family for another sixty-three years.[27] I asked Mavis Golder if she thought Mary's house should have stayed in her family. She answered, 'It would have been lovely.'

The Bates family went on to buy the little farm at Pigs Head Flat three years later.[28] Emma returned to her old house near Frenchman's Rock, which was transferred back into her name from her son Thomas's.[29] She was sixty-two years old and would live for another six years. Most of those years she would be alone, as all her children left the island.

Mildred and her older sister Clara 'worked for a couple of years in the hotel' in Penneshaw until their brother Thomas suggested 'we should go to Adelaide to find work'.[30] Thomas and Gilbert continued to work as labourers for the council until about

1917, but they eventually followed their sisters.[31] So too did their youngest brother Lewis, whom some in Penneshaw remember as 'the red–haired blackfella'. The nickname suggests another reason why they wanted to leave.

When I asked Agnes Marshall what she could remember about the Aboriginal people who once lived in Dudley, she told me that 'some of them used to live ... up beyond Frenchman's Rock'. I asked what their names were, and Agnes answered, 'I just remember hearing that the Barretts lived up there and I also remember that people used to refer to that part of the district as "The Aboriginal" because the Aborigines lived up there.'

It was the first time I had heard the name 'The Aboriginal' used for the area near Frenchman's Rock. When I did some further research, I found the name had been widely used, but that it had in fact preceded Emma and her family. Margaret Ayliffe, who grew up in Penneshaw, wrote in her 1951 history, *Flinders Land of the South*, that 'the east end' of Penneshaw 'was called "the Aboriginal" because it was there that the government allotted a block of land to a white settler who married a native woman'.[32] I then looked at the rough notes that the farmer on Nat's old property at Antechamber Bay had given me from his conversations with older Islanders in 1960. One of the Buicks, who had had a garden behind Frenchman's Rock, had told him that a resident called Wilkinson had been married to a 'mainland gin'.

When I went to research this further, I learnt that the original records of the land grant had been mislaid. But on 2 April 1860 the former Protector of Aborigines received a letter from a William Wilkins:

The land that I have been supporting my children that you ... told me to take is just taken for a sheep run by a man of the name of [Marshall] he tells me I must not grow any more grain which is the only means I have of supporting my Children and I have ten of them. I have been at great expence having built 2 good stones Houses, and I have to work very hard ... the mother of my children is Mary Monatto who I have had for 16 years. One of the Aborigines.[33]

The former Protector remembered the case. He wrote to the Surveyor General that William Wilkins had taken 'an aboriginal female as his wife', and 'settled upon a plot of land at Hogg Bay at a time when the Govt. were allowing such cases a section of land'. (From the 1840s the South Australian government had a policy of reserving lands for use by Aborigines to encourage European farming practices.[34]) While the land was officially leased to Mary Monatto, it was understood that Wilkins would in fact be farming the land and would be allowed to do so because he was married to her.

Mary Monatto had come to Kangaroo Island not with the sealers, but after official settlement. The name Monatto is probably an Aboriginal name or title from southern South Australia.[35] Wilkins remembered this title; she was not Mrs Wilkins in his letter. The former Protector felt sure that his office files would 'prove that Wilkins, so long as he lives with the Aboriginal female, has no right to be disturbed'.

Unfortunately, the reserve at Hog Bay had not been gazetted or surveyed when it was first issued to Wilkins. He had merely been promised that his (or more properly Mary Monatto's) lease would be more accurately defined 'at some convenient time'.[36]

Thomas Marshall had been granted two leases in 1860 in addition to his first lease of 1858. His holdings, also unsurveyed, went west from Antechamber Bay almost as far as Hog Bay. But the Surveyor General found in his records that Wilkins's grant, 'being numbered 100, containing 80 acres ... is not included in any Run'. Marshall had gone too far west when he told Wilkins to stop growing his grain.

Wilkins's crops and 'stones Houses' lay at the east end of Hog Bay beach, near where Captain Baudin's men had scratched their message in the rock. His land, the Surveyor General stated in late April 1860, had now 'been surveyed and made an aboriginal reserve'. This meant the land was reserved from sale and 'Wilkins will be left in possession'.

Four months after writing his letter, Wilkins fell ill with influenza. Mary Monatto travelled on foot to Cape Willoughby to request assistance from the lighthouse station. There, she was issued with one sack of flour and two 'pairs of Blanketts' from the store for natives, and tea, sugar, rice, vegetables and 'Medecine' from keeper McArthur's private stocks. McArthur reported that the family were in a state of 'sickness and destitution' and had no bedding or provisions.[37]

Wilkins died in October, leaving Mary with the care of nine children between the ages of ten months and fifteen years. It seems that one of their children had died since Wilkins wrote his letter. Some of the others were ill. The residents of Hog Bay, McArthur reported, 'could not support the family any longer'; the younger children were getting out of hand, having set fire to a tin of 'Camfor', threatening nearby grasslands and crops. McArthur issued a letter approving their removal and the requisitioning of their estate.[38] In a letter to the Commissioner of Crown Lands in March 1861, the sub-Protector of Aborigines advised that 'native woman Wilkins' had left for Yankalilla, north-west of Cape Jervis.[39]

Wilkins's old farm, although still an Aboriginal reserve, was commercially leased for farming. The lessees did not have to be Aboriginal or married to Aboriginal women. The land was first leased to Robert Davidson, then to Henry Bates in 1872 and to George James Bates three years later.[40]

Nineteen years later the Aboriginal reserve was cancelled by parliamentary declaration, and the land was divided into sixty-seven suburban blocks, ranging in size from a quarter of an acre to three-and-a-half acres.[41] In local Hog Bay vocabulary, the word 'reserve' was eventually dropped and the land behind Frenchman's Rock became known as 'The Aboriginal'.

After the jetty was built at Hog Bay beach in 1902, the town began to shift its focus from Christmas Cove to the headland just above it. Not long after, a pub was finally built there. For more than half a century, Penneshaw had been a town without a pub. The geographer Francis Bauer commented that this 'must have been almost unique in the annals of Australian settlement'.[42] When a shop was built opposite, a new town centre emerged. The road that ran between the two buildings and down to the jetty became a place to gather and talk, especially on Saturday afternoons.[43] But the Penneshaw school, two stores, the Methodist

Church, a boarding house and the post office were all in the old centre on the western side of Christmas Cove.[44]

'The Aboriginal' was far from all this activity; it was at the other end of Hog Bay beach, separated from the town by empty, grassy sand-dunes with a dirt road running behind them, known for years as 'Lovers' Lane'.[45] A natural well brought many to the beach, but it was not until the 1960s that the beach shacks that now overlook the bay began to be built. The dunes were not even surveyed until the 1980s.[46]

Now a tarmac road runs in front of the houses, and the name 'The Aboriginal' is little known. The east end of the beach now boasts some of the most up-market beach houses. The old cottages, including Emma and Frank's, are done up and rented to holiday-makers. Some locals even refer to the area as 'Snob Hill'.[47]

By the time Emma lived there, 'The Aboriginal' had lost its original meaning. The government reserve was now a locality for low-class blacks. Mary Monatto had lived there with her children until 1861. Emma and her family lived there thirty years later. It was the Barretts' presence that sustained the name 'The Aboriginal' and gave it new meaning. Their relative poverty was connected to their Aboriginal ancestry, and to the name and history of the place where they lived. 'The Aboriginal' also became known as 'Blackfella Town': a fringe dwelling, a place for outcasts.

To a little boy, as Dave Buick was in the 1910s, the east end of Hog Bay must have seemed a long way from his home west of Penneshaw. He recalls going with his mates on expeditions to 'have a look in Blackfella Town' and play pranks on the 'dark . . . old lady' who lived there and was known as 'the black boong'. Her name, John confirmed, was Emma Barrett.

'The Aboriginal of "The Aboriginal"?' I asked.

'Yeah,' he answered.

Mavis Golder's son Larry, who grew up in Kingscote, also remembers Blackfella Town. 'I remember when we were driving past there one day,' he told me. 'At that stage [there was] only a few beaten-up bloody houses and I think it was the old man who said, "That's what they call Blackfella Town up there".'

Penneshaw Hotel and main store. After the jetty was built in 1902, this became the town centre. Residents would meet on this corner on Saturday mornings. Rebe Taylor, 1994

Hog Bay beach, Penneshaw. At the far end is the white dome covering 'Frenchman's Rock'. Behind is 'The Aboriginal' where Emma Barrett and her family lived. It is now known to some as 'Snob Hill'. Rebe Taylor, 1994

Perhaps his father did not know, or chose not to tell Larry, that it was his great-aunt and her children who had sustained the name.

Mildred Chester was left one lot of land at 'The Aboriginal' when her mother Emma died.[48] But her daughter, Ellen Marks, grew up in Adelaide and did not know that this land was in 'Blackfella Town'. Indeed, she knew nothing of her Aboriginal ancestry. When I told her that her grandmother Emma was remembered as the 'black boong', as the Aboriginal of 'The Aboriginal', Ellen said to me: 'Probably it is the reason why my mother has not said a lot about her family.'

Those in Penneshaw old enough to remember still refer to the Barretts as the 'blackfellas', even if they had red hair. The land behind Frenchman's Rock retains this meaning for those who knew it when the little historic cottages were still ramshackle – when it was 'Blackfella Town' and not 'Snob Hill'. But the descendants of Nat Thomas do not know this. From indignity and derision, silence is born; and from silence comes inclusion some-where else, somewhere where red hair implies a white ancestry.

Hannah

Hannah Thomas was born in 1839, six years after her sister Mary, and died two years before her in 1912.[1] So no one could speculatively claim that Hannah was the 'first child born on Kangaroo Island' or the 'last Tasmanian half-caste' to die. Perhaps for this reason, Hannah never received the attention Mary did. She was never interviewed or photographed by anthropologists or ethnologists – indeed, I could find only one photograph thought to be of Hannah in the Penneshaw Folk Museum – and no one wrote an obituary for her when she died.

An image thought to be of Hannah Simpson, née Thomas.
The Penneshaw Folk Museum

Hannah's life was quite different from that of her sister. Mary was more years a widow than a wife, brought up three children on her own and was legally defined as an Aborigine by her poverty. She became, in Herbert Basedow's words, a woman with a 'determined will'. Hannah had a large family and was married for most of her life. She was defined as a mother and wife rather than by her individuality or race. Just as Hannah escaped the vulnerability and hardships that her sister suffered, so she also escaped becoming a rare racial specimen to be studied, speculated over and stripped of her assets.

Hannah was married in February 1860, at about the age of twenty-one, to Thomas Simpson, an Englishman almost twice her age. In Lincolnshire Thomas had been a butcher, the trade he put on his marriage certificate, but had also worked a sailor for several years before he settled on Kangaroo Island.[2] From 1859 he held the mail contract for Hog Bay.

Hannah was pregnant a month after their marriage, and by May Thomas Simpson was officially the owner of a new whitewashed cottage in Hog Bay. Their cottage was perched in the top corner of a 69-acre block surveyed only months earlier, a neat square of a hill that swept down to the road that ran along the sea.[3] Some still remember it today as 'Simpson's Hill'.[4]

Hannah's new home enjoyed a view no less spectacular than that from her father's cottage. She still looked over Backstairs Passage to the cliffs of the mainland, but from a different vantage point. And from her top corner she could see the few cottages and buildings clustered around Christmas Cove, where the boats landed to deliver goods and to take away produce for sale.

The Simpson house is remembered as the first post office in Hog Bay. Thomas rode his horse to the Cape Willoughby lighthouse, on the island's most eastern point, to deliver the mail to the eastern part of the Dudley Peninsula. He covered forty-two miles every week for twenty-seven years.[5] They called him 'Tommy the Penman', Roe Trethewey told me; 'the best scriber and the best swearer in South Australia'.

Thomas and Hannah moved to Hog Bay just as it was starting to attract interest as a place to settle.[6] Shortly after Hannah gave

Thomas and Hannah Simpson's home, also Penneshaw's first
Post Office, with a view of Backstairs Passage, 1991.
Courtesy of Bruce Bates

birth to Nathaniel Thomas Simpson in December 1860, the
Simpsons acquired neighbours on their hill.

The Bates family came from Melbourne and bought the 58-
acre block just above the Simpsons'.[7] Ephraim Bates, his wife
Martha and their seven children had arrived in Adelaide from
England in December 1858. Ephraim had at first found work as a
timber-cutter in the mill Henry Wallen had helped establish at
Cygnet River. Twelve months later he took his family to
Melbourne, and he and his older sons went in search of gold at
Ballarat. They did not make their fortune on the goldfields, and
the family soon returned to Kangaroo Island. Ephraim knew that
the soil was good, and Bruce Bates told me that in Melbourne
Ephraim's wife had 'missed the fleshpots of Kangaroo Island' –
namely the fresh wallaby.[8] Ephraim built a house on his block, and
for three generations – almost a century – the Bateses and Simpsons
lived next door to each other.

Early in the twentieth century the Bates family built a new,
bigger house and turned the old one into a shed. Many years later
Bruce Bates, combining a sense of history with a farmer's practi-
cality, built a large new shed over the original house. When I

visited Bruce, he showed me his family's first home and pointed
out the original floorboards. As the layers of Bates history continue to be laid down, Bruce Bates feels justified in claiming that
the hill has 'always' been known not as 'Simpson's' but as 'Bates's
Hill'. There are no Simpson descendants on the hill now to contradict him.

When my family drove up that hill out of Penneshaw to go to
the farm at Antechamber Bay, we always looked out for the little
white cottage near the road. We didn't know it had been the
Simpsons' cottage; we just loved the way it was almost completely covered by thorn-bush. But since then a doctor from
Adelaide has bought it and done it up as a holiday house.[9] Today
it looks very smart. The view from its tiny square windows must
be one of the best views in the world.

When I last went to visit Bruce Bates, I gave in to curiosity
and knocked on the door of the Simpsons' old house. It was
beautifully renovated, with polished floorboards and exposed
beams. Perhaps sizeable for its day, to me it seemed still small for
a family as large as Hannah's.

Hannah gave birth to ten children, nine of whom survived. By
the turn of the twentieth century Nathaniel had been followed by
Thomas, William, Stephen, Jane, Mary, Anne, John and Stamford;
only Joseph, born in 1872, had died. Thomas Simpson supported
his growing family on his meagre mail contractor's wage of £35 a
year.[10] Perhaps the need for money prompted Thomas in 1875 to
sell all but two acres of his original sixty-nine, keeping only the
top corner where the family cottage was situated.[11] He then
rented a 39-acre block opposite (owned by the South Australian
Company) and attempted to grow a small cereal crop there.[12]

By the time Thomas sold his land, Hog Bay and Kangaroo
Island had changed considerably. The island's population had
grown to about 340 people. There was rising interest in pastoralism and agriculture, and this interest was increasingly focused
on the eastern end of the island.[13] While Kingscote, surrounded
by poor soil but with a good harbour, became a commercial and
fishing centre, Hog Bay, with its good soils on the flats and slopes
near the coast, became the farming centre of the island. By the

mid-1870s the Simpsons looked out on a denser cluster of buildings around a busier Christmas Cove, which also included one of the island's three primary schools, founded in 1869.[14]

Thomas's land had doubtless increased in value, and its sale may have helped his finances. Five years later, however, he was apparently again struggling. His sons were growing up with little to inherit. So Thomas sought an alternative way to get more land.

In 1880 he applied for a land grant under Clause 11 of the Crown Lands Consolidation Act, proclaimed in 1877. Clause 11 stated that 'the Governor may demise to any aboriginal native, or the descendant of any aboriginal native, Crown lands not exceeding one hundred and sixty acres, for any term of years, and upon such terms and conditions as the Governor shall think fit'. Thomas explained that for more than twenty years he had been legally married to a 'descendant of a native of Tasmania', who had 'born to him' nine surviving children. He made particular effort to emphasise that, although of Tasmanian descent, Hannah was born on Kangaroo Island before the arrival of the South Australian Company. He wrote in his famously neat hand, 'Sir ... I beg to state that my wife's parents were residents on Kangaroo Island several years previous to South Australia becoming a separate dependency to the British rule'.[15]

Thomas also emphasised the 'length of time' his parents-in-law had been residents before 1836. He went on to explain that he had only a 39-acre holding, which had failed to produce any substantial crops. In conclusion Thomas expressed his concern that his young children risked becoming 'destitute' and a 'burden to the state' should his situation be allowed to continue.

While he was waiting for a reply, Thomas spoke about his application to a visiting reporter for the *South Australian Advertiser*. The reporter explained that Thomas, who had a 'fine healthy family of quadroons', was applying for a grant of land under the relevant parliamentary Act. 'The difficulty in this case', the journalist added, 'is that Mr. Simpson's mother-in-law was not an aboriginal native of this colony, but of Tasmania'. The reporter concluded that 'the Act does not authorise the granting of land to a person marrying any other than a South Australian aboriginal'.[16]

The Commissioner of Crown Lands came to the same conclusion. He passed Thomas's letter to the Protector of Aborigines,
who in turn advised the Commissioner to review the applicant's
eligibility. The Commissioner wrote in his memo of reply:

> I have no doubt in my mind that clause eleven of the Crown
> Lands Consolidation Act ... refers only to Aboriginal natives of
> South Australia proper and cannot be held to include one from
> Tasmania ... I therefore have no power to grant the request.[17]

How could the Commissioner, and the reporter, have had 'no
doubt' that Clause 11 could not 'include one from Tasmania'
when it stated that the Governor could demise Crown lands to
'any aboriginal native, or the descendant of any aboriginal native'?
Besides, when the same question of bloodlines had been raised by
the Minister for Agriculture in the case of Mary Seymour's request
for Destitute rations, the Protector had argued that it was 'the
practice to assist aborigines' from other colonies. This 'practice'
was here forgotten. It seems the Commissioner was rendered
powerless because it was economically expedient for him to be so.
He saved the government up to 160 acres of Crown land at a time
when demand for land from paying white settlers was increasing.

So Hannah was defined as indigenous to a place she had never
even visited, a place that did not even consider it had any
Aborigines. Kangaroo Island was thus stuck in an indefinable
position: it had Aboriginal people on it, but none were indigenous; if they were defined as Aboriginal Tasmanians, then they
were categorically part of a race that was officially extinct. The
descendants of Betty and Nat Thomas were caught in a Catch-22.
'Although Kangaroo Island retains no traces or proof of being able
to claim any aboriginal inhabitants', wrote E. H. Hallack in 1905,
'the bones of "the last of the Tasmanians" are buried there'.[18]

Thomas Simpson emphatically argued that his wife and her
family should qualify as 'natives' – as indigenous Islanders by virtue
of being born there. But it seems being born on the island before
it was proclaimed part of South Australia did not make Hannah
indigenous to it. In the late nineteenth century, bloodlines ran
according to European-constructed colonial boundaries. To be

Aboriginal within this definition was not only to be an indigene of a place, but also to continue to live at the original site of colonisation. This is not so different from the present laws that define Native Title – Aboriginality continues to be defined predominantly by place, by the continuing culture sustained by the relationship with the land. Both definitions disadvantage those who have been displaced.

In 1881 Thomas succeeded in applying for a scrub lease over 524 acres near his home.[19] Little of it had been cleared, and by then he was sixty years of age, still doing a demanding but poorly paid job in order to support a wife and nine children, ranging from an infant to a 20-year-old. Perhaps not a talented or knowledgeable farmer, he was unable to produce an ample crop on the small holding he rented. He had relatively little to pass onto his sons. But he need not have worried.

The Years of Success

Nat Thomas willed all his land to his eldest grandson, Nathaniel Thomas Simpson, after Sophia Newcombe's death. He wanted his namesake to inherit the place where he had lived for more than fifty years. Nathaniel, or Nat as he also became known, was more like a son to him than a grandson. Nat Thomas's own son, Sam, had left many years before, and young Nat had been helping his grandfather at Antechamber Bay since he was a boy. It seems he was already living and farming at Antechamber Bay in Nat's last years.[1]

Sophia Newcombe died soon after Nat Thomas, and the whole estate was passed on to Thomas Simpson as executor. Nat Simpson was not yet twenty-one years old, but the land was later put in his name.[2] Eighteen-year-old Nat might have already had a sense of excitement about starting on a career of farming. He had every reason to.

In 1882 Nat took up a credit agreement to buy sixteen acres of freehold. A year later he took up another for sixty-four acres. In the same year, his brother William (Bill) took up a credit agreement for a 288-acre section at Antechamber Bay, and soon afterwards a third brother, Stephen (Steve), took up the adjacent section on credit.[3] Then in 1888 'Thomas Simpson and Sons' – namely Thomas senior, Nat, Bill, Tom junior and Steve – were granted two leases comprising a total of 9606 acres of land running from Antechamber Bay south to Cape Hart.[4] It was a considerable expanse. Within another three years Thomas senior had been

Nat Thomas and Betty

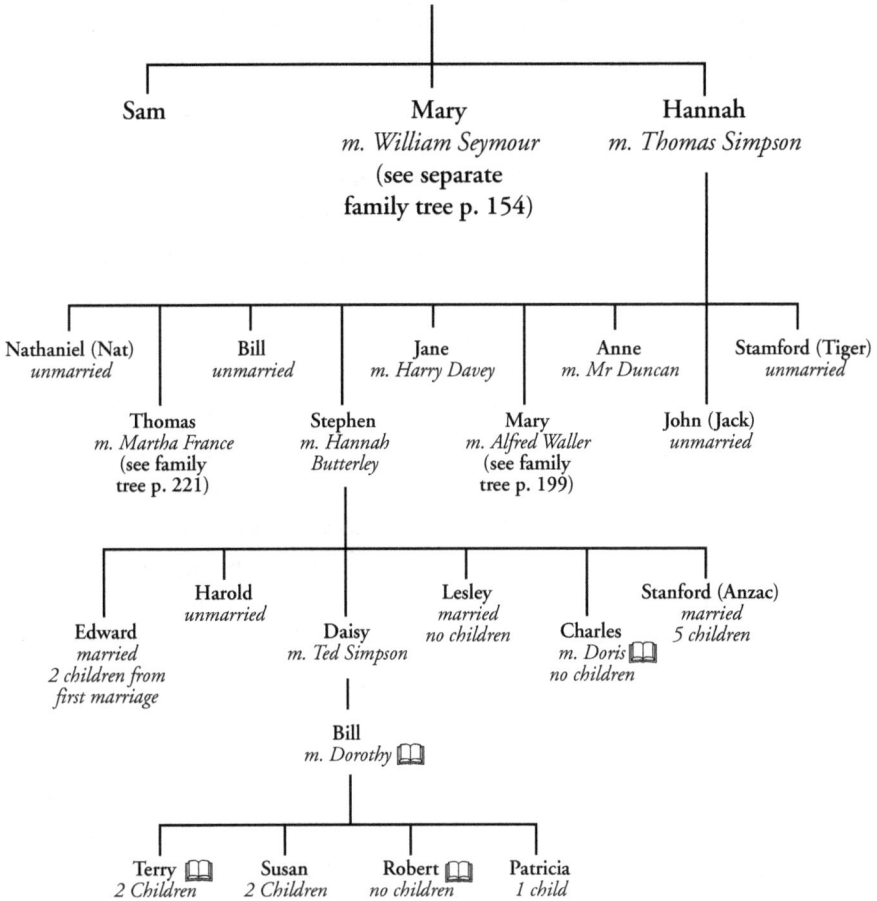

Sam

Mary
m. William Seymour
**(see separate
family tree p. 154)**

Hannah
m. Thomas Simpson

Nathaniel (Nat)
unmarried

Bill
unmarried

Jane
m. Harry Davey

Anne
m. Mr Duncan

Stamford (Tiger)
unmarried

Thomas
m. Martha France
**(see family
tree p. 221)**

Stephen
*m. Hannah
Butterley*

Mary
m. Alfred Waller
**(see family
tree p. 199)**

John (Jack)
unmarried

Edward
*married
2 children from
first marriage*

Harold
unmarried

Daisy
m. Ted Simpson

Lesley
*married
no children*

Charles
m. Doris 📖
no children

Stanford (Anzac)
*married
5 children*

Bill
m. Dorothy 📖

Terry 📖
2 Children

Susan
2 Children

Robert 📖
no children

Patricia
1 child

📖 = informants   * = pseudonym

issued a new lease on the substantial 524-acre block close to their family home in Hog Bay, giving him the option to buy it freehold. Another credit agreement for 423 acres of land near Antechamber Bay had also been taken up in his name, and Nat and Bill took out a lease for another twenty-eight acres on the coast.[5]

The Simpsons were not just expanding their holdings at Antechamber Bay, but were spreading across the district, adding acres and family members as they went. The local assessment records of 1896 list Steve Simpson as the owner of a 39-acre section opposite the original Simpson family home, the block his father had rented from the South Australian Company for so many years.[6] Its value must have increased considerably since Thomas senior first started renting it. In 1884 Hog Bay had been declared a town and renamed Penneshaw. In that same year the town acquired its own post office, and the following year St Columba's Protestant Church was built. The population of Kangaroo Island was now about 400 – seventy more than ten years earlier.[7]

Steve built a house facing the sea in the bottom corner of his thirty-nine acres, directly over the road from the Penneshaw School. His house was on the corner where the road turned away from the sea and up Simpson's Hill. It was called 'Simpson's Corner' for years. By 1902 Steve was married to Hannah Butterley (or Seymour as she had become by her mother's second marriage to Steve's cousin Joe) and had a daughter, Daisy. She was followed by five brothers: Harold, Charles, Lesley, Edward and Stanford, known to all as 'Anzac'.

In 1898 Steve bought ten suburban sections, a total of 130 acres, at Sapphiretown, a township on Strawbridge Point at the western end of Dudley. The township was surveyed and proclaimed in 1878.[8] Although the Strawbridge Point settlement was a failure, having been planned on a badly chosen site, Steve's sections made up a large block and he may have used it for grazing, as other farmers did.[9]

Steve's little sister, Anne, had gone to Western Australia and married there.[10] His sister Jane had married William Henry (Harry) Davey, who had replaced their father as the district mailman. In 1901 he and Jane rented a home near Christmas

Anne Duncan, née Simpson, who left the island and married in
Western Australia. Courtesy of the Waller family

Cove, within sight of her parents on the hill above, and the following year they moved to another house near American Beach,
south-west of Penneshaw. Three years later they moved again, this
time to a house near Antechamber Bay. 'Davey's Hill' became a
well-known placename.

Another sister, Mary, married Alfred James Waller, who had
come to Kangaroo Island in 1883 with his brother Henry and his
sister-in-law, and had settled near Pelican Lagoon.[11] Alfred took up
a credit agreement for 324 acres in 1888, leased another 25 acres
a year later and in 1890 took over an 87-acre lease from his
brother. He finally added another 15-acre lease in 1895.[12] He and
Mary built their own home near the mouth of Pelican Lagoon
and had seven children: William, Thomas, Amy, Charles, Wallace,
Norman – Adrian Waller's father – and John.

Henry Waller later transferred his first lease to his brother Alfred,
but he had also taken up a credit agreement over 109 acres and leased
another 438 acres in 1885. He had another 238 acres on a credit

Mary Waller, née Simpson, and her husband Alfred.
Courtesy of the Waller family

agreement by 1890.[13] Two years later Henry took up a large lease at Nepean Bay, in the Hundred of Haines where he farmed barley, merino sheep and raised thirteen surviving children. His descendants still own some of this land, but none live in Dudley. Henry's eldest son, James, continued to own land near Pelican Lagoon until 1955 when he sold it to the Willson family. Henry Waller's first home still stands on this land. It was another landmark my family always looked out for in the car on the way to Kingscote – a little abandoned cottage with orange paint peeling off its door. It has recently been done up by one of Henry Waller's descendants, and it seems tiny for the seven of his children who were born there.[14]

Henry's and Alfred's families were close, as were their connections with the Simpsons. Alfred leased Steve Simpson's Sapphiretown sections from 1891.[15] In 1894 Henry bought the part section next door to Mary Seymour that Joe Seymour had been renting from Frank Barrett.[16] Six years later, James took over Frank's leases near Pelican Lagoon and near Cape Hart, on the

Nat Thomas and Betty

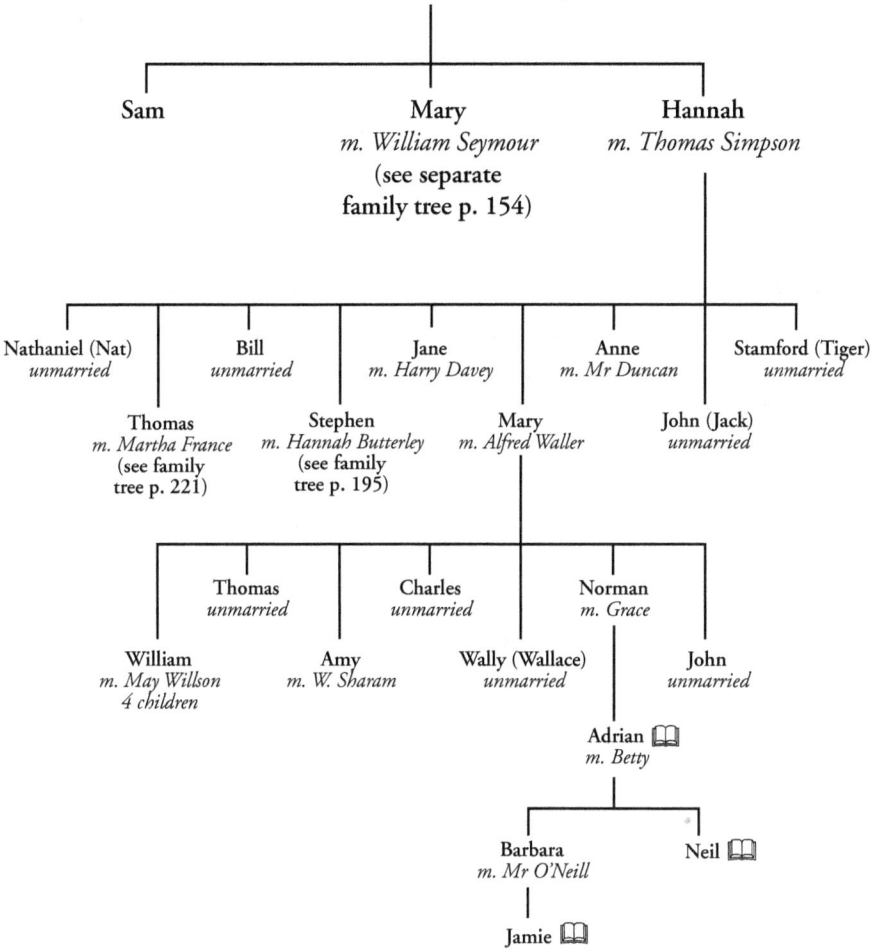

Sam

Mary
m. William Seymour
(see separate
family tree p. 154)

Hannah
m. Thomas Simpson

Nathaniel (Nat)
unmarried

Bill
unmarried

Jane
m. Harry Davey

Anne
m. Mr Duncan

Stamford (Tiger)
unmarried

Thomas
m. Martha France
(see family
tree p. 221)

Stephen
m. Hannah Butterley
(see family
tree p. 195)

Mary
m. Alfred Waller

John (Jack)
unmarried

Thomas
unmarried

Charles
unmarried

Norman
m. Grace

William
m. May Willson
4 children

Amy
m. W. Sharam

Wally (Wallace)
unmarried

John
unmarried

Adrian 📖
m. Betty

Barbara
m. Mr O'Neill

Neil 📖

Jamie 📖

📖 = informants

south-east corner of the peninsula – a total of 3000 acres.[17] But the Wallers' holdings were small compared to the Simpson empire.

In 1897 Stamford (Tiger), the youngest of Hannah Simpson's boys, joined his brothers at Antechamber Bay, taking up a 467-acre lease.[18] He never bought any freehold land, but by 1902 his older brothers had paid off most of their credit agreements. In 1904 Nat took up another credit agreement on 370 acres near Antechamber Bay, and he paid it off three years later, while Steve had paid off his 285 acres by 1909. By then the Simpsons had freehold title on over 1000 acres of coastal land near Antechamber Bay. Their 524-acre section near Penneshaw was also fully paid by 1911.[19]

In 1904, a year after their father's death, the Simpson brothers' total holdings across the peninsula were 12,300 acres. There were only two farming families in Dudley who owned more land than they did. The Willson brothers – Thomas's sons Thomas, Martin and Charles – owned about 13,700 acres between them. Most of this land was leased, and they had about the same amount of freehold land as the Simpsons. Their father had also leased some land in the Hundred of Haines, just over the isthmus, but most of the Willsons' holdings were along the Hog Bay River near the centre of Dudley, and on the north coast near Penneshaw. Their neighbours in both places were the Buick brothers, who had just over 14,000 acres in Dudley, with about 650 acres in freehold.

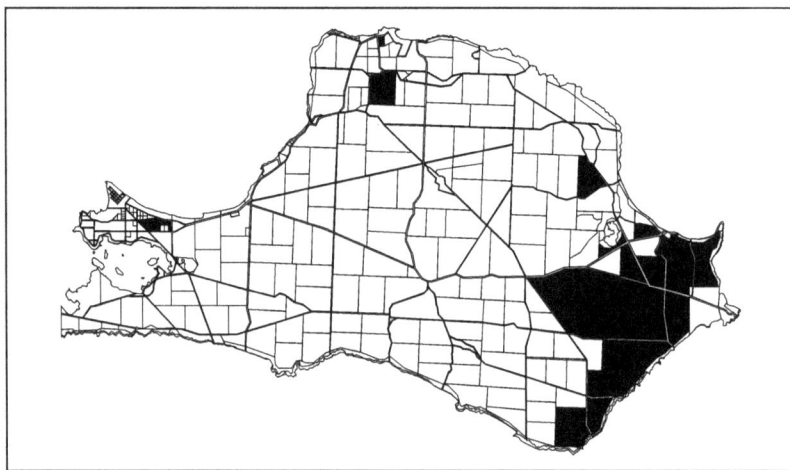

Land ownership of the Simpson family, Hundred of Dudley, 1904

The Simpsons' holdings dwarfed those of the Marshalls, Nat Thomas's old neighbours at Antechamber Bay. In the days of large, unsurveyed leases, the Marshalls, Nat Thomas, the Willsons and the Buicks had once leased most of the peninsula between them. Now the two Marshall brothers, Thomas and George, owned about 6500 acres between them, with about half in freehold.

The Simpsons also had more land than their Penneshaw neighbours, the Bateses. Near their original home in Penneshaw, the Bateses had just under 4000 acres, though most of it was freehold.[20] Some of their family members had settled on other parts of the island a long way from Dudley; because the peninsula was almost an island in itself, they were too distant to operate as one family business. Even the Bates family history only follows 'the family lines that remained and farmed in the Dudley district'.[21]

There are other settlers who should also be introduced in order to make up the picture of farming on the peninsula at the turn of the twentieth century. In 1877 John Trethewey, a Cornish miner who was working in the silver-lead mines at nearby Cape Jervis, made a successful joint application with his father-in-law to lease a section of land at Cuttlefish Bay, south-east of Hog Bay.[22] From 1885 Trethewey's son ran the store near Salt Lagoon, where they also took up some land. By the early twentieth century the Tretheweys owned over 4500 acres, and most of it was freehold.

William Howard, whose family had been farming in the Balaklava district from about 1856, heard that there was good land near Hog Bay and began farming there in 1883.[23] Many other farmers came to Kangaroo Island in the early 1880s, shifting from the dry areas on the mainland where they had been severely affected by the drought of 1881–82. By the turn of the twentieth century, the Howard family owned about 5000 acres of land, mostly behind the north-east coast of the peninsula. Only about 450 acres was freehold.[24]

Robert Clark, who had come to Kangaroo Island in 1873, settled at Antechamber Bay behind the Marshalls. By 1904 he owned nearly 5000 acres of land, with only a small portion in freehold. The Lyalls had 4000 acres of land on the stony soil near the south-west of the peninsula, all of which was leased.

The Barr family had almost 2500 acres, mostly near the isthmus, with a total of about 400 acres in freehold. The Neaves had about 1000 acres of good land on the flats near Hog Bay River, about a third of which was freehold, and about 600 acres of poorer land on the south-west coast. And the son of the new lighthouse-keeper, James McArthur, leased about 1500 acres near Cape Willoughby.[25]

The Simpsons entered the twentieth century as one of the largest landholders in Dudley. They had been farming their land for about twenty-five years, and had given their farm the rather English-sounding name of Holmesdale, disregarding the colloquial Creek Bay.[26] Holmesdale was a name without any clear origin, but it suggested an appropriate sense of achievement. The *Cyclopedia of South Australia* of 1907–09 claimed that Nat Simpson had 'met with considerable success' in raising merinos. In 1905 E. H. Hallack visited Holmesdale and found it an 'extensive property ... used principally as a sheeprun' with 'a small part' used 'for the cultivation of barley'.[27]

Hallack would have looked at a landscape considerably changed from W. A. Cawthorne's 1850s watercolour of 'Old Nat's'. The Simpson brothers had been working hard. Most of their land along the coast, south from their grandfather's homestead to Cape St Albans, would by now have been cleared of mallee.[28] This was a considerable achievement in the days before heavy farm machinery.

Thomas Willson had claimed in 1877 that Nat Thomas's land was 'the worst land hereabout'.[29] But surely Nat's grandsons would have disputed this claim – the farmer who owns the Simpsons' land today does, and so do Robin and Fiona Marshall, who live next door.[30] It is ironstone country, its soil formed from ancient sand-dunes that blew onto the land thousands of years before the seas separated the island from the mainland.[31] Where the narrow-leaf mallee grows, the soil is deep and sustains good pasture, but only if it is supplemented with fertilisers.[32]

These were also the days before superphosphate, so the Simpsons, like all the farmers on Dudley, had probably been content to clear the coastal land. They had learnt they could

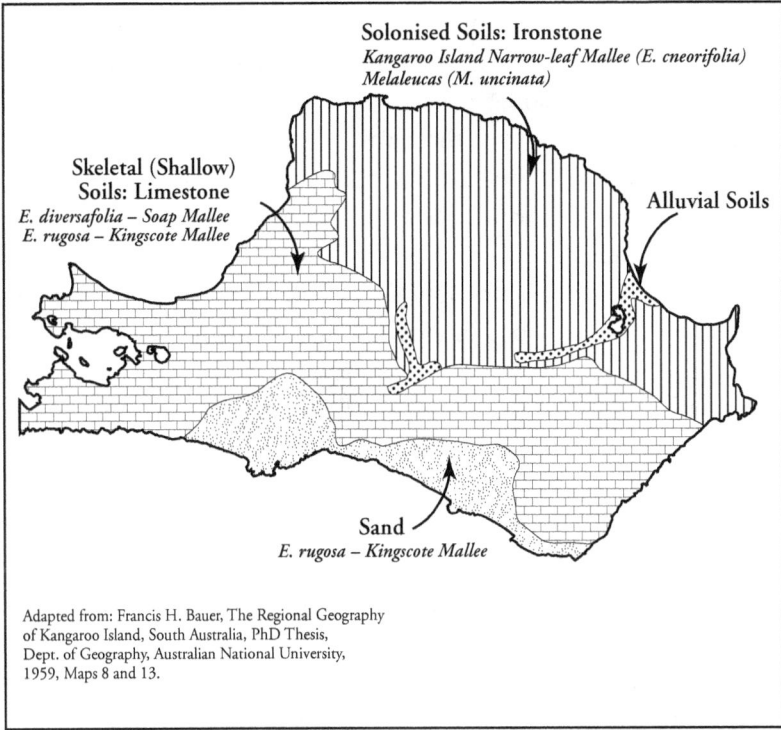

Solonised Soils: Ironstone
Kangaroo Island Narrow-leaf Mallee (E. cneorifolia)
Melaleucas (M. uncinata)

Skeletal (Shallow)
Soils: Limestone
E. diversafolia – Soap Mallee
E. rugosa – Kingscote Mallee

Alluvial Soils

Sand
E. rugosa – Kingscote Mallee

Adapted from: Francis H. Bauer, The Regional Geography
of Kangaroo Island, South Australia, PhD Thesis,
Dept. of Geography, Australian National University,
1959, Maps 8 and 13.

Dudley Peninsula soil and vegetation types

plant crops and graze sheep year-round only on the perimeters of their peninsula, looking out to sea, with their backs to the cursed mallee scrub. Yet most of the land was covered by mallee, and much of it was limestone country with shallow, stony soil.[33]

The farmers didn't own this land on poor limestone soil in south Dudley; they leased it. Like most of the farmers, the Simpsons had bought freehold title only to the good coastal land on ironstone soil in the north. The Simpsons' 9606 acres of leased land was issued in two 'Miscellaneous Leases', which would have been auctioned at an upset price fixed by the Commissioner of Lands to be used for grazing and cultivation for up to twenty-one years.[34] They could burn this cheap scrubby country and use it for grazing their sheep on the winter regrowth when the native pasture was green and tender, watered by the reliable rainfalls on Dudley.[35] Old fences can still be seen through much of this limestone country.[36] Sheep-grazing was an unsustainable practice, and the farmers needed a lot of scrub land to keep it up. With today's technologies, however, farmers can produce good crops even on the poor limestone soil.[37]

E. H. Hallack thought the Simpson brothers had made a sensible decision when he saw their 'extensive property ... used principally as a sheeprun'. Sheep could graze on relatively marginal and cheap land. Wool was also light to ship. The Simpsons, Marshalls and Clarks probably used bullocks to transport their wool. Nat Simpson had his own bullock team. No doubt he took it to the jetty at Antechamber Bay.[38] (The jetty stumps are all that is left of it today. My family used to marvel at the idea that it had been pulled down out of fear of Japanese invasion during the Second World War.)

In 1905 Hallack described the Simpsons' farm as extensive, but he didn't record their stock numbers. In the same year, it was recorded that Henry Waller had 400 sheep, the Marshalls had a flock of 700 and the Buicks had 3500.[39] Maybe the Simpsons had some number in between. Without knowing how much Kangaroo Island wool fetched during this period, it is also hard to estimate how much they might have earned. But presumably a 'gentleman' who met 'with considerable success' in growing merino wool earned significantly more than the average man's wage of about £150 a year.

Hallack also noticed that 'a small part' of Holmesdale was used 'for the cultivation of barley'. This was another dependable investment on the island. After early attempts to grow wheat, the first settlers who started farming in Dudley in the 1860s found the land better suited to barley. In 1870 a correspondent to the *Adelaide Observer* claimed 'Kangaroo Island grows the best barley in the world, and plenty to the acre'.[40] Malting barley was difficult to grow on the mainland, so the island's growers had a ready market there.[41] At this time island barley sold at about four shillings a bushel and averaged over sixteen bushels an acre – although the *Cyclopedia of South Australia* claimed Thomas Willson junior reaped forty bushels to an acre near Penneshaw. The *Cyclopedia* also reported that Henry Waller grew 'some fine crops of barley' on the Dudley Isthmus, where 'the climate and soil are peculiarly suited' to this crop. Bruce Bates's father remembered that he once filled a hundred bags of barley for James Waller out at Antechamber Bay, using Nat Simpson's bullock team to shift the barley and a threshing machine, perhaps so they could then ship the bags from the nearby jetty.[42]

The flats behind Antechamber Bay, where Hallack found the Simpsons growing barley, were also good and fertile,[43] but most of the good barley grew at the Penneshaw end of the peninsula. Perhaps the Simpsons also grew barley on the cleared portion of the 524 acres they leased behind their parents' home, and on Steve's 39-acre paddock near by. Their father's failure to get ample yields on that paddock might have said more about his farming skills than the quality of the soil. Before costs, that paddock alone could have earned Steve about £130 a year.[44]

Thomas Simpson, who had worried that his sons would become destitute, would have been proud of their success. He would have been proud to open the *Cyclopedia of South Australia* and see his eldest son featured along with other gentlemen who were the 'founders and builders' of the South Australian State. Nat

Nat Simpson as he appeared in the *Cyclopedia of South Australia*, 1907–09

Simpson's photograph shows him smartly attired in wing-collar and tie, with a handsomely curled moustache. He is described as an 'agriculturist and grazier'; he had been a Justice of the Peace for the past six years, and in that capacity his 'services' had been 'requisitioned on very many occasions'. He took 'a general interest in political matters' and 'also in all affairs of sport, etc. on the island', and had served two terms on the Dudley District Council in 1893–95 and 1900–02.[45]

William and Thomas junior, or Bill and Tom, also served as district councillors in 1889–90 and 1891–92 respectively. Nat had been the locally appointed constable in 1888, a position Steve took over in 1890, Tom in 1892 and their youngest brother Stamford in 1904.[46] A photograph in the Penneshaw Museum, taken at about the turn of the century, shows John and Stamford – or Jack and Tiger, as they were called – in suits and boaters as members of the

Bill Simpson, c. 1895.

The Penneshaw Folk Museum

Thomas Simpson Jnr, 1890.
The Penneshaw Folk Museum

The Hog Bay Cricket Team, c. 1899. Back row: Thomas Willson,
Charles Willson, Thomas Simpson Jnr, John Trethewey, Jack Jones.
Front row: Stamford (Tiger) Simpson, William Lyall, Thomas Clark,
John (Jack) Simpson, Harry Clark, Fred Buick.
The Penneshaw Folk Museum

local cricket team. A studio photograph taken about ten years later shows three of Steve's children looking very well dressed. It is said that Steve owned the first car in the Dudley district.[47]

The Simpsons had joined the 'gentry' of this almost-island within an island. With its fertile coastal lands, on which the rain dependably falls each year, the Dudley peninsula had at first dominated the rest of the island in population, wool and cereal production. Dudley became the first Hundred, and the only Hundred to have its own council – the rest of the island fell under Kingscote's jurisdiction. When pastoralism spread after 1900, however, Dudley eventually ran second to Kingscote and the rest of the island.

When Nat Simpson was first elected as a councillor in Dudley, he shared the chambers with brothers William and David Buick, his neighbour Robert Clark, and James Barr. Thomas Willson senior was their chairman. Together with the clerk and overseer, John Trethewey, they were responsible for collecting rates and fines, planning the development of the town and district, employing labourers to maintain public lands and letting the tenders to build roads.

Members of most farming families did road-work. The local council was just about the only employer in the district, and road-work contractors came from farming and labouring families alike.[48] Did Nat put in a good word when his brothers were tendering for work? Steve and Tom were both granted three road-working contracts in Nat's first elected year. Did Nat say anything when the council discussed giving his brother Bill permission to pasture six bullocks near the Neaves' property while he was working on a road near there? And when his Aunt Mary applied to the Destitute Board, did Nat and Thomas Willson talk together? Did Nat prompt Thomas Willson to write to, and even visit, the Board's chairman in Adelaide?

Thomas Willson died halfway through Nat's second term and was replaced by his son, Charles. By then Nat's nephew by marriage, James Waller, was also a councillor. Maybe he supported Emma Barrett's application to become District Ranger. When Frank Barrett died soon afterwards and the Destitute Board turned down Emma's application for rations, perhaps Nat and

Three of Steve Simpson's children (from left to right):
Charles, Harold and Daisy, c. 1910. The Penneshaw Folk Museum

Four generations: Mrs Hannah Simpson (nursing Daisy),
Mrs Rachel Seymour and Mrs Hannah Davidson (née Ebert).
The Penneshaw Folk Museum

James urged the Council to write to the Board arguing Emma Barrett's 'deserving' case.[49]

Serving on council was a position of influence in the community. Men could help their families as well as their neighbours, for both were their voters. Being civic-minded was an important attribute; it was quite a burden just to travel into Penneshaw for meetings twice a month. But to lobby for support, a candidate had to be respected and display some evidence of success.

On the other hand, there were no wool barons in Dudley. No one could afford to go to Adelaide and spend up in the finest shops. The large farmers had more than most — far more than those on Destitute rations. Yet perhaps when they looked over to the mainland they were reminded of their isolation. As they waited in the chambers before the resumption of a council meeting, or sat in the front bar of the new Penneshaw Hotel, they might have agreed that others had an easier life than they did. While the returns on barley were reliable, the crop needed good cleared land, and shipping costs were high. Although they had merinos, their sheep were not first-class; their wool was clean but lighter and coarser than most of the South Australian yields.[50] As these farmers looked out towards the mainland shore — pushed against the edges of their almost-island — they knew that their scrubby peninsula would never yield the same wealth as the verdant plains of western Victoria.

A century later the Willsons, Buicks and Marshalls are still looking out to the mainland. They never became *very* rich, but they are still the gentry of that peninsula, now superphosphated, cleared of much of its mallee and running three sheep to an acre. So too are other families who did not have as much land in 1901, and who were not even listed among the gentlemen in the *Cyclopedia of South Australia*. Members of the Trethewey, Howard and Bates families were elected to council generation after generation until Dudley was forced to merge with Kingscote in 1996. Even without autonomy, Dudley is still its own world, and the same six families still own most of it. Among them are descendants of the Barrs, Clarks, Neaves and even James McArthur — families who continue in all but name.

But no Simpsons or Simpson descendants own land in Dudley. There are no Simpsons to attend council meetings, to look out at the unchanged view through the pub windows and discuss the price of wool. There are no Simpsons to help build the roads, shear the sheep, mend the fences or fertilise the ancient, windswept dunes. There are no descendants of Nat Thomas and Betty even living in Dudley. Perhaps Thomas Simpson's fear of his children's destitution had become their curse.

Land ownership of the eight main colonial and Aboriginal descendant families, Hundred of Dudley 1904 and 1992–95

Bates 1904

Bates 1992–95

Buick 1904

Buick 1992–95

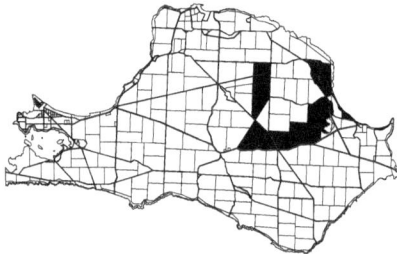

Marshall 1904

Marshall 1992–95

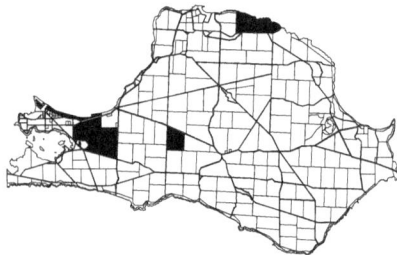

Trethewey 1904

Tretheway 1992–95

Howard 1904

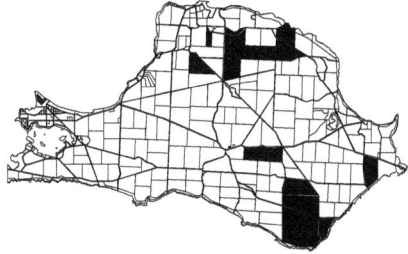

Howard 1992–95

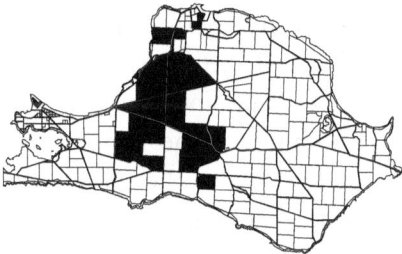

Willson 1904

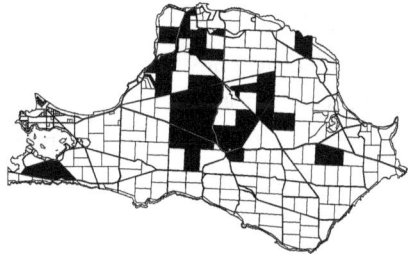

Willson 1992–95

Waller 1904

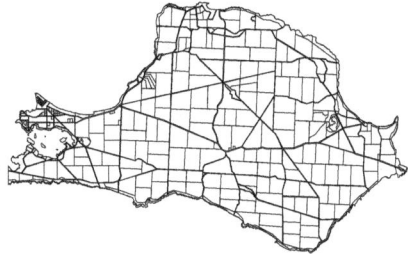

Waller 1992–95

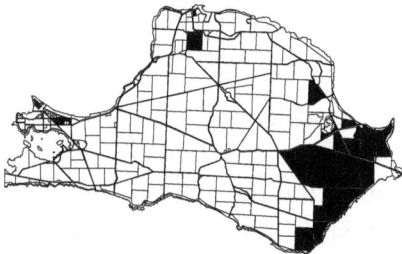

Simpson 1904

Simpson 1992–95

The Years of Decline

When Nat Simpson read of his success in the *Cyclopedia of South Australia*, he knew it talked of a time that had already past. Seeing his proud photo must have sent a pang of disappointment through him, matched only by the pain of walking into the Penneshaw Hotel and facing the other farmers. He knew what they all knew: that this 46-year-old man might have once 'met with considerable success' in raising merino sheep, but he no longer did. Nor was he any longer a councillor, a Justice of the Peace or a constable. His knowledge of the soils, the nature of mallee and the yearly rainfalls would not save him now. He was a doomed man.

The looks he met in the bar would have told him it was common knowledge that almost every acre of freehold that he and his brothers owned at Holmesdale was mortgaged to private lenders, and most of their leased land had been cancelled for failure to pay the rent. Perhaps if Nat bought a drink it was not from conviviality, to share the talk of wool prices and the weather as he perhaps once had, but to wet a mouth dry from hard, futile work. To drink in sadness.

Nat, Bill and Tom were young in the early 1880s, when they took up their credit agreements at Antechamber Bay. Nat was twenty-two and Bill was not yet twenty. Steve was a teenager, and Tiger and Jack only children. It seems the three eldest brothers worked hard together, and in their first decade they did well.

But 1893 saw a financial crisis hit the Australian colonies. Cereal and wool prices plummeted. The Bank of South Australia was unable to carry on business.[1] Perhaps suffering the effects of the depression, in 1896 Nat Simpson took out a private mortgage on the house and fifty-one acres that his grandfather had left him. He was thirty-five years old. It was probably not a big debt. Twelve years earlier the land had been valued at £51 and his mortgagee, Sarah Rankine of Adelaide, would probably have charged interest of just over five per cent.[2] Nat never cleared this debt.

Things did not get any easier for him. At the turn of the twentieth century, when Bill and Tom were nearing forty and Nat already was, his younger brother Steve married and moved with his new family to Penneshaw – a long way from Antechamber Bay. Tom had gone even further away. By 1900 he was on the mainland, and married to Mary O'Leary, from Kapunda, north of Adelaide, and had a daughter, Dorothy. Five years later they had a son, Horace (Horrie), and moved to Oodnadatta. Tom then went further north again, working in the Northern Territory with cattle and camels and rarely seeing his family. He never returned to Kangaroo Island.

It seems Nat and Bill had to manage more than ten thousand acres at Antechamber Bay alone. Tiger and Jack were old enough to help out, but Holmesdale was already in seemingly irreversible trouble. Nat and Bill had paid off their credit agreements by 1902, but within four years Bill had mortgaged his 288 acres of freehold land, and Nat had mortgaged another 439 acres. Roe Trethewey told me that he thought Bill might also have gone to work in the far north. If so, it was some time after 1905, because the Dudley council records show he was still regularly doing road-work then. And it seems that, unlike Tom, he came back; Roe Trethewey and others remember him as an old man on the island.[3]

In 1907 the Simpson brothers' large miscellaneous lease of almost 8000 acres was cancelled for non-payment of rent.[4] At first, most of this land stayed in the family: 6547 acres were transferred to their brother-in-law Harry Davey and another 1524 acres to their brother Jack. But Jack only had his lease for three years before it was cancelled.[5] The Simpsons' other lease of 1754 acres, also issued in 1888, was mortgaged in 1906 and ultimately sold to the Neaves in 1923.[6]

Steve Simpson had also begun to sell his holdings. He transferred his lease at Sapphiretown to John Trethewey in 1908. The following year he paid off the credit agreement on his 285 acres near Antechamber Bay, but immediately mortgaged it. He then sold it two years later to their neighbour, Robert Clark.

In the same year Nat Simpson mortgaged another sixty-four freehold acres.[7] Harry Davey also began to have a bigger interest in Holmesdale, buying the lease of twenty-eight acres on the coast, as well as becoming part-owner of 423 acres of Nat's mortgaged land. But in 1914–15 Kangaroo Island farmers experienced their worst ever drought. Nat was granted government drought relief for sixty-four acres near the homestead at Antechamber Bay. The relief money only increased the debt he already had on his land; although Nat managed to pay the government back within four years, the drought may have been the final nail in his coffin.

In 1912 the Simpson brothers had lost their mother. Hannah's home, occupied by the family from the year of Nat's birth, was transferred to Tiger and then to his sister Jane Davey a year later. In 1917 it was mortgaged to the neighbouring Bates family, who foreclosed on the mortgage in 1938.[8] Harry Davey's leases near Antechamber Bay had been cancelled five years earlier for failure to pay the rent.[9] The Simpson cottage stood empty for years, becoming covered in thorn-bush.

At Pelican Lagoon, Alfred Waller had sold one of his leases in 1906. Fourteen years later he sold two more leases to the Willson family, and in 1922 the lease for his last fifteen acres was cancelled.[10] In 1920, Alfred's nephew, James, transferred his 1402-acre lease at Antechamber Bay to Tiger Simpson, but within three years Tiger had sold it to the Bates family.[11] Alfred's brother Henry had sold his 238-acre lease to the Buick family in 1897, but had kept 547 acres of leased land, which he passed on to his sons. They sold it to the Willson family in 1957.[12]

In the council's Assessment Records for the year ending 30 June 1922, pencilled notes around Nat Simpson's section numbers at Antechamber Bay indicate that he could not even pay his rates. 'Hardly any of them paid their rates – the Tigers and Nats and Harry Daveys,' Roe Trethewey told me.

That year Nat, aged sixty-two, sold to the Neave family 131 acres of his land, including both the first credit agreements he had taken up in his early twenties and the fifty-one acres left to him by his grandfather.[13] It must have been heartbreaking for him. More than a hundred years of continuous occupancy of Nat's original homestead by the family was ended. The following year, 1923, Nat sold his last two sections of freehold land at Antechamber Bay, a total of 655 acres, to the Willson family. He had no more land to his name.

In the year his eldest brother became landless, Steve Simpson left the island and went to Adelaide with his wife and six children. He left his thirty-nine acres and his house in Penneshaw unsold – perhaps it was a sudden departure. The Bates family finally bought Steve's land in 1930.[14]

The only one of the Simpson brothers who still owned any land in Dudley was Tiger. He had a 76-acre portion of the land near Penneshaw that his father had first leased in 1881. After his mother died, the land was subdivided to the Neave and Willson families, and in 1923 it was subdivided between them again, leaving Tiger ten acres. By 1951, four years before his death, Tiger had sold all but one acre of his land. He had an old hut on it. Bruce Bates told me Tiger called it the 'Possum's Tail', because the section of land his family had first owned was once called 'The Possum', and Tiger was left with only the tail-end. When Tiger died, his nephew Les, one of Steve's children, inherited Tiger's one acre. He sold it in 1979, entirely ending the Simpsons' land ownership on Dudley.[15]

Why did the Simpsons lose all their land? Had the 1893 crisis sown the seeds for irreversible damage? Was the drought of 1914–15 the last straw? If so, why had these events not had the same detrimental effects on the other farming families? Was it simply that the Simpsons were bad farmers? If so, how had they initially been so successful in growing merino wool?

Farming on Kangaroo Island had never been easy or very profitable. Many farmers had to learn the limitations of the Dudley land the hard way. Bruce Bates explained to me that the mallee scrub was almost impossible to clear. It was so thick that the sheep couldn't get into it even if they could find something in it to eat. Before there was machinery to tear up the roots, the farmers could only roll or burn the scrub, and even then it simply grew back. If they grazed their sheep solely on the regrowth on limestone country, the animals got 'coast disease' – a mysterious condition of wasting and steely wool, later shown to arise from a lack of cobalt.[16]

If sheep farming had its problems, attempting to grow crops could prove even more difficult. In the 1880s some Kangaroo Island farmers tried to join the colony-wide wheat boom. The attempts to grow wheat were to their loss: without superphosphate the island soils could not produce wheat.

In 1888 Thomas Willson told the Lands Laws Commission that it cost him £2 to £5 an acre to clear the scrub, but it kept growing back. Ten other island farmers gave evidence; six were from Dudley.[17] The Simpsons were not among those giving evidence. When Hallack observed that the Simpsons had dedicated most of their land to sheep and a little to barley in 1905, they were following the best standard farming practices for the peninsula. Perhaps they had never tried to grow wheat. After more than a quarter of a century, the Simpsons had surely learnt their land – its capacity to hold stock and grow crops, the nature of its soils, the behaviour of the weather.

The Simpsons invested in a comparatively similar proportion of freehold land to the other families over a similar period. So it seems doubtful that they alone tried to buy too much land on credit too quickly.

Did they start out with less than the other Dudley farmers? While Nat Thomas did not leave much land to Nat Simpson, his aunt and uncle, William and Mary Seymour, may have left a few sheep from which he could have bred his merinos. Other settlers do not seem to have started out with much more. John Buick was a boat-builder wearing hand-made kangaroo moccasins at American River in the 1850s. Thomas Marshall was a butcher in outer Adelaide. The Bateses began with no more than the Simpsons did. In the 1870s John Trethewey was a tin miner, and William Howard a struggling farmer. Only Thomas Willson came with any significant capital, after owning a pub, shop and land at nearby Yankalilla. But it was not until the 1880s that any of these families began to expand their pastoral interests.

Yet there is a reason why the Simpsons failed so fast and so comprehensively, why *they* were so different. It is the reason that Tom left, that Steve and his family left, that Nat died in debt and that Jack and Tiger had no future on the land. For there was something that was different about the Simpsons, and it was a difference the other families would not accept.

Staying White

'So why do you think the Simpsons lost their land?' I asked Bruce Bates.

'Well ... because they were part Aboriginal,' he answered, 'they fell out of the social connection, and didn't marry easily.'

'*Because* they were part Aboriginal?' I asked.

'Yes,' he answered. 'A lot of them never married, and only one to my knowledge had many children, and that was Steve, and he didn't stick to any land anyway.'

The Simpsons had owned over 12,000 acres of land; Nat Simpson had become possibly South Australia's first Aboriginal Justice of the Peace; he was listed among South Australia's gentlemen of progress; he and his brothers had been voted on to council; they had joined the cricket team and wore boaters and suits. But they could not marry the local girls.

Nat, Bill, Jack and Tiger never married. Jane, Mary and Steve married in Dudley, and the latter two had families. But, as Bruce put it, they 'didn't stick to land'; they had not married into the 'social connection'. Tom and Anne both left the island.

Tom Simpson did in fact marry in Dudley before he left for the mainland. In about 1892 he married Martha France Cousin, who had come to teach in the Penneshaw School, and they had a child. Martha gave birth to Gladys France Simpson at her parents' home in April 1893.[1] If Martha brought her child back to Kangaroo Island, it was not for long. A year later Martha died of consumption. She was twenty-eight years old.[2] Gladys seems to

Nat Thomas and Betty

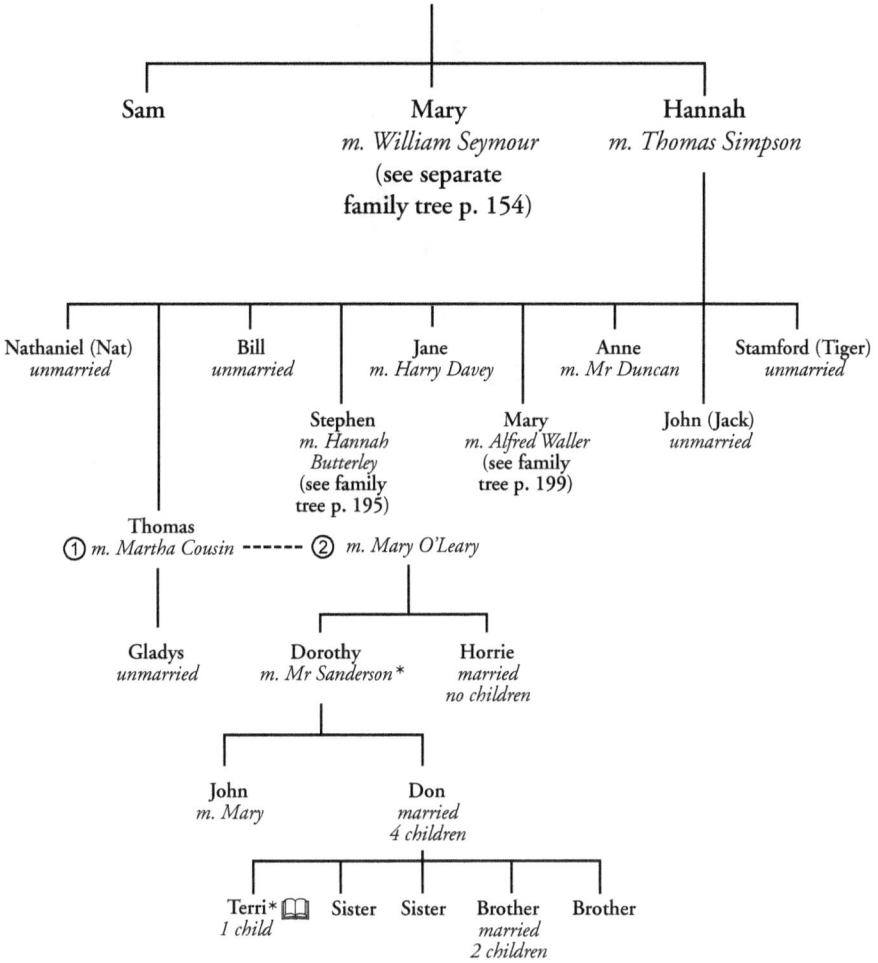

Sam

Mary
m. William Seymour
(see separate
family tree p. 154)

Hannah
m. Thomas Simpson

Nathaniel (Nat)
unmarried

Bill
unmarried

Jane
m. Harry Davey

Anne
m. Mr Duncan

Stamford (Tiger)
unmarried

Stephen
*m. Hannah
Butterley*
(see family
tree p. 195)

Mary
m. Alfred Waller
(see family
tree p. 199)

John (Jack)
unmarried

Thomas
① *m. Martha Cousin* ------ ② *m. Mary O'Leary*

Gladys
unmarried

Dorothy
m. Mr Sanderson *

Horrie
*married
no children*

John
m. Mary

Don
*married
4 children*

Terri* 📖
1 child

Sister

Sister

Brother
*married
2 children*

Brother

📖 = informants   * = pseudonym

Martha France Cousin, Tom Simpson's first wife. She died of
consumption only a year after they were married.
The Penneshaw Folk Museum

have grown up on the mainland, perhaps with her mother's family. I know little about her, other than the fact she became a nursing sister and died unmarried in an Adelaide nursing home in 1984. There was apparently no family to attend to her funeral or estate. It seems none of the other descendants of Nat Thomas and Betty even knew that she existed.[3]

'I had the impression', Agnes Marshall said of Tom and Martha's marriage, 'that people didn't think it would be a very good idea.' Agnes was referring to their racial difference. Such intolerance must have made Tom want to escape. How could he properly grieve for his lost wife in a community that had never approved of his marriage?

When Mary Thomas was married in 1849, there were only about eighty people on Kangaroo Island. When Hannah married eleven years later, there were about 175. Both were lawfully married; the Venerable Archdeacon Morse married Mary and

William in her father's house, and Hannah and Thomas went to Normanville, opposite Kangaroo Island, where a registrar presided. But Kangaroo Island then was still a long way from English civility, and perhaps more like the cross-cultural community of the pre-settlement years. Perhaps Thomas and William did not feel there was a society that their racially mixed marriages could offend.[4]

By the 1880s, Dudley society had changed. By the time the eldest Simpson children were of marriageable age, Dudley had become, as Francis Bauer put it, 'the most conservative and provincial portion of the Island'. There were churches, sports teams, a school and a council – a 'gentry' had emerged. The Simpsons could join it, but they could not marry into it, and marriage was the key to reproducing status.

'Marriage united the children of the earliest families', writes Jean Nunn in her history of Kangaroo Island. 'This helped to build a strong community which tended to exclude those without family connections'.[5] The fortunes of the Dudley gentry were sustained not only by their land ownership, but also by their marriages to each other. It was an exclusive social class created by exclusion. They stuck to land because they stuck together.

At the turn of the twentieth century there were thirteen families who owned at least a thousand acres in Dudley. By 1895 nine of these landowning families – the Willsons, Buicks, Marshalls, Clarks, Howards, Tretheweys, Barrs, Neaves and James McArthur – were related by several marriages. The third generation saw the inclusion of the Bateses into this group, as well as another five marriages between the same nine families. In the fourth generation, there were another eight in-marriages between the nine families, as well as a marriage between a Howard and one of the Southlyns*, who had been farming on Kangaroo Island (but not in Dudley) since the 1870s. The fifth generation saw two Southlyns marry into the Clark and Buick families and two Willsons marry into the Buick and Trethewey families.

After the third generation the colonial descendants began marrying relatives. A third-generation descendant, Ronald Willson, married his fourth cousin, Mildred Howard. And when two fourth-generation Howard siblings married a Willson and a

Buick, they were not only distantly related to their spouses, but their spouses were related to each other.

The filial relations were densest between the biggest land-owners – the Willsons, Buicks and Marshalls, who were related through several marriages by the early 1880s. The Simpsons, the third-largest landowners, were a notable exclusion. At the other end of the scale, the smaller landowners married some of the larger families, but not as often. There was one marriage between a Waller and a Willson, but otherwise the Wallers did not marry into any of the landowning families. Neither did the much smaller Lyall family. When I asked Bruce Bates why, he said it was not because the Lyalls were considered unacceptable marriage partners like the Aboriginal descendants, but that they simply made other choices.

There was a time when most people in Dudley were related by marriage. Today there remain six interrelated farming families whose histories date back to the colonial period. They also include descendants of almost every other family who farmed in Dudley in the nineteenth century. They are now a minority of the peninsula's population, but they still own most of the land. Their farms plot a genealogical map across the landscape. This is the Dudley 'social connection' that the Simpsons 'fell out' of.

Without that connection, the Simpson brothers' success faded as soon as they were past their physical prime. Throughout southern Australia, farming depended on the free labour of women and children. On Kangaroo Island, a single drought or financial downturn could spell ruin to an ageing farmer without family support.

When Nat, Tom and Bill mortgaged their land, they were in their forties and fifties. They had no sons to help them, and no wider network of family to call on. Other farmers had both. The Willsons, Buicks and Marshalls could enlist the unpaid labour of their offspring. They could call on relatives who were also neigh-bours. They could pool their resources, sharing equipment or providing each other with financial assistance. But the Simpsons had only their own ageing hands to shear their sheep, mend their fences, tend to the waterholes and maintain their buildings. Even if all the Simpson brothers had successfully married women from other island families, or from the mainland, they – and their children – would not have been part of the 'social connection'.

The Simpson brothers must have walked away from their land with a sense of despair. After years of hard work, what had been the point of trying to build a future here? The community had never fully accepted them because of their Aboriginal grandmother. Racial prejudice had denied them a future.

Did Dudley people, I asked Dave Buick, avoid marrying the Simpsons because they were Aboriginal?

'Yes,' he answered. 'It was something that was always avoided and I can speak for myself [that] I would dread to be mixed in the abo race ... I always say, stay white, keep away from any colour.'

'Do you think that is what other people in the community thought?' I asked.

'Yes, I do. I think it carried a long way through.'

I asked Agnes Marshall: 'When it came to the question of marriage, would it have been an issue for someone to marry a Simpson?'

'Oh, yes, I think so,' she answered. 'My husband's grandmother told me ... no white person, parents wouldn't have wanted their daughters to marry them.'

On a level of daily interaction in Dudley – at school and at work, in the shop and in the streets – the difference between the Aboriginal descendants and the colonial descendants went seemingly unnoted. Clara Bates's diary of 1940 includes numerous records of exchanging garden produce, cakes and jams, borrowing household items, visiting and sharing long conversations with Marshalls, Simpsons and Daveys alike.[6]

'We treated them all alike at school,' Monica Buick said.

'I thought they were all right,' Dave Buick remarked.

'I never heard they were ... dishonest, or bad people,' Agnes Marshall said of the Simpson men. 'They were respected as long as they didn't want to marry the daughters.'

'No one would make any fuss', Bruce Bates explained, 'until you start to talk of marrying one.'

There was a world of difference between sharing tea and cakes with the Aboriginal descendants and mixing their 'blood' with yours. Aboriginal blood was a dangerous contaminant, particularly frightening for its supposed potential to create 'throwbacks'. Agnes Marshall told me that two young women had once wanted to marry Simpson men, but their parents forbade the engagements on the grounds that the black genes might re-emerge in subsequent generations.

'The parents of the girls ... might have been afraid that their children would be black,' Agnes said, 'because it was commonly believed in those days that, even though the parents were perhaps only of quarter-caste, that any children could come back quite black. I know that's what my mother thought.'

Agnes Marshall's sister-in-law, Mildred Willson, knows what it is like to be on the receiving end of such prejudice. Mildred Wiullson's grandfather was a French national from Mauritius. His daughter went to Kangaroo Island as a dressmaker in 1909 and, breaking the conventions of acceptability, married Andrew Howard in 1914.

Bruce Bates said the marriage caused 'a certain stand-offishness' in the community. Mildred, however, put it more strongly. 'There was a very strong racist attitude' on Kangaroo Island, she said. When she was at the Penneshaw School in the 1920s, she was told that she couldn't be a fairy in the school play because she was too dark. When she grew up, she and her sisters experienced a more serious kind of exclusion. 'Having black grandchildren ... that's at the back of the minds of these Kangaroo Islanders,' she said. 'The boys saying, "You don't want to go for *her*, you want to try *her* family, they're all blonde there."' Mildred's sister was much fairer than her, 'but they know perfectly well ... they're saying, "They're all tarred with the same brush, they're dark like their mother."'

'She was very dark,' Monica Buick said of Mildred, '[but] she wasn't Aboriginal.' Perhaps that was why the Howard family did not 'fall out' of the 'social connection'. Their Mauritian ancestry might have denied Mildred and her sisters respectful treatment by several young men, but it did not deny their family their land and connections. They were dark, but they were not part of the 'abo race'. It was not simply dark skin that the Dudley families feared; it was crossing the line from coloniser to colonised. Aboriginality is more than just colour; it is, as historian Patrick Wolfe puts it, 'a matter of history'.[7]

This racism was a nationwide phenomenon. After years in the Victoria River district of the Northern Territory, Tom Simpson met and worked with Charlie Schultz, who established Humbert Station. Charlie was interested in the district's history, and listened keenly to the older bushmen. He put his memories on paper in *Beyond the Big Run*, co-authored by Darrell Lewis. Charlie remembers Tom Simpson:

> He was a character all of his own ... he was well into his sixties and seventies when I knew him. Tom was very good to me and I got on very well with him. I think most people did. He wasn't anything outstanding as a cook, but he was a happy-go-lucky bloke. Actually there was a dash of Maori in him.[8]

It is not clear if Tom told Charlie he had a 'dash of Maori in him', or if Charlie just thought it. To judge from a photo of Tom on the 1911 Barclay expedition, he would have been too dark to avoid giving some explanation. But, as Darrell Lewis explained to me, you wouldn't want to admit you were Aboriginal in the Northern Territory at that time. This was, as the subtitle of Charlie and Darrell's book put it, 'Australia's Last Frontier'. If racism was not expressed at a mundane level in Dudley, it was blatant in the Territory. It was better to be indigenous to any place other than Australia, especially since Maoris were generally considered more 'advanced' than Australian Aborigines.

Charlie also remembered that Tom 'used to help me along with any tucker' that was left over after the muster at Gordon Creek. 'He'd say, "Here, take this home with yer for yer blacks ... if you don't take it, we'll only skie it".'[9]

Tom's nieces and nephews on Kangaroo Island apparently did not look noticeably different from the descendants of the colonial settlers, yet they were still excluded on the basis of their race. The story of Steve Simpson's daughter, Daisy, is an example of this 'colourless' racism. It begins with an anecdote told to me by Dave and Monica Buick.

Three members of Barclay's exploration party, with Tom Simpson
in centre, 1911. The Mortlock Library of South Australiana,
State Library of South Australia

Steve and his family lived directly opposite the Penneshaw School, but Monica Buick told me that on one occasion 'he had a row with the schoolteacher and wouldn't let [his children] go across the road to the school any more, and sent them to American Beach on their tricycles. I don't think it lasted long, it was too far to go.'

'Poor little kids,' said Dave, laughing at the idea of sending children ten kilometres to school when there was one over the road.

When we met again a year later, I asked what had caused the argument. Dave was suddenly evasive. 'It's like every other community,' he said. 'Arguments crop up . . . I don't know what Mrs

Simpson [thought]; she was white . . . just a quarrel . . . the same quarrels are going on in many cases.'

But the nature of these apparently universal quarrels, and why it was relevant that Steve's wife was 'white', did not become clear until I spoke with Mildred Willson. Showing me a photo of her first year at the Penneshaw School in 1923, Mildred pointed to her classmates Charlie, Les and 'Anzac' Simpson, Steve's three youngest sons. They were the 'poor little kids' he temporarily sent to the American Beach school.

Mildred said she had not heard about Steve's argument with the schoolteacher, because she was very young at the time. She did, however, remember that Daisy Simpson had been going out with the teacher, John Murphy, who was from Adelaide. She pointed him out in the photograph. Murphy had been 'engaged to Daisy Simpson', Mildred explained, 'but as soon as he found out that she had Aboriginal blood . . . he just went away and left her there.' Perhaps he met the same community disapproval that Tom Simpson had experienced when he married a schoolteacher some thirty years earlier.

'You know, he could have upset the family by ditching the girl because of that reason,' Mildred reflected. Daisy was twenty-one in 1923. It seems likely that her broken engagement

Daisy Simpson as a teenage girl. Courtesy of the Golder family

had caused her father's argument with the schoolteacher. Dave Buick was also twenty-one at the time, and was quite possibly aware of the event. Evidently Daisy did not look very dark, for Murphy had to 'find out' about her ancestry. But, as Mildred Willson observed, knowing someone's ancestry could make a fair woman black.

Soon after this incident Steve and his family left Penneshaw to live in Thebarton, a suburb of Adelaide. This perhaps explains why Steve 'didn't stick to any land', as Bruce Bates had put it. After working as a cook in Whyalla, Daisy ultimately married a man who shared her family name, Ted Simpson. They had a son, Bill, in Victoria. 'I hope some day I will come over and see you all,' she wrote to her uncles Jack and Tiger Simpson, 'what is left at any rate'.[10]

Daisy and her son are no longer alive, but I spoke to her daughter-in-law, Dorothy Simpson, in Melbourne in 1998. Dorothy told me that Daisy never told her son or his family about their Aboriginal ancestry until six months before she died, when she was very ill.

'We were talking one night,' Dorothy explained, 'and she said, "We've got Aboriginal in the family", and I said. "Well, that's good", and she didn't go in any further than that . . . She [said she] had aunts who were Aboriginal, but she never owned up that she had it in her line, just that it was in her family.'

Dorothy also said that Daisy's looks had never given her away. 'You'd never pick it in a million years,' she said. Daisy had spoken of her broken engagement with John Murphy, but she had said that 'the reason they didn't get married was because she wasn't a Catholic and his people were'. But Dorothy added reflectively: 'As she was ashamed of being Aboriginal, then the other story might well be true.'

Dorothy's son Terry thought Daisy's deathbed announcement of their Aboriginal ancestry eased a longstanding sense of guilt that she had felt too ashamed to tell them earlier. Terry also thought Daisy would have been 'devastated' by her broken engagement and because of this, she 'did not want her son growing up with the same problems that she had experienced'.

Terry's Aunt Doris, who had been married to Daisy's brother Charlie, remembered Daisy's story of her broken engagement. She did not know the cause, but thought the story was very sad, 'because I think she really liked him . . . and he liked her too'.

Charlie, like four of his brothers and his sister, married in Adelaide. Mildred Willson told me that his brother Les came back to Penneshaw after his marriage and worked as a builder, helping construct the Anglican church. She told me that Anzac and Eddy (Edward) both married in Adelaide, and that Eddy played league football for West Torrens. Harold was the only brother who did not marry, but only Stan had children of his own; Eddy's wife had two children from a previous marriage, and Charlie's wife, Doris, told me she and Charlie had been unable to have children.

Doris still lives in Thebarton, the suburb Steve's family first moved to in the early 1920s. Charlie ended up working on the South Australian railways, which had a long history of employing Aboriginal labourers. But Doris told me she had had no idea her husband was of Aboriginal Tasmanian descent until Terry and I told her. Doris said Charlie had looked quite dark, but had simply told her he had 'dark blood in him' – 'he didn't say "black", he said dark', Doris explained. He used to joke, 'I'm just like an Italian, you know.'

Stephen and Hannah Simpson after they moved to Thebarton, Adelaide. Courtesy of Mrs Doris Simpson

Charlie Simpson (left) with fellow railway workers.
Courtesy of Mrs Doris Simpson

'We always said he was sunburnt,' she laughed. 'Ooh, did he have dark eyes! He was lovely.' But Doris said that Charlie had not wanted to tell her any more, so she had never asked.

Historian Jan Critchett writes that in pastoral Australia the colonial frontier ran as close between Indigenous and settler populations as the bed shared by an Aboriginal woman and a white man. Patrick Wolfe claims the frontier ran even closer; it is 'running through [the] veins' of those with mixed Aboriginal and non-Aboriginal ancestries.[11] In tightly knit communities, a single Aboriginal ancestor can place generations of descendants on the side of the colonised. It takes only one drop of Aboriginal blood to contaminate a white genealogy, if that one drop is common knowledge.[12]

Tom and Charlie Simpson were Aboriginal on Kangaroo Island, but they were Maori or Italian when they left. Although John Murphy did not want to marry Daisy in Dudley because of her Aboriginal 'blood', her son and grandchildren in Adelaide grew up never knowing about their Aboriginal ancestry. In Dudley, Lewis Barrett, Emma's youngest, was the 'redheaded blackfella', in Adelaide he just had red hair. To leave the island was to leave behind the common knowledge of their Aboriginal ancestry and gain a chance of acceptance, marriage, families and a future. On the mainland these families could hide their ancestry and escape the prejudice to which it exposed them.

Tom Simpson and his sister Anne both left before 1900. By the early 1920s all of Emma Barrett's five surviving children had followed, as had Steve Simpson and his family of six. So had three of Mary and Alfred Waller's six children: Bill, Amy and Norman Waller had left and married. Their sons Wally and Jack stayed, but remained bachelors, and Charlie Waller died at Gallipoli in the First World War. In 1908 Joe Seymour's daughter Annie wrote from Penneshaw to Tiger Simpson, who was working at the island's Cape de Couedic lighthouse: 'There is not many left now, nearly every one has cleared out and Hog Bay is dead.'[13]

'They would have to go away to the mainland,' Agnes Marshall explained, 'because [they] would have been known by people on the other end of the island'. Almost everyone knew everyone on Kangaroo Island; Agnes said her father-in-law had claimed to know the family name of every person on the island.

Joe Seymour's youngest daughter, Annie, was married in Kingscote, where, Agnes confirmed, 'they would have known'.

Amy Waller, who left and married off the island.
Courtesy of the Waller family

Wally Waller in World War One uniform. He returned to the island, but never married. Courtesy of the Waller family

Jack Waller in Second World War RAAF uniform. Jack returned to the island, but remained a bachelor. Courtesy of the Waller family

Annie Seymour before she married, Penneshaw.

The Penneshaw Folk Museum

Annie Harry (née Seymour) with her husband Arthur and their
daughter, Mavis, c. 1924. The Penneshaw Folk Museum

But her husband, Arthur Harry, was a new settler; he established the island's first ice-works, and was not part of the landed establishment. Moreover, Annie was eight months pregnant when they married. They did not tell their daughter, Mavis, about this, nor about her Aboriginal ancestry.

Annie's older sister Mary was the only Aboriginal descendant of her generation to marry and continue living in Dudley. Her husband, Frank Abell, came over from Norwood in Adelaide to work in the new Penneshaw brickworks. He was also a potter and artist. But Frank and Mary never had any children. Bruce Bates told me this was a deliberate decision they had made.

'It was generally understood', he said, 'that Frank and Mary had no children because Mary *chose* not to, because they were going to have Aboriginal descent and she herself had felt a bit ostracised because of her background ... She didn't want to have children who had stigma attached to them.'

I asked if perhaps Frank and Mary had been unable to have children. 'Perhaps', Bruce said, but people had thought she had deliberately chosen not to.

'Because she didn't want them to have a rough time?' I asked.

'That's right,' he answered.

'There wasn't any third generation,' Mildred Willson said of the Aboriginal families on Kangaroo Island. 'Mary ... married Frank Abell, but they didn't have any children. Mavis Golder seems to be a one and only.'

If the racism of the Dudley community could persuade a woman not to have children, it's hardly surprising that those living outside Dudley hid their Aboriginality and decided not to tell their children about their ancestry. It is quite possible that there are still descendants of Betty and Nat Thomas in South Australia, or across the nation, who are unaware that they are of Aboriginal Tasmanian descent.

As the families of Aboriginal ancestry were shrinking and disappearing from Dudley, the families of white colonial descent were growing. In 1913, when most of the Barretts, Wallers and Simpsons had left, the Willsons had their own cricket team – their family versus the rest of the community. Monica Buick told me: 'I thought

Mary Abell at her Penneshaw home, c. 1930.

Courtesy of the Golder family

Mary Abell in the doorway of her Penneshaw home, 1933.

Courtesy of the Golder family

Mary Abell fishing, possibly from rocks near Penneshaw, c. 1940.
Courtesy of the Golder family

Mary Abell. The Penneshaw Folk Museum

there were too many Willsons, so I married a Buick. There were
a lot more Buicks afterward because we had eight children.'

Mildred Willson quoted a saying of Tiger Simpson's: 'The
three "W"s of Kangaroo Island: the wall-rocket, the wallabies
and the Willsons. You can get rid of the wall-rocket and the wallabies, but you can't get rid of the Willsons!'

It was ironic that a Willson should have been quoting Tiger;
it was as if she was admitting that her family was the introduced
species that had wiped out the native fauna. The biggest families,
like the Willsons, owned the most land and mostly married other
landed families. Fiona Marshall, who did a lot of genealogical
work on the Dudley colonial families when she was curator of the
Penneshaw Folk Museum, and who gained a sharply analytical
perception of Dudley's social history, reflected: 'There were only
six or seven families, and they tended to marry in amongst themselves all the time. I mean, anyone will tell you that if you look
into any family tree you will find people from every other one of
those seven families represented on it. Names just keep cropping
up all the time.'

When I asked Fiona the source of the standard island joke that
people in Dudley have six toes, she said, 'Well ... because it was
a little isolated community [and] ... one of the oldest ... and there
was a lot of interbreeding ... and because of that there were ...
these [so-called] dangers of deformities cropping up a bit more
regularly.'

One of the reasons for the intermarriage in Dudley, I was told,
was a lack of choice. While there were about 1000 people on
Kangaroo Island by the early twentieth century, there were only
about 400 in Dudley. There was also a slight gender imbalance,
with marginally more men than women.[14] 'Among other things',
wrote an Adelaide *Register* journalist in 1907, 'Hog Bay is noted
for a jetty [and] the number of bachelors it possesses per square
inch.' The Hog Bay Bachelor Society, which was formed at the
turn of the century, focused its energies on advertising the need
for more single women in the district. 'Eligible young ladies are at
a premium here', the *Register* journalist reported after attending a
meeting of the society, 'and the society will be greatly obliged to

The Register if it will try to induce a nice shipment of them (no old maids need apply) to spend their next holidays in this town'.[15]

Despite these problems, almost all the sons of non-Aboriginal farming families managed to marry in Dudley. But only four of the twenty-one male descendants of Betty and Nat Thomas born on Kangaroo Island married there. The Bachelor Society was essentially a social club, an excuse for smart, landed young men to announce their availability to attractive young women. The gender imbalance as they presented it was essentially a problem of such men being unable to find women of their ilk. 'Girls of choice', Dave Buick explained, 'weren't that plentiful in my day. Eventually I got the best one.'

It was not only that these families were without choice, it was also that they were choosy. Fiona Marshall explained to me that men often preferred to wait, or even not marry at all, rather than marry a woman of lesser standing. Fiona identified what had once been essentially two groups of families in the community: the 'coarser', or 'lower-class', families, who included, among others, the Seymours and the Barretts, and the 'refined' or 'landed' families. When it came to marriage, the two groups rarely mixed.

'There were certain families that you just didn't associate with,' she reflected of the previous generation of 'landed' families, 'and there were those select families that were considered to be in your class, in your social standing ... You didn't really marry outside those families and if you didn't find anybody within those families that you wanted to marry ... often you stayed unmarried.'

Despite owning so much land, the Simpsons were denied the 'certain' families' 'social standing' because of their Aboriginal ancestry. When I pointed out to Fiona how the Simpsons' name never 'cropped up' in any of these genealogies, she admitted, 'No, they don't come into too many families.' She later wrote in the margins of the interview transcript I had sent her to read: 'Simpsons more associated with peripheral families; Eberts, Barretts, etc.; the "lower class" families'.

There was only one marriage between a member of the 'landed' families and a descendant of Betty and Nat Thomas. In 1914 Bill Waller, the eldest son of Hannah Simpson's daughter

Mary, married May Willson, the granddaughter of Thomas Willson. But Bill, it was felt, had managed to escape his 'lower class' background. May's cousin, Monica Buick, told me that Bill had 'worked himself up' and had become a sea captain. He worked in Port Adelaide and lived near by with his family of four children.

'There was a slight difference', Dave Buick said of the Aboriginal descendants. 'The abo got into them a bit.' But he conceded: 'You've got to give the abo credit; if he's trained a bit he's got as much intelligence as we have ... There *was* intelligence in the Waller family, you know. Bill Waller never had a day's schooling in his life, and he ended up being a deep-sea captain, in the big ships.'

Captain William (Bill) Waller. Courtesy of the Waller family

Bill had worked his way into a professionally more prestigious position than most of the members of the 'refined' families of Dudley. Progressing in class apparently made race less of an issue.

But Joe Seymour and Steve Simpson had not 'worked themselves up'. Their marriages indicated how their ancestry limited their eligibility. Joe's wife, Rachel Josephine Ebert (née Butterley), was not only born of a 'lower-class' family but had already married into one before her second marriage to Joe. When the death of her first husband left her alone with seven children, Josephine, as she was known, possibly needed a husband so much that she had no real choice. Steve Simpson married Hannah, Josephine's daughter by her earlier marriage. In effect, she was already part of the family, and was therefore unlikely to reject Steve for his Aboriginal ancestry.

While the smart young men in Hog Bay complained about the lack of available girls, none of them married the three Simpson sisters, the two Barrett sisters, the two Seymour sisters or Daisy Simpson. It seems these young women did not qualify as 'girls of choice'. A display panel in Penneshaw Museum tells how lighthouse-keepers' daughters and schoolteachers often married local men and became 'part of the community network of the Hog Bay district'. But the women of Aboriginal descent who were born there did not. Those Aboriginal-descendant women who did marry locally mostly married tradesmen with little or no land.

Emma Barrett's husband, Frank, had some land, but he was most often employed by the council as cemetery curator, district ranger and dayworker.[16] After examining the Dudley council records, Michael Golder observed that mostly his Penneshaw ancestors did the kind of work 'reserved for the lower strata of society ... If the council wanted a new septic tank dug it was Frank Barrett that they called on, or if something needed cleaning, or whatever else ... You wonder whether they were ... accepted.'

Harry Davey delivered the Dudley mail, like his father-in-law before him. He did own some land, but only what his brothers-in-law transferred to him, fully mortgaged. Frank Abell was a brickmaker, potter and artist. Mary Simpson's husband, Alfred Waller, owned land, but not very much of it. Arthur Harry set up the ice-works in Kingscote. These men were not considered of the 'lowest' class – Agnes Marshall thought Jane Davey had done very well to marry a 'well-educated white man' – they were just not among the most established within the Dudley community.

Race and class were two sides of the same coin. While the Aboriginal descendants could only marry into the 'coarser' families because of their race, association with those families made

Joe Seymour and his family (left to right): his daughter Annie,
his stepdaughter Rachel, his wife Rachel and his daughter Mary,
c. 1902. The Penneshaw Folk Museum

Joe Seymour's three daughters: Rachel (his stepdaughter),
Annie and Mary, c. 1900. The Penneshaw Folk Museum

them seem even more 'lower class'. And for those families, associ-ation with Aboriginal descendants confirmed their place among the 'coarser' families. In fact, 'lower-class' and 'Aboriginal' were almost synonyms, especially since they were all related by marriage.

The 'lower-class' families formed a marriage network parallel to that of the intermarried 'refined' families. The 'lower-class' family network was town-based and essentially formed around the three marriages of one woman, Hannah Charlesworth (1826–1907). Hannah's first marriage was to Richard Whyte, with whom she had three sons; among her grandsons was Ralph Whyte, the storekeeper who ripped off Mary Seymour. Hannah's second marriage was to Frederick Ebert, with whom she had three daughters and two sons, and her third marriage was to Robert Davidson. They didn't have any children, but he had three daughters from his first marriage. Josephine Ebert, a daughter of Hannah's second marriage, eventually married Joe Seymour, and her eldest daughter, Hannah Butterley, married Steve Simpson.

These two marriages meant that the names Whyte, Davidson, Butterley and Ebert became associated with an Aboriginal ancestry. In 1965, H. M. Cooper wrote to Norman Tindale about the Aboriginal Tasmanian descendants on Kangaroo Island, where he had been told (incorrectly) that 'Old Mrs Seymour' had been married twice, the first time to a 'Mr Butley' – seemingly a mis-spelling of Butterley.[17] When I asked Agnes Marshall what she could tell me about the Simpsons' land ownership, she replied that she knew only that Tony Ebert had owned some land at Cape Willoughby. Roe Trethewey said that Ralph Whyte had been 'associated with the Aboriginal mob'.

'Association with the Aboriginal mob' was precisely what the Bateses feared, for they knew its consequences. It was Bruce Bates who had told me the Simpsons had lost their land 'because they … didn't marry easily'. While the Bateses married into the 'refined' family network, they are part of the 'coarser' network as well, and are related to the Aboriginal descendants by marriage. Bruce Bates's great-grandfather was Robert Davidson, Hannah Charlesworth's third husband. Two of Robert's daughters from his first marriage married Bates men – including Bruce's grandfather.

Two generations later, Joe Seymour's stepdaughter Maria Butterley married Arthur Bates. Arthur, who was already his wife's step-cousin, became Joe's son-in-law and Steve Simpson's brother-in-law. Arthur Bates's sister, Clarissa, married William Butterley, and she became Joe and Steve's cousin-in-law, although she had already been their step-cousin too.

These relatives were also recognised by the Aboriginal descendants. Although Doris Simpson had been told little about her husband's ancestry, she knew that the Butterleys and the Bateses were relatives. Dorothy Simpson said she remembered that when Daisy went back to visit relatives on Kangaroo Island they included her aunts, Annie and Mary, and the Bateses.

But it seems the Bateses have wanted to disguise and divert attention from their relations with the Simpsons and Seymours. Throughout Bruce Bates's father's memoirs, the name Butterley is systematically crossed out. When I asked Bruce about the relations between his family and the Butterleys, he said they were a 'different' Butterley family from the one related to the Seymours and the Simpsons. This is simply not true.

In spite of several marriages to the Buicks (who in turn married into the other families), the Bateses are far more closely related to the so-called 'lower-class' network, which included the Aboriginal families, than any of the other established families.

Nonetheless, the Bates are still considered one of the 'refined' landed families of Dudley. This is because in Dudley among the six main families land does not only have monetary worth, but is also a passport to marriage into the right families; to the reproduction of success with each generation. The Bates family managed to continue to reproduce their land ownership because they were related to the Aboriginal descendants by law but not by blood.

Staying landed meant staying white. But a revelatory piece of information raises the question: how white were the Dudley colonial families? In 1960 Norman Tindale spoke to Bruce Bates's father, who told him that the Clark family of Antechamber Bay was of Aboriginal descent. Bruce's father thought that a Tom Clark had come from Tasmania and settled on the South

Australian mainland, where he had several Aboriginal partners. Exactly when, Bruce's father did not say. Tom's son, 'Bob', was claimed to have a white mother, but Bruce's father thought that 'the Clarks of Kangaroo Island all have some Encounter Bay aboriginal blood from Bob Clark'.

Bruce Bates's father asked Tindale that 'this matter be treated confidentially in a way that would not offend present day people'. Tindale 'assured' him that 'a dilute strain of Australian Aboriginal need worry no one'.[18]

But had it worried the people in Dudley? Robert Clark had settled in Dudley in 1873 and had about five thousand acres by the turn of the twentieth century as well as a large family. But from the early twentieth century there was a continuing feud between the Clarks and the Marshalls – about what, I was never told. By the 1920s the Clarks had sold most of their land. There are now only a few Clark descendants in name in Dudley, and they no longer own very much land.

But there are many Clark descendants among the six-family kinship group in Dudley. From the 1870s onwards, there were several marriages between the Clarks and the Marshalls, Tretheweys and Willsons. Those three families in turn married the Howards and Buicks, who in turn married the Bateses. Could it be that all the Dudley colonial descendants are of Aboriginal descent?

Bruce Bates thinks not. He had never heard of his father's claims, and thinks his father must have been wrong. Perhaps Tindale and Bruce's father were confused. Thirty years earlier, Tindale was told incorrectly by a 'local' on Kangaroo Island that Bob Clark was the grandfather of Mavis Golder's mother, Annie Harry; that he had 'brought in some dark blood' into their family.[19] But even if Bruce Bates's father had been right, the Clarks arrived on Kangaroo Island in 1873. They were not, like Nat Thomas and Betty, the local 'indigenes' to the first colonists.

∾

On the largest scale, white Australia's national story has been about a moving frontier, conquering a new land and spreading civilisation where before there was only emptiness, or a people too savage to tend the land properly themselves. On the Dudley Peninsula it was not so different. There it was told as a story about pioneer farmers settling an almost-island where there were only a few wild white men who could threaten to cut out a man's windpipe for the most trifling offence. When the Dudley farmers arrived, from the 1850s to 1880s, women like Sal, Betty and Suke could still be seen wandering the peninsula, apparently dejected and destitute, with grubs in their hair. They were remembered as mad children-eaters who begot children destined to collect rations as they had themselves. This was the ancestry of the Simpsons, Seymours, Wallers and Barretts.

The *Oxford English Dictionary* defines a 'throwback' as a 'reversion to an earlier ancestral type or character'. This suggests a reversion not only of genes – of colour or blood – but of a history: to an earlier type, an earlier time. After all, that 'savage' Nat Thomas, as the first settler Mary Thomas perceived him, was English.

The frontier line in Dudley was one of histories defined by ancestral blood; the blood of the 'landed gentry' and that of the pre-colonial Aboriginal families never mixed. It was a jagged frontier, winding its way through a complex of relations by marriage, but it did not run through the veins of those who continued to own land in Dudley. The Bateses were able to continue owning land and marrying the other landed families because they did not mix with Aboriginal blood. They did not fall victim to its domino effect. All the colonial families feared this pattern. Indeed, it was not only their fear of the 'throwback' but their fear of each other that bonded them and excluded Aboriginal families. Like the wall-rocket in Tiger's story, they eradicated the Aboriginal contaminant by isolation. Bonded in marriage, the colonial descendants are thus bonded in land, and it is land that sustains their sense of identity and their shared history and memory.

The colonial descendants still demonstrate Nat Thomas's shivery voice in Dudley. They still tell the stories of the old Aboriginal women collecting rations at their homestead doors.

They still remember the frontier line imagined by the first settlers. And so they explain the land loss of the Simpsons and the exodus of all the Aboriginal descendants from Dudley: that it was not caused by racial prejudice, but was an inevitable outcome – that failure was in their genes.

Images of Loss

Up in the Victoria River district of the Northern Territory Tom Simpson worked as a contractor, a well-sinker, a camel-driver and a cook. In 1911 he accompanied a survey expedition lead by Captain Henry Barclay from Adelaide to Borroloola via Charlotte Waters, Hermannsburg Mission, Alice Springs, Haasts Bluff and Newcastle Waters. It was no doubt Tom's job on the expedition to cook and tend the camels, but he was also interested in the country he saw. He wrote a lengthy journal, and took many photographs. Tom had not forgotten his family back in Oodnadatta, and sent the photos to his son, Horrie. But Horrie destroyed the journals in play with his friends. What did Tom write? Was he as disgusted with the conditions of Aborigines on Hermannsburg as Barclay was?[1] Apparently the only remaining text of Tom's journey is his name, scratched into Chambers Pillar, a well-known landmark.[2]

Despite his initial destructiveness, Horrie was inspired to start a journal himself in 1919, aged thirteen, and he kept it for seventy-one years. His journals in turn inspired his book *Horrie Simpson's Oodnadatta*, edited by John Dallwitz. Tom is hardly mentioned in the book. Horrie, his sister Dorothy and their mother Mary barely saw him. Horrie grew up with almost no memories of his father. He knew that Tom had come from Kangaroo Island, but certainly had no idea that he was of Aboriginal Tasmanian descent. Horrie was left with a few of Tom's objects: a bushman's shaving mirror, a cigarette case in which Tom kept fishhooks, and the birthday book of Tom's first wife, Martha Cousin. It includes the dates of birth and death of family members Horrie had never met or even heard of.[3]

Charlie Schultz, who had worked with Tom up north, knew more stories about Tom than his son did. In *Beyond the Big Run*, Charlie described Tom as 'a rough old bushman'. He also portrayed the life in the Victoria River district that made him so. Fights and shootings were not uncommon on the stations, 'but unless someone got shot nothing was ever made of it'.

In Wave Hill in 1919, someone did get shot. It was a dispute over 'a half-caste' girl. Tom Simpson had to act as witness in a Darwin court. He was asked by the judge: 'What was your opinion of the half-caste girl the row started over?' Tom answered, 'She's got a rattlin' fine figure, but she's about the ugliest thing yer ever clapped eyes on ... she's like the peacock – the beauty's all in her tail'.[4] Schultz remembers how everyone in the court fell about laughing.

Charlie had a fondness for Tom. The last time he saw Tom, he was heading south with mates to Tennant Creek to look for gold. He never made it, stopping instead to work at Newcastle Waters. Afterwards Tom kept going south to Oodnadatta. From there he wrote to Charlie asking for news of the Victoria River district. 'I really treasured that letter', writes Charlie, 'so I sat down then and wrote him four or five pages. About three months later the letter was returned unclaimed, and I heard he'd passed away.'[5] Tom died in March 1937.[6]

Back on Kangaroo Island, where Tom had once known relative wealth and success, his brothers also became 'rough old bushmen'. After they lost their land, Nat and Bill did manual labour. They worked in the shearing sheds and stockyards of their former peers. They worked for the council making roads, cutting and metalling, and repairing. Nat was fifty-eight when he carried out his last road contract.[7]

When Mildred Willson was a child, he was known as simply 'Old Nat'. She thought that he and his brother Bill might have also done 'yacca gumming' and 'cutting leaf'. Yacca gummers were useful to settlers who wanted their land cleared. Gum collected from the native yacca plants was shipped to Adelaide, where it was sold for export to Europe at about £3 a ton. 'Leaf' was cut to be used for distilling eucalyptus oil, a small-time island industry; the oil sold for about a shilling a pound on the mainland.[8] I was told that the Simpson brothers also snared wallabies for the meat, and may have also sold the hides.[9] This was the work of the landless – the same survival work that kept starvation at bay during the Great Depression. It meant camping and living in the bush for long periods of time. Mildred Willson thought that Nat and his brothers were 'sort of bushmen ... you'd see them occasionally', she told me, coming into town carrying swags.

Mildred remembers the last time she saw Nat Simpson. It was at a drawing competition in the Penneshaw Town Hall. 'I can remember Nat coming to the hall,' she told me. He didn't enter, but stood 'leaning up against the wall ... watching ... the party going on'. He had a beard and only one good eye.[10]

Nat soon became the subject of one of the drawings. 'I can just see that black-looking drawing', Mildred told me. 'They used black ... for his dark face ... I think they sort of thought that he mightn't be well and he died soon after that ... It really was rather pathetic, he really looked such a poor, haggard, old man.' Bruce Bates, as if echoing Mildred, thought Nat was a 'broken-down old man'.

Few people I spoke to could remember much about Bill. Mildred Willson said she couldn't remember Bill at all, other than that 'there *was* a Bill Simpson'. She thought that 'he worked in shearing sheds sometimes'. Her brother, Lindsay Howard, thought that he worked at Cape de Couedic lighthouse, and perhaps also at Cape Willoughby.[11] Roe Trethewey wondered if Bill, like Tom, might have spent some time up north camel-driving, but said that he certainly came back to the island to die. He was buried near his father in the Penneshaw Cemetery in 1936.

While many of the people I spoke to remembered that Nat and Bill spent most of their time at Antechamber Bay, Bruce Bates remembers that their brother Jack, and sometimes Tiger, lived next door to him in the old Simpson house with their sister Jane and her husband Harry Davey. Bruce thought they lived in 'very Aboriginal conditions'; that the house was unclean and had dirt floors. He told me that the whole family 'went to the dogs', and remembered that Jane died ill and 'neglected'. Bruce said that the Waller cousins also used to stay for periods of time. 'When things got difficult somewhere else,' Bruce told me, 'they'd appear back there, and then they'd be all in there.'

Tom, the son of Mary Waller, née Simpson, was one such cousin. He is well remembered by the people I spoke to. His own nephew and grand-nephew – Adrian and Neil Waller – described Tom Waller as 'eccentric'. They remember he used to travel over to Adelaide and stay in digs and walk every day to Adrian's place for breakfast. On one visit Tom decided to collect money for Nigerian refugees in the city's Victoria Square.

Dave Buick and Fiona and Robin Marshall thought Tom was 'eccentric', but John also said Tom was 'really simple' and Bruce Bates went so far as to say he was 'off his rocker'. Tom, I was told, was a religious zealot. Adrian Waller told me he was kicked out of his Adelaide digs for 'Bible-bashing' and had 'God is love' spelt out with cabbages in his garden in Penneshaw. Robin Marshall said Tom had biblical text written on his house, his shoes and his bicycle, and claimed to have a Bible the size of a twenty-gallon drum. On one occasion Tom dressed up as the Archbishop of Canterbury and paraded past the Penneshaw school. Dave Buick remembers calling in on Tom for some help drenching, only to find him applying lipstick in front of a mirror. Tom later fell in Dave's sheep dip and refused to wash or change his clothes for the rest of the day.

While Tom spent some years living in the old Simpson house, he lived much of the time in the bush. His homes included a tree-house and a hole in the ground. Robin Marshall told me that when he was camping on the roadsides in Dudley, he would scrape the leaves from under the trees into mounds like a bush turkey, then plant improvised roadside gardens; patches of flowers would appear in the most unlikely places. Bruce Bates's father told Norman Tindale in 1960 that Tom claimed he could 'work faster than a bulldozer' and often spent the whole night 'filling in wash-ways with a spade to prove his speed'. Tom 'was of Tasmanian extraction', Bates explained.[12]

One of Tom Waller's homes; his other abodes included a treehouse
and a hole in the ground. Courtesy of the Waller family

Two of the other Simpson cousins who lived in Penneshaw
were Emma Barrett, the 'boong' of Blackfella Town, and her
brother Joe Seymour. Joe outlived Emma by twenty-three years,
and remained next door to his mother's old house at Christmas
Cove. Some people remembered seeing Joe reading the paper
on his veranda. When Bruce Bates was a boy, Joe used to come
into his family's shearing shed to sit and chat – by then he was too
old to shear.

But Joe continued to work as a stonemason and a builder. He
worked hard, walking as far as Cape Willoughby to do a job. He
was over eighty when he built the stone foundations for Roe
Trethewey's first house. 'He'd come out every Monday night,' Roe
told me, '. . . with a couple of bottles of wine . . . and he'd say,
"Well, well, well, Roe, let's have a h-eye, h-eye, h-eye opener."'

Back when Roe was still at school, he recalled, an optician
had come to test the locals' eyes at the hotel. Joe, who was
building the fire station at the time, saw 'all these buggies outside
the pub' and 'went up to see what was going on'. When he got
there 'everyone bought him a drink'. From then on, whenever Joe
left the pub, he would pass the children in the school and, putting

Joe Seymour (holding the lamb) with Sam Neave and son, tailing lambs, c. 1905. Courtesy of the Golder family

Joe Seymour (far right) at a harvest, c. 1900.
The Penneshaw Folk Museum

his perhaps normally dropped 'h's in front of the wrong words, call out, 'I was h-only going down for an h-eye, h-eye, h-eye tester.'

'I don't think he ever went to an optician,' Roe reflected. 'He had one tooth in his head . . . he managed all right.'

'I can remember what he looked like,' Mildred Willson told me. 'He was dark, and he had a bushy beard. Sort of . . . smoke-stained beard . . . fairly grubby around the top.' Bruce Bates told me that Joe 'wore a beard and it was very silvery and he had a very strong Aboriginal appearance'. Mildred Willson said that 'years ago' some people had called him 'Old Black Joe'.

Joe Seymour aged about eighty; the photograph of Joe that Mavis Golder saw in *Walkabout* magazine in 1954 looks very similar to this, and may have been taken at about the same time. The Birdsell Collection, South Australian Museum

But Jack and Tiger Simpson, the youngest Simpson brothers, were among the best remembered of all the Aboriginal descendants. 'A lot of people knew them well because they worked on their farms,' Mildred Willson told me.

'Any building that had to be done, you got Tiger because he was good,' said Keith Southlyn, who was descended of an island colonial family from outside Dudley but had married a Buick. 'You wanted your sheep shorn, you got Jack.' But Thelma Buick thought Jack did more paid work than Tiger. 'Old Jack . . . used to come out to our place shearing for about forty years,' Roe Trethewey said.

'I knew Jack quite well,' Bruce Bates explained to me. Jack 'used to be our gardener for quite a while, he used to come up here every day'.

'Jack … I remember him, he used to work for my father,' Monica Buick told me. Agnes Marshall said Jack worked for her mother in about 1926. Lindsay Howard remembered that Jack 'preferred shearing when it was hot enough to fry an egg on the roof'. Keith Southlyn told me that Jack taught him how to shear with a blade.

Mildred Willson also remembered that Jack was 'extremely interested in the cricket'. She and her family would 'always' see Jack at local sports events, but she added: 'I wouldn't see more of him than to say "hello, Jack" if I came close by him.'

In the photograph of the 1899 Penneshaw cricket team, Jack Simpson is a handsome young man in jacket, tie and cap. But for those I spoke to who could remember him, he was a middle-aged or old man most famous for having never washed a shirt in his life.

'Every Saturday night he'd buy himself a new white shirt,' Monica Buick told me, 'and he'd wear it all the week and when it was dirty he'd throw it away … he never washed it.' Roe Trethewey told me that Jack would 'buy himself a new shirt … every night' when he finished working for Monica Buick's father and went to the pub. John said that the pub owner eventually found about twenty of Jack's shirts that he had left there, dirty but hardly worn. Mildred Willson also said that several bags of Jack's shirts were found in his living quarters at one of the Willson farms. Mildred's brother Lindsay thought Jack was 'very particular about cleanliness', because he 'always wore a white shirt, even when he was shearing'. But Mildred thought 'the brand-new shirt would get a grubby look because he wasn't really looking after himself very well'.

'I think Tiger was a lot cleaner than Jack,' Mildred told me. This was despite the fact that at best Tiger had only a hut to live in. 'He could hardly call it a hut,' she said. 'It was a real dump of a place.'

Like his cousin Tom Waller, Tiger spent much of his life camping in the bush. Carrying his possessions in a wheelbarrow,

Tiger would set up a humpy of wheat sacks or corrugated iron 'in the outback blocks', as Thelma Buick put it, where he collected yacca gum or went fishing, possum-hunting and wallabying.

Born Stamford, Tiger got his nickname 'because of his ferociousness', Roe Trethewey told me. He was often blackballed from the pub for bad language and brawling, while at fetes and sports matches he could get into an alcohol-induced rage that some recalled as being close to madness.

Over dinner with Fiona and Robin Marshall I reflected on my interviews with other colonial descendants in Dudley. 'They are surprised to learn that [the Simpsons] were councillors and that one was a JP,' I explained. 'They say that Jack Simpson never washed, Tiger Simpson . . .'

'. . . drunk all the time, the brawls outside parties and dances, that sort of thing', Fiona finished the statement for me.

Although the Simpsons were friends and locals, they feature in local gossip mainly for their hopelessness: Tiger, angry and drunken, with his barrow and humpy, the grubby Jack with his bags of unwashed shirts, the ill and neglected Jane Davey, the bushman Bill, the one-eyed, broken-down Nat, their absent camel-driving brother Tom and their cousins, crazy Tom Waller, Old Black Joe, and Emma the boong of Blackfella Town. These images have more in common with Mary Seymour collecting rations from the Aboriginal Protector, and her mother Betty collecting rations from the homesteads and lighthouse, than they do with a history of successful merino farming.

These images of hopelessness are remembered in the land, in the places where the Simpsons lived. On 'Davey's Hill', now Marshall land, overlooking the eastern end of Antechamber Bay, the remains of Harry and Jane Davey's house are almost completely overgrown. The empty shell of the house owned by Steve Simpson's brother-in-law, Anton Ebert, stands monumentally exposed at Cape Willoughby. Fiona and Robin Marshall have removed some of its stones to restore their ancestor's original Antechamber Bay homestead, as if taking the memories of the absent family to preserve their own. Henry Waller's old cottage remained abandoned in a sheep paddock opposite Pelican Lagoon, its windows sealed with corrugated iron. For many years Steve Simpson's old house lay neglected on the corner of the Willoughby Road turn-off in Penneshaw, but it has since been restored. To those who know, the place is still remembered as 'Simpson's Corner'.

Even Antechamber Bay is seen as a place where Aboriginal people once lived ('quite a settlement of black people', Agnes Marshall thought) and where Aboriginal people failed. Hannah Simpson's name is carved in an old fig tree, but her descendants are no longer there to see it. Lubra Creek, Wab's Gully, Simpson's Paddock – all these places continue to contribute to a notion of Aboriginal failure in that land: it is not their indigenous home, they die there alone, they are unable to farm it. Their absence continues to bespeak their inadequacy.

The Simpsons' old farm at Antechamber Bay is almost entirely surrounded by land that has been continuously owned by the same family for generations. It is the only substantial piece of farming land in the Dudley district settled in the nineteenth century that

Anton Ebert's house, Cape Willoughby, built c. 1894,
abandoned c. 1920. Rebe Taylor, 1994

Henry Waller's house on the East–West Highway,
opposite Pelican Lagoon. Rebe Taylor, 1994

Steve Simpson's house, on what is still referred to as
'Simpson's Corner', Penneshaw. Rebe Taylor, 1994

259

has changed hands outside the six-family kinship network. Like a missing tooth in an otherwise perfect smile, the Antechamber Bay farm is a gap – a black hole – in a landscape otherwise filled with stories of white success and continued habitation.

But these places are in fact the evidence of the Simpsons' one-time success. The land at Antechamber Bay, the derelict houses, the names 'Davey's Hill', 'Nat's Shed', 'Simpson's Cottage', 'Simpson's Paddock', 'Simpson's Corner' and 'Simpson's Hill' are like the remnants of a fallen empire. They testify to the extent of the Simpsons' entrenchment in the district. Yet the colonial descendants do not acknowledge these remnants as evidence of success. They remember the Aboriginal descendants as being in the same state of dilapidation as their houses.

Dave Buick told me: 'The abo, the coloured race as far as we were concerned here, never gave much for land holding at all. Although the Simpsons, I believe, got as far as managing the post office and this sort of thing, but I think that's about as far as they went.'

After Bruce Bates read my Masters thesis, he told me I had made too much of the Simpsons' one-time success: 'They certainly weren't ... successful, [but] it was before my time so I really can't tell you *why* ... but I think it's for the same reason that Aboriginal people don't seem to be very successful on the mainland, they prefer to live in a wurley some of them and just take things as they come. They didn't seem very motivated.'

Agnes Marshall described the Simpsons as 'detribalised' people for whom it was 'foreign ... alien ... to work on the land'. She added, with pity, that 'perhaps white people didn't understand that'.

Interestingly, Fiona Marshall thought 'the Simpsons were considered more white than the Seymours', but she added, 'I don't know why.'

'There shouldn't have been any difference,' her husband, Robin, said. Perhaps poverty is seen as 'more' Aboriginal; the Seymours had always been worse off than their cousins.

None of the colonial descendants I interviewed was old enough to remember the Simpsons' era of success. 'The Simpsons as farmers didn't mean a thing to us,' Keith Southlyn told me. 'It was only the next generation that weren't farmers that we knew ... people like Tiger and Jack.'

When the elderly Dudley residents of today were children, the Simpsons had already lost their land and joined the labouring poor. Their parents claimed this was a quintessentially Aboriginal condition. Most of them taught their children that the Simpsons had never had anything to lose. Yet the evidence of the Simpsons' one-time success lay all around them, in the placenames and empty houses.

When the colonial descendants try to explain this contradiction, a paradox emerges. The images of Tiger living in his humpy or Tom Waller in his hole are images of loss, but they are remembered as the cause of the loss, not as the effect. Poverty and failure have come to define the Thomas descendants' Aboriginality and, contradictorily, to justify their exclusion.

This paradox repeatedly emerged in the conversations I had with the colonial descendants. Mildred Willson said, 'The only thing I can remember Jack owning was a terrific bag of shirts.' Then she added, 'He must have used up a bit of his land money wasting it on those shirts.'

Mildred remembered that Steve Simpson owned the first car on Kangaroo Island, but when I asked her if this meant Steve was quite wealthy, she answered, 'Oh, no. I don't know what they did with their money.'

'Were they very poor?' I asked.

'No, no, they definitely weren't poor,' Mildred answered. She got out her old school photograph and pointed out that Anzac Simpson was wearing shoes and socks. 'A lot of kids' in the picture weren't, Mildred observed. 'The policeman's kids haven't got any boots on.'

While Bruce Bates thought the Simpsons 'certainly ... weren't successful', when I asked him why they lost all their land he said it was 'because they were part-Aboriginal' and 'didn't marry easily'. Mildred Willson thought that the Simpsons 'didn't own much at all', but said that this was because they had not been 'very good managers', having had a 'lack of training in the first place'. Dave Buick said that the Simpsons had 'gone to pot' because they 'didn't know anything about farming'.

Bruce Bates told me that the Simpsons 'wasted their inheritance through drinking'. All the Simpsons were drinkers, Monica Buick agreed: 'That's where their money went.' Agnes Marshall claimed 'they were drinkers … I guess there was nothing much else for them to do on the weekend.'

But no one remembered if Nat or Bill drank a lot. 'I don't remember Steve drinking,' Monica Buick told me, to which her husband added, 'No, Steve was a family man.' Roe Trethewey also didn't think Steve drank 'because he had a big family'. Roe mentioned that Jack Simpson went to the pub every night, but no one else ever mentioned his drinking. Keith Southlyn's memory of Jack was of a 'quiet and gentle' man, while Bruce Bates considered him 'quite placid'.

Only Tiger was famous for his drinking bouts. Only Tiger was blackballed from the pub for his drunken brawls. But to extirpate the memory of racial exclusion, Tiger has become 'all' the Simpsons.

'I'm a Blackfella'

'Most people knew Tiger,' Mildred Willson told me, 'I knew him right till he died and I knew him as a child.' Every Dudley colonial descendant I spoke to had a story to tell me about Tiger, or would simply smile or chuckle when his name was mentioned. When I asked Agnes Marshall why, she said, 'Well, he was just Tiger, he was just a character.'

People knew Tiger because he worked for them. Bruce Bates remembered that Tiger used to shear in his family's shed alongside his cousin Joe Seymour. Thelma Buick said Tiger 'did a lot of casual work for Dad'. 'We knew Tiger really well,' Monica Buick told me. 'He used to work for us. He helped to build this house.' 'He was a good worker,' Roe Trethewey said, then he added, 'He wouldn't kill himself.' But the people of Dudley knew Tiger as more than an employee; he was part of the district.

For many years Tiger lived on a patch of land just above the Penneshaw township, known to the locals as 'Tiger's Hill'. Mildred Willson remembered how 'on a mail day or shopping day' Tiger would start to walk into town, 'knowing that the people would be going shopping' and that those passing him would offer him a lift.

'He preferred it when it was horse and buggy days,' Mildred remembered, '. . . he was a bit dubious about motorised vehicles'. In fact, at one stage Tiger 'didn't like anybody with a car'. But when Tiger ultimately condescended to ride on the running board, Mildred said her family 'gave him lots and lots of rides'.

Tiger covered many miles on foot. His barrow loaded up

with gear, he would turn up on the 'outback blocks' of farms and set up camp to collect yacca gum, trap wallabies, fish or hunt possums. Roe Trethewey remembers that Tiger had 'a portable building he used to take around . . . two bits of iron. He used to put them up . . . never put any nails in it; used to be tied on with wire'. Bruce Bates thought Tiger used to camp in a tent 'made of . . . ordinary wheat sacks sewn together'. Dave Buick remembered Tiger arriving on his property 'with a cart-load of old bags and rag tent', unloading it and saying, 'I might be back one day to put up a camp here.'

Lindsay Howard told me how in 1938 he and some other farmers were fighting a bushfire near Antechamber Bay. The fire jumped the road and was going out of control when Tiger appeared out of the bush 'pushing a wheelbarrow loaded up with blankets, pots and pans, shovels, etc. . . . "There's fifty years gatherin' in that barrow,"' Tiger had said. Lindsay added: 'It was about all he possessed.'

Several people remembered Tiger for his musical performances at local dances in woolsheds or the town hall. 'Tiger used to play the musical saw,' Agnes Marshall told me. 'He was very popular.' Roe Trethewey told me Tiger could play the accordion and the violin as well. John thought he was a 'great musician'. 'He was a clever old bloke,' John also said; he could 'put his hand in anything'.

'Actually, he was a very well-read man,' Thelma Buick told me. 'He had no education, but he used to read a lot.' She recalled an evening when Tiger and her father sat talking in the family kitchen, their feet warming by the stove. They were imagining a future world with robots and machines that could store information. 'I've never forgotten that,' she told me, 'because Dad and Tiger were right.'

Tiger's nephew, Adrian Waller, said his uncle 'was very clever and very musical'. Adrian told me Tiger had fought in the First World War alongside fellow Kangaroo Islander 'Wacka' Daw of Kingscote. Wacka told Adrian that when he and Tiger were at the front, Tiger made a banjo out of biscuit tins and communication wire. 'To get the bass notes he'd probably wind two or three wires together and he'd have a single wire for the higher notes,'

Adrian told me, and then he would be 'strumming away in the trenches'. If a wire broke he'd call out, 'No bloody wire, Daw!' and Wacka 'had to go out in no man's land and get more wire'. Adrian said Tiger made 'trinkets out of shell cases ... He'd sit down for hours and he'd carve them—he used to give them to his girlfriends during the war.'

Back in Penneshaw, Mildred Willson didn't remember Tiger having any 'steady girlfriends', but she thought Tiger had 'a reputation of being a clean-looking man. He could look after himself.' Thelma Buick's sister, Margaret Southlyn, remembered that when she was a child Tiger visited their home every Saturday, always with a piece of wattle in his buttonhole, to be given jam tartlets by her mother. Her mother also cooked Tiger meals and made sure he was well fed.

Their family is remembered for their kindness to Tiger. 'Tiger's Hill' was close to their home, and as well as yarning with Thelma's father in the kitchen, Tiger did quite a lot of casual work for him. 'He always thought the world of our family,' Thelma told me. 'I suppose he considered us his family because he was so close.' Mildred Willson said Thelma and her five sisters all had the 'utmost respect' for Tiger, but she thought Thelma 'was his really close buddy'.

'What he was, was a dear old thing,' Thelma said to me. 'I used to love him.' She remembered that Tiger had once had a trap drawn by two horses—he called them 'the mice'—in which he took her 'cranberrying'. He also took Thelma out fishing in his boat, and cooked wallaby stew and billy tea for her in his hut. Tiger was 'nice to me', Thelma said; he 'more or less protected me'. When other children bullied Thelma, Tiger would look after her. She was 'his little baby'.

Thelma told me: 'He would have been well in his forties, and I was only thirteen, fourteen ... We used to go *right* around the coast ... in his little dinghy. We'd take a frying pan and some dripping and ... we'd have our lunch after we'd caught a few fish ... I often think now, my gosh, there's not too many teenage girls would be allowed to do that, but Mum trusted him, *I* trusted him, and there was never anything stupid, or anything like that.'

Roe Trethewey also had fond memories of fishing with Tiger, and considered him a close friend. When I asked Roe if he thought Tiger had any other close friends, he answered, 'I should think so, yes, a lot of people were very good to him.' 'He was a great friend of my father's,' Bruce Bates told me. 'They knocked around a lot.'

When Tiger was older, in the 1950s, he moved to a hut opposite the Penneshaw School. Robin Marshall told me that when he went to school there, some of the kids used to throw stones at Tiger's roof and run away before he came out to bellow at them. I asked Robin if he joined in the prank. 'No, I didn't do that,' he answered. 'I could never do that.'

'He was a great old friend,' Thelma told me, 'but he was temperamental, and he was an old fighter ... He was worse when he got a bit of drink in him.'

'He'd get on the grog and he'd spend all his money and then he'd get nasty and take it out on someone,' Roe Trethewey told me. 'Then he'd get on the water wagon, perhaps for six months, and come good, and he'd decide it was all right to happen again.'

'He'd always say things in a temper,' Thelma said, 'and then he'd be sorry afterwards. He was always sorry afterwards.'

Roe Trethewey thought that Tiger had 'quite a few fights with different ones, but I don't think he ever won one'. Dave Buick said he 'was harmless, really. He used to make a noise, but there wasn't that much to it ... He never committed anything in the way of a crime.'

But Adrian Waller said his Uncle Tiger was often 'blackballed' from the pub or 'put under the blackfellas act' for bad behaviour or foul language. In 1914, Bruce Bates's father, as Justice of the Peace, signed a summons for Tiger to appear in the local police house for 'indicent [sic] language in a certain public place to witt the Main Road at Penneshaw'.[1] Adrian Waller remembers that Tiger used to swear 'like a trooper'. When Adrian introduced Tiger to his wife on the Penneshaw jetty, Tiger said to her, 'You'll have to excuse me, ma'am, I can't talk without swearing.'

People remembered that Tiger had more than a foul mouth. Agnes Marshall told me how at one of the local dances, 'Tiger had

had one too many and he started to fight with somebody.' While it was 'apparently ... quite normal' for fights to happen at the dances, on this occasion the local policeman couldn't control the brawl, and 'called on volunteers in the name of the Queen to help him'. Agnes told me, laughing, that her 'tight-laced' auntie fainted, 'and they had to go to a neighbour's place to borrow a knife to cut the stays so that she could breathe again'.

Roe Trethewey said that at one dance in the Town Hall, 'they threw [Tiger] out the front door because he was going mad, and he'd race around and come in through the back door and hop on to the stage and they'd chuck him out again'. Perhaps it happened on Strawberry Fete day, the same annual occasion when, according to another colonial descendant, Tiger ran into the Town Hall and jumped onto the stage, covered in blood, biting his collar and making noises, having been in another 'scrape'.

This same man, who can't be named here even by pseudonym, said the first word that came to mind when he thought of Tiger was 'violent'; it was his 'biggest impression'. He remembered Tiger was always talking about 'beating up this person and that person'. While he was the 'old Tiger' when sober, he was violent when drunk, 'and that was often enough'.

This man also remembered an incident in 1940 when Tiger travelled with the Penneshaw football club on the school bus to Kingscote. For some reason he decided to 'pick on Bill Willson, pummelling him again and again, and Bill let him do it, because Tiger was an old man'. This man said that Tiger's cousin by marriage, James (Jim) Waller, 'never came into Penneshaw if Tiger was around, because Tiger would beat him up, even if Jim was a foot taller than him'.

When I asked this man why, he said, 'Tiger would beat up anyone he could.'

'What would make him mad?' I asked Roe Trethewey.

'Who knows? He might be full,' he answered.

'He had a chip on his shoulder,' Monica Buick told me. When I asked her why, she answered, 'They owned quite a lot of land, the Simpsons. They gradually sold it all, and got rid of it, and then they were envious of the people who had bought it.'

When I then asked Dave and Monica Buick if they thought Tiger's anger was also related to any racial stigma he may have experienced in the community, they answered, 'No, no,' in unison.

'No, I think that it was because he lost his land, sold it and drank, and then resented the people who had it,' Monica explained.

'So it was not a matter of race, but of the "haves and have-nots"?' I asked.

'Yes,' Monica answered.

'He had a chip on his shoulder, very definitely,' Mildred Willson agreed.

In the memoirs of Bruce Bates's father I found a story about Tiger shearing for him and refusing to continue because he said the lambs were wet. Bruce's father told Tiger the lambs had to be dry, because they been inside since the rain had started. But Tiger told him, 'You wouldn't know enough about sheep to know a wet one from a dry one', to which Bates retorted, 'Well, at least I know how to keep them.' Tiger then stormed out.

I read this story sitting in Bruce Bates's living room. Afterwards, Bruce explained to me that 'the reference there would be to the fact the Simpson family sort of wasted their inheritance through, er, drinking'.

Just as Tiger's alcoholic binges are used to justify why his whole family lost their land, his violent outbursts explain their collective envy. '*They* gradually sold it all,' was how Monica Buick explained Tiger's temper. '*They* were envious'.

Tiger grew up knowing only paid labour and life in a 'dump of a place'. His plight was a result of his family's loss, and so he became its perfect cause.

'The native instinct ... continually came out in him', Dave Buick told me. 'He'd get the darkie impulse and go to the scrub and camp for a few days.'

'He went walkabout,' Monica confirmed.

I asked Dave if he thought Tiger would have kept his land if he hadn't gone 'walkabout'.

Dave found it hard to imagine Tiger *not* going walkabout. 'He couldn't help it,' he said.

'I can't recall him doing much there,' Bruce Bates said of

Tiger's patch of land near Penneshaw. 'He would sooner go yakka gumming.'

Bruce Bates told me how his father used to keep some sheep at Cape Hart on Dudley's south coast, and that he regularly had to move them north to prevent them getting coast disease. Tiger, whose brothers had once leased land at Cape Hart, always wanted to go with him. He was forever asking, 'When are you goin' out? I wanna come out!' Bruce said that when they got to Cape Hart, Tiger would 'want to go to crayfishing or fishing and do what Aborigines would do; it suited him to do *that*'. Bruce said that even years after his father stopped going out to Cape Hart, whenever he rode past Tiger on his horse, 'Tiger would scream out, "When are you goin' out?"'

In 1936 Tiger and his cousin Joe Seymour took Norman Tindale to Cape Hart and told him that Suke was buried near by. Tindale noted on his map that Cape Hart had a 'post European occupation site with Tasmanian women of the sealer period'. Betty, Suke and Sal quite possibly camped there. Maybe Tiger was not only remembering his Aboriginal Tasmanian crayfishing tradition when he went to Cape Hart, but also revisiting a place that was important to his grandmother's memory. He remembered where his grandmother used to camp and was buried, and spoke at least some words of her language. He spent much of his life in the bush hunting and fishing, as his mother and Aunt Mary had done with Betty almost a century before.

When Tiger remembered his Aboriginal traditions, however, the colonial descendants perceived these as innate 'native instincts' coming out. His behaviour proved to them how land ownership was 'alien' to Aborigines, how they 'prefer to live in a wurley'. For them, Tiger provides the perfect example of the Aborigine with no understanding of land ownership.

But there is a catch. To some degree Tiger was playing to the gallery. He called going bush 'going walkabout', Dave and Monica Buick told me. They remembered that Tiger was proud to call himself a 'darkie'. 'He was very proud of his Aboriginal blood,' Thelma Buick told me. 'He was Tasmanian Aboriginal origin, he was very, very proud of that.' When I asked Thelma how Tiger expressed his pride, she replied, 'He'd say ... "I'm an Aborigine" ... "I'm a black man", or "I'm a blackfella".'

Tiger's Aboriginal identity was in part synthesised from the projections of failure placed upon him; in a 1988 essay, Julie Carter called this process 'incorporating stigma'.[2] Roe Trethewey told me that Tiger called himself the 'scrapin' of the bowl', the last child with the least. His camp at 'Tiger's Hill' was on the 'Possum's Tail': the tail end of the large section of land his family had once owned.

Tiger was constantly reminding people of his ancestry, his displacement and his exclusion. While Dave and Monica Buick thought Tiger had never experienced any racist stigmatisation, I was told that Tiger's standard response to taunts about being a black man was to lift up his shirt, point to his belly and call out, 'I'm not black, I'm custard!'

Mildred Willson remembered how Tiger said he was only 'one-sixteenth', a reference to the racist definitions of Aboriginality by a blood percentage, which was halved in each generation. In a community where a redhead was still called a blackfella, Tiger's retort reminded them of his family's continuing exclusion, no matter how fair they were.

After meeting Tiger, Tindale wrote in his journal that Tiger had 'deep set' eyes like his cousin Joe Seymour, but his features were 'more European, his skin colour fair, his hair practically straight and ... one time it was fair. As a child his eyes were blue.'[3]

But Dave Buick thought Tiger 'had all the features' of an Aborigine, the 'stubby nose and different setting in the face'. When I asked John if he thought Tiger 'was more of a Tasmanian than a Kangaroo Islander', he answered, 'I think he would be, yeah.'

Tiger also told people he was 'more of a Tasmanian'. When he got angry, he would say 'I've got my Tassie up.' It was because, Bruce Bates said, 'he was a Tasmanian native'.[4] When Tiger explained his anger to the people of Dudley as genetic, he reminded them they had deemed his family's genes unacceptable. If someone called him black, he called himself custard, but no doubt if someone called him custard then Tiger 'got his Tassie up' and proudly told them: 'I'm a blackfella.' Tiger was a master of subversion.

'He was a bad-tempered old cow,' Dave Buick said to me. Dave thought that what had also made Tiger particularly angry were his experiences of war and feelings of injustice that he went while others stayed at home. 'He called [us] all cold-footed and deserters,' Dave remembered. 'He used to lose his head and go cranky ... but we were only boys!' Dave was thirteen when the First World War broke out.

'Anyone that didn't go to war he called cold-footed,' Monica Buick explained. Keith Southlyn told me that Tiger would always ask people he 'didn't like': 'Where's your badge?' 'If you weren't a returned serviceman you weren't very big in Tiger's eyes,' Keith explained. Mildred Willson said specifically that Tiger 'couldn't tolerate the white boys here who didn't go to war'.

John McQuilton, in his book *Rural Australia and the Great War*, observes that in north-eastern Victoria 'almost two-thirds ... of the applications for exemption from the call-up came from farming communities', because farmers did not want to lose the labour of their sons. While McQuilton found that almost all these applications failed, he also observed how in the Exemption Court in Rutherglen, a usually 'severe' presiding Police Magistrate 'allowed class to govern his decisions' by exempting the son of a prominent local.[5] I have no idea if there were any such cases on Kangaroo Island, but if there were, they would further explain Tiger's anger.

Tiger was sent to the front twice, and saw the hells of France and Gallipoli. 'That was the big thing in his life,' said Roe Trethewey. But he returned to nothing: no house and almost no land. Instead he had to work for Dave Buick's father, who would pass on hundreds of acres to Dave. If Dave and all the other 'white boys' worked hard on the land, they had the opportunity to. They were able to marry and have large families, while Tiger remained a childless bachelor. They refused 'to be mixed in the abo race', taunted Tiger for his colour, and then told him his family lost their land because they didn't know how to farm.

Tiger was also treated differently as a soldier because of his Aboriginal ancestry. 'I think he found himself pretty labelled in the army,' Mildred Willson told me. He was put in the cook-house,

Dave Buick told me, because he was a 'darkie'. Dave thought Tiger had actually wanted to work in the cook-house because the trenches had 'scared' him. Dave explained that Tiger had 'told them he was of Aboriginal extraction, and they shifted him from the front-line'.

But Tiger told people in Dudley that he was treated unequally. He also told them how he rebelled against this treatment, and against the authority of the army. Roe Trethewey said that Tiger claimed to have fired only one shot from his rifle during the war – and then 'he put it straight up in the air and pulled the trigger'.

'Never fired a shot in anger' was one of Tiger's famous sayings. He 'wouldn't salute anyone if he didn't have to', Mildred Willson remembered. She and her brother Lindsay told me a story about Tiger's time in France, when he was sent to look for kerosene tins with two other soldiers. A 'pommie major came along', said Lindsay, but Tiger and his mates failed to salute. When asked why, Tiger answered, 'I wasn't looking for officers, I was looking for kerosene tins.' Dave Buick remembered Tiger joking that in the cook-house he made jam-rolly puddings using the bed-sheets from blown-out houses. John quoted Tiger: 'You didn't wash it or anything. The troops wouldn't know.'

Telling stories about the war was important to Tiger. Roe Trethewey told me there were 'two things' that were an 'obsession' with Tiger as he got older: being an Anzac and having an 'Aboriginal background'. Ironically, no two things had probably caused Tiger more pain. He had cried when sent to the front for a second time during the First World War, but back home he would save up all year for his annual trip to the Adelaide Anzac Day parade. His Aboriginal ancestry had caused his family's land loss and displacement, but he incorporated this loss into his Aboriginality and, most significantly, re-invested it back into the land.

'I've camped in every three-quarters of a mile of road in the Dudley district,' Tiger used to boast. He seems to have left an indelible mark wherever he went. The placenames and rituals he bequeathed continue to be recognised today. There are the places named after where he lived – 'Tiger's Hill' and 'Possum's Tail' – and the places he named to commemorate an event or situation. 'Stagger Juice Corner' is the place where Tiger and his yacca-

Tiger Simpson in uniform, Penneshaw, c. 1915. The Penneshaw Folk Museum

Tiger Simpson trapping wallabies at Cape Hart, c. 1950. The Penneshaw Folk Museum

gumming gang opened a keg and shared a drink. 'Tiger's Knob' is a cairn Tiger built near Pelican Lagoon to celebrate the end of the First World War.[6] When the road between sections 120 and 459 was cleared, Tiger named it 'Jews' Highway' because he considered the contractors mean with money. The name continues to be used even on modern government maps of Dudley. A bend midway between Penneshaw and Kingscote on the East–West Highway where Tiger once found a felt hat is named 'Felt Hat Corner'. The spot is marked by a signpost, usually with a hat nailed to it.

When Tiger did stonemasonry or cement work, he always engraved his name in it. As far away as American River, west of Dudley, I found 'Tiger' chiselled in large letters on one of the stones above the dining room of Linnett's Resort. Today, those aware of the tradition write 'Tiger' in newly laid concrete. When

Felt Hat Corner on the East–West Highway, between Penneshaw and Kingscote. Tiger Simpson gave the corner its name after he found a hat there. I was told that someone always ensures there is a hat nailed to the sign. Rebe Taylor, 1994

I spoke to Keith Southlyn, he said that the Penneshaw Golf Club had 'just done some cementing and sure enough there is Tiger's name etched in the cement again'. Tiger's name can also be found in the boat-ramp of Christmas Cove, in the pub veranda and even on the cement covering his grave.

Tiger has become a Dudley legend. He is the final chapter in the chronicle of remnants known only to the 'true' Kangaroo Islanders. His placenames and catchphrases help to make up the language and knowledge that set the dyed-in-the-blood Dudley locals apart from the mere residents. They remember his war stories. They laugh at his punch-lines and at the sharpness of his commentary. 'He had some funny old sayings,' Roe Trethewey told me. They were 'weird and wonderful', Thelma Buick thought.

The locals imitated his voice with a uniform booming bass. 'Never fired a shot in anger,' Roe Trethewey sang out. 'When are you goin' out?' called Bruce Bates. Like Bruce's demonstration of Nat Thomas's 'menacing, shivery kind of voice', Tiger's voice is echoing in the homes of the colonial descendants. Through Tiger they remember his grandfather's antagonism towards the 'official' settlers; by imitating him they also reaffirm their legitimacy.

When the colonial descendants pass 'Possum's Tail' or write 'Tiger' in cement, they are carrying out the same process of signification as when they pass through Lubra Creek or 'The Aboriginal'. Indeed, the way they remember Tiger as blackfella has shaped how they remember these places; they have become images of loss through his self-identification with loss. Tiger demonstrated his ancestry; it is in his image that the 'detribalised' image is constructed, much like that of the vagrant Aboriginal women wandering the island in search of rations. He exposes the 'lack of training in the first place', as Mildred Willson put it.

Dudley people were fond of Tiger. 'No family would ever have looked down on him,' Mildred told me. 'Everybody liked him.' When Tiger was close to death, Roe Trethewey took him to the island's only hospital in Kingscote, and Bruce Bates said he went to visit him there. Tiger had already made several visits to the hospital when he was older, simply walking in and getting into one of the beds. He knew that his old friend Thelma Buick, by then the nursing sister, would look after him. Thelma told me she even bought him new pyjamas, and she was with him when he died.

Thelma Buick and Roe Trethewey were particularly close to him, and both wanted to place on record their memories of his intelligence, kindness and sober times.

'Could Tiger be misrepresented?' I asked Roe Trethewey.

'Oh, quite easily I should say, yes,' he answered.

'How would you like Tiger to be remembered?' I asked Thelma.

'I'd like to see something in Penneshaw ... perhaps a little plaque or something,' she told me.

Tiger was not, I was also instructed, to be described as either derelict or violent. The colonial descendant who had described Tiger as 'violent' in an interview wrote to me later: 'We have a problem with Tiger.' He said that he had spoken to some of the people who knew Tiger well and they would prefer not to have him remembered as a violent man.[7]

But Tiger's anger cannot be hidden – it is remembered in his nickname. It is an integral part of the Aboriginal identity he constructed. Tiger 'wanted to be remembered', Roe Trethewey told me; it was his 'greatest ambition'. He wanted to be remembered as an Aborigine and an Anzac; his anger shaped these identities as he protested against the racial prejudice he had experienced at war and at home.

Dave Buick thought Tiger's Aboriginal ancestry 'carried out more' in him than it did in the rest of his family because 'he didn't like us *really*. He knew he was abo and he had it, *really* had it. He seemed to resent it in his own mind that he had it.' Dave not only interpreted Tiger's Aboriginality as a fate he resented, but also saw his anger as quintessentially Aboriginal.

Bruce Bates told me, 'He was Aboriginal, but I think ... he inherited [his anger] from his white ancestors.' Bruce was thinking of Nat Thomas's famously ferocious temperament, as demonstrated in the story of the snares. But Tiger reminded them of his Aboriginal ancestors with his threat 'I'll get my Tassie up.'

Tiger was an Aboriginal man who constructed his own Aboriginal identity. That it was in part a self-portrait of failure shows how contradictory it is to use this identity to deny that his family was excluded from marriage. But to the Dudley colonial descendants, Tiger's failure must be an innate Aboriginal trait. To remember Tiger as violent, however, is to remember that he had good reason to be angry: he failed because his family was racially excluded. So I was not to present Tiger as violent. I was to use only the verbose, exuberant, happy-go-walkabout images of Tiger that signify a naturally impeded, fringe-dwelling and landless Aboriginality, not a once-landed and excluded Aboriginality.

These withdrawals are, nonetheless, the chinks through which the Aboriginal descendants' exclusion is revealed. The colonial descendants want to sweep the Aboriginal history up into a time long ago; put it safely in a plaque or museum display and call it the 'distant past'. But they also want to remember the funny stories, placenames and rituals bequeathed by Tiger and his ancestors. For these are testimony to the colonial descendants' entrenchment in

Kangaroo Island history, their consistent engagement with and ownership of the land.

If these remnants are also evidence of the Aboriginal descendants' entrenchment and ownership, this contradiction is concealed in the reconstruction of their identity and history. In the colonial retelling, the Aboriginal descendants' history has become a story of generic failure and unfortunate loss. As Agnes Marshall told me: 'Nobody feels guilty about anything.'

This history of the Aboriginal Tasmanians of Kangaroo Island, however, is as alive as the land in which it is invested. While the places continue to exist, while the threads can be found and the layers beneath exposed, their history remains a record of exclusion.

Identity

Memory

In Dudley a name can ring up a five-generation genealogy with the speed of a cash register. While Mavis Golder struggled to name all her uncles, aunts and cousins, the colonial descendants knew her forebears' nicknames, where they lived and who they worked for. 'Everyone knew everyone,' Monica Buick explained.

I asked Agnes Marshall if this included everyone's histories.

'Oh, yes!' she laughed, 'right back to their great-grandparents!'

'So there weren't many secrets?' I asked.

'No!' she exclaimed.

There were no strange faces, even in Kingscote. For Dudley colonial descendants, the history of your family is a history of your community. Those who can claim a part in that history form an exclusive group within the present community in Dudley. Only they can call themselves 'true' Kangaroo Islanders.

Fiona Marshall: 'To call yourself a Kangaroo Islander implies that you [are] . . . from a long-established family on the island.'

Robin Marshall: 'In my case I feel that way because maybe we are still working some of the land that was taken up before it was ever surveyed.'

Margaret Southlyn explained to me that there are two historically divided groups within Dudley, the 'locals' and the '*local* locals': those who live in Dudley and those who have '*always*' lived in Dudley. Margaret admitted that the *local* locals are a difficult group to penetrate. They share a collective memory of rituals, placenames and stories born from generations of owning land in

Dudley. From the land comes a language of memory; speaking it is an act of identification.[1]

It is also an act of appropriation. When I asked her how it was that people knew to write 'Tiger' in newly laid concrete, Margaret explained, 'You'd have to be a *local* local to know.' Only *local* locals could tell me why the Simpsons lost all their land; a history of exclusion has become part of an exclusive identity. While the Aboriginal descendants' history is part of the '*local* local' identity, the later generations of Aboriginal descendants do not share it. They are not even locals.

Pigs Head Flat

In the pre-1836 days, when KI was inhabited by all sorts of runaway sailors and escaped convicts with their Aboriginal wives, George Bates ... and Nat Thomas were living at Antechamber Bay. They heard that there was a ship anchored in Nepean Bay, probably to get salt and trade for wallaby and kangaroo skins, so it was decided that George would walk to where Kingscote now stands and trade for whatever they needed, particularly nails and tobacco. The tobacco was for Nat Thomas, and he was keen to get some – he was probably running short.

George had done his trading and was well on his way home, and had in fact reached Pigs Head Flat on his walk through the scrub, when he remembered he had not brought Nat's tobacco. He knew that Nat, who could be a bit violent at times, would be very nasty if he didn't get his tobacco, so he decided to leave the nails under a tree on the flat which he marked with an old pig's skull which he found there. After walking all the way back for the tobacco, he searched and searched for the nails, and was never able to find them. But the spot from that time on was always called Pigs Head Flat.

Bruce Bates told me this tale on the same winter's day in 1993 when he read the story about his grandfather and Nat Thomas's wallaby snares. In that story Bruce remembered Nat Thomas's frightening behaviour and imitated his shivery voice. In the story of Pigs Head

Flat, Nat is again remembered for his bad temper. This story is also part of Bruce's inheritance – Bruce now owns Pigs Head Flat, which has been handed down from his great-grandfather. The story of Pigs Head Flat is well known to the other colonial descendants, and the council has put up a sign near the flat with the name 'Pigs Head Corner'. But Bruce has written the story down, and he could also tell me what he called its 'sequel'.

'My father and I were digging a strainer-post hole on this flat,' he said, 'and a few inches under the surface we found a mass of rusty iron, and in the middle of it we found a couple of undamaged, hand-made, wrought-iron, three-inch nails . . . I still have the nails in my possession.'

Bruce showed them to me; they were hanging on display in his shed, with a paper tag attached stating that they were George Bates's lost nails.

Earthed in the land, the buried nails of the Pigs Head Flat story confirm the notion that land secretes memory. Finding the nails brought the story to life, just as working on land owned for four or five generations brings the colonial descendants' history to life. The reality of work meets the mythology of the past; the mundane blends with the memorial.

History is the death of memory, theorist Pierre Nora claims. While memory is spontaneous and unconscious, history is critical and reconstructed.[2] For the colonial descendants, working their ancestors' land is predominantly an unconscious interaction with the past. In that context they are living, as Nora defines it, 'within memory'. If such an existence were total, then:

> Each gesture, down to the most everyday, would be experienced as the ritual repetition of a timeless practice in a primordial identification of act and meaning. With the appearance of the trace . . . of distance, we are not in the realm of true memory but of history.[3]

For Bruce Bates, going into his shed is an act of 'true memory', but telling me about it is not. While Bruce will go in there daily without thinking about his ancestors, my presence as visiting historian introduces a distancing 'trace'. Similarly, the colonial descendants drive past Pigs Head Corner without considering its history, but at one stage they decided to memorialise its story by erecting a signpost. Could it be that, left totally 'alone', without visiting historians, tourists or even 'locals', the colonial descendants would be a 'people of memory', similar to Nora's example of the Jews?[4]

The question is immaterial. For, while the story of Pigs Head Flat is contained in the colonial descendants' land, it pre-dates their arrival; it tells of the 'pre-1836 days'. While they tell the story to remember their narrative of continual habitation, it is also a reminder that they were not there first. This contradiction is resolved in the land: Pigs Head Flat is both a historical site and part of a working farm. While the colonial descendants consciously memorialise the 'pre-1836' history, they also work the land unconscious of its history. From this work comes the honest belief that the 'pre-1836' history has become theirs to tell.

This belief stems from walking in two worlds: the world of constructed linear history, of signposts and museums, and the world of digging post-strainer holes on their ancestors' land. The colonial descendants are not totally 'within memory', nor are they totally 'within history'. If the Bateses were to sell their land and leave the area, ultimately they would have only their history, which, as Nora points out 'belongs to everyone and no one', a mere share in a public asset. Memory, on the other hand, Nora explains, 'is blind to all but the group it binds'.[5]

The colonial descendants are aware of the role land plays in sustaining this balance between history and memory. Robin Marshall feels like a 'Kangaroo Islander' because his family is 'still working some of the land that was taken up before it was ever surveyed'. In her family history manuscript, Jayne Bates writes that she endeavoured to write 'not a history of the people' but a history of 'the land the family have farmed since first arriving at Hog Bay'. The people only appear because their lives 'have been interwoven with the land'. Jayne continues:

I hope to make the reader of these pages, particularly my children, appreciate the land. The value is not its financial worth, or the amount of production it is capable of, but the fact that five generations of the same family have survived because of it . . . It is the only enduring link we have with our forebears. It gives us a sense of belonging and continuity.[6]

The land provides history – the 'enduring link', the narrative of progress, of pioneering hardships and success – but it also provides memory, the 'sense of belonging and continuity'. It provides the pre-1836 stories that demonstrate the success of that 'enduring link'. Therefore, with land as the buffer, the polarities of history and memory can co-exist. Memory can indeed 'crystallise', as Nora calls it, into history, but it can also exist in a fluid, dynamic form.[7] The buried nails of Pigs Head Flat are a crystallised memory in that they are part of a myth, but their material presence brings the memory to life. As the land is living and growing, so too is the identity of the colonial descendants.

Michael Golder

When young Michael Golder found out that his great-great-grandmother was the same Mrs Seymour whom the *Australian Junior Encyclopaedia* described as the 'Last Tasmanian', he thought that she 'must have been a princess'. But he was disappointed when he went to look for remnants of this fantastic past within his family and home. He noticed that his great-aunt Mary Abell (née Seymour) had a 'darker complexion' and 'almost Aboriginal features'. He remembered seeing some hand-woven baskets in his grandmother's house that looked vaguely 'Aboriginal', but he supposed 'my grandmother might have bought them at the East End Market'. His discovery, Michael concluded, 'didn't change anything, because I couldn't find anything'.

Even the stories his grandmother told him about his ancestors on Kangaroo Island, now half-forgotten, made no sense in his home in Kingscote. 'I still can't recall . . . if [my grandmother] was talking about her father or her grandfather; someone who went to the mainland in a boat . . . came back and was carrying a keg of nails and must have had a heart attack in the sand-dunes . . . and they went looking for him and found him with a keg of nails lying alongside him.'

This seems to be the keg of nails from the Pigs Head Flat story, mixed up with the story of the death of Nat Thomas's son-in-law, William Seymour, in the sand-dunes of Antechamber Bay. But it was Fiona Marshall who told me that when Mary Seymour heard her husband had died, all she said was: 'Trust the old bugger to die there!' This, Fiona explained, was evidence of the popularly held belief that William had been a lazy sod while Mary had been a true battler who, after his death, continued to live and farm alone at Antechamber Bay with three small children.

While Michael was imagining his great-great-grandmother as a princess of a lost Tasmanian tribe, the colonial descendants were remembering her as a hard-working woman with a sardonic sense of humour and a lazy husband. Michael did not know where Pigs Head Flat was, but through its story the colonial descendants remember his great-great-great-grandfather's violent temper. They know Michael's ancestors as they know their land.

Beyond the details, the colonial descendants realise that knowing the intricate details of old Kangaroo Island history defines their identity. For Michael, however, the stories are merely something his grandmother once told him. His Aboriginal, pre-colonial Kangaroo Island ancestry is abstract, only tangentially relevant to his personal interest in history.

'It's no different to finding out your great-great-great-grand-mother was Welsh or Finnish or whatever else,' he told me, 'except to the extent that it does make me feel a little closer to where I live. If I was to find out that she was a North American Indian, I would probably feel closer to Arizona than I do right now.'

Michael is right; blood carries fewer memories than land. His ancestry makes him feel 'a little closer', only not to Antechamber Bay or the land Nat Thomas once owned, but to Kangaroo Island and Tasmania. He says he is no less interested in the history of his father's family, who are descendants of a Tasmanian convict. Because Michael cannot find 'any *thing*', cannot feel or touch his Aboriginality, it is as if it were not there. And how do you iden-tify with a numbness, with a lack of identity?

Mavis Golder[†]

When I first met Mavis in 1993, one of the first things she said to me was how sorry she was she did not know more about her Aboriginal history. She was sorry that she did not have more to show, not even dark skin. 'I only wish I had known,' she said. 'I could have asked such a lot of questions.'

'Do you know why you weren't told?' I asked Mavis.

'I think that it was the mode of the day,' she answered. 'People were, I wouldn't say ashamed of, but ... they didn't like to talk about somebody, their background, an Aboriginal ... I don't know why ... and of course I didn't ask. I didn't ask any questions even about my grandfather. I just went on living and didn't think to ask any questions. I wish I had.'

When I asked Mavis if she knew her grandfather well, she answered, 'Grandfather Seymour? Oh, I loved him, I loved him, I didn't even notice that his skin was dark. It wasn't *that* dark, it was olive.'

Mavis's love for her grandfather, Joe Seymour, and her apparent inability to notice his dark skin seemed to run close together. Pointing to her grandfather's picture – the one used in the 1954 *Walkabout* article – she said, 'You can see the likeness there to an Aboriginal, and the older he got – I didn't notice it when I was young, I just loved him.'

'But you weren't looking?' I asked.

'No, I wasn't looking,' Mavis answered, 'and my mother never told me.' Mavis said she was 'never, ever told'. 'I don't know what people thought about dark people in those days,' Mavis explained, 'but I couldn't pick it, otherwise I might have asked something.'

'Didn't she know she had Aboriginal blood?' Monica Buick exclaimed when I told her that Mavis had not been told about her Aboriginal ancestry. 'Oh, goodness me!' Monica paused, then concluded, 'I suppose it never hit her.' Agnes Marshall was also at first surprised, then reasoned, 'I suppose people didn't really care about it.'

[†] Mavis Golder passed away before she could read the following account, but her sons have read it, and have given their support for it to be published.

Mavis Harry as a little girl.
Courtesy of the Golder family

Mavis Harry in 1942. On the back was written 'Yours very lovingly, Mavis': Les Golder carried this photo in his wallet throughout World War Two.
Courtesy of the Golder family

When I asked Roe Trethewey if it surprised him that Mavis didn't know, he answered, 'No, it doesn't, because I think ... they were brought up as white people in a white community and there was no other Aboriginal people on Kangaroo Island so that they could hardly realise they were different from anyone else.'

Monica Buick went on to compare Mavis's situation with that of Mrs Howard: 'Like Old Mrs Howard, she was Mauritius, or half-caste Mauritius ... She wasn't Aboriginal, but she was very dark. Of course, nobody here took any notice, she was just like everybody else, but my mother said when she'd go to Adelaide and she might meet Mrs Howard in the street and talk to her, everybody used to turn around and look at her, talking to this dark woman, because you never saw them in those days. You wouldn't associate with them!'

This was testimony enough for Monica that there was no racism in the Dudley community. It makes ignorance the measure of acceptance. But Mrs Howard's daughter, Mildred Willson, told me that she and her sisters were never dated by the local boys. According to Bruce Bates, the family's 'Negro background', as he described it, caused 'a certain stand-offishness' in the community. For fear of offending the Howard family, Bruce even declined to name them in this context.

'It's a far bigger issue than what it used to be,' Roe Trethewey told me. 'Bit like Cathy Freeman running around with an Aboriginal flag ... There [was a] time when people with Aboriginal blood tried to disguise the fact. Nowadays it's just the opposite, isn't it?'

'Do you think ... Joe Seymour tried to disguise that fact?' I asked.

Mrs Mavis Golder in the late 1950s.
Courtesy of the Golder family

'He couldn't very well if you had seen him!' said Roe, laughing.

'He didn't speak about it?' I asked.

'Well ... I knew him very well ... and he never spoke about that to me,' Roe replied. 'He wasn't concerned about that, I don't think, he didn't consider himself to be any different from anyone else. The fact that he had Aboriginal blood in him probably never even occurred to him much.'

Though he could never 'disguise' his Aboriginal looks – Bruce Bates remembered he 'had a very strong Aboriginal appearance' – Joe supposedly never thought about his Aboriginal 'blood'. Perhaps it 'occurred' to him, though, when he was called 'Old Black Joe', or when Ernestine Hill interviewed him as 'the last half-caste Tasmanian', or when Norman Tindale asked him to show him where his grandmother was buried. When Mavis emphasised that she had never noticed how dark he was, it seemed that to remember him as different would have been to discriminate against him.

I pointed out to Mavis that Joe's mother would have spoken a different language and had a different culture. I asked, 'You don't think he inherited it and showed it at all?'

'No, no, no, nothing,' Mavis insisted. She said her grandfather was 'just part of normal Penneshaw life', and so were her mother and her Auntie Mary. 'I don't think there was any discrimination,' she said. 'I don't think it was even mentioned . . . in Penneshaw, because my mother was a good tennis player, in fact she held the championship of the island for many years. Well, they joined in with everything exactly the same as everybody else, and there was nothing different about them. Of course, my mother was fair-skinned, but Auntie Mary was absolutely *loved* in Penneshaw. If you're going to John and Monica Buick, you ask Monica about my Auntie Mary, and she'll soon tell you that she was absolutely loved.'

Monica Buick did remember Mavis's aunt and mother very well. Many people in Penneshaw and Kingscote remembered the sisters fondly. Mary Abell taught Bruce Bates at Sunday school, and she played the organ in the church and piano at the local dances. But while Mavis's mother was 'of course . . . fair skinned', her Aunt Mary was 'absolutely *loved*'. It seems the emphasis was necessary because she was darker. It had to be emphasised that

Penneshaw Tennis Club, probably in the 1920s; Mary Abell is in the back row on the far left. Courtesy of the Golder family

Mary Abell, second from right, at the Country Women's Association's twenty-first birthday, Kingscote, 1961. Courtesy of the Golder family

nobody noticed and it never made any difference: they 'joined in', so there was 'no discrimination'. The sisters were 'brought up as white people,' Roe Trethewey had put it, suggesting that in fact they weren't white. While the fact that Mavis grew up not knowing about her Aboriginal ancestry seemed at first surprising to them, it was soon presented to me as proof of her family's acceptance in the community.

After Mavis had passed away in 1995, I went to see her husband, Les. He said he had 'heard things about the very dark past' relating to Mavis's family. He added, 'They might have been a bit, um, you-know-what in Penneshaw about it, but I couldn't say for sure.'

When I asked what exactly he meant, he said there was nothing in particular that he could put his finger on.

But earlier, when I had asked Mavis if she thought that by 'hiding' their Aboriginal ancestry her family was protecting her she answered, 'Maybe ... in those days Aboriginals were thought of in a different way than they are today. That's why my mother didn't tell me, I'm sure.' Mavis thought this 'was a shame,' but she added: 'In those days they wouldn't think it was a shame, because they just wanted to live normally.'

I asked if they would have had to hide their Aboriginal ancestry in order to 'live normally' in Penneshaw.

'They were a very tight-knit community in Penneshaw,' was her careful answer.

Mavis had said she remembered her mother speaking with anger about how Mary Seymour was treated by the storekeeper. 'People didn't worry about whether she was the first or anything in those days,' Mavis had said. 'They weren't given the opportunities of, perhaps if you was a Buick or a Willson,' she had also said, referring perhaps more broadly to her whole family.

But Mavis repeated emphatically that her grandfather, mother and aunt were accepted as equals in the Dudley community. She even said at one point, 'I think it was only themselves who thought it was bit of a stigma.'

'I don't think there was any discrimination,' Mavis repeated to me, 'even [towards] my grandfather, whose skin I noticed after I was told ... was a little bit olive'. At first I did not hear anything different from other, similar statements Mavis had made. Then, later, I reread her words: 'whose skin I noticed *after I was told*'. Joe Seymour had died in 1945. Mavis did not read the *Walkabout* article until 1954. Did Mavis in fact know something about her Aboriginal ancestry before then? What did she know, and how?

Mavis's second son, Larry Golder, whom I met in Adelaide in 1998, thought his mother 'must have' known about her Aboriginal ancestry. Looking at the photograph of his great-grandfather Joe used for Ernestine Hill's *Walkabout* article in 1954, Larry said to me: 'I look at that now; how in the hell could Mavis not know?'

Larry said he 'always used to notice' how his great-aunt Mary 'had dark skin' when he was a child. He told me that he remembers 'lying in bed one night and it was just going through my mind – how come Auntie Mary looks like an abo, and yet she's Nanna's sister? ... I must have been at most seven years old, and if it occurred to me ... at the age of seven, surely at some stage Mavis must have asked the same question of herself.'

Mary Abell (left) and Annie Harry (right) with a friend in Kingscote.
Courtesy of Brentley Golder and his partner, who wrote to me that
'Mary certainly looks darker in skin colour than her sister'

Larry thought he had once asked his older brother Michael why Auntie Mary was so dark, and that Michael had said 'something along the lines of all that throwback stuff – you know, when you get white people and black people marrying and every now and again, two or three or four generations you'd get a throwback – that was the popular phrase in those days.'

Larry also remembers his mother taking him to the doctor when he was suffering conjunctivitis for the third time in a year. The doctor said to his mother that it was 'a very common complaint with Aboriginals'. 'The way he said it,' Larry explained to me, 'he knew that she knew ... and she didn't argue about it.'

On another occasion Larry was getting ready to go fishing after school with a mate. His mate waited impatiently while Larry took off his shoes – a long-standing summer habit.

His mate then said to Larry, 'You're always taking your bloody shoes off, it must be the abo in you.'

Larry, astonished, asked, 'What are you talking about?'

His mate replied, 'Well, it's the abo come out in you.'

Larry asked again what he meant, and his mate said, 'Well, you've got abo blood in you, everyone knows that.'

'I didn't want to appear ignorant,' Larry told me, 'so I said, "Oh, yeah . . . I knew that."'

I told Larry that Les, his father, had remembered Joe Seymour coming to visit them, and had described Joe as 'a real gentleman', and a 'very nice old fella'. When I asked if he had noticed that Joe was dark, Les had said, 'Oh, I believe I did, but I never put any significance to it.' He explained that a lot of people looked dark in those days from the work they did out in the sun.

Larry just laughed at this. We also talked about the way Mavis had emphasised how Aunt Mary was 'absolutely *loved*', and 'joined in' with everything in Penneshaw. Larry said that his mother had said that 'all the time' because 'she was very strong with the family'.

When I told him how the people in Penneshaw also echoed this sentiment, Larry said, 'It's like they protest too much . . . I just wonder why they would go to such lengths to stress what a lovely lady she was.' Larry also thought his great-aunt Mary was 'a lovely old lady' and 'a respected citizen' and that 'no one put shit on her or anything like that'. But he added that she 'wasn't like Annie', her sister. Saying almost the opposite of his mother, Larry thought that Mary 'was never in the crowd . . . My recollections of her in my childhood [are that] she wasn't in the CWA [Country Women's Association] . . . She did a few things with Annie . . . She played the organ and church now and again . . . but she was very much a loner.'

Larry thought this was because Mary 'was really freaked out by the fact everyone must have known that she was a bloody abo. I mean she just obviously looked like it.'

Larry remembers how when Mavis was ill, Mary would come and stay and 'get us out of bed in the morning and get us off to school and cook breakfast for us'. She 'sort of took over the role of being mother', Larry said. But he also said that 'she was a very stern mother' and 'was very hard, which, now I look back, was just the way those people of her generation were'.

She was tough enough to decide against having children for fear that they too might be stigmatised. Larry's younger brother, Brentley, thought that Annie, his grandmother, was also 'a fairly hard sort of woman' who 'obviously had a hard upbringing'. He had also been told that his great-grandfather Joe was 'a bit of a hard one'.

Larry said that 'apparently' Joe 'was a bit of a bloody piss-pot. Apparently he used to go down to the pub and get absolutely smashed and come home quite aggressive.' Brentley said that Annie 'left Penneshaw never to return . . . She . . . even never went around there to visit.' Mary visited her in Kingscote, and eventually came to live with her. There was perhaps a hardness to Joe Seymour and his daughters that was both the cause and the result of a stoic silence.

Mavis had apparently respected a tacit agreement in her family that their Aboriginal ancestry would go unmentioned and unexplained. 'There's skeletons in the closet,' Larry said, 'and I get the feeling that the whole thing just wasn't discussed between Annie and Mary and Mavis . . . It was never discussed.' Brentley thought his grandmother Annie 'was not the kind of person who would have spoken to anyone about it' and agreed 'it was never discussed', not 'any sort of aspect of it' while she and his Aunt Mary were alive. This was how they survived the stigma of being of Aboriginal descent in a small town where 'everyone knew everyone'.

In 1993 Michael Golder described his mother as still being 'less secure' than he was about their ancestry. Mavis had said that she 'was horrified that they had the names wrong' in the 1954 *Walkabout* article that identified her Grandfather Joe and Aunt Mary as 'Tom Simpson', the 'well known . . . last Tasmanian half-caste of Kangaroo Island', and his daughter. She said she wasn't horrified about the Aboriginal Tasmanian reference because she 'didn't take it in'. Mavis said she did not 'take it in' until the late 1970s, when Michael did his archival research into their genealogy. Then, Mavis said, 'there was no way I wanted to push it under the carpet. I wanted more and more and more.'

But it had taken Mavis almost thirty years before she felt she could speak about it openly even with her family. 'Looking back on it now,' Larry said, 'I can only think that . . . Mavis must have known about it . . . In the forties and fifties I think she probably stuck her head in the sand because she was frightened there was going to be stigma.'

Perhaps the 1954 article was the first time Mavis saw written down what had lain under the surface of everyday social and family life. Mavis said the fact the names were wrong 'shocked' her. Or perhaps what shocked her was that the names were no longer relevant. There, on the printed page, her family had become significant, not for their names, lives and personalities, but for their blood, for being 'The Last Tasmanians'.

But it was not their blood that had been important to Mavis. She 'loved' her grandfather. 'He taught me how to reverse waltz,' she reminisced, 'and he sang "Waltz Around Again, Willie".' He played the violin well, and accompanied the local dances, as did Tiger Simpson, Annie, and also Mavis herself and her husband. Even her son Larry was a professional musician. It was an ancestral tradition Mavis was proud of.

Mavis also remembered how her grandfather told her: 'Never eat cucumbers, they're pigs' food', and how he would 'mix a little dry mustard on the side of his plate' with a drop of tea from his cup at every meal. 'Little silly things like that you remember, you know?' She had been left these 'silly' memories by her grandfather, but not the stories his mother and grandmother might have told him, nor a word of the language they spoke to each other. 'Michael always said to me, "Why didn't you ask your grandfather things?"' Mavis lamented. 'I believe his mother Mary used to sing songs to him, but I didn't know!' 'He was just Grandfather to me,' she added.

'How I would have taken it as a child I don't know,' she pondered. 'I don't think it would have made any difference.'

'What the hell is the difference what colour you are?' her husband Les chimed in.

'I don't think it made any difference whenever I heard it,' Mavis answered. 'I'm only sorry I didn't hear it earlier so I could have asked more questions.'

In 1937 Norman Tindale had written that Joe Seymour 'complained of loss of memory and it was difficult for him to talk for long on one subject, but it was felt that much could have been learned if time had permitted'. But time had not permitted, and Tindale had returned to Adelaide. From there he wrote to Tiger

Simpson saying that it was of 'great interest' to him that Tiger and Joe knew some of their grandmother's language. He was 'sorry' that he did 'not know of this earlier' so he could have written more down. 'We know very little about the language of the Tasmanian', he added with regret. Tindale asked Tiger to 'look me up' and 'have a yarn ... about your grandmother' if he was coming to Adelaide.[8] But Tiger did not look Tindale up, and no more of Betty's language was recorded.

Just as the people in Dudley pointed to the dark skin of Mavis's grandfather and aunt, but said they never noticed, so did Mavis. But it seemed to me that Mavis knew that the community had always 'noticed' they were of Aboriginal descent. The 1954 *Walkabout* article told her that the national media 'noticed' them too, and not because they played tennis or music. Mavis had lived on Kangaroo Island with people who had known her grand-father, her mother, her aunt and herself since she was a child. She had to live with the silence about her past ringing in her ears – with the tension of knowing why the silence had been created, and that it was also used as a marker of acceptance.

❧

Larry, Brentley and Michael Golder, Kingscote, 1962.
Courtesy of the Golder family

It is perhaps ironic that when Michael Golder started to research his family history, Norman Tindale's 1937 article proved one of his most important sources. There he read about his great-great-great-grandmother 'Betty, Polecat or Old Bet' and learnt her 'Hobart Town Speak' words. In December 1975 Michael wrote to Tindale, who was then in California, and asked him if he had any more detailed genealogical information about his family.

In his letter of reply, Tindale wrote that he was pleased to hear from Michael:

> I would be very happy to receive any notes that you are able to compile showing the following generations of people who have the blood of the Tasmanian people in their veins. The Tasmanians represent one of the most exciting and interesting peoples since they were the first inhabitants of the Australian part of the world and their nature shows wonderful light on the development of modern man. New researches that are going on suggest that they may have been in the Australian area for more than fifty thousand years.[9]

Tindale sent Michael a photocopy of his genealogies of the Seymours and Simpsons, after having added the words 'fullblood' and '1/4 caste' to 'make them clearer'. He also included the journal entries of the time he met Tiger Simpson and Joe Seymour on Kangaroo Island in 1936. So Mavis and Michael read Tindale's description of Joe as 'a man of perhaps 80 years of age' who showed 'severe traces of his Tasmanian ancestry':

> His nose is broad, his skin has a brown tinge, his ears are large and long, his jaw is massive, eyes brown and deep set while his beard is very [sic] and his hair moderately frizzy.[10]

Tindale did not send Michael the journal entries from his trip to Kangaroo Island six years earlier, when he was researching Kartan stone-tool sites. Then he saw Mavis's mother, Annie, in the street in Kingscote. He had been told that she was 'partly Tasmanian', so he noted her physical appearance. He guessed she was 'about 30–36 years of age', and thought 'her features are remarkably like those depicted by Perons artists'. (Péron's journal from Baudin's

1802 voyage, first published in 1807, included illustrations of
Aboriginal people in Van Diemen's Land.) Tindale continued his
description of Mavis's mother in his rough notes:

> The nose is relatively prominent, broad. In build she is short
> and stout but her legs whose lower extremities are very thin.
> Her skin is olivine and she has deeply waved very fine hair
> worn relatively short.

Arthur and Annie Harry, Kingscote, at about the time Tindale
noted Annie's Aboriginal looks from seeing her in the street.
Courtesy of the Golder family

'A local' even told Tindale what he thought was Annie's
genealogy, claiming that she was descended from a white man
called 'Seymour' and Bob Clark, who 'brought in some dark
blood', but the latter point is not true.[11]

While Annie had not spoken to her daughter of her
Tasmanian ancestry, I could read Tindale's notes in the South
Australian Museum, saying that her looks were reminiscent of the
people the French explorers drew in 1802. As well as learning that
Tindale saw 'severe traces' of Joe's 'Tasmanian ancestry', Michael

and his mother found out who in their family had been 'full-blood', 'half-' or 'quarter-caste', and were told that in their own 'veins' ran the blood of a people who had been in Australia for more than fifty thousand years, people who were 'exciting', 'interesting' and 'first inhabitants'.

Michael also showed his mother W. A. Cawthorne's 1853 article, in which Nat Thomas was described as a 'sailor, sealer, farmer and wild man'. He showed her Alexander Tolmer's journal, which claimed Nat and Betty's three children 'combined the intelligence of the white with the activity of the native', and also Basedow's 1914 obituary of Mary Seymour, 'Relic of the Lost Tasmanian Race'.

How did Mavis feel about all this? 'It certainly didn't worry me at all,' Mavis said to me. 'In fact, I suppose I more or less brought it all out in the open once I first heard about it.' This was no longer the 1950s; the 'mode of the day' had changed, and Mavis no longer had to 'push it under the carpet'. In the late 1970s and 1980s people generally became interested in their heritage. Many began to display their convict ancestry with pride, whereas previous generations hid it in shame. An Aboriginal ancestry also, for some, became a matter of pride. Perhaps the silence and oppression had distanced the history enough for it to be 'rediscovered' and reborn in a new context.

Mavis told me about the first time that she realised this. 'We was out on a picnic . . . and we met some new people . . . and they started to talk about it . . . and they said, "Oh, you're going to be famous, we're going to take your photo," and I said, "Whatever for?" and they said, "Well, you've come down from the first child born on Kangaroo Island," and . . . I thought, Oh, gee, I am somebody, and from then on I went on talking about it, and I wasn't ashamed of it, or it didn't worry me.'

Mavis realised that to 'new people' her history was not about whether her aunt or mother were 'accepted' in Penneshaw, about whether her grandfather was noticeably dark or whether the storekeeper ripped off her great-grandmother. It was about being 'first', about her having the longest antiquity. While Tindale wrote about being descended from the 'first inhabitants of the

Australian part of the world', Mavis was more proud about being descended of the first child born on Kangaroo Island. 'That's the start of everything, isn't it?' she had asked me. History, she realised, could be presented as a neat line dating back from herself and her sons to the 'beginning'.

How this 'beginning' might be imagined was also important to Mavis. One of the last things she said to me was that she wanted Nat to be remembered as 'an intelligent man'. Michael had also said Mavis wanted Nat to be 'given the benefit of the doubt'. His youngest brother, Brentley, remembered that, while the Aboriginal ancestry was kept 'fairly quiet' when he was a child, Nat Thomas was often talked about with pride.

Larry Golder said that after his mother became involved in the Pioneers Association in the 1980s, 'the main thing she used to talk about was what a successful farmer ... this Nat Thomas was'. He continued, 'I might not be correct, and I'd like to think I'm not ... but it's all part of the stigma thing. By going around and saying that Nat Thomas was this really decent, intelligent man who did this and did that ... what she is trying to do is apologise for the fact that he actually married a "black bitch".'

But Mavis had a way of expressing her pride for Betty as well. She told me that there were 'two kinds' of Aborigines: the aggressive types and the kind and gentle types. She claimed that she was descended of the latter.

'There you go,' said Larry when I told this to him. 'That's Mavis to a T, she was frightened shitless to think there was anything bad in her family; they were only beautiful, loving, charming ... people.' Larry later wrote to me and asked if I would include the following statement here, to make his meaning clearer: 'I'm only saying this about Mavis because I believe a lot of those "charming, loving, beautiful" European people over the years have tacitly forced her and other descendants of Nat and Betty into a "conspiracy of silence".'[12]

Mavis initially broke this silence by asserting that her ancestors were the 'first' on Kangaroo Island, and for this she did in fact become 'famous'. In 1984 she contacted the Kangaroo Island Pioneers Association, two years before their re-enactment of the landing of the South Australian Company. While many of the Association members are descended from Company settlers, they also thought Mavis's history was special and they made her their first patron. The local paper, the *Islander*, reported this event in an article headed 'Family's Unique Link with Island History'.[13] It was as a result of this article that a local suggested erecting a plaque on Mary Seymour's unmarked grave – the plaque that claimed she was 'the first white girl born on K Is'. Four years later, *Australian Geographic* interviewed Mavis as part of a feature on Kangaroo Island. 'I found out only a few years ago that I have Tasmanian Aborigine blood in me,' she was quoted as saying. 'I think that makes me a bit special, don't you?'[14]

Feeling special and accepted, Mavis used her involvement in the Pioneers Association to promote a more public representation of her history in Dudley. She asked the Dudley District Council that a street be named after Mary Seymour, to celebrate her being the 'first child born' on Kangaroo Island. Although the council declined this request, they did name a street after Nat Thomas. It was also at about this time that Fiona Marshall curated the new displays in the Penneshaw Museum on Nat Thomas – 'sailor, sealer, farmer and wildman' – as well as Mary Seymour and Hannah Simpson. The Penneshaw school began to teach its pupils about the island's pre-colonial history, including the Aboriginal women and the men who brought them.

It was through the Pioneers Association that Mavis met her second cousin Adrian Waller and his son Neil properly for the first time. Together they organised two plaques to honour Nat Thomas: one to be placed in Penneshaw at the end of Nat Thomas Street, and one at his farm at Antechamber Bay. Two years later Neil Waller was the main force behind having a plaque erected near Betty's grave.

But when the bus with sixty Pioneers bumped along the dusty road to open the plaque at Antechamber Bay, there was no memorial to Betty by the roadside.

Adrian Waller told me how, on that day, Les Trethewey, a retired Dudley farmer, joined the Pioneers in Penneshaw for their journey. At the Penneshaw plaque opening, Les spoke about

Mavis and Adrian's uncle, Tiger Simpson, and on the bus Les continued to tell funny and entertaining stories about him. When the bus pulled up the steep hill out of Penneshaw, Les pointed out the place where Tiger had lived, and mentioned that the hill was named after him. While 'everyone' in Dudley remembered Tiger very well, Adrian had known him reasonably well, and Mavis had only ever vaguely known him.

Perhaps Mavis did not want to be outdone. After all, this was her day. When the bus passed the turn-off to Chapmans River, at the eastern end of Antechamber Bay, Mavis remembered what her son Michael had told her. She explained to everyone that her ancestor Betty was buried near by. She later told me that since then everyone in Dudley had talked about Betty's burial site as if they'd always known about it, even though she was the one to tell them. But they *had* always known about it. In Dudley, Mavis's history is not 'special'; it's just a part of the landscape.

∾

Some months after Mavis had opened the plaques in Dudley, the Adelaide *Advertiser* contacted her and asked if they could photograph and interview her at the Antechamber Bay plaque. Mavis agreed, and so she again stood by the Hills hoist on the back lawn near the spot where Nat Thomas is apparently buried. The interviewer asked her how she felt to be standing so close to the 'burial site' of her ancestor.

'I felt nothing,' Mavis told me. 'Nothing.'

Afterwards Mavis went back to the Antechamber Bay property several times to revisit the sites she knew. She stood near the graves of Nat Thomas and William Seymour. She looked at the few stones that are the remains of Mary Seymour's cottage and thought of her life there with a farm, three children and no husband. After this, Mavis told me, she found she could not 'help but feel an affiliation with the land'.

Mavis's affiliation had to be learnt. She did not inherit it along with generations of storytelling, as the colonial descendants did. She had inherited a fear of stigma; she had inherited her mother's and aunt's silence. But, however 'insecure' Mavis may still have felt about her family's exclusion, she had broken the silence of her Aboriginal past.

'Perhaps [her mother] didn't want her to know, or perhaps she took it for granted they were white,' Monica Buick said to me, then added, 'She's very proud of it now.'

'She's proud of it,' Mildred Willson also said. 'She's quite wonderful, really, the way she talks about it.'

'I think it's good that she's proud,' Agnes Marshall said. 'We were very proud when they decided to name our street Nat Thomas Street ... That was ... very fitting ... that he should be remembered.'

A member of the Pioneers Association remembered her first meeting with Mavis. She had asked Mavis when her people got to Kangaroo Island. '1819,' said Mavis, the year it is thought that Betty arrived. Surprised, the woman said to Mavis that her ancestors must have been Aboriginal. 'Yes!' said Mavis. 'She was very proud,' I was told.

In 1994, a year before she died, Mavis published a short auto-biography. Titled *Gentlemen . . . Take your Partners*, it focused on Mavis's life playing music for dances, both on the island and on the mainland. Mavis wrote:

> I feel as if I was almost brought up in a dance hall and lived half my life in one.
>
> . . . [M]usic and dance halls started with my grandfather playing violin. According to my mother he only had to hear a tune and would be able to play it straight away.
>
> I only wish I knew if any music was in the generation before that, because my great grandmother was a big part of history. She was the firstborn on Kangaroo Island, in 1833, being the daughter of whaler Nat Thomas and a Tasmanian aboriginal. That was the Penneshaw end of Kangaroo Island and my mother being also born in Penneshaw was playing for dances in the early 1900's.[15]

Several people I spoke to commented how brave it had been for Mavis to publish the fact that she was of Aboriginal descent. Then, when Mavis died, the front page of the *Islander* ran the heading

'Tribute to true Islander' with a photograph of her at her book launch. She was described as being 'proud of her heritage as a 5th generation Islander' and someone who 'took a great interest in the history of the Island'. The article recalled her involvement in the CWA, Lions Club, tennis and especially her music. On behalf of the Pioneers Association, Adrian Waller wrote that Mavis was a descendent of Nat Thomas and his Tasmanian Aboriginal 'wife', Betty.[16]

Mavis learnt to feel an affinity with the land where her ancestors lived. She learnt to talk about them, and to feel proud of them; she even came to wish that she had inherited their dark skin. She could do this because she felt secure in the interpretation of her family history as the 'start of everything' in Kangaroo Island's shared history. It made her special, but not separate from her community. It was a friendly challenge to the colonial descendants, reminding them that they were pre-dated by Mavis's family. But they had always known that. It was why they had placed Mavis's ancestors on the other side of their colonial frontier – on the side of the illegitimate. It was why they had excluded them.

Many of the colonial descendants claim that they never noticed Mavis's family was Aboriginal, and that was why Mavis grew up not knowing. If Mavis had never been bothered to ask, why did she give it so much attention when she realised she could be open about it without shame or stigma? Why were the Dudley residents so impressed by Mavis's ability to talk about it openly with pride? And why did they agree to name a street, curate new displays, mount new plaques and teach in their school a history supposedly so inconsequential?

The subsequent noise of celebration has made the initial silence all the more significant. But in the centre of the noise, a silence still reigned: Mavis did not want to discuss her family's exclusion. Nor did she want to assert a political Aboriginality. This would have been an alien idea, and radical too. One Dudley resident told me that 'anyone less than a half-caste' had 'no right to call themselves an Aborigine'. But Mavis's sons have emphasised the importance of having their mother's story told, including her reticence to challenge the local community. I hear Larry Golder's words: 'There's skeletons in the closet.'

Adrian Waller

In 1960, when Adrian Waller read Edward Bates's letter to the *Chronicle* and learnt that his Uncle Tiger was of Aboriginal Tasmanian descent, it was a moment of real surprise. But, he said to me, 'I had an inkling that I was involved. I knew that my grandmother was a Simpson, and as soon as I read the article I said, "Yes, I'm connected".' Adrian, now in his eighties, was born in Adelaide, where he has spent most of his life. But he lived on Kangaroo Island with his grandparents between the ages of three and thirteen. He told me he remembered going to visit his Aunt Annie Harry, Mavis's mother, in Kingscote, and seeing his other aunt, Mary Abell.

Adrian Waller, aged eleven months.
Courtesy of the Waller family

He said that to his knowledge Mary Abell was 'the only one who showed any colour, because I used to go around to Mrs Harry's and there used to be this dark lady there and I used to wonder who that dark lady was – I didn't know they were related.'

Seeing 'that dark lady' must have made a lasting impression on Adrian; reading Bates's letter forty years later confirmed an 'inkling'. But in 1960 Adrian, like Mavis, had put the question of his ancestry aside. The 'mode of the day' was not exclusive to Kangaroo Island. It was not until his son, Neil, did some archival

Adrian Waller with his parents, Norman and Grace.
Courtesy of the Waller family

research about twenty years later that Adrian learnt more about his history. In 1986 Adrian attended his first meeting of the Pioneers Association and presented his handwritten genealogy. This was two years after Mavis had been made patron, and it was the first time they realised they shared a common story.

But in the Pioneers Association their story was not about why an aunt was dark, or why she was not even known. The Pioneers Association is concerned with beginnings. The personal became academic; the immediate memories were subordinated to distant history. The year 1836 has become a marker in a debate about whose ancestors were chronologically on the 'right side'. The marker has become an anchor for insecurities, helping shape a new sense of identity. Just as Mavis had said that Mary Seymour's birth was 'the start of everything', Adrian told me, 'We go back to the very beginning. Nat Thomas was there in 1827 ... [and] ... Betty ... was there in about 1819 ... They were some of the earliest ... pioneers on the island'.

The Association's annual dinner is held on 27 July, the day the *Duke of York* arrived at Nepean Bay in 1836. But Adrian told me his ancestors 'were there to *meet* the *Duke of York*, so the South Australian Company were not the beginning by any means'.

If talk of beginnings was fundamental to Mavis's sense of security, Adrian could talk, and even joke, with me about how the colonial descendants had excluded his ancestors. When I went to interview him and Neil in their home, Adrian asked his wife, laughing: 'Would you have married me if you'd known I was part-Aboriginal?' Adrian later wrote several long and thoughtful letters in response to the interview transcripts and the drafts of my work that I sent him. In one such letter in 1994, he clearly stated his opinion on the question of his ancestors' marital exclusion:

> White women could pick and choose and therefore were not prepared to marry a half-caste or quarter-caste, consequently there were no children to hand property on to.

Adrian was also quick to agree that he grew up not knowing his genealogy because of the negative feelings about having an Aboriginal ancestry. 'If you were a pure-blood,' he said, meaning pure *white*, 'someone would be interested enough to make up a family tree.' He pointed to a family member who still felt that way: 'This cousin ... when she was told, only a few years ago ... she said, "I wouldn't shout that to the tree-tops," much to say, "I don't feel I would like people to know I have black blood in me."' Adrian ultimately saw the longer story of exclusion and loss that had led to his discovery reading the *Chronicle*. After I sent him a draft of this chapter in early 1998, he wrote to me: 'You make a big thing of memory or the loss of memory, but to me it doesn't mean a thing. All I know is history.'[17] He could not have put it more succinctly.

When we met again three months later, Adrian said the notion of 'losing memory' was still not clear to him. So I asked him what he knew of the land at Antechamber Bay. He said he knew only where the plaque was erected in front of Nat's house. I told him that this is what I meant by having lost memory.

He then realised. 'If they had been accepted,' he said, 'then ... it would have been like the colonial [descendants] ... They talk about their ancestors ... well, had they been accepted they may have talked about their ancestors too.'

Without the 'talk about the ancestors', the Aboriginal descendants were left with only the talk of beginnings and being first. Mavis spoke of these things because she felt too insecure to talk of anything else. But Adrian knew of nothing else. He did not live with the people who had grown up with his parents and grand-parents, the people who knew his ancestry. Adrian had lost even the harsh memory of fear that Mavis lived with – a memory that sustained the silence her ancestors had established.

Neil Waller

Neil has also been involved in the Pioneers Association, where he has been president since 1997. He assists in conserving significant sites and establishing new memorials relating to all areas of Kangaroo Island history. But Neil is particularly keen to have his ancestors recognised as pioneers too, and he is forthright about it.

'I don't mind stirring up a bit of political trouble,' he said to me. As a result of his lobbying, he says, there is now an informal but clear division in the association between those who recognise a 'pre-1836 beginning' and those who do not. Among the latter group, who once defined the association, are the descendants of the first official settlers to step onto the beach at Nepean Bay. Neil explained to me that they think 'the whole history goes back to 27th of July [1836] and that's it . . . Nothing happened before then.'

Neil is aware that the focus of both these groups has little relevance to the history of settlement in Dudley, or to the way Dudley people remember their past. When I asked him if he thought an 'aristocracy' of landowning colonial families still exists in Dudley, he immediately named the major families with a sardonic air, and observed that these families have not only dominated land ownership and the District Council, but also how his own history is represented.

The two plaques remembering Nat Thomas in Penneshaw and at Antechamber Bay were markers of his descendants' return. So too was the plaque erected to honour Betty's gravesite. But this plaque, organised primarily by Neil, offered a more direct political challenge. Neil gained support not only from the Dudley Council, but also from Department of State Aboriginal Affairs. It was erected in 1993, the International Year of the World's Indigenous People, a fact that was considered relevant to the application.

The plaque, fenced and mounted on a large granite rock, stands by the Cape Willoughby Road near the Chapmans River turn-off. Neil had chosen the site because it was closest to where Joe Seymour had told Norman Tindale that Betty was buried. Drivers can clearly see it and choose to stop and read it. Its text includes the words: 'while not always well treated, the Aboriginal companions of the pre-1836 settlers made a significant contribution to the early development of the island'.

Neil told me he wanted women like his ancestor Betty to be remembered in a 'positive' way. He gave as an example of their 'significant contribution' the fact that Kangaroo Islanders are still trapping wallabies in the way the women originally did. Bruce Bates had told me that his grandfather used to snare, and explained that trapping was something the Aboriginal women had passed on to the white men. But he also claimed that trapping 'was [a] traditional thing' in his family. A pre-colonial practice had become a colonial tradition. Robin Marshall said he grew up trapping wallabies too. He also told me that Betty's plaque was 'about two miles out'. He knew this because his father had told him where she was buried.

Neil does not trap wallabies; he erects plaques in the 'wrong' place. He has only textual references, not handed-down stories. The memorial to Betty is also a memorial to his inheritance: his outside-ness, his lack of lived tradition, his loss of knowledge. Just as when Mavis Golder stood at Antechamber Bay and felt 'nothing', just as Michael Golder couldn't find 'anything' to ground him to his Aboriginal ancestry, this lack is Neil's inheritance of exclusion, land loss and displacement. When he and his father speak of who the first settlers were, they inhabit their inheritance.

Ellen Marks

Ellen Marks is Mavis and Adrian's second cousin. Her mother was Mildred Chester, the daughter of Emma Barrett, 'the Aboriginal of "The Aboriginal"', as some remember her in Dudley. Ellen, who grew up in Adelaide, told me she knew that her mother came from Kangaroo Island and that she had spoken about Nat Thomas 'and that he was a sealer ... but that's all she told me'. But in recent years Ellen's son began 'pestering me to find out more about my lineage, so I thought I'd better look into that a bit more'. She said finding out more was 'difficult at first', but with her husband and daughter, who is a historian, they eventually found the books, articles and records that the Golders and Wallers had discovered before her. Slowly Ellen worked out that Betty was her great-great-grandmother.

Ellen not only followed the footsteps of Mavis and Adrian and their children through the same historical sources, but she decided to visit Kangaroo Island and went to Antechamber Bay. 'I decided to look up the house where Nat ... was living,' she explained. But the resident family was not at home, and Ellen and her husband 'didn't want to wander all over the place'. Anyway, she said, 'we weren't sure what we were looking for'. Ellen saw the big old fig tree, but not the inscription that Hannah Simpson had made. She stood near Nat's grave, but only unwittingly, and didn't see the plaque dedicated to him near the Hills hoist. 'Had they been home, they could have directed us to all these things.'

Ellen visited Mary Seymour's grave in the Penneshaw cemetery, but she didn't go to the eastern end of Hog Bay where her grandmother had lived and her mother had grown up. She didn't know where it was; there were no plaques or signs remembering 'The Aboriginal'.

'All I can remember', said Ellen of her grandmother, 'is her standing at the doorway of this house ... a tall thin woman ... She was standing in the doorway waving us goodbye.'

'I haven't got any stories to tell you,' Ellen later explained apologetically, 'because ... Mother didn't talk very much.'

Ellen had asked her mother to write down some of her memories before she died. That was when Mildred wrote of the Barretts' farm at Pigs Head Flat with its apple and almond trees, the cranberry bushes and also of the 'nice beach' near their home in Penneshaw where she and her brothers and sisters played and fished. But she didn't write that their house was on what was known as 'The Aboriginal'. Ellen said her mother had also told her some things about her grandmother, Mary Seymour; that 'she was a very very hard-working woman and she managed a farm'.

But did she mention their Aboriginal ancestry?

'No, no,' Ellen answered. 'I never really asked her directly,' she explained, '. . . I knew her mother was Emma and I didn't know much about her. It was just one of those things you just didn't talk about it, but . . . it all comes out in the wash.'

And how did she feel about it now it had 'come out in the wash'?

'I think it was great!' Ellen answered. She not only had written sources, but she had met previously unknown relatives. Ellen found Mavis Golder, who had 'oceans of stuff' about their family history to show her. Back in Adelaide, Ellen went to visit Adrian Waller, who gave her 'quite a bit of literature' as well. Ellen even attended a Pioneers Association dinner, although she did not become a member.

Learning about her Aboriginal ancestry, Ellen explained, has led her to give more considered thought to the history of Australian colonisation. She doesn't think it was 'right . . . the white people coming out here and thinking that they own the place . . . They're still not doing anything about it,' she added, 'not the ones that should.' Thinking of Betty and Nat Thomas, Ellen reflected how they had managed to 'fare' pretty well before the colonists arrived. 'I suppose they thought . . . they were as good as the others,' said Ellen, 'but evidently from the start they weren't, in the opinion of the colonials.'

When I left, I lent Ellen a copy of my Masters thesis to read before I went to Kangaroo Island. Two weeks later I went to see her again to pick it up. She gave me the following written statement as her response:

> Thank you Rebe for allowing me to read your thesis. It was most enlightening. I think I can now understand my Mother's reticence to talk about her history, although maybe she did not know herself of her family beginnings. I was amazed to read of the ostracism and downright meanness of a small group of colonials. Who were they to judge the culture and way of life of a people who had eked out a life, a very rough and a very tough existence for many years before their own arrivals.

To judge on colour and blood alone, where was their Christian ethics?

I enjoyed meeting you Rebe and only sorry I did not have more information for you.

Ellen understood why her mother would not talk about their ancestors. She saw how a history of 'ostracism' now meant apologising to me for not having 'any stories to tell me'.

∾

The last time I went to the island was in April 1998. I had lunch with Neil Waller, who has a cottage facing Nepean Bay, left to him by his great-uncle. It is around the corner from Mavis Golder's home, where her youngest son Brentley lives and still runs the ice-works established by his grandfather. Neil and I talked about what I had written about him – about the importance of 'beginnings' and his involvement with the Pioneers' Association.

'It doesn't matter who was here first,' he said, surprising me. 'I see myself . . . as a showman,' he explained of his involvement with the Pioneers Association, '. . . trying to keep the troops happy . . . and I don't mind being a bit mischievous . . . with the history'.

The next day we went together to Lubra Creek with Neil's nephew, Jamie O'Neill, and also with Mildred Willson. On the way we stopped and looked at the places where Neil and Jamie's family had lived, the small Waller farms near Kingscote. Mildred pointed out the cairn near Pelican Lagoon that Tiger Simpson built to celebrate the end of the First World War. At Antechamber Bay I directed them to the farmhouse, and then to Lubra Creek. Our memories and connections with the land were joined.

Neil had never been to Lubra Creek before. He was completely awe-struck; by the Aboriginal flint stones we picked up, the stories of the woman 'beaten for her troubles', and most of all by the sense of peace he felt there.

When Ellen had told me that she went to Antechamber Bay to see where Nat Thomas lived, I asked her, 'Did you have a sense you were somewhere special?'

'Yes,' she answered.

Adrian stood in the same place and saw the view Nat Thomas had once looked upon. He chose a beautiful spot, Adrian thought. Mavis could not 'help but feel an affiliation with the land'. Neil Waller learnt from a book where Betty was buried, but he went there and celebrated her memory with a plaque.

'It really doesn't matter where it is,' Neil had told me. 'It's the symbolic thing that's more important.' He stood at the crossing in Lubra Creek and felt at peace.

The descendants of Nat Thomas and Betty may have inherited a mere share in a public asset: pieces of paper, references in books, archival notes and a hand-made genealogy. But they have translated, transplanted these bits of paper into the land. They have returned.

Memory lost, a history unearthed. In the freshly turned earth, new memories are seeded. And the roots grow deep.

'How Aboriginal Am I?'

There are probably many descendants of Nat Thomas and Betty whom I have never met, and among them several who have no idea about their ancestry. But among those descendants I have met, there are many who have not returned to Antechamber Bay, or joined the Pioneers Association, or been a part of the push to erect plaques or name streets. How do they understand and identify with their history?

Mavis Golder's three sons grew up on Kangaroo Island, but have not been to Antechamber Bay; Steve Simpson's great-grandchildren and Tom Simpson's great-granddaughter, Terri Sanderson*, have never been to Kangaroo Island. But they have all given careful thought to their history, in particular to what it means to have an Aboriginal ancestry.

Larry Golder† said he first started thinking about his Aboriginal ancestry when he was 'six or seven', lying in bed wondering why his Aunt Mary looked 'like an abo'. He said he 'became *very* consciously aware of it' in his early teens, particularly after his friend said that going barefoot was 'the abo come out' in him. But it wasn't until Larry left Kangaroo Island in 1970 to live in Adelaide that he began to '*really*' think about what it meant to have an Aboriginal ancestry.

When I spoke to him, he still found it difficult to form a clear idea of what that means. 'I really don't know what to think,' he

---

† Larry Golder passed away suddenly in April 2002, just before the first edition of this book went to press.

told me. 'At many times in the last twenty years I've thought to myself, am I perturbed by this? Am I stigmatised by it? Do I feel ashamed of it? Do I feel proud of it? *What* do I *feel* about it? And it's probably one of the most elusive feelings I've ever had in my life. I don't know *what* to *feel* about it. I don't know whether to go and jump up and down and say, "I'm Aboriginal", or whether to say ... "my great-great-great-grandfather could have been a postman or the milkman for all I know".'

Larry's older brother Michael has veered towards the second opinion. 'To me your background is a whole jumble of things,' he said to me. If finding out who his great-great-great-grandmother was made him feel closer to Kangaroo Island, it was only because he had deliberately chosen to focus on that part of this family history. 'I do like to be identified with [it],' he admitted. But as someone 'generally interested in history', Michael said of his Aboriginal ancestry, 'I don't regard that as being important ... Where I come from wasn't just Nat and Betty [but] that whole fan, that whole spectrum ... there is nothing more or less important.'

Larry pondered this more academic summary of their history and said, 'If I really just wanted to be rational and objective about it ... I would have to say a similar thing to what Michael said: "Well, I was brought up as a white Caucasian and ... I was never taught anything about Aboriginal culture from my family."'

But for the last twenty years Larry has not been so 'objective'. He says that he has at times 'thought of myself as being an Aboriginal' and has told people so. Larry says their reactions can be 'funny' because they often 'really recoil'. 'A lot of people say, "You're joking, aren't you?" ... [or] "You're as white as driven snow, you've got no Aboriginal blood in you".' Larry said that even if he tells them he can trace his ancestry right back to the 1820s on Kangaroo Island, they still say, 'You're bullshitting me, you're not a bloody *abo*.' To this, Larry replies, 'I know I'm not a bloody *abo*; I've got Aboriginal *blood* in me.'

The difference is apparently significant; admitting to having some Aboriginal 'blood' means remembering one's genetic ancestry, but *being* an '*abo*' means embracing an identity with an agenda and beliefs somehow different from white society's. For, as

Larry went on to explain, 'They're just thinking, what is he getting at? Why is he saying this? Is he setting up something to get some land rights? Does he want to come and pinch my back yard? Was one of his tribal descendants bloody buried there or something?'

While Larry said that had often 'thought of' himself as 'being an Aboriginal', he wondered if in fact the thinking has made him so. 'I've often thought that maybe I've subconsciously tried to *make* myself Aboriginal,' Larry explained. He remembers how his friend saw his need to take off his shoes as the 'abo come out' in him. Looking down at his still-bare feet, Larry wondered at the significance of this, then added, 'I'm not a great believer in those sorts of traits being passed on down genes; I'm more nurture than nature.'

But Larry then thought about his life as a musician, working on the margins of mainstream society, and said: 'I don't want to get too personal about this, but I'm a bit of a failure, I'm a bit of an itinerant. I work really hard sometimes and then I sort of go walkabout ... I don't know if ... this is something I've trained to myself to do because I think, I've got Aboriginal blood in me maybe I should act a bit like a bloody Aboriginal ... [and] this is why am living in this beaten-up house – the gas has been cut off for two weeks.'

When I asked Larry where his toilet was, he said 'follow your nose'. Passing through the kitchen, I noticed that dirty plates were piled up. Larry said he hadn't done the washing up in about three years. I thought he was joking until I saw a weed growing through the sink plughole. The longstanding view that Aboriginal people are poor, itinerant and marginal has such power that being like that was in some way intrinsic to Larry's sense of connection to Betty: having Aboriginal ancestry gave sense to being a so-called 'failure'.

After we'd been talking for about half an hour, Terri Sanderson knocked on Larry's door, as arranged. Larry and Terri had never met before. Terri was born in Peterborough, north of Adelaide, and is descended from Tom Simpson, who left Kangaroo Island in about 1900. Her great-uncle was Horrie

Simpson, who was born in Kapunda in 1905 to Tom Simpson and Mary O'Leary.

Not only had Terri grown up totally unaware of her Aboriginal ancestry, but so had her father, and so, it seems, had Horrie. The family's Aboriginal ancestry came to light shortly before Horrie's death, when he decided to compile a genealogy. But Terri told me that when Horrie got to Nat Thomas, 'He stopped doing it. Just stopped dead . . . And then he said in a very brushing-aside sort of way, "Oh, you know, touch of the tar brush in the family . . . don't want to talk about that any more."'

Perhaps the idea of tracing his family history through Nat Thomas to England might have been acceptable to Horrie, but plunging into the abyss of two thousand generations of Aboriginal Tasmanians was frightening and undesirable, not to mention near-impossible. 'He couldn't cope with it at all,' Terri said, laughing. 'He had a really bad attitude.'

But Terri also respected her uncle's feelings. 'It wasn't until he died, because he had such strong feelings, that I went and pursued it and tried to find out more information,' she explained. Terri went to the South Australian Museum and was advised to talk to Philip Clarke, who has researched and published on the early history of Kangaroo Island, including the descendants of Nat Thomas and Betty.[1] He had a 'mountain of information', Terri said, and since 'no one knew anything' about her 'bit' of the genealogy, she said he was also 'quite pleased to meet with me'.

That was only two years before I met Terri. I asked her what it had been like learning that she had Aboriginal ancestry. 'Well, I had a bit of a panic,' she said to me. 'Two years ago I also turned forty. So I wasn't quite sure whether it was a forty thing or coming to terms with that.'

Reflecting, Terri said that there had in fact 'been a bit of an Aboriginal theme all through my life', from having a good Aboriginal friend at school to working with Aboriginal people and issues in her job with the South Australian government. She also told us that ever since she was young she had claimed she had 'Aboriginal legs' because of how they 'bow out'. 'It turns out I have!' Terri laughed.

The first time I had spoken to Terri was on the telephone. She then told me that what had really 'blown her away' about her discovery was that for her whole life she had assumed she was associated only with the white history of Australia, and now she realised she had a connection to the black history as well. When we later met, I asked what this meant for her, and if, in particular, it meant feeling she was no longer in the so-called guilty but the aggrieved party.

'I don't think I ever felt guilt,' Terri answered. 'I've felt outrage.' She explained, 'There is nothing I could have done to have changed the things that happened to Aboriginal people ... I don't feel guilt as a white person.' Terri then stopped, realising what she had said, before adding, 'I still feel outraged.' Indeed, like Ellen Marks, Terri said that discovering her Aboriginal ancestry has made her angrier about the injustices in Australia's colonial history.

'I get very outraged about the genocide that has been committed by the white people against the Aboriginals of this country in the last two hundred years,' Larry agreed, 'but I don't know how to bloody feel about it ... Sometimes ... I feel ashamed to be a white man, and then other times I think they did it to my bloody people, and then I think, is it my people? ... Or have I got to maintain that shame of being a white man? Because I'm probably more white than I am black now, because I've had more white influence over the last six generations than black, so basically I'm the bloody culprit!'

With the unresolved history of colonial settlement, Larry and Terri both felt the choice about their identity had, quite literally, to be a black-or-white decision. Terri said that an Aboriginal woman had told her, 'You're either Aboriginal or you're not.' Terri then said, 'So what I've been trying to do over the last two years is find out: What am I?'

She found that making the decision was not easy. 'I thought I was a fairly tolerant person,' she said, 'but I'm finding myself thinking if I tell people I've got Aboriginal blood in me they're going to think differently of me, and they *do* think differently of you. It will affect the way people look at me, it will affect my opportunities ... I want to know more before I commit myself one way or the other, because I can't sit on the fence all the time; I have to say either I *am* or I'm *not*.'

Terri said that if she were to say 'I *am*,' there would be several important things to consider. 'I think of things like the kinship obligations,' she told me, 'I think if I call myself Aboriginal and find out who my Aboriginal family is, does that then mean that I have to take on the responsibility for all those people?' Terri also worried: 'I know how Aboriginal people have to live, and that's the struggle I have with myself, whether I get drawn into that.'

I said that perhaps it is a lot easier to be white.

'It is!' Terri answered. 'Incredibly easier.'

But in the 1996 national census Terri reached the question: 'Is the person of Aboriginal or Torres Strait Islander origin?' and faced three possible answers: 'No', 'Yes, Aboriginal' and 'Yes, Torres Strait Islander'. After sitting there, her 'pen over the box', Terri ticked the second answer. 'So I'm that far towards acknowledging it,' she said.

Larry said that he has not acknowledged his Aboriginal ancestry in any census, but in recent years has begun to wonder exactly what the question in the form means. Does it refer to 'one generation' back, or to 'two, three, four, five, eight, nine, ten, twelve?'

Terri said, 'It doesn't matter how far it goes back. That's where I started from, so in the end I ticked the box.' Then she added, 'The census is nice and anonymous.'

Larry replied, 'I'm not worried about people knowing. I've just often thought to myself, how Aboriginal *am* I? I've been doing that in my own way. I'm not too worried about what ... some bureaucratic mob think about it; I think to myself, how Aboriginal am *I*? – because I'm six generations away from a full-blooded Aboriginal.'

'I actually believe that it's not about colour,' Terri responded, 'it's about the spirituality ...'

'I'm not talking about colour,' Larry answered.

But Terri continued, '... and the sense of belonging-ness and a connection to the land ... It's a state of mind.'

Terri spoke of feeling a 'strong need' to go to Tasmania and learn more about Betty, or 'Old Bet', as she calls her. While she knew her search might be long and difficult, if not impossible, she said that trying to find this 'connection' was important, while learning about Nat Thomas and the other descendants on Kangaroo Island was not.

'Kangaroo Island is nothing to me ... as a place,' she told us. 'I have no knowledge of ... or connection with Kangaroo Island,' she reiterated. 'The one person I need to know about is Old Bet, because that's who I'm descended from; bugger all these other people!'

But Kangaroo Island is the place Larry grew up. He also wanted to know more about Betty and her ancestors, but he was dubious about the idea of being interested only in her. He said he had never really thought about 'where the *white* side of me comes from ... that just in this country alone [there are] two thousand generations ... that *is* a bit of an attraction! Is that because I'm trying to be exclusive? Is it some sort of morbid thing? "Yeah, that's bit different than the boring old bloody Anglo-Celtic."'

Larry had criticised his mother for privileging Nat Thomas for opposite reasons, but he understood why she had done it – he understood his mother's silence and nervousness. Larry knew how small and insular that community had been. While he had not been to Antechamber Bay, for him his past was still located on the island where his family had been living for six generations.

He told us how his mother used to talk about his great-grand-father, Joe Seymour, especially how he played the violin. 'She said you could whistle a tune and he could play it right away.' We then talked about how his grandmother Annie and great-aunt Mary were both musical, as was Tiger Simpson, and Mavis, and now Larry and also his brother Brentley.

Terri then said, 'Listening to you talk about the stories you've got back to the great-greats ... I felt a sadness ... I've got none of that.' Terri said she felt a 'sense of dislocation'. 'I wouldn't have a clue if that side of the family was musical or not musical or whatever.'

Terri was born hundreds of kilometres north of Kangaroo Island. She has few family or community members who share her story. While Mavis Golder found her sense of confidence by focusing on the beginnings on Kangaroo Island, Terri is seeking a sense of 'belonging-ness' in Tasmania, a place far from where she was born. She knows that her journey to find it is not over.

Perhaps one day she will be able to say 'I *am*' to her question of whether she is Aboriginal. But if someone was to ask her now how she might describe herself: 'I would describe myself as an Australian ... a true Australian, and feel connected to the nation of Australia, and know that I am an amalgam of just about every settler that ever landed on the shores ... I can truly and confidently and proudly call myself an Australian. I can't, I don't feel that confidence about calling myself Aboriginal.'

Larry agreed he couldn't either. 'I can't find a niche for it, I can't,' he said.

'No Matter How Sly'

My first contact with Steve Simpson's great-grandchildren was through their mother, Dorothy Simpson. Her late husband, Bill Simpson, had been the only child of Daisy Simpson, who was jilted by the Penneshaw schoolteacher in 1923 and later went to Victoria and married there.

Bill Simpson grew up in Melbourne totally unaware of his Aboriginal ancestry. His mother did not tell her family about it until months before her death. 'I think my husband was shocked,' Dorothy told me. 'He did not know.' Dorothy led the journey to find out more about his genealogy. She had a chance meeting with Adrian Waller's wife at a bingo game, and was given some more information by Adrian. After Bill died, Dorothy went to Kangaroo Island, and even visited Antechamber Bay.

None of her four children have been to Kangaroo Island. 'I personally feel my children have been robbed,' said Dorothy, reflecting on how little information about their ancestry had been passed on to them. But she then added: 'They know where their lines are, they know where they come from ... They are true Australians and it doesn't matter that there is other [European] blood there, they are true Australians.' Dorothy also told me that her granddaughter has on her birth certificate that she is Aboriginal, 'because she *is*', Dorothy claimed. 'I mean, no matter how sly, it's there.'

Dorothy said that while her children did not know about the Aboriginal ancestry until they were grown up, they always had interests and connections with Aboriginal culture and people. Her oldest daughter used to go 'walkabout' from the age of twelve, 'and that's no joke'. Dorothy explained, 'She just walks and walks and walks.' She also told me her younger daughter used to do volunteer work for the Aboriginal League in the Melbourne suburb of Westmeadows, and had always been 'pro-Aboriginal'. Dorothy said that her son Terry's first wife had always joked that he had 'Aboriginal legs', just as Terri Sanderson had joked about herself.

Dorothy told me how her son Robert had recently gone up to the Northern Territory to work with an Aboriginal Community Government Council on issues of infrastructure and planning.

I wrote to Robert, asking him if he might tell me how he found working with Aboriginal people and how he felt about his own Aboriginal ancestry.[2]

'I identify myself as of Aboriginal heritage,' Robert wrote back, 'and not as Aboriginal. It is the Aboriginal people that I work and socialise with that consider me as Aboriginal.'

I had sent Robert some of my research, including the story of how his grandmother Daisy had been jilted. It was a story he had not heard before, but he said it 'brought back some bad memories to myself, as I have been victimised for having the very same descent'. While Robert did not tell me any specific details, he said that he has found 'racial hatred' to be 'very strong', with South Australians being among the 'worst offenders'. Robert said that their racism 'extends to those that are of Aboriginal descent', and also those who 'are associated with Aboriginals, and ... have some compassion towards Aboriginals'.

He explained:

I, like my grandmother Daisy, show no signs of having any Aboriginal descent, yet we have both suffered because of the small mindness of some people. When they learn that you may have an ounce of black blood, their unintelligent brain tells them there is a 'Black fellow' before them. A person to be feared with hatred.[3]

It seems that Terri Sanderson's fear of telling people about her Aboriginal ancestry was not unfounded.

The only one of Dorothy's children I met was Terry, who is living in Adelaide. I called him and asked if I could meet him, and he kindly invited me to dinner with his partner.

I first asked Terry to tell me how he found out about his ancestry. He said he had always known that his grandmother Daisy was born on Kangaroo Island, and that she used to tell him about what it was like growing up there. Terry said he was given 'the general impression' that being 'the only daughter of a very strict mother' and having five brothers meant that Daisy 'had a very hard life as a younger girl in Penneshaw'. Terry thought that she had 'decided that she wanted to be a lady and that they were certain things she wanted to achieve', and that was precisely what she did.

'She didn't drink, smoke or swear, and . . . she had a nice, comfortable home where everything was running like a clock . . . She was a very content lady.' Terry thought that Daisy's 'middle-class' ambition had led her to 'suppress' her Aboriginal 'blood'. He remembered she had 'some . . . typical Aboriginal bits and pieces' in her home, such as boomerangs, so he considered 'it was not as though she tried to bury the whole thing totally'. (Particularly in the 1950s and '60s, it was fashionable in many Australian homes to have Aboriginal-inspired knick-knacks on display. Concrete Aboriginal warriors stood sentinal over many a suburban home. Because of this, I think it is unlikely Daisy was remembering her Aboriginal Tasmanian ancestry; furthermore, boomerangs were not traditionally used in Tasmania.)

Terry did say Daisy 'certainly saw [her Aboriginal ancestry] as something that would get in her way . . . a threat . . . to where she wanted to be'. He also thought her discretion had come at a cost – that since Daisy 'confessed . . . on her death-bed', hiding her ancestry 'must have weighed heavy on her conscience'.

Learning of his Aboriginal ancestry, Terry explained, had 'affected me and my brother, particularly my brother'. He said that Robert took identifying with his ancestry more seriously, despite the fact that his skin was even fairer than Terry's, 'and you can't look me and say, "Yes, you have Aboriginal blood".'

Terry said you could also not look at him, or listen to his accent, and decide he was any of the other nationalities that make up his varied ancestry – French, German or Scottish. So, Terry concluded, no one of these ancestral lines was more significant than the other.

In contrast, Terry said, Robert understands his 'Aboriginal blood as an anchor', that it makes him 'closer to home'. 'I can understand this,' Terry conceded, 'because the only thing I ever did with my father was to hunt.' When he was out in the bush, he felt that he 'came alive'. He had 'always wondered, is that a male thing?' until he found out he had Aboriginal 'blood'. Then he wondered, 'Well does *that* have a bearing on it? ... I like to think that it's ... that Aboriginal content that comes alive when I'm out there'.

Seeing the contradictions in what he'd said to me, Terry explained, 'It's been really hard since you rung me up. I've really been going through a lot within myself. You've really caused me to churn myself over ... a person looks for identity.' Terry used to see himself as 'mainly having Scottish blood', because he liked to think of his red beard and being 'tight' with money as intrinsically Scottish. So, Terry joked, when he found out he also had Aboriginal ancestry, 'I thought I'd be the only fellow on the earth that's entitled to wear a bark sporran, and that if I went caber tossing it may come back.'

More seriously, Terry reflected how, in his opinion, Aboriginal people were 'more in touch with their environment', and were 'the true environmentalists'. 'If any of that influence is in me,' he said, 'I'm really thankful for it.' He had studied natural resources management at university, and felt it was important to look after the environment. 'I don't see it as a disgrace, as my grandmother would have seen it,' he said of his Aboriginal ancestry, 'but ... more as a bonus for myself.'

'At the same time,' Terry continued, 'I have a real trouble with Aboriginal activists, a majority of whom are not full-blooded ... pushing Aboriginal rights and land rights.' Terry said he thought that those people simply had their hands out 'for money' while the 'true Aboriginal fella' could put no price on his culture.

'I'm disturbed by the way the Aboriginal culture is fighting to stay alive,' Terry explained, 'that it's not really the true Aboriginal culture the way I see it.' He said, 'The true Aboriginal culture which I would like to identify with is pretty much dead or dying, or it's alive in very remote areas only.' Terry imagined that when that culture originally 'influenced' his family, 'it would have been untainted, it would have been genuine'.

He concluded, 'If somebody asks me today, "Are you Aboriginal?" I say, "No, I'm not Aboriginal." If they ask me if I'm French, no I'm not French, I'm not German, I'm not Scottish. But I have got all that blood in me. That only leaves one place and that's Australia, so I say "I am Australian." But I don't hide the fact that I have Aboriginal blood, and nor do I jump up and down and say, "Well, I've got Aboriginal ancestry, therefore you must give to me." Every form that I sign ... that says "Are you an Aboriginal or a Torres Strait Islander?" ... I always tick "no". I'm not. I do have some of that influence in me, but I don't think that gives me the right four or five generations down the road to be a parasite on the community.'

The history and perception of Aborigines' dependency on government support is so entrenched that the notion of a modern Aboriginal identity is seen by its relationship with the welfare state, by its 'parasitical' nature. But Terry has also found a personal understanding of his Aboriginal ancestry – it explained for him why he loved hunting and the environment. 'It certainly did clear up a few things for me,' he added later. 'I felt like there was a whole big area that I hadn't been told ... I found it really significant,' he explained. 'I felt proud ... I felt *good* ... I really did, I felt *good* about it.'

Terry then continued: 'I got typical Aboriginal features, not in my face like a flattened nose ... but I've got these really skinny sort of legs and everybody goes "Oh, they're Aboriginal legs", and I squat a certain way ... it's a typical Aboriginal squat ... I'm a firm believer that genetic information carries on certain ways people do things.'

These features, like his love of hunting, are perhaps the traits of the 'true Aboriginal culture' Terry would 'like to identify with'. But they do not seem to relate to how he feels about his immediate experiences of his ancestry – the reflections of his grandmother's repressive ambitions and his opinions of his brother's identity.

'I'm confused, I'm confused,' he said to me as I left that evening. 'We were taught at school that Aborigines were people with boomerangs who ate kangaroo [but] ... there is a lot more to it ... I can't make sense of it yet.'[4]

Terry's confusion comes after a lifetime of seeing Aboriginal people and culture as distant and estranged, a lifetime of respecting only what is 'untainted' and 'genuine'. While he can respect the boomerangs and kangaroo hunting, he cannot sympathise with contemporary Aboriginal politics. Though he believes that white settlement was a wrongful invasion, he does not believe that white Australians today should say they are sorry for what happened.

'What happened, happened,' he told me. 'I didn't do it. My forefathers did it, and yet my forefathers were also ...' He paused, then gave voice to the realisation. 'I'm on both sides!'

The Dinner

The day I was leaving Kangaroo Island in April 1998, Neil Waller dropped me at Penneshaw so I could have dinner with the Tretheweys before catching the ferry back to Cape Jervis. Just before I got out of his car, he asked me if I would address that year's Kangaroo Island Pioneers Association annual dinner. 'Are you *sure*?' I asked him. He was.

So on 27 July, the day the South Australian Company landed at Nepean Bay, I stood in a pub in my childhood suburb of North Adelaide before members of the Pioneers Association and told them some of the story you have read. I told them about the arrival of Nat Thomas and Betty, about how the Simpsons had once owned a lot of land but lost it because the Dudley people feared their black 'blood', and about why their members Mavis Golder and Adrian Waller grew up not knowing their ancestries.

I was really nervous. There were people in the audience with Dudley colonial family names on their cardboard name-tags, and I felt a tense hush when I quoted their cousins, uncles and aunts: 'Stay white, keep away from any colour'; 'No white person, parents wouldn't have wanted their daughters to marry them.' At the end, as I had planned, I thanked the descendants of Nat Thomas and Betty for giving me the opportunity to tell their story and be a part of their journeys. I was shocked at how moved I suddenly felt. This was the end of a personal journey for me too.

Adrian and Neil Waller were there, of course; they'd been to these dinners for years. But Mavis Golder was missing, and was missed. Terry Simpson had come with his partner, and had also brought his Aunt Doris. Doris told me that she was sure her husband, Charlie, would have loved to be there. Terri Sanderson also came. She met some of more of her family for the first time. It seemed that her journey to Tasmania was taking her via Kangaroo Island and its history after all.

When I finished, I welcomed questions. An older lady with a Dudley colonial descendant name-tag stood up and told us: 'I would like to say that Mavis Golder's Auntie Mary ... and ... my mother corresponded ... for years ... And my grandmother used to walk up that hill to where Mavis's mother used to live and play bridge with them. And they did that in the 1930s!'[1]

It was a testimony to the friendship between two women. It was supposed to be a evidence that the Dudley she grew up in had not been racist. But then Adrian Waller stood up. He told everyone how he remembered, when he was living on Kangaroo Island as a boy, he used to visit his Auntie Annie, Mavis Golder's mother. He said that there always used to be 'this dark lady' there, and he did not know who she was. He had never been told that she was his Auntie Mary.[2]

While the elderly colonial descendant boasted of how well her mother knew Mary *despite* her colour, Adrian told us he had not known his own aunt *because* of her colour. 'If they had been accepted,' Adrian had said to me, 'then ... they may have talked about their ancestors too'.

❧

Five months after the dinner, I emailed Neil Waller with some of my work to read. He told me there were Pioneers Association members who had been disturbed by my talk, but that he had tried to explain to them the differences between 'overt' and 'covert' racism, and that it had been the latter that had caused his family's exclusion.

Finally he told me: 'You have to say [this story] is important and [that] it must be told. The same story must exist across Australia ... but for those [who are] the subject of the story it can be difficult to do the telling. It must come from the outside.'[3]

Neil also wrote that for a while now he and his father had thought about 'proclaim[ing]' their Aboriginal 'heritage', but in the current climate of 'overt racism' people might look at their 'apparent' whiteness and assume they were trying to claim benefits.

To Nat

When I met Mavis Golder's youngest son, Brentley, in Kingscote in April 1998, I asked him how he felt to be the only descendant of Nat Thomas and Betty living permanently on Kangaroo Island. 'Proud,' he answered.

Brentley and his partner had a son in 1999. They called him Nathaniel Thomas. This new Nat was born only a short walk from the beach where the first Nathaniel Thomas first stood in early 1825.

I wonder if young Nat will grow up and stand on that same beach, and remember the moment when his great-great-great-great-grandfather arrived 174 years before his birth. I wonder if he will try to imagine his great-great-great-great-grandmother's journey from the island where she was born to the island where he was born. Will he make her journey in reverse with a sense of returning to an ancestral home? Will Kangaroo Island always remain his home and the home of his children? Will they continue to tell this story of their family? Or will it again have to be unearthed?

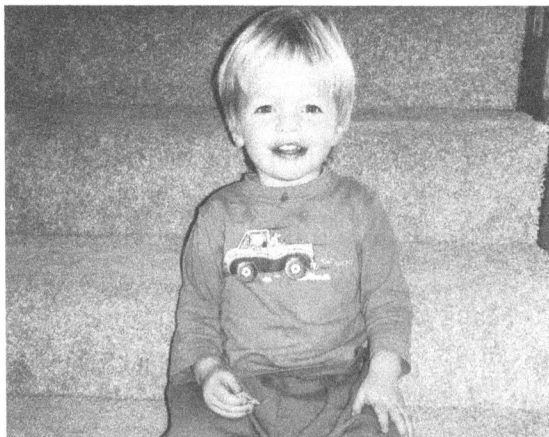

Nathaniel Thomas Golder, 2001. Courtesy of the Golder family

Epilogue to the
Second Edition

Since the first edition of this book was published in 2002 the way in which the Tasmanian Aboriginal history is publicly remembered on Kangaroo Island has undergone a significant shift.

In February 2008 I returned to Kangaroo Island for the first time in ten years. On the ferry from Cape Jervis I found, hanging in the passengers' lounge, a large framed photograph of Tiger Simpson in his army uniform. The accompanying text remembers a well-loved and intelligent Aboriginal man who fought for his country, but who never married. The RSL will soon erect a memorial to Tiger at the cairn he built on Kangaroo Island to commemorate the First World War.

In Penneshaw I found that Frenchman's Rock had been beautifully reinterpreted with bronze sculptural installations by artist Catherine Truman including a drinking fountain set into a wall built by local stonemason Thomas Appleby. It was created in consultation with the local community and funded by Country South Australian Arts Trust as part of a Statewide 'Waterworks' project between 1997 and 1999.

But for me the most important new memorial is to the Aboriginal women brought to Kangaroo Island by sealers before 1836. The 'Contemplation Seat' above Frenchman's Rock demonstrates a new level of thought, care and respect for the Island's Aboriginal history.

It was conceived and organised by Bev Willson, with assistance from Keryn James, on behalf of the Penneshaw Progress

Association. The seat was carved by local artist Indiana James from a fallen gum found at Hog Bay River (now Willson's River) where Mary Seymour was born. It rests on washed pebbles from Chapman's River and what was once the flagged floor of the cottage where William Wilkins and his Aboriginal wife Mary Monatto lived. In each of the steps leading up to the seat is inscribed the name of an Aboriginal woman taken to Kangaroo Island.

The seat overlooks Backstairs Passage. The idea is to sit and contemplate that stretch of water that turned the women into prisoners – that one-way journey from the nearby mainland and, looking west, from Tasmania.

The Contemplation Seat was dedicated in April 2002. Present were descendants of the Kaurna and Ngarrandgeri women who were taken to Kangaroo Island. Adrian Waller and his children Neil and Barbara were also there, as was Les Golder. It was one of his last acts in life; he died only days later. A smoking ceremony spiritually cleansed the site. The haunting voice of Fanny Cochrane Smith singing a traditional Tasmanian Aboriginal song was played from the wax cylinder recordings made in the last years of her life.

Next to the seat is a sign with Mary Seymour's photograph on it. It remembers how the women's unpaid work helped secure the success of Australia's first colonies. It acknowledges how the women 'made shelters, hunted, gathered and cooked food, found water, made clothes and rugs, tracked missing people and acted as sexual partners for the men'.

> They were often brutally treated but women like Sally, Big Sal, Suke, Betty, Old Wauber and many others will be remembered as strong, adaptable and resourceful survivors who continued their cultural traditions even though they were far from their homes and families.
>
> This seat initiates a process of reconciliation and healing for Ngarrindgeri, Kaurna and Palawa [Tasmanian Aboriginal] people and the community of Kangaroo Island and recognises the contribution of the women.

The Contemplation Seat marks a new beginning. This history unearthed no longer has so many dark secrets.

Rebe Taylor with her son, Hugo, on the Contemplation Seat overlooking Backstairs Passage, Penneshaw. Ariette Taylor, 2008

Acknowledgements

As I wrote this book, I often thought of the moment when I would write my acknowledgements. This was not only because I knew it would be one of the last things I would do, but because I knew it would be an opportunity to think of the many people who have made *Unearthed* possible.

It has been ten years since I began researching Kangaroo Island's history. With me all that time was Chris Blackall. This book has been a journey that I could not have travelled without him. Chris is also responsible for designing the maps and genealogies in this book, and I thank him for his hours of work.

This book began as a Masters thesis at the University of Melbourne, supervised by Patrick Wolfe. My thanks go not only to Patrick, but also to Don Garden, Stuart Macintyre, Patricia Grimshaw and Peter McPhee.

There have also been those who have given me encouragement and advice in how to turn my thesis into a book: Tom Griffiths, Henry Reynolds, Paul Turnbull, Ann Curthoys, Gordon Briscoe and Bain Attwood. Thanks also to Greg Dening and Donna Merwick for giving me the courage to fly.

Jenny Lee's support and work as editor has been simply fantastic. She has been a vital source of wisdom on both writing and Australian history. Everyone at Wakefield Press has also been extraordinarily supportive and my thanks go to them.

I am also very grateful for the funding this book has received from the University of Melbourne, Arts SA and the Centennial Committee of the Australian Historical Association.

My heartfelt thanks go to the Aboriginal Tasmanian descendants of Kangaroo Island. To the late Mavis Golder and her sons, Larry, Michael and Brentley; to Adrian and Neil Waller, to Dorothy, Terry, Robert and Doris Simpson, and to the women I call Terri Sanderson and Ellen Marks, thank you all for your friendship, your letters, photographs, phone calls and for your shared feelings.

I would also like to acknowledge the invaluable contribution of many Kangaroo Islanders, in particular Fiona and Robin Marshall, Agnes Marshall, Keith and Margaret Southlyn, Bruce Bates, Jayne Bates, Roe and Kim Trethewey, Mildred Willson, Bev Willson, Lindsay Howard, Thelma Buick, and Dave and Monica Buick. I made some very close friendships among you, and I appreciate the hours you spent talking with me, and the meals and beds you offered after the hours of driving. Many thanks also for photographs, phone calls and the long letters and faxes filled with genealogical information and local history.

Also on Kangaroo Island, my thanks goes to Ian Gilfillan and Andy and Kate Gilfillan for their information and for the memories. Thanks also to the curators of the Penneshaw Folk Museum for the photographs, the research and the access to the building. Many thanks also to the former Dudley District Council, in particular Council Chief Executive Officer Terry Winter, for the hours of researching and photocopying done for me at no charge, and for allowing me to climb into the attic and go through old Council records.

There are several other people and institutions whom I also thank: Philip Clarke at the South Australian Museum for the hours of his time, copies of his own articles and the many photocopies he sent me of Norman Tindale's journals. The staff of the Lands Office in Adelaide let me spend a fortnight behind their counters; a very special thanks to Michael Sincock for the hours of work he did researching the land ownership of the Aboriginal descendants. Thanks also for the expert advice and information from Philip Clarke, Jean Nunn, Lyndall Ryan, Patsy Cameron,

Tom Gara, Keryn James, Julie-Ann Ellis, Brian Dickey, Alex Castles, Pat Stretton, Nigel Wace, Ian McFarlane, Rob Amery, Graham Deane Miller and Rick Hosking. I would also like to thank the Public Records Office of South Australia, in particular Senior Archivist Andrew Boucher, and the State Records of South Australia for their responses to so many queries. Thanks also to the Hon. Ian Gilfillan and Coral Baines. And many thanks for the professional expertise of the librarians in the Mitchell Library, the State Library of New South Wales, the National Library of Australia and the State Library of South Australia.

I would also like to acknowledge the support of the History Program in the Research School of Social Sciences at the Australian National University, in particular the encouragement of the late Paul Bourke and also of Pat Jalland and Barry Higman. Also many thanks to Darrell Lewis and to the Program's administrative staff: Bev, Janice and Kay.

Lastly, my thanks must go to my family: to Ariette and John for their support and the roof over my head when I was a student, to Juliet for being there, to Ingmar and Louise for the holiday, and for Louise's research in the Mitchell Library. Thanks to all my friends, especially Team and his family. And my special thanks to Peter for his kindness, love and support.

Thank you all.

Rebe Taylor, Melbourne, 2008

Notes

Three Beginnings

1   Ernestine Hill, 'Last of the Tasmanians', *Walkabout*, 1 July 1954, p. 20.
2   Thomas Dunabin, 'The Old Sealing Days', in Charles Barrett, ed., *The Australian Junior Encyclopaedia*, Australian Educational Foundation, Sydney, 1959, vols. 1–3, 1, pp. 304–6, p. 306.
3   Letter from Edward Bates, *Chronicle*, 22 September 1960.

Exploring

1   Matthew Flinders, *A Voyage to Terra Australis; Undertaken for the Purpose of Completing the Discovery of that Vast Country, and Prosecuted in the Years 1801, 1802 and 1803*, G. & W. Nicol Booksellers, London, 1814, vols 1–2, 1, p. 169.
2   Flinders, pp. 168–9. Flinders may not have been the first English-speaking man to butcher meat on Kangaroo Island. In 1836 an Islander showed visitor W. H. Leigh a tree near Nepean Bay in which were scratched the words: 'This is the place for fat meat, 1800'. It seems someone else had been grateful for so seasonable a supply (W. H. Leigh, *Reconnoitering, Voyages, Travels and Adventures in the New Colonies of South Australia*, Smith Elder & Co., London, 1839, p. 126).
3   Flinders, p. 49.
4   Flinders, p. 164.
5   Inspired by Flinders' description of Pelican Lagoon, James Montgomery wrote the 167-page poem 'The Pelican Island', *The Pelican Island and Other Poems*, Longman, Rees, Orrne, Brown & Green, London, 1827.
6   Flinders, pp. 182–4.
7   Nicolas Baudin, *The Journal of Post Captain Nicolas Baudin Commander-in-Chief of the Corvettes* Geographe *and* Naturaliste *Assigned by Order of the Government to a Voyage of Discovery*, trans. Christine Cornell, Libraries Board of South Australia, Adelaide, 1974, p. 379.
8   Baudin, p. 380.
9   Flinders, p. 189.
10 Baudin, pp. 11, 1.
11 Comte de Fleurieu, *Plan of Itinerary for Citizen Baudin*, written for the Institut National, *The Journal of Post Captain Nicolas Baudin*, p. 1.

12 Susan Hunt and Paul Carter, *Terre Napoléon: Australia Through French Eyes 1800–1804*, Historic Houses Trust of New South Wales, Sydney, 1999, p. 21; Carter quotes Frank Horner who claims there were twenty-two scientists and artists on board. Horner also explains that some ten scientists stayed in Mauritius rather than go on to Australia, and another eight were lost – only five returned to France; 'The Baudin Expedition to Australia, 1800–1804', in Jacqueline Bonnemains, Elliott Forsyth and Bernard Smith, eds, *Baudin in Australian Waters*, Oxford University Press in association with the Australian Academy of Humanities, Melbourne, 1988, pp. 1–14.

13 Flinders, p. 189.

14 Baudin, p. 380.

15 Flinders, p. 190.

16 Flinders, pp. 193–5.

17 Baudin, p. 381.

18 Baudin, p. 384.

19 François Péron, *Voyage De Decouvertes Aux Terres Australes*, Paris, 1816, vols. 1–2, 2, pp. 156–7; Jean Nunn, *This Southern Land: A Social History of Kangaroo Island 1800–1890*, Investigator Press, Adelaide, 1989, pp. 18–19.

20 Baudin, pp. 458–60.

21 Baudin, pp. 458, 462.

22 Baudin, pp. 467–8.

23 The original rock, once on display in the Mortlock Library, Adelaide, is now on display at the Information Centre in Penneshaw.

24 Baudin, p. 468.

25 H. M. Cooper, 'Kangaroo Island's Wild Pigs – Their Possible Origin', *The South Australian Naturalist*, vol. 28, 3, 1954, pp. 57–61. Cooper believes Baudin first introduced the now wild pigs on Kangaroo Island.

26 Baudin, p. 469.

27 Baudin, p. 473.

28 Baudin, p. 489.

29 Cumpston quotes this number of Americans when he states that in June 1804 the *Union* arrived in Sydney with twenty-two men on board and her consort and the *Independence* with sixteen (J. S. Cumpston, *Kangaroo Island 1800–1836*, Roebuck Series, Roebuck Society Publication, Canberra, 1970, p. 28). Cumpston's number contradicts H. A. Lindsay, who claims there were about fifty Americans; H. A. Lindsay, 'American Settlement Kangaroo Island 1803', *Quadrant*, vol. 5, 1961, pp. 43–7.

30 Baudin, pp. 488–9.

31 Péron, pp. 153–7.

32 Baudin, p. 489.

33 Edmund Fanning, *Voyages and Discoveries in the South Seas 1792–1832*, Marine Research Society, Salem, Massachusetts, 1924, p. 232.

34 Parry Kostoglou, 'Sealing in Tasmania: historical research project – a report for the Parks and Wildlife Service', Department of Environment and Land Management, Hobart, 1996, p. 56.

35 Cumpston, p. 27.

36 Nunn, p. 20.

37 Cumpston, p. 28.

38 Cumpston, p. 30.

39 *Manning Clark's History of Australia*, abridged by Michael Cathcart, Melbourne University Press, Carlton, 1997, p. 387.

40 Cumpston, pp. 27–9.

41 Fanning, pp. 234–8.

42 Cumpston, p. 29. Lindsay, 1961, tells the story of Pendleton and Lord in the South Pacific seas differently, but his account is not in accordance with shipping records.

43 Fanning, p. 239.

44 Cumpston, p. 30.

45 Cumpston, pp. 30–1.

46 Cumpston, p. 31.

47 Walter Howchin, *The Geography of South Australia, Historical, Physical, Political and Commercial*, Whitcombe & Tombs, Auckland, 1917.

48 Norman B. Tindale and Brian G Maegraith, 'Traces of an Extinct Aboriginal Population on Kangaroo Island', *Records of the South Australian Museum*, vol. 4, 1928–32, pp. 275–87; Norman B. Tindale, 'Relationship of the Extinct Kangaroo Island Cultures of Australia Tasmania and Malaya', *Records of the South Australia Museum*, vol. 6, 1937–41, pp. 39–59; H. M. Cooper, 'Large Stone Implements from South Australia', *Records of the South Australian Museum*, vol. 7, 1941–43, pp. 345–69.

49 Tindale, 1937–41, p. 55.

50 Tindale, 1928–32, p. 285.

51 Ronald Lampert, 'The Great Kartan Mystery', *Terra Australis*, vol. 5, 1981, pp. 1–185; James Knight, 'The Great Kartan Myth', in possession of James Knight, Department of State Aboriginal Affairs, South Australia, 1995, p. 1.

52 Rhys Jones, 'Man as an Element of a Continental Fauna: The Case of the Sundering of the Bassian Bridge', in J. Allen, J. Golson and R. Jones, eds, *Sunda and Sahul: Prehistoric Studies in Southeast Asia, Melanesia and Australia*, Academic Press, New York, 1977, pp. 316–86. Many of these ideas were also put forward by Francis H. Bauer, 'The Kartans of Kangaroo Island, South Australia: A Puzzle in Extinction', in Arnold R. Pilling and Richard A. Waterman, eds, *Diprotodon to Detribalization: Studies of Change Among Australian Aborigines*, Michigan State University Press, East Lansing, Michigan, 1970, pp. 198–216.

53 Diane Bell, *Ngarrindjeri Wurruwarrin: a world that is, was, and will be*, Spinifex, Melbourne, 1998, pp. 92–3, 427.

54 Bell, pp. 91–2.

55 Flinders, p. 187.

Arriving

1 Cumpston, p. 74.

2 'Journal of a Trip to Kangaroo Island', *Adelaide Observer*, 15 January 1853. While this article is not attributed to W. A. Cawthorne, it does appear among newspaper clippings in his diary in 1859. Also, his diary entry of 30 December 1852 states: 'returned with mother from Kangaroo Island after a 19 day visit sundry adventures – a short Report of which will appear in the papers', W. A. Cawthorne, 'Diary', 1849–1859, B230 (CY2141), Mitchell Library, State Library of New South Wales.

3 Cumpston, p. 127; Nunn p. 39.

4 Michael Golder, 'Nat Thomas's Chronology 1818–1824', in possession of Michael Golder, Reynella, South Australia.

5 Cumpston, pp. 68–75.

6 Nunn, p. 31.

7 Nunn, pp. 45–6.

8 Cumpston, p. 79.

9 Philip A. Clarke, 'Early European Interaction with Aboriginal Hunters and Gatherers on Kangaroo Island, South Australia', *Aboriginal History*, vol. 20, 1996, pp. 51–81, p. 59.

10 Letter from John Hart to Governor La Trobe, Melbourne, 24 April 1854 in Thomas Francis McBride, *Letters From Victorian Pioneers*, Published for Trustees of Public Library by Robert S. Brain, Government Printer, Melbourne, 1898, p. 302.

11 Cumpston, p. v.

12 Parry Kostoglou, 1996, pp. 21–2, 45–9, 17.

13 Letter from John Hart to Governor La Trobe, p. 302.

14 Cumpston, p. 72.

15 *Nat Thomas' Chronology 1818–1824*; Cumpston, p. 170.

16 Irynej Skira, Tasmanian Aborigines and Mutton-birding: A Historical Examination, PhD Thesis, Department of Geography and Environmental Studies, University of Tasmania, 1993, p. 118.

17 *The Australian*, 9 March 1826, in Cumpston, p. 79.

18 *Hobart Town Gazette*, 10 June 1826, in Cumpston, p. 85.

19 Peter Cunningham, *Two Years in New South Wales*, Henry Colburn, London, 1827, vols. 1–2, 2, p. 206, quoted by Cumpston, p. 86.

20 Letter from John Hart to Governor La Trobe, p. 302.

21 Cumpston, p. 128.

22 *Hobart Town Gazette*, 10 June 1826, in Cumpston, p. 85.

23 Cumpston, pp. 85, 170; N. J. B. Plomley, *Friendly Mission: The Tasmanian Journals and Papers of George Augustus Robinson, 1829–1832*, Tasmanian Historical Research Association, 1966, Appendix 7, 'The Sealers', p. 1010.

24 Cumpston, p. 168.

25 Cumpston, p. 53.

26 Cumpston, pp. 70–1.

27 Cumpston, p. 70.

28 Cumpston, p. 71.

29 Norman B. Tindale, 'Tasmania and the Part Aborigines of the Bass Strait Islands and Kangaroo Island, 1936–1965', South Australian Museum, p. 307.

30 'Death of George Bates', *Adelaide Observer*, 14 September 1895.

31 Cumpston, p. 127. Also, in a story passed on to Bruce Bates, Bates was living with Nat Thomas at Antechamber Bay; interview with Bruce Bates, 28 June 1993, Penneshaw, Kangaroo Island.

32 Newspaper clipping entitled '"Tiger" Simpson Of K.I.' from the early 1950s, possibly from the *Chronicle*, kindly copied for me by Jean Nunn.

33 Nunn, pp. 31–2; Leigh, p. 102; Cumpston, p. 127.

34 Nunn, p. 45.

35 Cumpston, p. 108.

36 Cumpston pp. 70, 110, 127, 131, 171; Plomley, 1966, p. 1012.

37 Nunn, p. 29.

38 Letter from John Hart to Governor La Trobe, p. 302.

39 Cumpston, p. 79.

40 Philip A. Clarke, 'The Aboriginal presence on Kangaroo Island, South Australia', in Jane Simpson and Luise Hercus, eds, *History in Portraits – Biographies of nineteenth century South Australian Aboriginal people*, *Aboriginal History*, Monograph 6, Southwood Press, Sydney, 1998, pp. 14–48, p. 35.

41 B. C. Mollison, *The Tasmanian Aborigines*, University of Tasmania, Hobart, 1977, no page number.
42 A. L. Meston, 'Halfcastes of the Furneaux Group', *The Records of the Queen Victoria Museum, Launceston*, 1946, issued separately 1947, pp. 47–52, p. 50.
43 Wynnis J. Ruediger, *Border's Land, Kangaroo Island 1802–1836*, published by the author, Morgan, South Australia, 1980, p. 52. Sandy Alexander claims Nat arrived 'with another man' in 1824 and that both of them had 'Aboriginal wives' in her book *Kangaroo Island – A Brief Chronological History*, published by author, Kingscote, 1997, p. 14.
44 Interview with Bruce Bates, Penneshaw, Kangaroo Island, 28 June 1993.
45 Norman B. Tindale, 'Tasmanian Aborigines on Kangaroo Island South Australia', *Records of the South Australian Museum*, vol. 6, no. 1, 1937, pp. 29–37, p. 33.
46 Cumpston, pp. 53, 110, 115, 140; in an interview with Tindale, Ted Bates claims that on Wallen's headstone is the name 'Robert Wallen Perkey', in 'Tasmania and the Part Aborigines of the Bass Strait and Kangaroo Island 1936–1965', p. 303, see also Tindale, 1937, p. 31. There is a transcript of Wallen's headstone in Nunn, pp. 100–1. Mary Seymour mentioned a 'whaler' called 'Pirkey' to Dr Herbert Basedow, 'Relic of the Lost Tasmanian Race – Obituary of Mary Seymour', *Man*, vol. 14, no. 10, 1914, pp. 160–2, p. 161.
47 'Native Women on Kangaroo Island', 'Loose Notes', Tindale collection, South Australian Museum, accession numbers 65, 73, 74, 75; Jane Isabella Watts, *Family Life in South Australia Fifty-three Years Ago Dating From October 1837*, Libraries Board of South Australia, Adelaide, 1978 (first published by W. K. Thomas & Co., Adelaide, 1890), p. 17.
48 Tindale, 1937, p. 31.
49 Cumpston, p. 53.
50 Clarke, 1998, p. 46.
51 Lyndall Ryan, *The Aboriginal Tasmanians*, Allen & Unwin, Sydney, 1996, 2nd ed., p. 71; Plomley, 1966, pp. 1017–20.
52 Henry Ling Roth, *The Aborigines of Tasmania*, F. King & Sons, Halifax, 1899, pp. xli, vi.
53 Clarke, 1998, pp. 34–5.
54 Henry Reynolds, *Fate of a Free People*, Penguin, Ringwood, 1995, pp. 27–52.
55 Ryan, p. 67.
56 Ian McFarlane, *Aboriginal Society in North West Tasmania: Dispossession and Genocide*, PhD Thesis, School of History and Classics, University of Tasmania, 2002, pp. 59–60.
57 Rhys Jones, Rocky Cape and the Problem of the Tasmanians, PhD Thesis, University of Sydney, 1971, p. 11.
58 Ryan, p. 71.
59 Jones, p. 11.
60 Graeme Davison, John Hirst and Stuart Macintyre, eds, *The Oxford Companion to Australian History*, Oxford University Press, Melbourne, 1998, p. 651.
61 Plomley, 1966, pp. 1011, 1018.
62 Clarke, 1998, pp. 33–4.
63 Plomley, 1966, pp. 1010, 1013, 1016; Cumpston, p. 170.
64 W. A. Cawthorne's 'The Islanders' first appeared in print in the *Melbourne Illustrated Post* as a monthly serial from 25 January 1865 to 18 February 1866. This quotation is taken from the edition published as a novel and renamed *The Kangaroo Islanders, The Story of South Australia Before Colonization, 1823*, Rigby, Adelaide, 1926, p. 80.
65 Cumpston, p. 113.
66 Tindale and Maegraith, p. 286.
67 Clarke, 1998, p. 19.

68 'Death of George Bates', *Adelaide Observer*, 14 September 1895.

69 'Old George Bates', *South Australian Advertiser*, 27 December 1886.

70 Bell, p. 427.

71 George Taplin's Diary, 9 March 1867, PRG 186, Mortlock Library, State Library of South Australia.

72 Clarke, 1998, pp. 25–6.

73 John W. Bull, *Early Experiences in South Australia*, E. S. Wigg & Son, London, 1884, p. 5.

74 'The Last of the Tasmanians', interview with Augustus Reeves, 'the oldest resident on the island', *Adelaide Observer*, 1 April 1905.

75 Clarke, 1998, p. 26.

76 'Old George Bates', *South Australian Advertiser*, 27 December 1886.

Judging

1 'Report of a Voyage from Sydney to Kangaroo Island' by Captain Sutherland, in Edward Gibbon Wakefield, *Plan of a Company to be Established for the Purpose of Founding a Colony in Southern Australia Purchasing Land Therein, and Preparing the Land so Purchased for the Reception of Immigrants*, South Australian Facsimile Editions, No. 6, Public Library of South Australia, Adelaide, 1962 (first published by Ridgway & Sons, London, 1832), p. 73.

2 Major Lockyer, 'Expedition Sent from Sydney in 1826 to Found a Settlement at King George's Sound, Western Australia', in H. P. Moore, 'Notes on the Early Settlers in South Australia Prior to 1836', *Royal Geographical Society of Australia, South Australian Branch*, vol. 25, 1923, pp. 81–135, p. 125.

3 Wakefield, p. 73.

4 Moore, p. 125.

5 *Hobart Town Gazette*, 26 August 1826.

6 *Hobart Town Gazette*, 26 August 1826.

7 *Hobart Town Gazette*, 26 August 1826.

8 *Hobart Town Gazette*, 26 August 1826.

9 Lloyd L. Robson, *A History of Tasmania: Van Diemen's Land from the Earliest Times to 1855*, Oxford University Press, Melbourne, 1983, vols. 1–2, 1, pp. 48–9, 86, 100–1; T. E. Wells, *Michael Howe: The Last and Worst of the Bushrangers of Van Diemen's Land*, Angus & Robertson, Sydney, 1926; James Bonwick, *Mike Howe, The Bushranger of Van Diemen's Land*, Henry S. King & Co., London, 1873; James Bonwick, *The Bushrangers: Illustrating the Early Days of Van Diemen's Land*, Fullers Bookshop, Hobart, 1967; Charles Barrett, *White Blackfellows: The Strange Adventures of Europeans Who Lived Among Savages*, Hallcraft, Melbourne, 1948, pp. 1–32; George Boxall, *An Illustrated History of Australian Bushrangers*, Viking O'Neil, Ringwood, 1988, pp. 18–19.

10 Kostoglou, p. 18.

11 James Bonwick, *The Lost Tasmanian Race*, Sampson Low, Marston, Searle & Rivington, London, 1884, p. 191.

12 'On Kangaroo Island', *Hobart Town Gazette*, 10 June 1826.

13 'On Kangaroo Island', *Hobart Town Gazette*, 10 June 1826.

14 John West, *The History of Tasmania*, A. G. L. Shaw, ed., Angus & Robertson in association with the Royal Australian Historical Society, Sydney, 1971 (first edition, Henry Dowling, Launceston, Tasmania, 1852), p. 274.

15 Cawthorne, 1926, p. 26.

16 Joan Kerr, ed., *The Dictionary of Australian Artists – Painters, Sketchers, Photographers and Engravers to 1870*, Oxford University Press, Melbourne, 1992, pp. 141–2.

17 W. A. Cawthorne, 'Diary', 1852–1859 and Log book for Sturt Lighthouse, 1853–1867, 10 March and 1 August 1853, D26, National Archives, South Australia.

18 'Journal of a Trip of Kangaroo Island', *Adelaide Observer*, 13 January 1853; 'Early South Australia', *Adelaide Observer*, 20 October 1906. This is a reprint of a letter from 'W. A. C.', 15 September 1856. On 4 October 1857, Cawthorne wrote in his diary that Nat Thomas was dismissed from the lighthouse, indicating that he knew him.

19 'From our Hog Bay Correspondent', *Adelaide Observer*, 3 June 1865.

20 Christopher Nance, 'Two South Australian Writers', *Tradition*, vol. 20, December 1979, pp. 19–22, p. 20.

21 Clark, 1997, p. 187.

22 Clarke, 1998, p. 29.

23 Geoffrey Blainey, *The Tyranny of Distance: How Distance Shaped Australia's History*, Sun Books, Melbourne, 1966, pp. 106–7.

24 John Molony, *The Penguin History of Australia*, Penguin, Ringwood, 1988, 2nd. ed., p. 31.

25 Robert Hughes, *The Fatal Shore: A History of the Transportation of Convicts to Australia, 1787–1863*, Collins Harvill, London, 1987, p. 333.

26 Clarke, 1998, p. 29.

27 John Jones, 'Port Adelaide River. Its First Reported Discovery', *Proceedings of the Royal Geographical Society of Australasia, South Australian Branch*, vol. 34, 1920–21, pp. 73–5, p. 75.

28 Letter from John Hart to Governor La Trobe, p. 302.

29 Cumpston, p. vi.

30 Gustav Jahoda, *Images of Savages: Ancient Roots of Modern Prejudice in Western Culture*, London, Routledge, 1999, p. 11.

31 Jahoda, p. 5.

32 Cawthorne, 1926, p. 25.

33 Easton's 1897 Bible Dictionary: http://www.ccel.org/e/easton/ebd/ebd.html. Online edition based on: M. G. Easton, *Illustrated Bible Dictionary*, Thomas Nelson, 3rd. ed., 1897.

34 Jahoda, pp. 40–1.

35 In the Preface of the 1926 Rigby edition of the renamed *The Kangaroo Islanders*, the publisher claims that W. A. Cawthorne first published the novel as a serial in 'about the year 1854'. While this information may have been told to the Rigby's publisher by W. A. Cawthorne's niece who gave permission for Rigby to republish her uncle's book, W. A. Cawthorne, 'Sketches, manuscripts and memorabilia 1840–1979', FM4/8474–8475, Mitchell Library, State Library of New South Wales. However, there is no available evidence of any publication of 'The Islanders' until it appeared in the *Illustrated Melbourne Post* as a monthly serial from 25 January 1865 to 18 February 1866. It was republished as a serial in the *Adelaide Illustrated Post*, which Cawthorne himself published, two years later.

36 Margarette Lincoln, 'Shipwreck Narratives of the Eighteenth and Early Nineteenth Century: Indicators of Culture and Identity', *British Journal for Eighteenth-century Studies*, vol. 20, 1997, pp. 155–72, p. 155.

37 Daniel Defoe, *The Life and Strange and Surprizing Adventures of Robinson Crusoe of York, Mariner: who lived eight and twenty years, all alone in an uninhabited island on the coast of America, near to mouth of the great river or Oroonoque; having been cast on shore by shipwreck, whereon all the men perished but himself. With an account of how he was at last as strangely deliver'd by pyrates. Written by himself*, W. Taylor, London, 1719.

38 Cawthorne, 1926, p. 28.

39 Leigh, p. 102. There are various books regarding the story of Alexander Selkirk: Woodes Rogers, *A Cruising Voyage Round the World [including] an Account of Alexander Selkirk's Living*

Alone Four Years and Four Months in an Island, printed for Bernard Lintot & Edward Symon, London, 1726; Captain Edward Cooke, *A Voyage to the South Sea . . . Wherein an Account is given of Mr. Alexander Selkirk . . . during the Four Years and Four Months he liv'd upon the Uninhabited Island of Juan Fernandes*, printed by H. M. for B. Lintot & R. Gosling, A. Bettesworth & W. Innys, London, 1712; R. L. Megroz, *The Real Robinson Crusoe: being the Life and Strange Surprising Adventures of Alexander Selkirk of Largo, Fife, Mariner*, Cresset Press, London, 1939.

40 G. F. Angas, *Savage Life and Scenes in Australia and New Zealand*, Smith Elder, London, 1847, vols. 1–2, 1, p. 184.

41 Tom Griffiths with assistance from Alan Platt, eds, *The Life and Adventures of Edward Snell: The Illustrated Diary of an Artist, Engineer and Adventurer in the Australian colonies 1849 to 1859*, Angus & Robertson with The Library Council of Victoria, North Ryde, New South Wales, 1988, p. 42.

42 Daniel Defoe, *The Life and Adventures of Robinson Crusoe of York, Mariner*, Gall & Inglis, London, 1847, p. 158.

43 Clarke, 1998, p. 17.

44 James Bonwick, *The Last of the Tasmanians Or the Black War of Van Diemen's Land*, Sampson Low, Son & Marston, London, 1870, p. 295.

45 Buckley's story has been written many times over: James Bonwick, *William Buckley: The Wild White Man, and his Port Phillip Black Friends*, George Nichols, Melbourne, 1856 (republished as *The Wild White Man and the Blacks of Victoria*, Fergusson & Moore, Melbourne, 1863); William T. Pyke, *Savage Life in Australia: the Story of William Buckley the Runaway Convict who Lived Thirty-two Years among the Blacks of Australia*, E. W. Cole, Melbourne, 1889, republished as *Thirty Years among the Blacks of Australia: the Life and Adventures of William Buckley, The Runaway Convict*, George Routledge & Sons, London, 1904, and again under the same title by Routledge, 1912. George Sutherland's abridged account of the story for children, 'The Wild White Man', was included in his *Sixteen Stories of Australian Exploration and Settlement*, James Ingram, Melbourne, 1901[?]. There have also been many papers, novels and poems inspired by Buckley: Kevin Hayden, *Wild White Man: A Condensed Account of the Adventures of William Buckley who Lived in Exile for 32 Years (1803–35) Amongst the Black People of the Unexplored Regions of Port Phillip*, Marine History Publications, Geelong, 1976[?]; Cecily M. Tudehope, *William Buckley*, Hall's Book Store, Prahran, 1962; Craig Robertson, *Buckley's Hope: the Story of Australia's Wild White Man*, Scribe, Fitzroy, 1980; Barry Hill, *Ghosting William Buckley*, Heinemann, Port Melbourne, 1993; and Alan Garner, *Strandloper*, Harvill Press, London, 1996.

46 John Morgan, *The Life and Adventures of William Buckley, Thirty-two Years a Wanderer Amongst the Aborigines of the then Unexplored Country round Port Phillip, now the Province of Victoria*, Archibald Macdougall, Hobart, 1852.

47 Morgan, pp. 91–2, 14–16, 82, 146–7.

48 John Morgan, *Life and Adventures of William Buckley*, edited and introduced by Tim Flannery, Text Publishing, Melbourne, 2002.

49 John Morgan, *Ein Australischer Robinson: Leben und Abenteuer des William Buckley*, trans. Helmut Reim, F. A. Brockhaus Verlag, Leipzig, 1964; and John Morgan, *Uil'iam Bakli, Avstraliiskii Robinzon: Zhizn' i Prikliucheniia Uil'iama Bakli Rasskazannye Dzhonom Morganom*, Nauka, Moscow, 1966.

50 Morgan, 1852, pp. 91–2.

51 Barrett, p. 1; Sutherland, 1901[?], p. 31.

52 Bonwick, 1856, p. 3.

53 Bonwick, 1856, p. 1.

54 Barrett, p. 29.
55 Sutherland, 1901[?], pp. 31–2.
56 Jahoda, p. 118.
57 Bonwick, 1870, p. 296.

Knowing
1 'Journal of a Trip to Kangaroo Island', *Adelaide Observer*, 13 January 1853.
2 Jones, 1921, pp. 74–5.
3 Clarke, 1996, p. 65.
4 Police Inspector Alexander Tolmer arrested Sal and Suke on Kangaroo Island for Meredith's murder in 1844; Clarke, 1998, pp. 34–5.
5 Cumpston, p. 115.
6 Bull, pp. 32–3.
7 Cumpston, p. 115.
8 'Old George Bates', *South Australian Advertiser*, 27 December 1886.
9 'Death of George Bates', *Adelaide Observer*, 14 September 1895.
10 'Old George Bates', *South Australian Advertiser*, 27 December 1886.
11 Leigh, p. 162.
12 Leigh, p. 160.
13 Leigh, pp. 160–1.
14 Cumpston, p. 127.
15 Clarke, 1998, pp. 43–6.
16 Clarke, 1998, p. 46.
17 Leigh, p. 86; Clarke, 1996, p. 65.
18 Leigh, pp. 129–30.
19 Cawthorne, 1926, p. 72.
20 Leigh, p. 90.
21 Nunn, p. 84; Clarke, 1996, p. 60; Cumpston, p. 165.
22 Leigh, p. 104.
23 Letter from John Hart to Governor La Trobe, p. 302.
24 Clarke, 1998, p. 35.
25 Cawthorne, 1926, p. 87.
26 Cawthorne, 1926, pp. 85–6.
27 Cawthorne, 1926, pp. 87–8.
28 Ryan, p. 11.
29 Cawthorne, 1926, pp. 87–8.
30 Nunn, pp. 95–97.
31 Tindale, 1937, p. 33.
32 Basedow, p. 161.
33 Francis H. Bauer, The Regional Geography of Kangaroo Island, South Australia, PhD Thesis, Department of Geography, Australian National University, 1959, Appendix ix, p. 667.
34 Ryan, p. 71.
35 Australian Census of 1996, Australian Bureau of Statistics, http://www.abs.gov.au.
36 Ryan, pp. 251–3, 263.

Settling
1 Bull, p. 8.
2 Adelaide *Advertiser*, 27 July 1926; Nunn, p. 52.

3   Adelaide *Advertiser*, 27 July 1926.
4   Bull, p. 8.
5   Nunn, p. 54.
6   Leigh, p. 124.
7   Leigh, p. 125.
8   'Old George Bates', *South Australian Advertiser*, 27 December 1886.
9   Nunn, p. 60; Cumpston, p. 135.
10 Bauer, Appendix ix, p. 667.
11 South Australian Colonization Commission, *Report of the Colonization Commissioners for South Australia to Her Majesty's Principal Secretary of State for the Colonies*, 1836–1838, London, 1836, vols. 1–3, 1, p. 9.
12 Henry Reynolds, *The Law of the Land*, Penguin, Ringwood, 1987, p. 107.
13 Reynolds, 1987, p. 114.
14 South Australian Colonization Commission, p. 9.
15 South Australian Colonization Commission, pp. 8–9.
16 South Australian Land Company, *Evidence Respecting the Soil, Climate and Productions of the South Coast of Australia, between the 132nd and 141st degrees of East Longitude*, South Australian Facsimile Editions No.11, Public Library of South Australia, Adelaide, 1962 (first published by William Nicol, London, 1832) p. 37.
17 South Australian Land Company, *Proposal to His Majesty's Government for Founding a Colony on the Southern Coast of Australia*, South Australian Facsimile Editions No. 10, Public Library of South Australia, Adelaide, 1962 (first published by W. Nicol, London, 1831) p. 39.
18 South Australian Colonization Commission, 'Appendix'.
19 Bull, pp. 10–11.
20 South Australian Colonization Commission, 'Appendix'.
21 Bauer, p. 667.
22 Nunn, p. 58.
23 'Old George Bates', *South Australian Advertiser*, 27 December 1886.
24 Nunn, p. 58.
25 Clarke, 1996, p. 71.
26 'Old George Bates', *South Australian Advertiser*, 27 December 1886.
27 Cumpston, pp. 127, 165–6.
28 Bull, pp. 32–6.
29 Cumpston, p. 128.
30 Bauer, pp. 666–7.
31 Leigh, p. 124.
32 Bauer, p. 669.
33 Leigh, pp. 123–4.
34 Nunn, p. 67.
35 South Australian Land Company, Facsimile, 1962 (1831), p. 34.
36 Nunn, pp. 54–5.
37 South Australian Land Company, Facsimile, 1962 (1831), p. 36.
38 Cumpston, p. 137.
39 Cumpston, pp. 136–40.
40 Nunn, p. 60. See also 'Lost on Kangaroo Island, An Incident of the Pioneer Days', *Adelaide Observer*, 20 May 1899; Alfred Austin Lendon, *Kangaroo Island: The Tragedy of Dr. Slater and Mr. Osborne: a Story of Ninety Years Ago*, Adelaide[?], 1925[?] (the cover states: 'reprinted from the *Proceedings of the Royal Geographical Society, South Australian Branch* – session 1924–5').

41 Cumpston, p. 134.

42 Minutes of Proceedings of the Commission of Inquiry into the Lawless State of Society on Kangaroo Island, 1837, GRG 24/90/342, State Records, South Australia.

43 Leigh, p. 107.

44 J. C. Beaglehole, ed., *The Journals of Captain James Cook on his Voyages of Discovery*, vols. 1–2, 1, Cambridge University Press, London, 1955, pp. 361–2.

45 John Lort Stokes, *Discoveries in Australia; with an Account of the Coasts and Rivers Explored and Surveyed during the Voyage of H.M.S. Beagle 1837–1843*, T. & W. Boone, London, 1846, vols. 1–2, 2, pp. 296–7.

46 Lynette Peel, ed. *The Henty Journals – A Record of Farming, Whaling and Shipping at Portland Bay, 1834–1839*, The Miegunyah Press in association with The State Library of Victoria, Melbourne, 1996, p. 205.

47 The street names include Angas, Rundle, Currie, Hindley, Waymouth and Pirie; Alexander, pp. 15–16.

48 Alexander, p. 16.

49 South Australia, *Parliamentary Debates*, Legislative Council: Motion moved by the Hon. Ian Gilfillan and amended by the Hon. M. J. Elliott and the Hon. Anne Levy, 'That this Council officially recognises – a) human occupation of South Australia for many thousands of years; b) European habitation in South Australia from early in the nineteenth century; c) Kangaroo Island as the first South Australia Company Settlement in the Province of South Australia in July 1836; d) the Inauguration of Government at Glenelg, proclaimed on 28 December 1836. Moved 9 October 1991, carried 26 November 1991, 961–6, 2276–8.

Lubra Creek

1 Nunn, p. 57.

The Hundred of Dudley

1 Nunn, p. 135.

2 Letter from Penneshaw resident, to remain unnamed, 6 November 1994.

3 Leigh, p. 124.

4 W. A. Cawthorne made several visits to Kangaroo Island between 1852 and 1859. He also wrote in his diary on 14 January 1859 that he was 'painting my journey to K. Isd'., which he made a few weeks earlier; Nunn, p. 91.

5 E. H. Hallack, *Kangaroo Island, Adelaide's Sanatorium*, W. K. Thomas & Co., Adelaide, 1905, p. 41.

6 Cumpston, p. 163.

7 *The Church Chronicle*, Diocese of Adelaide, 20 March 1863, p. 531; newspaper clipping entitled '"Tiger" Simpson of K. I.'

8 Ruediger, p. 54.

9 Mildred Chester [pseudonym], 'This is My Life', in possession of Ellen Marks, Lockleys, South Australia.

10 Letter from Thomas Willson, *The South Australian Register*, 21 February 1877.

11 Ruediger, p. 53.

12 Hallack, p. 41.

13 Mary Seymour apparently told Professor Berry that Mrs Cawthorne taught her to read and write English; Richard J. A. Berry, 'A Living Descendant of an Extinct (Tasmanian) Race', *Proceedings of the Royal Society of Victoria*, vol. 20, pt. 1, 1907, pp. 1–21 p. 4; Mary Seymour

apparently also told Hallack in 1905 that Mrs Cawthorne taught her how to write English, p. 44; Basedow simply claims that Mary was 'educated by the lighthouse-keepers and learnt to read and write', p. 161; Ruediger claims Mrs Cawthorne taught Mary and Hannah to read and write English, p. 54.

[14] Nunn. p. 88; Log book for Sturt Lighthouse, 1853–1867, 10 March and 1 August 1853, D26, National Archives, South Australia.

[15] Log Books and Daily Journals, Trinity Board Miscellaneous Papers, 30–31 October and 2 November 1857, GRG 51, State Records, South Australia.

[16] 'Journal of a Trip to Kangaroo Island', *Adelaide Observer*, 15 January 1853.

[17] W. A. Cawthorne, 'Diary', 4 October 1857. The word 'unsettled' was barely legible and may not be the correct interpretation.

[18] Nunn, p. 99.

[19] Log Books and Daily Journals, Trinity Board, 9 October 1857.

[20] Nunn, p. 99.

[21] Log Books and, Daily Journals, Trinity Board, 9 October 1857 and 26 February 1858.

[22] Nunn, p. 88.

[23] Log Books and Daily Journals, Trinity Board, 19 and 20 December 1859.

[24] Log Books and Daily Journals, Trinity Board, 25 January 1860.

[25] Pastoral lease 660, issued to Nat Thomas 1 January 1859, Minutes forming enclosure to Department of Lands, no. 5489, vol. 8, f. 4, 1946, Lands Office, South Australia.

[26] Alex C. Castles, *An Australian Legal History*, The Law Book Company Ltd., Sydney, 1982, p. 459.

[27] Bauer, pp. 324, 331–2.

[28] Bauer, p. 332.

[29] Bauer, pp. 33, 344.

[30] Minutes forming enclosure to Department of Lands, no. 5489.

[31] Minutes forming enclosure to Department of Lands, no. 5489.

[32] Minutes forming enclosure to Department of Lands, no. 5489.

[33] Nunn, p. 135.

[34] Bauer, p. 345, Appendix VI.

[35] *Waste Lands Alienation Act 1872*, (SA).

[36] *The South Australian Register*, 21 February 1877.

[37] Section 63, CT 445/43 was issued to Nathaniel Wallace [sic] Thomas, 4 February 1884 [NB: This is five years after his death; the date of issue does not always correspond with the date of the grant].

[38] Nunn, p. 101.

[39] 'Journal of a Trip to Kangaroo Island', *Adelaide Observer*, 15 January 1853.

[40] Nunn, p. 168.

[41] Cumpston, p. 165.

[42] 'Death of George Bates', *Adelaide Observer*, 14 September 1895.

[43] Tindale, 1937, p. 31.

[44] Ruediger, p. 52. This confusion meant that when Mavis Golder and Adrian Waller organised the plaque to be erected at Antechamber Bay, it originally honoured Nat Thomas and his Aboriginal Tasmanian 'wife' Sophia. The mistake was realised in time, and the plaque was remade. As recently as 1997, Alexander made this same mistake in her book, *Kangaroo Island – A Brief Chronological History*, in which she claimed Nat arrived on Kangaroo Island with his Aboriginal wife 'Sophie', p. 14.

[45] Copy of Last Will and Testament of Nathaniel Walles Thomas, 29 July 1879, the Penneshaw Folk Museum, Kangaroo Island.

46 Dorothy Simpson showed me a copy of Sophia's death certificate in an interview with her at Parkville, Victoria, 25 February 1998.

47 Letter from Michael Golder, 5 December 1994.

48 Alexander, p. 14.

The Shadows

1 Cumpston, p. 127; 'Kangaroo Island', *Adelaide Observer*, 18 September 1844.

2 Clarke estimates that there were about nine women living on Kangaroo Island (excluding Mary Seymour and Hannah Simpson) in the 1860s, 1998, pp. 30–43.

3 South Australia, *Aborigines Department Return*, Parl Paper 198, 1866.

4 Clarke, 1998, pp. 40, 42.

5 Clarke, 1996, p. 75; 'Tasmanian Aboriginals', *Adelaide Observer*, 7 October 1871.

6 Cumpston, pp. 123, 158.

7 'Journal of a Trip to Kangaroo Island', *Adelaide Observer*, 15 January 1853.

8 Plomley, 1966, p. 1020.

9 Alexander Tolmer, *Reminiscences of an Adventurous and Chequered Career*, Sampson Low, Marston, Searle & Rivington, London, 1882, vols. 1–2, 1, p. 321.

10 Clarke, 1998, p. 43.

11 Clarke, 1998, p. 42.

12 Basedow, p. 161.

13 Cawthorne, 1926, p. 87.

14 Plomley and Henley give a list of baptised 'native children' who had been appropriated by settlers in Tasmania, N. J. B. Plomley and Kristen Anne Henley, *The Sealers of Bass Strait and the Cape Barren Island Community*, Blubber Head Press, Sandy Bay, Tasmania, 1990, pp. 25–6; Ryan, pp. 79, 196.

15 Fiona is referring to Basedow's obituary of Mary Seymour, in which Mary tells how she grew up hunting with her mother, brother and sister on the south coast of the island, and spoke their mother's language, p. 161.

16 Fiona Marshall, 'History Research Notes', copy in possession of Rebe Taylor, Canberra.

17 Letter from W. C. Cawthorne to the Trinity Board, Adelaide, 23 June 1859, GRG 51/14, State Records, South Australia.

18 Letter from secretary of Trinity Board to Treasurer, 21 July 1859, GRG 45/1/1859/327, State Records, South Australia.

19 Letter from Treasurer's Office to Secretary of Trinity Board, 25 August 1859, GRG 51/14, State Records, South Australia.

20 Alexander, p. 14.

21 Nunn, p. 108.

22 Bauer, p. 5.

23 Nunn, pp. 101, 84.

24 Cumpston, p. 165.

25 Ruediger, p. 53.

26 Cumpston, p. 172.

27 Interview with Agnes Marshall, 27 August 1994, Penneshaw. Hallack notes in 1905 that wallaby skins 'are not plentiful, albeit they are still quoted in the Adelaide market'. He considered wallabies ought to be protected, p. 17.

28 Joy Seager's memories of being a doctor on Kangaroo Island from the 1920s include meeting a farmer who was wallaby snaring when she was visiting Penneshaw; Joy Seager, *Kangaroo Island Doctor*, Rigby, Adelaide, 1980, pp. 102–3.

29 Bauer, p. 425.

30 'Kangaroo Island', *Adelaide Observer*, 18 September 1844; Cumpston, p. 163.

31 'Thinks He Can Find Sal', Adelaide *News*, 17 March 1932.

32 Hill, p. 20.

33 Bauer, p. 5; Cumpston, p. 165.

34 Tolmer, p. 321; Cumpston, p. 163.

35 *Adelaide Observer*, 13 October 1906 (reprinted article from 13 September 1856).

36 *Adelaide Observer*, 20 October 1906 (reprinted article from 15 September 1856).

37 Clarke, 1998, p. 23.

38 'Thinks He Can Find Sal', Adelaide *News*, 17 March 1932.

39 Nunn, pp. 105–6.

40 Letter to Tindale from H. C. Derek [?], 18 April 1932, enclosing typed notes of information about Aboriginal women on Kangaroo Island that had been given to him by early settler George Bell, in 'Loose Notes', Tindale Collection, South Australian Museum.

41 'An Official Trip to Kangaroo Island', *South Australian Advertiser*, 20 March 1880.

42 'Tasmanian Aboriginals', *Adelaide Observer*, 7 October 1871.

43 'Tasmanian Aboriginals', *Adelaide Observer*, 7 October 1871.

44 'Australian Aborigine', Adelaide *News*, 19 March 1932, in Tindale, 'Journal of Anthropological Researches on Kangaroo Island, South Australia, 1930–1974', South Australian Museum. Nunn also makes this claim, p. 108, based on Hill's, 'Last of the Tasmanians', p. 20; Hill has cited H. A. Lindsay, 'American Settlement on Kangaroo Island 1803', *Quadrant*, vol. 5, 1961, pp. 43–7. In this article Lindsay refers to an unnamed Aboriginal woman who collected rations from Middle River, Stokes Bay, in the 1890s. Hill makes the assumption it is Suke.

45 Letter to W. C. Cawthorne from the Trinity Board, GRG 51/26/3 No. 25/1859. In 1866 the South Australian Parliament stipulated that rations should only be granted to those unable otherwise to procure food, *Aborigines Department Return*, Parl Paper No. 198, 1866.

46 Log Books and Early Journals, Trinity Board, 12 March 1863; store for natives sent up on the *Blanche*.

47 Interview with Jim Marshall, Penneshaw, 24 August 1994.

48 Clarke, 1998, p. 23.

Outlasting

1 Ryan, p. 258.

2 Ryan, p. 203; 'Tasmanians', *Encyclopaedia Britannica CD 98: Knowledge for the Information Age*, CD-ROM, Chicago, 1998.

3 Colleen Coy, 'Fanny Cochrane Smith', in *Tunapi Three: From Family to Community*, ALBE Resources Unit, Tasmania, 1994, pp. 4–5.

4 Cassandra Pybus, *Community of Thieves*, William Heinemann Australia, Port Melbourne, 1991, pp. 180–2.

5 'Tasmania – Frequently Asked Questions': http://www.tased.au/tasfaq/people/aborig.html.

6 H. A. Lindsay, 'Australia's First Human Population', *Walkabout*, 1 January 1954, pp. 34–5, p. 34.

7 Memorandum from the Protector of Aborigines, 8 September 1894, GRG 29/3/280/1894, State Records, South Australia.

8 Tindale, 1937, p. 30.

9 Lindsay, 1961, p. 47.

10 Ryan, p. 220.

11 Nunn, pp. 108, 110.

12 'Tasmanians', *Encyclopaedia Britannica CD 98*. It seems the Encyclopedia is referring to Norman B. Tindale, with an Appendix on Tasmanian Tribes by Rhys Jones, *Aboriginal Tribes of Australia*, Australian National University Press, Canberra, 1974, pts. 1–2, 1, p. 318.

13 'An Official Trip to Kangaroo Island', *South Australian Advertiser*, 20 March 1880; Clarke, 1998, p. 35.

14 Clarke, 1998, p. 35.

15 Stefan Petrow, 'The Last Man: The Mutilation of William Lanne in 1869 and its Aftermath', *Australian Cultural History*, no. 16, 1997/98, pp. 18–44.

16 Petrow, p. 26.

17 'Thinks He Can Find Sal ... Will Look Soon', Adelaide *News*, 17 March 1932, in Tindale, 'Journal of Anthropological Researches on Kangaroo Island', p. 61.

18 'Hot on the Trail of Our Vanished Race', Adelaide *News*, 24 March 1932, in Tindale, 'Journal of Anthropological Researches on Kangaroo Island', p. 64.

19 'Who was the Last to Die – Betty, Bumble Foot or Old Suke?', Adelaide *News*, 23 March 1932, in Tindale, 'Journal of Anthropological Researches on Kangaroo Island', p. 63.

20 Tindale, 'Journal of Anthropological Researches on Kangaroo Island', p. 134.

21 Ryan, p. 218.

22 Hallack, p. 44.

23 Tindale, 1937, p. 33.

24 Tindale, 1937, pp. 33–6.

25 Meaghan Morris, who has researched Hill's life, explained to me that her notes were almost all taken in a very rare style of shorthand few people can decipher.

26 Thomas Gill regretted that there were no Aboriginal Tasmanian skulls or skeletons to be found in the Adelaide Museum with which to do any comparative work with mainland Aborigines; Thomas Gill, 'Some Anthropological Notes on the South Australian Aborigines', in *A Cruise in the Steamer 'Governor Musgrave' Among the Islands in Spencer's Gulf, January 1907*, J. L. Bonython & Co., 'The Advertiser' Office, Adelaide, 1909, pp. 132–60, p. 157.

27 Margaret Ayliffe, *Flinders Land of the South: Early and Later History of Kangaroo Island*, first published by the author in Penneshaw, 1951, 2nd ed: Advertiser Printing Office, Adelaide, 1953 (first published by the author, Penneshaw, Kangaroo Island, 1951), p. 24.

Mary

1 Basedow, p. 161.

2 Basedow, p. 161.

3 Clarke, 1998, p. 45.

4 Basedow, p. 161.

5 'Early South Australia', *Adelaide Observer*, 13 October 1906 (reprinted from 13 September 1856). The same story was repeated in "Came from the Mainland, Old Resident Gives History', Adelaide *Mail*, 19 March 1932, in Tindale, 'Journal of Anthropological Researches on Kangaroo Island', p. 62.

6 Basedow, p. 161.

7 Interview with Roe Trethewey, Penneshaw, Kangaroo Island, 27 August 1994.

8 Hallack, p. 44.

9 H. T. Burgess, ed., *The Cyclopedia of South Australia*, Cyclopedia Company, Adelaide, 1907–09, vols. 1–2, 2, p. 1021.

10 Section 112, Credit Agreement 8672. For some reason this Credit Agreement is not listed in the name of Mary Seymour, but as 'widow'. But Mary told Basedow that she 'bought 268

acres of land near Hog Bay', p. 161. Section 112 is the only 268-acre section in Dudley.
The number of shillings owed in interest is nearly illegible so it may not be correct here.

11 Mary Seymour surrendered her Credit Agreement on 12 June 1883. Credit Agreement
21273 was issued to Thomas Willson on 3 March 1886 and the purchase completed
in 1905.

12 Nunn, p. 157. Tindale wrote in his journal that he travelled to 'Penneshaw (the new name;
Hog Bay is too vulgar)', 'Journal of Anthropological Researches on Kangaroo Island',
10 December 1934, p. 109.

13 Section 2, Penneshaw, CT 403/138, issued 4 September 1885.

14 Section 2, Penneshaw, portion transferred to F. T. Barrett, 6 March 1886, CT 403/138.

15 District of Dudley Assessment for year ending 30 June 1894, District of Dudley Assessment
1888–1904, vol. 1, MRG 81, State Records, South Australia. The Assessments for years
ending 30 June 1890 and 1891 state that Joe Seymour was occupying Part Section 108, near
Penneshaw; the Assessments for years ending 30 June 1892 and 1893 state that he was
occupying Section 42, Penneshaw.

16 South Australia, *Rules and Regulations of the Destitute Board*, Parl Paper No. 35,
South Australian Parliamentary Records, 1883–84.

17 Minutes of the Dudley Council, 6 June 1891 and 6 July 1891.

18 Tenders for contract 7A, Minutes of the Dudley Council, 12 September 1891.

19 Rachel Seymour, 'Birthday Book', in possession of Brentley Golder, Kingscote,
Kangaroo Island.

20 Minutes of the Dudley Council, 4 August 1894.

21 Letter from Thomas Willson, 6 August 1894, GRG 29/3/280/1894, State Records,
South Australia.

22 Similar cases can be found in the Minutes of the Destitute Board vol. 12, GRG 28/1/1894,
GRG 29/3/1895 and GRG 29/3/1921, State Records, South Australia. The case of
Susannah Godrey of Burnside is comparable in some way to Mary Seymour's. In 1887 her
property was transferred to the Destitute Board in return for rations until 1909 when she was
eligible for the Old Age Pension. Her letter to the Board in 1887 shows she was aware that
the cost of her maintenance would be taken from the proceeds from the sale of her house
and land. She had been receiving rations from the Board since 1884 and the cost up until
1909 was £182.11.10. This was in fact more than the value of her property, which in 1887
was given at £100–£120, GRG 29/3/591/1895, State Records, South Australia.

23 *The Destitute Persons Act*, 1881 (SA), pp. 10, 3.

24 *Rules and Regulations of the Destitute Board*; *The Destitute Persons Act*, 1881.

25 This was explained to me in a personal conversation with Brian Dickey. See also Brian
Dickey, with contributions from Elaine Martin and Rodney Oxenberry, *Rations, Residence,
Resources – A History of Social Welfare in South Australia Since 1836*, Wakefield Press, A South
Australian Jubilee 150 Publication, Adelaide, 1986.

26 Letter from Thomas Willson, 6 August 1894.

27 Dickey, p. 51.

28 This correspondence in a series of internal memoranda concerning the request from
Thomas Willson, GRG 29/3/280/1894, State Records, South Australia.

29 Minutes of the Dudley Council, 1 September 1894.

30 The Memorandum of Transfer was signed by Mary on 12 November 1894,
GRG 52/1/390/1894, State Records, South Australia.

31 Minutes of the Dudley Council, 16 May 1896.

32 The following notes appear in the Minutes of the Dudley Council: F. T. Barrett paid to cart 36 gallons a week for 3/, 5 February 1898; F. T. Barrett paid £1.11.8 for carting water for Mrs Seymour, Minutes, 20 May and 10 June 1899; Mary Seymour waited on council to ask for clothes for winter, council resolved to attend to matter, 22 March 1902; J. Seymour repaired Mary Seymour's house, paid 30 shillings, 14 February 1903; S. Jones supplied Mary Seymour with firewood, 13 January 1906; Council to write to Protector of Aborigines to apply for a new 600-gallon iron tank for Mary Seymour, 25 January 1908; new water tank approved, 8 February 1908; Council to write to Protector to request money to purchase more firewood for Mary Seymour, 29 May 1909; Clerk to inspect Mary Seymour's house and report if it needs repairs, 1 June 1912. Also from the records of the Protector of Aborigines, store ledger: Penneshaw, Kangaroo Island, blankets, etc. for Mary Seymour, 1909 and 1910, GRG 52/25, pp. 85–6, State Records, South Australia.

33 Minutes of the Dudley Council, 18 November 1899.

34 Minutes of the Dudley Council, 18 July 1903.

35 Notes provided to me from the Penneshaw Folk Museum. Roe Trethewey, descendant of the original storekeeper and farmer, told me that he did not know that 'Ralph' worked for his ancestor, and thought that when Ralph ran his own shop in Penneshaw, he may have bought it from either Sammy Harris or Mr Bottomley, both of whom sold their businesses at about this time, telephone conversation, 14 December 1999.

36 The District of Dudley Council have compiled lists of the Council's Clerks and Overseers, Councillors and Chairmen as well as details concerning the cemetery, which they kindly made available to me. The position of Pound-keeper is noted in Minutes of the Dudley Council, 12 June 1915 and 16 July 1916; 'We Honour [Ralph Whyte] JP', *The Islander*, 1981, kindly copied for me by the Penneshaw Folk Museum.

37 Section 84, Penneshaw was transferred to Ralph Whyte's father [pseudonym] on 17 April 1906.

38 Letter from Ralph Whyte's daughter [pseudonym] to Mildred Willson, 14 September 1992.

39 'Rules and Regulations of the Destitute Board'.

40 Mary's house was sold in 1914 for £60.5.0, Memorandum from Lands Office, 10 May 1946, GRG 52/390/1894, State Records, South Australia. My estimate here is based on the costs incurred by Destitute Board to support Susannah Godrey of Burnside from 1887–1909: £182.11.10 for 25 years of rations, GRG 29/3/591/1887.

41 Parkside Chronological List of Deaths 1911–1919, Admission no. 212/13, GRG 34/120, State Records, South Australia. This record claims that Jane Seymour was admitted on 2 February 1913, that she was born in England and died in the Asylum aged 62 in June 1914. It seems that some of these details are not correct. Jane's death certificate claims she was born in Penneshaw and died in the Parkville Asylum aged 61, 1 June 1914, Death Certificate no. 381, District of Norwood.

42 Telegram from J. Watson, Penneshaw, 9 September 1913, GRG 52/1/390/1894, State Records, South Australia.

43 South Australia, *Rules and Regulations of the Destitute Board*, Parl Paper No. 27, 1867.

44 *A Cruise in the Steamer 'Governor Musgrave' Among the Islands in Spencer's Gulf, January 1907.*

45 Berry, pp. 1–21.

46 Berry, pp. 4, 8.

47 Berry, pp. 4–5.

48 Berry, p. 8; Hallack, p. 44.

49 Basedow, pp. 160–2.

50 Plomley and Henley, p. 26.

51 Dunabin, p. 306.

Emma, 'The Aboriginal'

1   'This is My Life', notes by Mildred Chester [pseudonym].
2   Lot 84, Penneshaw, Land Grant 411/47, transferred to F. T. Barrett, 13 September 1892; Lots 85 and 86, Penneshaw, CT 395/190; CT 411/119 registered to Emma Barrett 6 April 1893.
3   'Barrett's Corner' was referred to in the Minutes of the Dudley Council, 23 March 1907; 'This is My Life', notes by Mildred Chester [pseudonym].
4   Sections 354, 355, 370 and 371 – 1402 acres – 377, 361, 292 and 372, amount not given, Right to Purchase lease 8235, issued to F. T. Barrett, 20 August 1895.
5   Lots 85 and 86, Penneshaw, CT395/190 and CT 411/119 were transferred to Charlotte Jones, 10 May 1899; Lot 52, Penneshaw, CT 639/47, transferred to J. R. Walker [not pseudonym], 8 October 1898.
6   Lot 73, Penneshaw, CT 283/64, issued 21 March 1900.
7   Sections 22, 23, 28, 29 and 32, CT 679/110, registered to Emma Barrett, 27 August 1901.
8   Frank Barrett 'chained' the cemetery (cleared it by dragging a chain), Minutes of the Dudley Council, 7 June 1890, and supplied water to Mary Seymour, Minutes, 5 February 1898 and 20 May 1899. Frank was Curator of the Cemetery from 13 December 1890 until 2 May 1896. He was re-appointed District Ranger on 12 September 1891 and again on 14 July 1894 and 1 September 1897 until he resigned 8 September 1900. Emma Barrett was then District Ranger until August 1904. Minutes of the Dudley Council.
9   Frank Barrett requested Destitute help for his son, Minutes of the Dudley Council, 2 July 1892. Letter received from Destitute Board with form to supply one quarter of rations to F. T. Barrett, Minutes of the Dudley Council, 9 April 1894.
10 It was noted that a letter from the Destitute Board declining to supply rations to Emma Barrett had been received and that the Clerk was to write and state the case is 'deserving', Minutes of the Dudley Council, 9 August 1902. Clerk reports that the Destitute Board refuses rations to Emma Barrett, Minutes of the Dudley Council, 4 October 1902.
11 Right to Purchase lease 8235 transferred to James Waller 26 April 1900.
12 Section 84, Penneshaw, was registered in 1892 to F. T. Barrett, who died on 6 April 1901. The land was transferred to Emma Barrett on 20 October 1901 then to Ralph Whyte's father [pseudonym] on 17 April 1906. The cottage on this section is still referred to as 'Dick's', which was Ralph's father's name.
13 Minutes of the Dudley Council, 10 September 1904; Section 122s [south], 32 acres, Right To Purchase Lease 6897, granted to F. T. Barrett, 23 February 1893, transferred to Emma Barrett, 1901, purchase completed. Land Grant 943/12 was issued to Emma Barrett, 31 December 1912. Transferred to Gilbert Barrett, 22 October 1913.
14 Lot 73, Penneshaw, area one rood, CT 483/64, registered 21 March 1900, transferred to Thomas Francis Barrett, October 1911. Thomas Barrett listed as owner and occupier of Lot 73, District of Dudley Assessment for year ending 1912, Kangaroo Island Council, Kingscote.
15 Memorandum from Protector of Aborigines, GRG 52/1/390/1894.
16 Letter from W. & G. Gunson Solicitors, 27 September 1913, GRG 52/1/390/1894, State Records, South Australia.
17 Letter from W. & G. Gunson Solicitors, 27 September 1913.
18 Memorandum from Protector of Aborigines, 29 September 1913, GRG 52/1/390/1894, State Records, South Australia.
19 The figure here of £35 is barely legible in the original and may not be correct. The £50 is, however, clearly legible.
20 Letter from W. & G. Gunson Solicitors, 16 December 1913, GRG 52/1/390/1894, State Records, South Australia.

21 Memorandum from Protector of Aborigines, 22 December 1913, GRG 52/1/390/1894, State Records, South Australia.

22 Memorandum from Protector, 18 June 1914, GRG 52/1/390/1894, State Records, South Australia.

23 Memorandum from Lands Office, 27 August 1914, GRG 52/1/390/1894, State Records, South Australia.

24 Letter from Emma Barrett, Hog Bay, 10 July 1914, GRG 52/1/390/1894, State Records, South Australia.

25 Letter from W. & G. Gunson Solicitors, Adelaide, 8 January 1914, GRG 52/1/390/1894, State Records, South Australia.

26 Letter from Joseph Seymour to the Surveyor General, 31 August 1914, GRG 52/1/390/1894, State Records, South Australia.

27 Memorandum from Lands Office, 10 May 1946, GRG 52/1/390/1894, State Records, South Australia; Section 2E, Penneshaw, Land Grant 1021/110 was held by different members of the Bates family until 27 May 1977.

28 Memorandum from Lands Office, 10 May 1946, GRG 52/1/390/1894, State Records, South Australia. Section 122s [south], Right To Purchase Lease 6897, transferred to E. L. Bates in 1917.

29 Lot 73 transferred from Thomas Barrett back to Emma Barrett May 1916; Section 32 transferred to Thomas Barrett 4 May 1916. The other four sections then became part of CT 1052/37.

30 'This is My Life', notes by Mildred Chester [pseudonym].

31 Thomas and Gilbert Barrett were both listed as owners and occupiers of their properties – Thomas of Section 73 in District of Dudley Assessment for year ending 30 June 1912 and Gilbert for Section 122s for year ending 30 June 1916. They were also employed by the Council: Gilbert as day worker (Minutes of the Dudley Council, 10 April 1915) and Thomas as day worker (Minutes of the Dudley Council, 10 September 1916). Gilbert applied to be District Ranger on 10 November 1917, Minutes of the Dudley Council. Ellen Marks told me that Gilbert and Thomas eventually lived in Adelaide like their sisters.

32 Ayliffe, p. 24.

33 Letter to M. Moorhouse from William Wilkins, received 2 April 1860, GRG 35/1/374/1860, State Records, South Australia.

34 Julie-Ann Ellis, Public Land and the Public Mind: Origins of Public Land Policy in South Australia 1834–1929, PhD Thesis, Faculty of Social Sciences, Flinders University, 1995, p. 78.

35 Linguist Rob Amery of the University of Adelaide told me he thinks the name Monatto is almost without doubt from *Munato*, a Kaurna birth-order name meaning third-born and female. Email from Rob Amery, 1 September 1999.

36 Letter to Surveyor General from M. Moorhouse, received 4 April 1860, GRG 35/1/374/1860, State Records, South Australia. According to the Land Titles Office, Section 100 was set aside at the time of survey (March 1860) as a Aboriginal Reserve, but Julie-Ann Ellis, who has a database of the Aboriginal Reserves in South Australia, explained to me that Section 100 was not properly gazetted until 1861, although lands reserved in South Australia in this period were not always formally gazetted.

37 Log Books and Daily Journals, Trinity Board Miscellaneous Papers, 17 September 1860.

38 Log Books and Daily Journals, 15 October 1860.

39 Letter from the Sub-Protector of Aborigines, 11 March 1861, GRG 35/1/374, 1861, State Records, South Australia.

40 Aboriginal Lease No. 34, issued to Robert Davidson 1 March 1865 and expired 29 February 1872. Aboriginal Lease No. 78 was then issued to Henry Bates in March 1872 (gazetted 4 April 1872) and transferred to George James Bates in 1875 and expired 31 January 1879, Land Titles Office and State Records, South Australia.

41 South Australia, *Cancellation of 'Aboriginal Section, Kangaroo Island'*, Parl Paper No. 78, 1880: Section 100, east of Section 101 and north and north-west of portions of Section 99, Hundred of Dudley, lease 78, cancelled in terms of clause 6 of the Crown Lands Consolidation Act, 1877. Field Book 1237, September 1881, Department of Lands, South Australia.

42 After more than a decade of lobbying to government, work began on the Penneshaw jetty in August 1902 and was completed four months later; Bauer, pp. 423, 431, 392.

43 Roe Trethewey remembers how people met and talked on the corner opposite the pub on Saturdays, interview, 27 August 1994.

44 Hallack, p. 7.

45 Interview with Roe Trethewey, 25 June 1993.

46 Interim Land Tenure Map, Town of Penneshaw, 110201, Local Government Area 52, Dudley, deposited 28 November 1986, Department of Lands. The sections overlooking Hog Bay were surveyed in 1982.

47 Interview with Mildred Willson, 4 September 1994.

48 Section 23 transferred to Mildred Chester [pseudonym], Section 29 transferred to Thomas Barrett, Section 28 transferred in 1924 and Section 22 transferred in 1968, both outside the Barrett family. Lewis Barrett acted as executor, 6 July 1922.

Hannah

1 Basedow, p. 161; Section 109, CT877/163 states that Hannah died on 11 March 1912.

2 Marriage Certificate 049, District of Yankalilla, Book 41, p. 223; Burgess, p. 1021.

3 Minutes forming enclosure to Department of Lands, 5489, vol. 8, f. 4, 1946.

4 Mildred Willson told me this on a (recorded) trip to Antechamber Bay with Neil Waller and his nephew Jamie O'Neill, 4 April 1998. Simpson's Hill is also referred to in the Minutes of the Dudley Council regarding the construction of a road, 2 July 1906.

5 Nunn, p. 210.

6 Bauer, p. 345.

7 Minutes forming enclosure to Department of Lands, 5489.

8 Jayne Bates, 'A History of the Wells Family', in possession of Jayne Bates, Penneshaw, Kangaroo Island, pp. 6–8; Nunn, p. 115.

9 Section 105, CT201/105 transferred 23 January 1974.

10 Post Office Masters received £140–210 annually, while messengers received a wage of only £30–39. This indicates that Thomas Simpson, with an annual wage of £35, was a messenger; *The South Australian Register*, Robert Thomas & Co., Adelaide, 1839–1900, 1873, pp. 20–4; Bauer, p. 371.

11 Section 105, CT14/54, subdivided and portion to T. Simpson 9 January 1875.

12 District Of Dudley Assessment for year ending 30 June 1889; Letter from Thomas Simpson, Hog Bay, Kangaroo Island, 5 April 1880, GRG 52/1/125, State Records, South Australia.

13 Bauer, pp. 344, 340.

14 Bauer, pp. 345–7.

15 Letter from Thomas Simpson, 1880.

16 'An Official Trip to Kangaroo Island', *South Australian Advertiser*, 20 March 1880.

[17] Memorandum from Commissioner of Crown Lands, 13 April 1880, GRG 52/1/125, State Records, South Australia.

[18] Hallack, p. 18.

[19] Section 109, Scrub Lease 1045, issued to Thomas Simpson, 1 October 1881.

The Years of Success

[1] Burgess, p. 1021.

[2] Section 63, CT 1221/38, issued to N. T. Simpson, 23 September 1896.

[3] Section 62, Credit Agreement 14603, issued 24 January 1882; Section 64, Credit Agreement 15855 issued 24 April 1883; Section 391, Credit Agreement 15857, issued 24 April 1883; Section 390, Credit Agreement 21403, issued 8 September 1896 (although Section 390 is listed in the District of Dudley Assessment for year ending 30 June 1889 as 'Credit Selection' for Stephen Simpson).

[4] Sections 360–366, 373–379, 382–386, miscellaneous lease 4287; Sections 387–388, 389, 392, 61 and 65, miscellaneous lease 4286, both issued on 1 April 1888.

[5] Section 109, Scrub Lease 2480, surrendered for Right of Purchase Lease 5384, issued 15 December 1890; Sections 66 and 380 (adjacent) Credit Agreement 21201, issued 1891 and Block V, Miscellaneous Lease 4851, transferred to W. V. and N. T. Simpson in 1891.

[6] District of Dudley Assessment for year ending 30 June 1896 lists Stephen Simpson as 'owner' of Section 7 but CT607/144 states Thomas Simpson snr was granted Section 7 on 29 September 1897.

[7] Nunn, p. 157; Bauer, pp. 371, 382, 386, 390.

[8] Sections 262–268, 271–273, Miscellaneous Lease 5324, issued 1898; Nunn, p. 141.

[9] Telephone conversation with Roe Trethewey, 16 December 1998; Bauer, p. 387.

[10] Interview with Adrian and Neil Waller, 15 August 1994.

[11] Email from Adrian Waller, 2 October 1999. They possibly also came with their younger brothers Benjamin and William, as Sections 54 and 55, Credit Agreement 20845 and Sections 56 and 57, Credit Agreement 17986, were issued to Benjamin in 1885 and 1888 respectively; they were both surrendered and a Selector's Lease was issued to Benjamin in 1889, and then transferred to his brother Henry. Section 315 was issued to William on 1 October 1885, transferred to Benjamin, date unknown, and then transferred to Henry in 1888.

[12] Section 316, Credit Agreement 17799, issued 4 July 1888, Section A1 Miscellaneous Lease 6039 transferred to Alfred Waller 1899; Sections 306 and 308, Credit Agreement 17800 was issued to Henry in 1884 and transferred to his brother Alfred in 1890; Section 269, Homestead Perpetual Lease 4139, issued 1 October 1895.

[13] Sections 51 and 314, Credit Agreement 18050, issued 16 January 1885, Section 315, Miscellaneous Lease 2773, issued 1 October 1885. For Sections 54–57, Credit Agreements 17986 and 20845, see note above.

[14] Burgess, p. 1022; letter from Adrian Waller, 31 December 1997; Letters from Graham Deane Miller 25 January 2003, 14 and 23 May 2006; District of Dudley Assessment for years ending 1939–1940 and 1955–1956.

[15] Sections 262–268 and 271–273, Miscellaneous Lease 5324, issued 1 October 1891. Thomas Simpson jnr was also granted Homestead Perpetual Lease 153 for Section 269 in Sapphiretown in 1886 according to the *South Australian Government Gazette*. This lease was issued to Alfred Waller 1 October 1895.

[16] Part Section 2, CT496/185, transferred from F. T. Barrett to Henry Waller 20 March 1894. The District of Dudley Assessment for years ending 30 June 1905–1907 lists Henry as owner and Joseph Seymour as occupant of part Section 2.

[17] Sections 354, 355, 370 and 371, Right of Purchase Lease 8235 was issued to F. T. Barrett 29 August 1895, transferred to James Waller 26 April 1900.

[18] Section 77, Perpetual Lease 3911, issued to Stamford Simpson, 28 July 1897.

[19] Sections 62, CT685/33, issued 4 January 1902, Section 64 CT694/140, issued 6 August 1902; Section 391, CT692/99, issued 9 July 1902; Section 381, Credit Agreement 5647, issued 1 October 1904, completed and Land Grant 765/133, issued 13 June 1907; Section 390, CT808/24, issued 3 June 1909; Section 109, CT857/90, issued 2 January 1911.

[20] The landholding details for the Willson, Buick and Marshall [pseudonym] families all come from the Interim Land Tenure Maps for East and West Dudley, discontinued 3 February 1992, Department of Lands, South Australia, the District of Dudley Assessment for year ending 30 June 1904 and the cadastral map of Dudley number 177–005, deposited 1899 and withdrawn 1928, Lands Office, South Australia. The latter two references also give the details for Robert Clark. The Willson and Buick leases in Haines can also be found in Bauer, Map 17.

[21] Bates, p. 10.

[22] Nunn, p. 160.

[23] Bauer, p. 363; Nunn, p. 160.

[24] The landholding details for the Bates, Trethewey and Howard families all come from the Interim Land Tenure Maps for East and West Dudley, cadastral map of Dudley, 177–005 and the District of Dudley Assessment for year ending 30 June 1904.

[25] The landholding details for the Clark, Lyall, Barr, Neave and McArthur families comes from the District of Dudley Assessment for year ending 30 June 1904; cadastral map of Dudley, 177–005. There are details on Albert Neave, James McArthur and William Lyall in Burgess, pp. 1011, 1022, 1025.

[26] Burgess, p. 1021.

[27] Hallack, p. 41.

[28] Bauer, Map 19.

[29] Letter from Thomas Willson, *South Australian Register*, 21 February 1877.

[30] Conversation with the current owner of the Simpsons' farm, 15 December 1998; interview with Fiona and Robin Marshall, 3 September 1994.

[31] Bauer, Map 8; H. C. T. Stace and others, *A Handbook of Australian Soils*, Rellim Technical Publications, Adelaide, 1968, pp. 191–5; conversation with geographer Nigel Wace of the Australian National University, who has studied Kangaroo Island's geography, 17 December 1998.

[32] Bauer, Maps 8, 13; M. I. H. Brooker and D. A. Keinig, *Field Guide to Eucalypts*, Melbourne, Inkata Press, 1990, vols. 1–3, 2, p. 228; telephone conversations with Bruce Bates, 15 and 23 November 1999.

[33] Telephone conversations with Roe Trethewey, 16 December 1998 and Bruce Bates, 15 and 23 November 1999; Bauer, Maps 8, 13; Brooker and Keinig, pp. 79, 345.

[34] Bauer, p. 351.

[35] Dudley received 20–28 inches of rain per year; Bauer, Appendix VI, Map 12, pp. 363, 258. Hallack had also learnt in 1905 from Thomas Willson that he had recorded the rainfall near the south coast of Dudley in 1902–1904 as being between 20.42 and 25.97 inches, p. 39.

36 Telephone conversations with Roe Trethewey, 16 December 1998, and current owner of Simpsons' farm, 15 December 1998. The current owner has been through this land and has seen the old fences.

37 Telephone conversations with Roe Trethewey, 16 December 1998; Bruce Bates, 15 and 23 November 1999; current owner of Simpsons' farm, 15 December 1998.

38 Ted Bates, 'Memoirs', in possession of Bruce Bates, Penneshaw, Kangaroo Island, pp. 11–12; Bauer, p. 340.

39 Wilson lists the numbers of sheep held by some of the Kangaroo Island graziers in 1905, p. 14. Burgess lists numbers of sheep held by Henry Waller (p. 1022) and other Island families.

40 'The Wants of Kangaroo Island', *Adelaide Observer*, 13 April 1870.

41 Bauer, p. 342 and telephone conversation with Roe Trethewey, 16 December 1998.

42 Ted Bates, 'Memoirs', pp. 11–12.

43 Bauer, p. 345.

44 Bauer, pp. 414, 404.

45 Burgess, Preface, p. 1021; Minutes of the Dudley Council 1893–1902.

46 Minutes of the Dudley Council, 1889–1904.

47 Interview with Mildred Willson, 4 September 1994.

48 Records of road-work contracts tendered, Minutes of the Dudley Council, 1888–1919.

49 Dudley Council Minutes, 9 August 1902 and 4 October 1902.

50 Bauer, pp. 414, 360.

The Years of Decline

1 T. A. Coghlan, *Labour and Industry in Australia: From the First Settlement in 1788 to the Establishment of the Commonwealth in 1901*, Macmillan, Melbourne, 1969, vols. 1–4, 3, pp. 1633–1789; 4, p. 2170.

2 Section 63, CT445/43, value given in the Certificate of Title records, mortgage for CT 1221/38 registered 23 September 1896. In 1895 the State Bank of South Australia could make advances to farmers on the security of their freehold or leasehold lands. The maximum rate of interest was 5%, but private lenders usually had higher lending rates than the public institutions.

3 Minutes of the Dudley Council, 1893–1905.

4 *South Australian Government Gazette*, 24 January 1907, p. 281.

5 Sections 360, 361 and 365 transferred to Henry Clark, Sections 362, 363, 364 and 379 transferred to George Abotomey, Sections 373–375, 378, 382, 383 transferred to Harry Davey, Sections 366, 376, 377 and 384 transferred to John Simpson, Sections 385 and 386 transferred to Stephen Fraser, all in 1907.

6 Perpetual Lease 8674, issued 1903, mortgaged in 1906 to Susan Hall and transferred to the Neaves in 1923.

7 Sections 66 and 380 mortgage registered 1905, Sections 391 and 62, mortgages registered 1906; Perpetual Lease 8613 transferred to J. Trethewey, 18 March 1908; Section 390, mortgage registered 1909, Section 390 transferred to Robert Clark 1911; Section 64 mortgage registered 1911.

8 Section 105, CT201–105, mortgaged registered to V. S. Bates, 8 June 1917: foreclosed 17 October 1938.

9 Sections 373–375, 378, 382 and 383, portion of Miscellaneous Lease 2487 was cancelled 22 December 1933 for failure to pay rent, *South Australian Government Gazette*, p. 281.

10 Sections 306 and 308 transferred to William Gray, 21 August 1906; Sections A1 and 316 transferred to T. Willson in 1921; Section 269 lease cancelled in 1922.

11 Sections 354, 355, 370 and 371, Right of Purchase Lease 8235, transferred to S. W. Simpson 29 September 1920, and then to E. S. Bates 11 December 1923.

12 Sections 54–57 transferred to M. L. Buick 24 June 1897; Sections 51, 314 and 315 were transferred to several of Henry Waller's children until 1957, when they were all transferred to T. Willson.

13 Sections 62, 63 and 64 were transferred to Harry and Frederick Neave in 1922.

14 Steve's address changed from Penneshaw to Adelaide in the District of Dudley Assessment for year ending 30 June 1923; Section 7, CT1578/9 transferred to V. Bates 4 July 1930.

15 Section 109, CT857/90, issued to Hannah Simpson, 2 January 1911; CT877/163 transferred to S. W. Simpson, 1 August 1912; CT1293/107, issued to S. W. Simpson, 20 July 1923; CT2152/172, issued to S. W. Simpson, 13 July 1951; transferred to Leslie Victor Simpson as executor of S. W. Simpson, who died 21 October 1955, then transferred 13 November 1979; District of Dudley Assessment for years ending 30 June, 1911–1954.

16 Bauer, pp. 259–466.

17 One farmer told the Lands Law Commission of 1888 that 'the crops came up beautifully, but yielded nothing', South Australia, *Report of the Commission on the Land Laws of South Australia; Together With Minutes of Proceedings, Evidence, and Apendices*, Parl Paper No. 28, 1888, pp. 53–69; Bauer, pp. 364–5; Nunn, pp. 167, 187.

Staying White

1 Birth Certificate for Gladys France Simpson, born 27 April 1893, Carrington Street, Adelaide, number 110, District of Adelaide.

2 Death Certificate for Martha France Simpson, died 23 April 1894, number 322, District of Yankalilla.

3 Death Certificate for Gladys France Simpson, died 5 October 1984, Campbelltown, number 7590, District of Norwood.

4 Similarly, Jan Critchett, in her book *Untold Stories*, tells of Wilmot Abraham of Warrnambool who, after growing up with his Aboriginal mother, returned to his white father's family, where he was welcomed and cared for. But after his death in 1916, 'Wilmot's membership of the family, obviously once accepted, became something best not talked about'. Wilmot was famously remembered as the last 'full-blood' of his tribe. Jan Critchett, *Untold Stories, Memories and Lives of Victorian Kooris*, Melbourne University Press, Melbourne, 1998, pp. 36–47.

5 Nunn, p. 150.

6 Clara Bates, 'Diary', the Penneshaw Folk Museum.

7 Patrick Wolfe, *Settler Colonialism and the Transformation of Anthropology*, Cassell, London, 1999, p. 185.

8 Charlie Schultz and Darrell Lewis, *Beyond the Big Run: Station Life in Australia's Last Frontier*, University of Queensland Press, St Lucia, 1995, p. 83.

9 Schultz and Lewis, p. 83.

10 Letter from Daisy Simpson, Victoria, to Stamford and Jack Simpson, no year given. Found among letters belonging to Stamford Simpson, the Penneshaw Folk Museum.

11 Patrick Wolfe, 'Nation and MiscegeNation: Discursive Continuity in the Post-Mabo Era', *Social Analysis*, 36, pp. 93–152, p. 95, in response to Jan Critchett, *A Distant Field*

of Murder: Western District Profile, 1834–1848, Melbourne University Press, Melbourne, 1990, p. 23.

12 Wolfe argues that it was the 'colour not the Aboriginality' that was being assimilated in the twentieth-century government policies – Aboriginality was 'left behind in the camp', 1994, pp. 116–17.

13 Postcard from Annie Seymour, Penneshaw, to Stamford Simpson, Cape de Couedic, 25 April 1908, found among letters belonging to Stamford Simpson, the Penneshaw Folk Museum.

14 Bauer, p. 430.

15 *The Register*, 3 June 1907.

16 Minute Books of the Dudley District Council, 1890–1917.

17 Norman B. Tindale, 'Tasmania and the Part Aborigines of the Bass Strait Islands and Kangaroo Island, 1936–1965', pp. 324–33.

18 Tindale, 'Tasmania and the Part Aborigines of the Bass Strait Islands and Kangaroo Island, 1936–1965', p. 311.

19 Tindale, 'Journal of Anthropological Researches on Kangaroo Island', p. 17.

Images of Loss

1 'Henry Vere Barclay', David Carment, Robyn Maynard and Alan Powell, eds, *Northern Territory Dictionary of Biography*, Darwin, NTU Press, 1990, pp. 11–14.

2 Telephone conversation with John Dallwitz, 9 October 2000. John was quoting a 1995 letter from Keith Mooney Smith, who had researched Tom Simpson.

3 John Dallwitz and Susan Marsden, 'Introduction', John Dallwitz ed., *Horrie Simpson's Oodnadatta*, Oodnadatta Progress Association, Oodnadatta, South Australia, 1990, pp. ix–xi.

4 Schultz and Lewis, p. 114.

5 Schultz and Lewis, p. 84.

6 Telephone conversation with John Dallwitz, 9 October 2000.

7 District Council of Dudley Minutes, 1893–1918.

8 Bauer, pp. 417–19.

9 Interview with Keith Southlyn, 28 June 1993.

10 Letter from Lindsay Howard, 3 July 2000.

11 Letter from Lindsay Howard.

12 Tindale, Tasmania and the Part Aborigines of the Bass Strait Islands and Kangaroo Island, 1936–1965, p. 315.

'I'm a Blackfella'

1 Summons for 'Standford [*sic*] W. Simpson, laborer, Penneshaw', 11 June 1914, photocopy kindly given to me by Jayne Bates, Penneshaw.

2 Julie Carter, 'Am I too Black to Go with You?', in Ian Keen, ed., *Being Black: Aboriginal Cultures in 'Settled' Australia*, Aboriginal Studies Press for Australian Institute of Aboriginal Studies, Canberra, 1988, p. 65.

3 Tindale, 'Journal of Anthropological Researches on Kangaroo Island', p. 131.

4 Ruediger also tells the story of how Tiger said he would 'get his Tassie up', p. 56. Bruce Bates thinks that she probably learnt this from his father.

5 John McQuilton, *Rural Australia and the Great War, from Tarrawingee to Tangambalanga*, Melbourne University Press, Melbourne, 2001, pp. 70, 66.

6 Letter from Robin and Fiona Marshall, 10 November 1995.

7 Letter from Keith and Margaret Southlyn, 5 August 1993.

Memory

1 Maurice Halbwachs, *On Collective Memory*, trans. F. J. Ditter and V. Y. Ditter, Harper & Row, New York, 1980. In their introduction, Ditter and Ditter discuss the 'impassable barrier' between people who do not share enough of the same collective memories, pp. 21–5. See also Paula Hamilton, 'The Knife Edge: Debates About History and Memory', in Kate Darian-Smith and Paula Hamilton, eds, *Memory and History in Twentieth Century Australia*, Oxford University Press, Melbourne, 1994, p. 19.

2 Pierre Nora, 'Between Memory and History: Les Lieux de Mémoire', *Representations*, vol. 26, 1989, pp. 7–25. John Frow gives a summary of Nora's *Lieux de Mémoire* in *Time and Commodity Culture, Essays in Cultural Theory and Postmodernity*, Oxford University Press, New York, 1997, pp. 219–23. Frow imagines postmodernity as a 'fall from memory into history, or from history into amnesia'. For Frow this is a 'state of loss', which 'is repeatedly linked to . . . the world of commodity culture'. This book was inspired before I had the opportunity to read Frow's interpretation of Nora.

3 Nora, p. 8.

4 Nora, p. 8.

5 Here Nora is quoting Halbwachs's notion that there are as many memories as there are groups, Halbwachs, p. 22.

6 Bates, p. 1

7 Nora, p. 7.

8 Letter to Mr Stamford Simpson from Norman B. Tindale, 31 March 1936, in 'Loose Notes', Tindale Collection, South Australian Museum.

9 Letter from Michael Golder to Norman Tindale, 16 December 1975, note concerning letter and reply from Tindale, 24 December 1975, in 'Journal of Anthropological Researches on Kangaroo Island', pp. 174–76.

10 Tindale, 'Journal of Anthropological Researches on Kangaroo Island', p. 131.

11 Tindale, 'Journal of Anthropological Researches on Kangaroo Island', p. 17.

12 Letter from Larry Golder, 23 September 2001.

13 'Family's Unique Link with Island History', *Islander*, 6 June 1984.

14 Paul Mann, 'Kangaroo Island – the pirate fortress that retains its free spirit', *Australian Geographic*, April/June, 1988, p. 33.

15 Mavis Golder, *Gentlemen . . . take your partners*, Kingscote, Kangaroo Island, published by the author, 1994, pp. 2–3.

16 'Tribute to true Islander', *The Islander*, 1 June 1995.

17 Letter from Adrian Waller of Hawthorn, Adelaide, 14 January 1998.

'How Aboriginal Am I?'

1 Clarke, 1996, 1998.

2 Letter from Rebe Taylor to Robert Simpson, 3 August 1998.

3 Fax from Robert Simpson, 11 August 1998.

4 Rebe Taylor's field notebook for Kangaroo Island and Adelaide, 13–19 April 1998, p. 46.

The Dinner

1 Rebe Taylor, 'Address to the Kangaroo Island Pioneers Association Annual Dinner', Adelaide, 17 July 1998, audio and visual recordings in possession of Rebe Taylor, Canberra.

2 Rebe Taylor, 'Address to the Kangaroo Island Pioneers Association Annual Dinner'.

3 Email from Neil Waller, 29 September 1998.

Bibliography

Interviews

* = *pseudonym*

All interview tapes and transcripts are in possession of Rebe Taylor, Melbourne.

Bruce Bates, Penneshaw, Kangaroo Island, 28 June 1993 & 15 April 1998.

Dave Buick, Kingscote, Kangaroo Island, 26 August 1994.

Dave and Monica Buick, Penneshaw, Kangaroo Island, 26 June 1993.

Thelma Buick, Kingscote, Kangaroo Island, 15 April 1998.

Brentley Golder, Kingscote, Kangaroo Island, 16 April 1998.

Larry Golder, Glenelg, Adelaide, 18 April 1998.

Les Golder, Kingscote, Kangaroo Island, 16 April 1998.

Mavis Golder, Kingscote, Kangaroo Island, 26 June 1993 & 2 September 1994.

Michael Golder, Reynella, Adelaide, 19 June 1993.

Lindsay Howard (with Agnes Walker*), Kingscote, Kangaroo Island, 15 April 1998.

Ellen Marks*, Lockleys, Adelaide, 12 April 1998.

Agnes Marshall*, Penneshaw, Kangaroo Island, 27 August 1994.

Robin and Fiona Marshall*, Antechamber Bay, Kangaroo Island, 27 June 1993 &
    3 September 1994.

Jim Marshall*, Penneshaw, Kangaroo Island, 23 June 1993 & 24 August 1994.

Jamie O'Neill, Kingscote, Kangaroo Island, 13 April 1998 & trip to Antechamber Bay,
    Kangaroo Island, with Neil Waller and Agnes Walker* 14 April 1998.

Terri Sanderson* (with Larry Golder), Glenelg, Adelaide, 18 April 1998.

Doris Simpson, Thebarton, Adelaide, 19 April 1998.

Dorothy Simpson, Parkville, Victoria, 25 February 1998.

Terry Simpson, Para Hills West, Adelaide, 17 April 1998.

Keith and Margaret Southlyn*, Antechamber Bay, Kangaroo Island, 28 June 1993 &
    2 September 1994.

Neil Waller, Springfield, Adelaide, 21 June 1993, Kingscote, Kangaroo Island, 13 April 1998 &
    trip to Antechamber Bay, 14 April 1998.

Roe Trethewey, Penneshaw, Kangaroo Island, 25 June 1993, 27 August 1994 & 15 April 1998.

Neil and Adrian Waller, Hawthorn, Adelaide, 15 August 1994 & 15 August 1998.

Mildred Willson, near Kingscote, Kangaroo Island, 4 September 1994, Kingscote, 14 April 1998
    & (with Lindsay Howard) 15 April 1998 and trip to Antechamber Bay, 14 April 1998.

Archival records

Correspondence concerning Mary Seymour's initial application for Destitute Board Rations, GRG 29/3/280/1894, State Records, South Australia.

Correspondence concerning Mary Seymour's rations from the Aborigines Office, including the sale of her house, GRG 52/1/390/1894, State Records, South Australia.

Correspondence concerning William Wilkins and The Aboriginal Reserve at Hog Bay (Penneshaw), Kangaroo Island, GRG 35/1/374/1860 & GRG 35/1/374/1861, State Records, South Australia.

District of Dudley Council Assessments, 1888–1904, vol. 1, MRG 81, State Records, South Australia.

Log book for Sturt Lighthouse (at Cape Willoughby) 1853–1867, D26, National Archives, South Australia.

Minutes of Proceedings of the Commission of Inquiry into the Lawless State of Society on Kangaroo Island, 1837, GRG 24/90/342, State Records, South Australia.

Minutes of the Destitute Board, GRG 28/1/1894, GRG 29/3/1895, GRG 29/3/591/1895 & GRG 29/3/1921, State Records, South Australia.

Parkside Chronological List of Deaths 1911–1919, GRG 34/120, State Records, South Australia.

The Protector of Aborigines, store ledger: Penneshaw, Kangaroo Island, 1909–1910, GRG 52/25, State Records, South Australia.

Trinity Board papers (concerning the Sturt Lighthouse at Cape Willoughby) GRG 51/14, GRG 51/26/3 No. 25/1859 & GRG 45/1/1859/327, State Records, South Australia.

Land and council records

Cadastral map of Dudley number 177–005, deposited 1899 and withdrawn 1928, Lands Office, South Australia.

Certificates of Title, Certificates of Lease, Credit Agreements and mortgage and transfer records for lots in the Hundred of Dudley, Lands Office, South Australia.

District of Dudley Council Assessments 1905–1954, Kangaroo Island Council, Kingscote (for Assessments 1888–1904, see 'archival records' listed above).

Interim Land Tenure Maps for East and West Dudley, discontinued 3 February 1992, Department of Lands, South Australia.

Interim Land Tenure Map, Town of Penneshaw, 110201, Local Government Area 52, Dudley, deposited 28 November 1986, Department of Lands, South Australia.

Minutes forming enclosure to Department of Lands, 5489, vol. 8, f. 4, 1946, Lands Office, South Australia.

Minutes of the District of Dudley Council, 1888–1920, Kangaroo Island Council, Kingscote.

Library, museum and private records

Bruce Bates, 'Grandfather's Stories', in possession of Bruce Bates, Penneshaw, Kangaroo Island.

Clara Bates, 'Diary', the Penneshaw Folk Museum, Kangaroo Island.

Jayne Bates, 'A History of the Bates Family', in possession of Jayne Bates, Penneshaw, Kangaroo Island.

Jayne Bates, 'Family History Research Notes', copy in possession of Rebe Taylor, Canberra.

Ted Bates, 'Memoirs', in possession of Bruce Bates, Penneshaw, Kangaroo Island.

W. A. Cawthorne, 'Diary', 1849–1859, B230, (CY2141), Mitchell Library, State Library of New South Wales.

W. A. Cawthorne, 'Sketches, manuscripts and memorabilia', 1840–1979, FM4/8474–8475, Mitchell Library, State Library of New South Wales.

Mildred Chester [pseudonym], 'This is My Life', in possession of Ellen Marks, Lockleys, South Australia.
James Knight, 'The Great Kartan Myth', in possession of James Knight, Department of State Aboriginal Affairs, South Australia, 1995.
Michael Golder, 'Nat Thomas' Chronology 1818–1824', in possession of Michael Golder, Reynella, South Australia.
Fiona Marshall, [pseudonym] 'History Research Notes', copy in possession of Rebe Taylor, Canberra.
Rachel Seymour, 'Birthday Book', in possession of Brentley Golder, Kingscote, Kangaroo Island.
Stamford (Tiger) Simpson, 'Correspondence', the Penneshaw Folk Museum, Kangaroo Island.
George Taplin, 'Diary', PRG 186, Mortlock Library, State Library of South Australia.
Rebe Taylor, 'Field Notebooks' and 'Correspondence with Interviewees', 1992–1998, in possession of Rebe Taylor, Canberra.
Rebe Taylor, 'Address to the KIPA Annual Dinner', Adelaide, 17 July 1998, audio and visual recordings, in possession of Rebe Taylor, Canberra.
Norman B. Tindale, 'Journal of Anthropological Researches on Kangaroo Island, South Australia, 1930–1974', South Australian Museum.
Norman B. Tindale, 'Tasmania and the Part Aborigines of the Bass Strait Islands and Kangaroo Island, 1936–1965', South Australian Museum.
Norman B. Tindale, 'Loose Notes', Tindale Collection, South Australian Museum.

Theses
Francis H. Bauer, The Regional Geography of Kangaroo Island, South Australia, PhD Thesis, Department of Geography, Australian National University, 1959.
Julie-Ann Ellis, Public Land and the Public Mind: Origins of Public Land Policy in South Australia 1834–1929, PhD Thesis, Faculty of Social Sciences, Flinders University, 1995.
Rhys Jones, Rocky Cape and the Problem of the Tasmanians, PhD Thesis, University of Sydney, 1971.
Ian McFarlane, Aboriginal Society in North West Tasmania: Dispossession and Genocide, PhD Thesis, School of History and Classics, University of Tasmania, 2002.
Irynej Skira, Tasmanian Aborigines and Mutton-birding: A Historical Examination, PhD Thesis, Department of Geography and Environmental Studies, University of Tasmania, 1993.

Parliamentary publications
South Australia, Aborigines Department Return, Parl Paper No. 198, 1866.
South Australia, Rules and Regulations of the Destitute Board, Parl Paper No. 27, 1867.
South Australia, Cancellation of 'Aboriginal Section, Kangaroo Island', Parl Paper No. 78, 1880.
South Australia, Rules and Regulations of the Destitute Board, Parl Paper No. 35, 1883–84.
South Australia, Report of the Commission on the Land Laws of South Australia; Together With Minutes of Proceedings, Evidence, and Appendices, Parl Paper No. 28, 1888.
South Australia, Parliamentary Debates, Legislative Council, 9 October 1991, 26 November 1991, 961–6, 2276–8 (Ian Gilfillan, MLC).

Electronic sources
Australian Census of 1996, Australian Bureau of Statistics, http://www.abs.gov.au.
'Tasmania – Frequently Asked Questions', http://www.tased.au/tasfaq/people/aborig.html.
Easton's 1897 Bible Dictionary: http://www.ccel.org/e/easton/ebd/ebd.html. Online edition based on: M. G. Easton, Illustrated Bible Dictionary, Thomas Nelson, 3rd ed., 1897.

Books, reports and pamphlets

Sandy Alexander, *Kangaroo Island – A Brief Chronological History*, published by the author, Kingscote, Kangaroo Island, 1997.

J. Allen, J. Golson and R. Jones, eds, *Sunda and Sahul: Prehistoric Studies in Southeast Asia, Melanesia and Australia*, Academic Press, New York, 1977.

G. F. Angas, *Savage Life and Scenes in Australia and New Zealand*, Smith Elder, London, 1847, vols. 1–2.

Margaret Ayliffe, *Flinders Land of the South: Early and Later History of Kangaroo Island*, Advertiser Printing Office, Adelaide, 1953, 2nd. ed. (first published by the author in Penneshaw, Kangaroo Island, 1951).

Charles Barrett, *White Blackfellows: The Strange Adventures of Europeans Who Lived Among Savages*, Hallcraft, Melbourne, 1948.

Charles Barrett, ed., *The Australian Junior Encyclopaedia*, Australian Educational Foundation, Sydney, 1959, vols. 1–3.

Francis H. Bauer, 'The Kartans of Kangaroo Island, South Australia: A Puzzle in Extinction', in Arnold R. Pilling and Richard A. Waterman, eds, *Diprotodon to Detribalization: Studies of Change Among Australian Aborigines*, Michigan State University Press, East Lansing, Michigan, 1970, pp. 198–216.

Nicolas Baudin, *The Journal of Post Captain Nicolas Baudin Commander-in-Chief of the Corvettes* Geographe *and* Naturaliste *Assigned by Order of the Government to a Voyage of Discovery*, trans. Christine Cornell, Libraries Board of South Australia, Adelaide, 1974.

J. C. Beaglehole, ed., *The Journals of Captain James Cook on his Voyages of Discovery*, Cambridge University Press, London, 1955, vols. 1–2.

Diane Bell, *Ngarrindjeri Wurruwarrin: a world that is, was, and will be*, Spinifex, Melbourne, 1998.

Geoffrey Blainey, *The Tyranny of Distance: How Distance Shaped Australia's History*, Sun Books, Melbourne, 1966.

Jacqueline Bonnemains, Elliott Forsyth and Bernard Smith, eds, *Baudin in Australian Waters*, Oxford University Press in association with the Australian Academy of Humanities, Melbourne, 1988.

James Bonwick, *William Buckley: The Wild White Man, and his Port Phillip Black Friends*, George Nichols, Melbourne, 1856 (republished as *The Wild White Man and the Blacks of Victoria*, Fergusson & Moore, Melbourne, 1863).

James Bonwick, *The Last of the Tasmanians Or the Black War of Van Diemen's Land*, Sampson Low, Son & Marston, London, 1870.

James Bonwick, *Mike Howe, The Bushranger of Van Diemen's Land*, Henry S. King & Co., London, 1873.

James Bonwick, *The Lost Tasmanian Race*, Sampson Low, Marston, Searle & Rivington, London, 1884.

James Bonwick, *The Bushrangers: Illustrating the Early Days of Van Diemen's Land*, Fullers Bookshop, Hobart, 1967.

George Boxall, *An Illustrated History of Australian Bushrangers*, Viking O'Neil, Ringwood, 1988.

M. I. H. Brooker and D. A. Keinig, *Field Guide to Eucalypts*, Melbourne, Inkata Press, 1990, vols. 1–3.

John W. Bull, *Early Experiences in South Australia*, E. S. Wigg & Son, London, 1884.

H. T. Burgess, ed., *The Cyclopedia of South Australia*, Cyclopedia Company, Adelaide, 1907–09, vols. 1–2.

David Carment, Robyn Maynard and Alan Powell, eds, *Northern Territory Dictionary of Biography*, Darwin, NTU Press, 1990.

Julie Carter, 'Am I too Black to Go with You?', in Ian Keen, ed., *Being Black: Aboriginal Cultures in 'Settled' Australia*, Aboriginal Studies Press for Australian Institute of Aboriginal Studies, Canberra, 1988, pp. 65–76.

Alex C. Castles, *An Australian Legal History*, The Law Book Company Ltd., Sydney, 1982.

W. A. Cawthorne, *The Kangaroo Islanders, The Story of South Australia Before Colonization, 1823*, Rigby, Adelaide, 1926 (first published as 'The Islanders', *Melbourne Illustrated Post*, 25 January 1865–18 February 1866).

Manning Clark, *A History of Australia*, abridged by Michael Cathcart, Melbourne University Press, Carlton, 1997.

Philip A. Clarke, 'The Aboriginal presence on Kangaroo Island, South Australia', in Jane Simpson and Luise Hercus, eds, *History in Portraits – Biographies of nineteenth century South Australian Aboriginal people, Aboriginal History*, Monograph 6, Southwood Press, Sydney, 1998, pp. 14–48.

T. A. Coghlan, *Labour and Industry in Australia: From the First Settlement in 1788 to the Establishment of the Commonwealth in 1901*, Macmillan, Melbourne, 1969, vols. 1–4.

Captain Edward Cooke, *A Voyage to the South Sea . . . Wherein an Account is given of Mr. Alexander Selkirk . . . during the Four Years and Four Months he liv'd upon the Uninhabited Island of Juan Fernandes*, printed by H. M. for B. Lintot & R. Gosling, A. Bettesworth & W. Innys, London, 1712.

Colleen Coy, 'Fanny Cochrane Smith', in *Tunapi Three: From Family to Community*, ALBE Resources Unit, Tasmania, 1994, pp. 4–5.

Jan Critchett, *A Distant Field of Murder: Western District Profile, 1834–1848*, Melbourne University Press, Melbourne, 1990.

Jan Critchett, *Untold Stories, Memories and Lives of Victorian Kooris*, Melbourne University Press, Melbourne, 1998.

J. S. Cumpston, *Kangaroo Island 1800–1836*, Roebuck Series, Roebuck Society Publication, Canberra, 1970.

Peter Cunningham, *Two Years in New South Wales*, Henry Colburn, London, 1827, vols 1–2.

John Dallwitz and Susan Marsden, 'Introduction', in John Dallwitz ed., *Horrie Simpson's Oodnadatta*, Oodnadatta Progress Association, Oodnadatta, South Australia, 1990.

Kate Darian-Smith and Paula Hamilton, eds, *Memory and History in Twentieth Century Australia*, Oxford University Press, Melbourne, 1994.

Graeme Davison, John Hirst and Stuart Macintyre, eds, *The Oxford Companion to Australian History*, Oxford University Press, Melbourne, 1998.

Daniel Defoe, *The Life and Strange and Surprizing Adventures of Robinson Crusoe of York, Mariner: who lived eight and twenty years, all alone in an uninhabited island on the coast of America, near to mouth of the great river or Oroonoque; having been cast on shore by shipwreck, whereon all the men perished but himself. With an account of how he was at last as strangely deliver'd by pyrates. Written by himself*, W. Taylor, London, 1719.

Daniel Defoe, *The Life and Adventures of Robinson Crusoe of York, Mariner*, Gall & Inglis, London, 1847.

Brian Dickey, with contributions from Elaine Martin and Rod Oxenberry, *Rations, Residence, Resources: A History of Social Welfare in South Australia since 1836*, Wakefield Press, A South Australian Jubilee 150 Publication, Adelaide, 1986.

Thomas Dunabin, 'The Old Sealing Days', in Charles Barrett, ed., *The Australian Junior Encyclopaedia*, Australian Educational Foundation, Sydney, 1959, vols. 1–3, 1, pp. 304–6.

Edmund Fanning, *Voyages and Discoveries in the South Seas 1792–1832*, Marine Research Society, Salem, Massachusetts, 1924.

Matthew Flinders, *A Voyage to Terra Australis; Undertaken for the Purpose of Completing the Discovery of that Vast Country, and Prosecuted in the Years 1801, 1802 and 1803*, G. & W. Nicol Booksellers, London, 1814, vols 1–2.

John Frow, *Time and Commodity Culture, Essays in Cultural Theory and Postmodernity*, Oxford University Press, New York, 1997.

Alan Garner, *Strandloper*, Harvill Press, London, 1996.

Thomas Gill, 'Some Anthropological Notes on the South Australian Aborigines', in *A Cruise in the Steamer 'Governor Musgrave' Among the Islands in Spencer's Gulf, January 1907*, J. L. Bonython & Co., 'The Advertiser' Office, Adelaide, 1909, pp. 132–60.

Mavis Golder, *Gentlemen . . . take your partners*, Kingscote, Kangaroo Island, published by the author, 1994.

Tom Griffiths with assistance from Alan Platt, eds, *The Life and Adventures of Edward Snell: The Illustrated Diary of an Artist, Engineer and Adventurer in the Australian Colonies 1849 to 1859*, Angus & Robertson with The Library Council of Victoria, North Ryde, New South Wales, 1988.

Maurice Halbwachs, *On Collective Memory*, trans. F. J. Ditter and V. Y. Ditter, Harper & Row, New York, 1980.

E. H. Hallack, *Kangaroo Island, Adelaide's Sanatorium*, W. K. Thomas & Co., Adelaide, 1905.

Paula Hamilton, 'The Knife Edge: Debates About History and Memory', in Kate Darian-Smith and Paula Hamilton, eds, *Memory and History in Twentieth Century Australia*, Oxford University Press, Melbourne, 1994, pp. 9–31.

John Hart, Letter to Governor La Trobe, Melbourne, 24 April 1854, in Thomas Francis McBride, *Letters From Victorian Pioneers*, Published for Trustees of Public Library by Robert S. Brain, Government Printer, Melbourne, 1898, p. 302.

Kevin Hayden, *Wild White Man: A Condensed Account of the Adventures of William Buckley who Lived in Exile for 32 Years (1803–35) Amongst the Black People of the Unexplored Regions of Port Phillip*, Marine History Publications, Geelong, 1976[?].

Barry Hill, *Ghosting William Buckley*, Heinemann, Port Melbourne, 1993.

Frank Horner, 'The Baudin Expedition to Australia, 1800–1804', in Jacqueline Bonnemains, Elliott Forsyth and Bernard Smith, eds, *Baudin in Australian Waters*, Oxford University Press in association with the Australian Academy of Humanities, Melbourne, 1988.

Walter Howchin, *The Geography of South Australia, Historical, Physical, Political and Commercial*, Whitcombe & Tombs, Auckland, 1917.

Robert Hughes, *The Fatal Shore: A History of the Transportation of Convicts to Australia, 1787–1868*, Collins Harvill, London, 1987.

Susan Hunt and Paul Carter, *Terre Napoléon: Australia Through French Eyes 1800–1804*, Historic Houses Trust of New South Wales, Sydney, 1999.

Gustav Jahoda, *Images of Savages: Ancient Roots of Modern Prejudice in Western Culture*, London, Routledge, 1999.

Rhys Jones, 'Man as an Element of a Continental Fauna: The Case of the Sundering of the Bassian Bridge', in J. Allen, J. Golson and R. Jones, eds, *Sunda and Sahul: Prehistoric Studies in Southeast Asia, Melanesia and Australia*, Academic Press, New York, 1977, pp. 316–86.

Ian Keen, ed., *Being Black: Aboriginal Cultures in 'Settled' Australia*, Aboriginal Studies Press for Australian Institute of Aboriginal Studies, Canberra, 1988.

Joan Kerr, ed., *The Dictionary of Australian Artists – Painters, Sketchers, Photographers and Engravers to 1870*, Oxford University Press, Melbourne, 1992.

Parry Kostoglou, 'Sealing in Tasmania: historical research project – a report for the Parks and Wildlife Service', Department of Environment and Land Management, Hobart, 1996.

W. H. Leigh, *Reconnoitering, Voyages, Travels and Adventures in the New Colonies of South Australia*, Smith Elder & Co., London, 1839.

Thomas Francis McBride, *Letters From Victorian Pioneers*, Published for Trustees of Public Library by Robert S. Brain, Government Printer, Melbourne, 1898.

John McQuilton, *Rural Australia and the Great War, from Tarrawingee to Tangambalanga*, Melbourne University Press, Melbourne, 2001.

Alfred Austin Lendon, *Kangaroo Island: The Tragedy of Dr. Slater and Mr. Osborne: a Story of Ninety Years Ago*, Register Office, Adelaide[?], 1925[?] (the cover states: 'reprinted from the *Proceedings of the Royal Geographical Society, South Australian Branch* – session 1924–5').

R. L. Megroz, *The Real Robinson Crusoe: being the Life and Strange Surprising Adventures of Alexander Selkirk of Largo, Fife, Mariner*, Cresset Press, London, 1939.

B. C. Mollison, *The Tasmanian Aborigines*, University of Tasmania, Hobart, 1977.

John Molony, *The Penguin History of Australia*, Penguin, Ringwood, 1988, 2nd. ed.

James Montgomery, *The Pelican Island and Other Poems*, Longman, Rees, Orrne, Brown & Green, London, 1827.

John Morgan, *The Life and Adventures of William Buckley, Thirty-two Years a Wanderer Amongst the Aborigines of the then Unexplored Country round Port Phillip, now the Province of Victoria*, Archibald Macdougall, Hobart, 1852.

John Morgan, *Life and Adventures of William Buckley*, with an introduction, explanatory notes, maps and illustrations by R. Schicht, published by the author, Sydney, 1996.

John Morgan, *Life and Adventures of William Buckley*, edited and introduced by Tim Flannery, Text Publishing, Melbourne, 2002.

John Morgan, *Ein Australischer Robinson: Leben und Abenteuer des William Buckley*, trans. Helmut Reim, F. A. Brockhaus Verlag, Leipzig, 1964.

John Morgan, *Uil'iam Bakli, Avstraliiskii Robinzon: Zhizn' i Prikliucheniia Uil'iama Bakli Rasskazannye Dzhonom Morganom*, Nauka, Moscow, 1966.

Catherine Murphy (writer) and Italo Vardaro (photographer), *Waterworks: an exploration of water through public art by five regional communities, initiated by the South Australian Country Arts Trust*, South Australian Country Arts Trust, Port Adelaide, 1999.

Jean Nunn, *This Southern Land: A Social History of Kangaroo Island 1800–1890*, Investigator Press, Adelaide, 1989.

Lynette Peel, ed. *The Henty Journals – A Record of Farming, Whaling and Shipping at Portland Bay, 1834–1839*, The Miegunyah Press in association with The State Library of Victoria, Melbourne, 1996.

François Péron, *Voyage De Decouvertes Aux Terres Australes*, Paris, 1816, vols. 1–2.

Arnold R. Pilling and Richard A. Waterman, eds, *Diprotodon to Detribalization: Studies of Change Among Australian Aborigines*, Michigan State University Press, East Lansing, Michigan, 1970.

N. J. B. Plomley, *Friendly Mission: The Tasmanian Journals and Papers of George Augustus Robinson, 1829–1832*, Tasmanian Historical Research Association, 1966.

N. J. B. Plomley and Kristen Anne Henley, *The Sealers of Bass Strait and the Cape Barren Island Community*, Blubber Head Press, Sandy Bay, Tasmania, 1990.

Cassandra Pybus, *Community of Thieves*, William Heinemann Australia, Port Melbourne, 1991.

William T. Pyke, *Savage Life in Australia: the Story of William Buckley the Runaway Convict who Lived Thirty-two Years among the Blacks of Australia*, E. W. Cole, Melbourne, 1889 (republished as *Thirty Years among the Blacks of Australia: the Life and Adventures of William Buckley, The Runaway Convict*, George Routledge & Sons, London, 1904, and again under the same title by Routledge, 1912).

Henry Reynolds, *The Law of the Land*, Penguin, Ringwood, 1987.

Henry Reynolds, *Fate of a Free People*, Penguin, Ringwood, 1995.

Craig Robertson, *Buckley's Hope: the Story of Australia's Wild White Man*, Scribe, Fitzroy, 1980.

Lloyd L. Robson, *A History of Tasmania: Van Diemen's Land from the Earliest Times to 1855*, Oxford University Press, Melbourne, 1983, vols. 1–2.

Woodes Rogers, *A Cruising Voyage Round the World [including] an Account of Alexander Selkirk's Living Alone Four Years and Four Months in an Island*, printed for Bernard Lintot & Edward Symon, London, 1726.

Henry Ling Roth, *The Aborigines of Tasmania*, F. King & Sons, Halifax, 1899.

Wynnis J. Ruediger, *Border's Land, Kangaroo Island 1802–1836*, published by the author, Morgan, South Australia, 1980.

Lyndall Ryan, *The Aboriginal Tasmanians*, Allen & Unwin, Sydney, 1996, 2nd ed.

Jane Simpson and Luise Hercus, eds, *History in Portraits – Biographies of nineteenth century South Australian Aboriginal people, Aboriginal History*, Monograph 6, Southwood Press, Sydney, 1998.

Charlie Schultz and Darrell Lewis, *Beyond the Big Run: Station Life in Australia's Last Frontier*, University of Queensland Press, St Lucia, 1995.

Joy Seager, *Kangaroo Island Doctor*, Rigby, Adelaide, 1980.

H. C. T. Stace and others, *A Handbook of Australian Soils*, Rellim Technical Publications, Adelaide, 1968.

South Australian Colonization Commission, *Report of the Colonization Commissioners for South Australia to Her Majesty's Principal Secretary of State for the Colonies*, 1836–1838, London, 1836, vols. 1–3.

South Australian Land Company, *Evidence Respecting the Soil, Climate and Productions of the South Coast of Australia, between the 132nd and 141st degrees of East Longitude*, South Australian Facsimile Editions No.11, Public Library of South Australia, Adelaide, 1962 (first published by William Nicol, London, 1832).

South Australian Land Company, *Proposal to His Majesty's Government for Founding a Colony on the Southern Coast of Australia*, South Australian Facsimile Editions No. 10, Public Library of South Australia, Adelaide, 1962 (first published by W. Nicol, London, 1831).

John Lort Stokes, *Discoveries in Australia; with an Account of the Coasts and Rivers Explored and Surveyed during the Voyage of H.M.S. Beagle 1837–1843*, T. & W. Boone, London, 1846, vols. 1–2.

George Sutherland, *Sixteen Stories of Australian Exploration and Settlement*, James Ingram, Melbourne, 1901[?].

Norman B. Tindale, with an Appendix on Tasmanian Tribes by Rhys Jones, *Aboriginal Tribes of Australia*, Australian National University Press, Canberra, 1974, pts. 1–2.

Alexander Tolmer, *Reminiscences of an Adventurous and Chequered Career*, Sampson Low, Marston, Searle & Rivington, London, 1882, vols. 1–2.

Cecily M. Tudehope, *William Buckley*, Hall's Book Store, Prahran, 1962.

Edward Gibbon Wakefield, *Plan of a Company to be Established for the Purpose of Founding a Colony in Southern Australia Purchasing Land Therein, and Preparing the Land so Purchased for the Reception of Immigrants*, South Australian Facsimile Editions, No. 6, Public Library of South Australia, Adelaide, 1962 (first published by Ridgway & Sons, London, 1832).

Jane Isabella Watts, *Family Life in South Australia Fifty-three Years Ago Dating From October 1837*, Libraries Board of South Australia, Adelaide, 1978 (first published by W. K. Thomas & Co., Adelaide, 1890).

T. E. Wells, *Michael Howe: The Last and Worst of the Bushrangers of Van Diemen's Land*, Angus & Robertson, Sydney, 1926.

John West, *The History of Tasmania*, ed. A. G. L Shaw, Angus & Robertson in association with the Royal Australian Historical Society, Sydney, 1971 (first published by Henry Dowling, Launceston, Tasmania, 1852).

Patrick Wolfe, *Settler Colonialism and the Transformation of Anthropology*, Cassell, London, 1999.

Journal and magazine articles

See Notes for newspaper articles.

Herbert Basedow, 'Relic of the Lost Tasmanian Race – Obituary of Mary Seymour', *Man*, vol. 14, no. 10, pp. 160–2.

Richard J. A. Berry, 'A Living Descendant of an Extinct (Tasmanian) Race', *Proceedings of the Royal Society of Victoria*, vol. 20, pt. 1, 1907, pp. 1–21.

Philip A. Clarke, 'Early European Interaction with Aboriginal Hunters and Gatherers on Kangaroo Island, South Australia', *Aboriginal History*, vol. 20, 1996, pp. 51–81.

H. M. Cooper, 'Large Stone Implements from South Australia', *Records of the South Australian Museum*, vol. 7, 1941–43, pp. 345–69.

Ernestine Hill, 'Last of the Tasmanians', *Walkabout*, 1 July 1954, p. 20.

John Jones, 'Port Adelaide River. Its First Reported Discovery', *Proceedings of the Royal Geographical Society of Australasia, South Australian Branch*, vol. 34, 1920–21, pp. 73–5.

Ronald Lampert, 'The Great Kartan Mystery', *Terra Australis*, vol. 5, 1981, pp. 1–185.

Margarette Lincoln, 'Shipwreck Narratives of the Eighteenth and Early Nineteenth Century: Indicators of Culture and Identity', *British Journal for Eighteenth-century Studies*, vol. 20, 1997, pp. 155–172.

H. A. Lindsay, 'American Settlement on Kangaroo Island 1803', *Quadrant*, vol. 5, 1961, pp. 43–7.

H. A. Lindsay, 'Australia's First Human Population', *Walkabout*, 1 January 1954, pp. 34–5.

Major Lockyer, 'Expedition Sent from Sydney in 1826 to Found a Settlement at King George's Sound, Western Australia', in H. P. Moore, 'Notes on the Early Settlers in South Australia Prior to 1836', *Royal Geographical Society of Australia, South Australian Branch*, vol. 25, 1923, pp. 81–135, pp. 125–127.

Paul Mann, 'Kangaroo Island – the pirate fortress that retains its free spirit', *Australian Geographic*, April/June, 1988, pp. 27–42.

A. L. Meston, 'Halfcastes of the Furneaux Group', *The Records of the Queen Victoria Museum*, Launceston, 1946, issued separately 1947, pp. 47–52.

H. P. Moore, 'Notes on the Early Settlers in South Australia Prior to 1836', *Royal Geographical Society of Australia, South Australian Branch*, vol. 25, 1923, pp. 81–135.

Christopher Nance, 'Two South Australian Writers', *Tradition*, vol. 20, December 1979, pp. 19–22.

Pierre Nora, 'Between Memory and History: Les Lieux de Mémoire', *Representations*, vol. 26, 1989, pp. 7–25.

Stefan Petrow, 'The Last Man: The Mutilation of William Lanne in 1869 and its Aftermath', *Australian Cultural History*, no. 16, 1997/98, pp. 18–44.

Norman B. Tindale, 'Tasmanian Aborigines on Kangaroo Island South Australia', *Records of the South Australian Museum*, vol. 6, no. 1, 1937, pp. 29–37.

Norman B. Tindale, 'Relationship of the Extinct Kangaroo Island Cultures of Australia Tasmania and Malaya', *Records of the South Australia Museum*, vol. 6, 1937–41, pp. 39–59.

Norman B. Tindale and Brian G. Maegraith, 'Traces of an Extinct Aboriginal Population on
   Kangaroo Island', *Records of the South Australian Museum*, vol. 4, 1928–32, pp. 275–87.
Patrick Wolfe, 'Nation and MiscegeNation: Discursive Continuity in the Post-Mabo Era', *Social
   Analysis*, no. 36, 1994, pp. 93–152.

Index

This index is arranged alphabetically, word for word. Illustrations are in *italics*.
Bold entries denote those references with the fullest information.

Wakefield Press is an independent publishing and
distribution company based in Adelaide, South Australia.
We love good stories and publish beautiful books.
To see our full range of books, please visit our website at
www.wakefieldpress.com.au
where all titles are available for purchase.
To keep up with our latest releases, news and events,
subscribe to our monthly newsletter.

Find us!

Facebook: www.facebook.com/wakefield.press
Twitter: www.twitter.com/wakefieldpress
Instagram: www.instagram.com/wakefieldpress

www.ingramcontent.com/pod-product-compliance
Lightning Source LLC
Chambersburg PA
CBHW060020030426
42334CB00019B/2120